Citroën CX Owners Workshop Manual

J H Haynes Member of the Guild of Motoring Writers
and A K Legg T Eng MIMI

Models covered
All Citroën CX models with ohv petrol engines (including fuel injection and Turbo models)
CX 2000, CX 2200, CX 2400 & CX 25
1985 cc, 2175 cc, 2347 cc & 2500 cc

Does not cover 1995 cc or 2165 cc ohc engines fitted to CX 20 & CX 22, Athena & some Reflex models, or Diesel-engine models

ISBN 1 85010 449 2

Printed in England *(528–12N3)*

ABCDE
FGHIJ
KLMNO
PQ

2

THE BOOK

Haynes Publishing Group
Sparkford Nr Yeovil
Somerset BA22 7JJ England

Haynes Publications, Inc
861 Lawrence Drive
Newbury Park
California 91320 USA

British Library Cataloguing in Publication Data
Legg, A. K. (Andrew K.), *1942-* Citroen CX owners workshop manual. 1. Cars. Maintenance & repair – Amateurs' manuals I. Title   II. Series 629.28'722 ISBN 1-85010-449-2

Acknowledgements

Thanks are due to the Société Anonyme Automobiles Citroën of France for the supply of technical information and the use of certain illustrations, and to Citroën U.K. Ltd for the loan of the Turbo model used in preparing the updated edition of the book. The Champion Sparking Plug Company supplied the illustrations showing the various spark plug conditions. Sykes-Pickavant provided some of the workshop tools. Thanks are also due to all those people at Sparkford who helped in the production of this manual.

About this manual

Its aim

The aim of this manual is to help you get the best value from your car. It can do so in several ways. It can help you decide what work must be done (even should you choose to get it done by a garage), provide information on routine maintenance and servicing, and give a logical course of action and diagnosis when random faults occur. However, it is hoped that you will make use of the manual by tackling the work yourself. On simpler jobs it may be even quicker than booking the car into a garage, and having to go there twice, to leave and collect it. Perhaps most important, a lot of money can be saved by avoiding the costs the garage must charge to cover its labour and overheads.

The manual has drawings and descriptions to show the function of the various components so that their layout can be understood. Then the tasks are described and photographed in a step-by-step sequence so that even a novice can do the work. Where special tools are essential to carry out the job their use is detailed, and the Citroen part number quoted. Because of the cost and limited use of special tools you may find it more economic to let your Citroen agent carry out the tasks requiring special equipment.

Its arrangement

The manual is divided into thirteen Chapters, each covering a logical sub-division of the vehicle. The Chapters are each divided into consecutively numbered Sections and the Sections into paragraphs (or sub-sections), with decimal numbers following on from the Section they are in, eg 5.1, 5.2, 5.3 etc.

It is freely illustrated in those parts where there is a detailed sequence of operations to be carried out. There are two forms of illustration; figures and photographs. The figures are numbered in sequence with decimal numbers, according to their position in the Chapter: eg, Fig. 6.4 is the 4th drawing/illustration in Chapter 6. Photographs are numbered (either individually or in related groups) the same as Section or sub-section of the text where the operation they show is described.

There is an alphabetical index at the back of the manual as well as a contents list at the front.

References to the 'left' or 'right' of the vehicle are in the sense of a person in a seat facing towards the front of the vehicle.

Vehicle manufacturers continually make changes to specifications and recommendations, and these, when notified, are incorporated into our manuals at the earliest opportunity.

Unless otherwise stated, nuts and bolts are removed by turning anti-clockwise, and tightened by turning clockwise.

Whilst every care is taken to ensure that the information in this manual is correct no liability can be accepted by the authors or publishers for loss, damage or injury caused by any errors in, or omissions from, the information given.

Introduction to the Citroën CX

The Citroen CX was first introduced in France in late 1974 and the CX 2000 was made available in the UK in July 1975. The CX 2200 followed in September 1975 and the CX 2400 in August 1976. Estate models were introduced in 1976.

The CX range models are equipped with all the modern instruments and gauges available, including a pneumatic oil level gauge, a brake pad wear warning lamp, and a battery condition meter. The manufacturers have also included many safety features in the design, including minimum stopping distances marked on the speedometer.

The models are also extremely comfortable to ride in, thanks to the hydropneumatic suspension and luxurious interior trim. The unique design suspension is self-levelling and the ride height is maintained automatically over all road conditions. A ground clearance lever inside the car may be used to adjust the ride height when travelling over rough ground, and also makes changing a roadwheel much simpler.

The engine/gearbox unit is mounted transversely and drives the front wheels through two driveshafts. The gearbox is available in a four or five-speed manual version or a three-speed semi-automatic version.

Contents

Citroën CX in native maritime setting

Side view of the Citroën CX Pallas

General dimensions, weights and capacities

For modifications, and information applicable to later models, see Supplement at end of manual

Overall length
CX 2000 saloon	4.63 m (182.5 in)
CX 2200 saloon	4.66 m (183.5 in)
CX 2200 estate	4.92 m (193.75 in)
CX Prestige	4.916 m (193.5 in)
CX 2400 saloon and Pallas	4.66 m (183.5 in)
CX 2400 estate	4.92 m (193.75 in)
CX 2400 GTi	4.67 m (183.75 in)
CX 2400 ambulance	4.985 m (196.25 in)

Overall width
CX 2000, CX 2200 and CX 2400 saloon	1.73 m (68.0 in)
CX 2000 estate, CS Prestige, CX 2400 estate, CX 2400 GTi and CX 2400 ambulance	1.734 m (68.25 in)

Overall height (normal)
CX 2000, CX 2200, CX Prestige, CX 2400 saloon and CX 2400 GTi	1.36 m (53.5 in)
CX 2000 estate and CX 2400 estate	1.465 m (57.75 in)
Ambulance	1.875 m (73.75 in)

Kerb weight
CX 2000	1265 kg (2789 lb)
CX 2200	1285 kg (2833 lb)
CX 2000 estate	1385 kg (3053 lb)
CX Prestige and Pallas	1450 kg (3197 lb); Auto. 1455 kg (3208 lb)
CX 2400	1300 kg (2866 lb)
CX 2400 estate	1405 kg (3097 lb)
CX 2400 GTi	1345 kg (2965 lb)
CX 2400 ambulance	1530 kg (3373 lb)

Maximum trailer weight
With one cooling fan	900 kg (1984 lb)
With twin cooling fans	1301 kg (2866 lb)

Capacities
Engine oil (including filter)	5.3 litre (9.3 Imp pt)
Gearbox oil:	
4-speed manual	1.6 litre (2.8 Imp pt)
5-speed manual	1.7 litre (3.0 Imp pt)
Automatic transmission fluid:	
2-speed	5.5 litre (9.7 Imp pt)
3-speed:	
From dry	6.5 litre (10.4 Imp pt)
Refill	2.5 litre (4.4 Imp pt)
Fuel tank	68.0 litre (15.0 Imp gal)

Buying spare parts and vehicle identification numbers

Buying spare parts

Spare parts are available from many sources, for example: Citroen garages, other accessory shops, and motor factors. Our advice regarding spare parts is as follows:

Officially appointed Citroen garages – This is the best source of parts which are peculiar to your car and otherwise not generally available (eg complete cylinder heads, internal gearbox components, badges, interior trim etc). It is also the only place at which you should buy parts if your car is still under warranty; non-Citroen parts may invalidate the warranty. To be sure of obtaining the correct parts it will always be necessary to give the storeman your car's engine and chassis number, and if possible, to take the old part along for positive identification. Many parts are available under a factory exchange scheme – any parts returned should always be clean. It obviously makes good sense to go straight to the specialists on your car for this type of part for they are best equipped to supply you.

Other garages and accessory shops – These are often very good places to buy material and components needed for the maintenance of your car (eg oil filters, spark plugs, bulbs, drivebelts, oils and grease, touch-up paint, filler paste etc). They also sell accessories, usually have convenient opening hours, charge lower prices and can often be found not far from home.

Motor factors – Good factors stock all of the more important components which wear out relatively quickly (eg clutch components, pistons and liners, valves, exhaust systems, brake pipes/seals and pads, etc). Motor factors will often provide new or reconditioned components on a part exchange basis – this can save a considerable amount of money.

Vehicle identification numbers

Modifications are a continuing and unpublished process in vehicle manufacture quite apart from major model changes. Spare parts manuals and lists are compiled upon a numerical basis, the individual vehicle numbers being essential to correct identification of the component required.

When ordering spare parts, always give as much information as possible. Quote the car model, year of manufacture, body and engine numbers as appropriate.

The car identification plate is in the engine compartment on the right-hand side wheel arch.

The engine number is on the right-hand side of the cylinder block towards the bulkhead.

The gearbox number is on the top of the gearbox casing.

The body code number is in the engine compartment on the front panel.

Car identification plate

Engine number plate

Tools and working facilities

Introduction

A selection of good tools is a fundamental requirement for anyone contemplating the maintenance and repair of a motor vehicle. For the owner who does not possess any, their purchase will prove a considerable expense, offsetting some of the savings made by doing-it-yourself. However, provided that the tools purchased meet the relevant national safety standards and are of good quality, they will last for many years and prove an extremely worthwhile investment.

To help the average owner to decide which tools are needed to carry out the various tasks detailed in this manual, we have compiled three lists of tools under the following headings: *Maintenance and minor repair*, *Repair and overhaul*, and *Special*. The newcomer to practical mechanics should start off with the *Maintenance and minor repair* tool kit and confine himself to the simpler jobs around the vehicle. Then, as his confidence and experience grow, he can undertake more difficult tasks, buying extra tools as, and when, they are needed. In this way, a *Maintenance and minor repair* tool kit can be built-up into a *Repair and overhaul* tool kit over a considerable period of time without any major cash outlays. The experienced do-it-yourselfer will have a tool kit good enough for most repair and overhaul procedures and will add tools from the *Special* category when he feels the expense is justified by the amount of use to which these tools will be put.

It is obviously not possible to cover the subject of tools fully here. For those who wish to learn more about tools and their use there is a book entitled *How to Choose and Use Car Tools* available from the publishers of this manual.

Maintenance and minor repair tool kit

The tools given in this list should be considered as a minimum requirement if routine maintenance, servicing and minor repair operations are to be undertaken. We recommend the purchase of combination spanners (ring one end, open-ended the other); although more expensive than open-ended ones, they do give the advantages of both types of spanner. All nuts, bolts screws and threads on the Citroën are to metric standards.

Combination spanners - 10, 11, 13, 14, 17 mm
Adjustable spanner - 9 inch
Spark plug spanner (with rubber insert)
Spark plug gap adjustment tool
Set of feeler gauges
Brake bleed nipple spanner
Screwdriver - 4 in long x $\frac{1}{4}$ in dia (flat blade)
Screwdriver - 4 in long x $\frac{1}{4}$ in dia (cross blade)
Combination pliers - 6 inch
Hacksaw, junior
Tyre pump
Tyre pressure gauge
Oil can
Fine emery cloth (1 sheet)
Wire brush (small)
Funnel (medium size)

Repair and overhaul tool kit

These tools are virtually essential for anyone undertaking any major repairs to a motor vehicle, and are additional to those given in the *Maintenance and minor repair* list. Included in this list is a comprehensive set of sockets. Although these are expensive they will be found invaluable as they are so versatile - particularly if various drives are included in the set. We recommend the $\frac{1}{2}$ in square-drive type, as this can be used with most proprietary torque wrenches. If you cannot afford a socket set, even bought piecemeal, then inexpensive tubular box spanners are a useful alternative.

The tools in this list will occasionally need to be supplemented by tools from the *Special* list.

Sockets (or box spanners) to cover range in previous list
Reversible ratchet drive (for use with sockets)
Extension piece, 10 inch (for use with sockets)
Universal joint (for use with sockets)
Torque wrench (for use with sockets)
'Mole' wrench - 8 inch
Ball pein hammer
Soft-faced hammer, plastic or rubber
Screwdriver - 6 in long x $\frac{5}{16}$ in dia (flat blade)
Screwdriver - 2 in long x $\frac{5}{16}$ in square (flat blade)
Screwdriver - 1$\frac{1}{2}$ in long x $\frac{1}{4}$ in dia (cross blade)
Screwdriver - 3 in long x $\frac{1}{8}$ in dia (electricians)
Pliers - electricians side cutters
Pliers - needle nosed
Pliers - circlip (internal and external)
Cold chisel - $\frac{1}{2}$ inch
Scriber (this can be made by grinding the end of a broken hacksaw blade)
Scraper (this can be made by flattening and sharpening one end of a piece of copper pipe)
Centre punch
Pin punch
Hacksaw
Valve grinding tool
Steel rule/straight edge
Allen keys
'Torx' keys (later models)
Selection of files
Wire brush (large)
Axle-stands
Jack (strong scissor or hydraulic type)

Special tools

The tools in this list are those which are not used regularly, are expensive to buy, or which need to be used in accordance with their manufacturers' instructions. Unless relatively difficult mechanical jobs are undertaken frequently, it will not be economic to buy many of these tools. Where this is the case, you could consider clubbing together with friends (or a motorists' club) to make a joint purchase, or borrowing the tools against a deposit from a local garage or tool hire specialist.

The following list contains only those tools and instruments freely available to the public, and not those special tools produced by the vehicle manufacturer specifically for its dealer network. You will find occasional references to these manufacturers' special tools in the text of this manual. Generally, an alternative method of doing the job without the vehicle manufacturer's special tool is given. However, sometimes, there is no alternative to using them. Where this is the case and the relevant tool cannot be bought or borrowed you will have to entrust the work to a franchised garage.

Valve spring compressor
Piston ring compressor
Balljoint separator
Universal hub/bearing puller
Impact screwdriver
Micrometer and/or vernier gauge
Dial gauge
Stroboscopic timing light
Dwell angle meter/tachometer
Universal electrical multi-meter
Cylinder compression gauge
Lifting tackle
Trolley jack
Light with extension lead

Buying tools

For practically all tools, a tool factor is the best source since he will have a very comprehensive range compared with the average garage or accessory shop. Having said that, accessory shops often offer excellent quality tools at discount prices, so it pays to shop around.

There are plenty of good tools around at reasonable prices, but always aim to purchase items which meet the relevant national safety standards. If in doubt, ask the proprietor or manager of the shop for advice before making a purchase.

Care and maintenance of tools

Having purchased a reasonable tool kit, it is necessary to keep the tools in a clean serviceable condition. After use, always wipe off any dirt, grease and metal particles using a clean, dry cloth, before putting the tools away. Never leave them lying around after they have been used. A simple tool rack on the garage or workshop wall, for items such as screwdrivers and pliers is a good idea. Store all normal spanners and sockets in a metal box. Any measuring instruments, gauges, meters, etc, must be carefully stored where they cannot be damaged or become rusty.

Take a little care when tools are used. Hammer heads inevitably become marked and screwdrivers lose the keen edge on their blades from time to time. A little timely attention with emery cloth or a file will soon restore items like this to a good serviceable finish.

Working facilities

Not to be forgotten when discussing tools, is the workshop itself. If anything more than routine maintenance is to be carried out, some form of suitable working area becomes essential.

It is appreciated that many an owner mechanic is forced by circumstances to remove an engine or similar item, without the benefit of a garage or workshop. Having done this, any repairs should always be done under the cover of a roof.

Wherever possible, any dismantling should be done on a clean flat workbench or table at a suitable working height.

Any workbench needs a vice: one with a jaw opening of 4 in (100 mm) is suitable for most jobs. As mentioned previously, some clean dry storage space is also required for tools, as well as the lubricants, cleaning fluids, touch-up paints and so on which become necessary.

Another item which may be required, and which has a much more general usage, is an electric drill with a chuck capacity of at least $\frac{5}{16}$ in (8 mm). This, together with a good range of twist drills, is virtually essential for fitting accessories such as wing mirrors and reversing lights.

Last, but not least, always keep a supply of old newspapers and clean, lint-free rags available, and try to keep any working area as clean as possible.

Spanner jaw gap comparison table

Jaw gap (in)	Spanner size
0·250	$\frac{1}{4}$ in AF
0·276	7 mm
0·313	$\frac{5}{16}$ in AF
0·315	8 mm
0·344	$\frac{11}{32}$ in AF; $\frac{1}{8}$ in Whitworth
0·354	9 mm
0·375	$\frac{3}{8}$ in AF
0·394	10 mm
0·433	11 mm
0·438	$\frac{7}{16}$ in AF
0·445	$\frac{3}{16}$ in Whitworth; $\frac{1}{4}$ in BSF
0·472	12 mm
0·500	$\frac{1}{2}$ in AF
0·512	13 mm
0·525	$\frac{1}{4}$ in Whitworth; $\frac{5}{16}$ in BSF
0·551	14 mm
0·563	$\frac{9}{16}$ in AF
0·591	15 mm
0·600	$\frac{5}{16}$ in Whitworth; $\frac{3}{8}$ in BSF
0·625	$\frac{5}{8}$ in AF
0·630	16 mm
0·669	17 mm
0·686	$\frac{11}{16}$ in AF
0·709	18 mm
0·710	$\frac{3}{8}$ in Whitworth; $\frac{7}{16}$ in BSF
0·748	19 mm
0·750	$\frac{3}{4}$ in AF
0·813	$\frac{13}{16}$ in AF
0·820	$\frac{7}{16}$ in Whitworth; $\frac{1}{2}$ in BSF
0·866	22 mm
0·875	$\frac{7}{8}$ in AF
0·920	$\frac{1}{2}$ in Whitworth; $\frac{9}{16}$ in BSF
0·938	$\frac{15}{16}$ in AF
0·945	24 mm
1·000	1 in AF
1·010	$\frac{9}{16}$ in Whitworth; $\frac{5}{8}$ in BSF
1·024	26 mm
1·063	$1\frac{1}{16}$ in AF; 27 mm
1·100	$\frac{5}{8}$ in Whitworth; $\frac{11}{16}$ in BSF
1·125	$1\frac{1}{8}$ in AF
1·181	30 mm
1·200	$\frac{11}{16}$ in Whitworth; $\frac{3}{4}$ in BSF
1·250	$1\frac{1}{4}$ in AF
1·260	32 mm
1·300	$\frac{3}{4}$ in Whitworth; $\frac{7}{8}$ in BSF
1·313	$1\frac{5}{16}$ in AF
1·390	$\frac{13}{16}$ in Whitworth; $\frac{15}{16}$ in BSF
1·417	36 mm
1·438	$1\frac{7}{16}$ in AF
1·480	$\frac{7}{8}$ in Whitworth; 1 in BSF
1·500	$1\frac{1}{2}$ in AF
1·575	40 mm; $\frac{15}{16}$ in Whitworth
1·614	41 mm
1·625	$1\frac{5}{8}$ in AF
1·670	1 in Whitworth; $1\frac{1}{8}$ in BSF
1·688	$1\frac{11}{16}$ in AF
1·811	46 mm
1·813	$1\frac{13}{16}$ in AF
1·860	$1\frac{1}{8}$ in Whitworth; $1\frac{1}{4}$ in BSF
1·875	$1\frac{7}{8}$ in AF
1·969	50 mm
2·000	2 in AF
2·050	$1\frac{1}{4}$ in Whitworth; $1\frac{3}{8}$ in BSF
2·165	55 mm
2·362	60 mm

Jacking and towing

To change a roadwheel, remove the spare wheel and tool kit from the engine compartment. Apply the handbrake, start the engine, and move the ground clearance lever fully forwards to the maximum height position. Locate the jack in the slot beneath the body sills and extend it to the ground. If the rear wheel is being removed, withdraw the rear wing lower panel. Remove the wheel embellisher and loosen the wheelnuts, then raise the jack until the wheel is off the ground and remove the wheel.

Fit the spare wheel using a reversal of the removal procedure. Remember to reset the ground clearance lever to the normal driving position before moving off.

When jacking-up the car with a trolley jack, never place the jack under the underframe side-members nor under the front or rear subframes. Use only the strengthened areas adjacent to the front lower suspension arm mounting points or at the rear under the main cross-tube or at the strengthened area used for attachment of a towing bracket. Always position axle stands beneath the outer strengthened sections of the subframes.

Towing eyes are provided beneath the front subframe extensions for towing the car with the hydraulic system pressurised; **do not** use these eyes for lifting the car. If it is necessary to lift the front of the car, cables must be attached to the eyes located beneath the wheel arches, and a length of wood must be located as shown in the illustration together with padding to protect the bumper. Eyes are provided below the rear bumper for lifting the rear of the car or towing another vehicle.

If it is necessary to tow a CX with fully automatic transmission, this should ideally be done with the front wheels raised. If this is not possible, make sure that the transmission fluid level is correct, and do not exceed 30 mph (48 km/h), nor tow further than 30 miles (48 km).

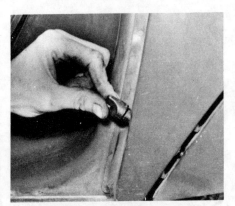
Removing rear wing lower panel

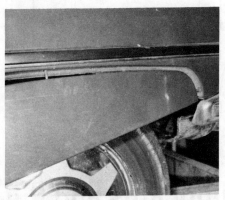
Removing rear wing lower panel

Front towing eye

Rear towing eye

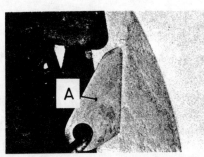
Location of the front lifting brackets (A)

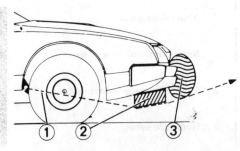
Method of lifting the front of the car for towing
1   Cable 2   Wooden beam 3   Padding

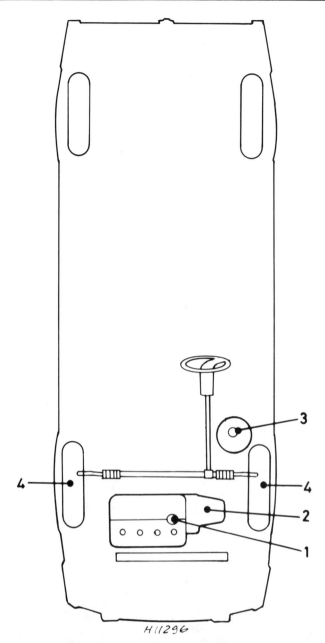

H11296

Recommended lubricants and fluids

Component	Lubricant or fluid
1 **Engine**	SAE 15W/40, 15W/50 or 20W/50 engine oil
2 **Manual gearbox**	SAE 75W/80 or 80W/85W gear oil
2 **Semi-automatic transmission**	Total Fluid T
2 **Fully automatic transmission**	Dexron ®II
3 **Hydraulic system**	Green LHM fluid
4 **Wheel bearings**	Multi-purpose grease

Safety first!

Professional motor mechanics are trained in safe working procedures. However enthusiastic you may be about getting on with the job in hand, do take the time to ensure that your safety is not put at risk. A moment's lack of attention can result in an accident, as can failure to observe certain elementary precautions.

There will always be new ways of having accidents, and the following points do not pretend to be a comprehensive list of all dangers; they are intended rather to make you aware of the risks and to encourage a safety-conscious approach to all work you carry out on your vehicle.

Essential DOs and DON'Ts

DON'T rely on a single jack when working underneath the vehicle. Always use reliable additional means of support, such as axle stands, securely placed under a part of the vehicle that you know will not give way.

DON'T attempt to loosen or tighten high-torque nuts (e.g. wheel hub nuts) while the vehicle is on a jack; it may be pulled off.

DON'T start the engine without first ascertaining that the transmission is in neutral (or 'Park' where applicable) and the parking brake applied.

DON'T suddenly remove the filler cap from a hot cooling system – cover it with a cloth and release the pressure gradually first, or you may get scalded by escaping coolant.

DON'T attempt to drain oil until you are sure it has cooled sufficiently to avoid scalding you.

DON'T grasp any part of the engine, exhaust or catalytic converter without first ascertaining that it is sufficiently cool to avoid burning you.

DON'T allow brake fluid or antifreeze to contact vehicle paintwork.

DON'T syphon toxic liquids such as fuel, brake fluid or antifreeze by mouth, or allow them to remain on your skin.

DON'T inhale dust – it may be injurious to health (see *Asbestos* below).

DON'T allow any spilt oil or grease to remain on the floor – wipe it up straight away, before someone slips on it.

DON'T use ill-fitting spanners or other tools which may slip and cause injury.

DON'T attempt to lift a heavy component which may be beyond your capability – get assistance.

DON'T rush to finish a job, or take unverified short cuts.

DON'T allow children or animals in or around an unattended vehicle.

DO wear eye protection when using power tools such as drill, sander, bench grinder etc, and when working under the vehicle.

DO use a barrier cream on your hands prior to undertaking dirty jobs – it will protect your skin from infection as well as making the dirt easier to remove afterwards; but make sure your hands aren't left slippery. Note that long-term contact with used engine oil can be a health hazard.

DO keep loose clothing (cuffs, tie etc) and long hair well out of the way of moving mechanical parts.

DO remove rings, wristwatch etc, before working on the vehicle – especially the electrical system.

DO ensure that any lifting tackle used has a safe working load rating adequate for the job.

DO keep your work area tidy – it is only too easy to fall over articles left lying around.

DO get someone to check periodically that all is well, when working alone on the vehicle.

DO carry out work in a logical sequence and check that everything is correctly assembled and tightened afterwards.

DO remember that your vehicle's safety affects that of yourself and others. If in doubt on any point, get specialist advice.

IF, in spite of following these precautions, you are unfortunate enough to injure yourself, seek medical attention as soon as possible.

Asbestos

Certain friction, insulating, sealing, and other products – such as brake linings, brake bands, clutch linings, torque converters, gaskets, etc – contain asbestos. *Extreme care must be taken to avoid inhalation of dust from such products since it is hazardous to health.* If in doubt, assume that they *do* contain asbestos.

Fire

Remember at all times that petrol (gasoline) is highly flammable. Never smoke, or have any kind of naked flame around, when working on the vehicle. But the risk does not end there – a spark caused by an electrical short-circuit, by two metal surfaces contacting each other, by careless use of tools, or even by static electricity built up in your body under certain conditions, can ignite petrol vapour, which in a confined space is highly explosive.

Always disconnect the battery earth (ground) terminal before working on any part of the fuel or electrical system, and never risk spilling fuel on to a hot engine or exhaust.

It is recommended that a fire extinguisher of a type suitable for fuel and electrical fires is kept handy in the garage or workplace at all times. Never try to extinguish a fuel or electrical fire with water.

Note: *Any reference to a 'torch' appearing in this manual should always be taken to mean a hand-held battery-operated electric lamp or flashlight. It does NOT mean a welding/gas torch or blowlamp.*

Fumes

Certain fumes are highly toxic and can quickly cause unconsciousness and even death if inhaled to any extent. Petrol (gasoline) vapour comes into this category, as do the vapours from certain solvents such as trichloroethylene. Any draining or pouring of such volatile fluids should be done in a well ventilated area.

When using cleaning fluids and solvents, read the instructions carefully. Never use materials from unmarked containers – they may give off poisonous vapours.

Never run the engine of a motor vehicle in an enclosed space such as a garage. Exhaust fumes contain carbon monoxide which is extremely poisonous; if you need to run the engine, always do so in the open air or at least have the rear of the vehicle outside the workplace.

If you are fortunate enough to have the use of an inspection pit, never drain or pour petrol, and never run the engine, while the vehicle is standing over it; the fumes, being heavier than air, will concentrate in the pit with possibly lethal results.

The battery

Never cause a spark, or allow a naked light, near the vehicle's battery. It will normally be giving off a certain amount of hydrogen gas, which is highly explosive.

Always disconnect the battery earth (ground) terminal before working on the fuel or electrical systems.

If possible, loosen the filler plugs or cover when charging the battery from an external source. Do not charge at an excessive rate or the battery may burst.

Take care when topping up and when carrying the battery. The acid electrolyte, even when diluted, is very corrosive and should not be allowed to contact the eyes or skin.

If you ever need to prepare electrolyte yourself, always add the acid slowly to the water, and never the other way round. Protect against splashes by wearing rubber gloves and goggles.

When jump starting a car using a booster battery, for negative earth (ground) vehicles, connect the jump leads in the following sequence: First connect one jump lead between the positive (+) terminals of the two batteries. Then connect the other jump lead first to the negative (–) terminal of the booster battery, and then to a good earthing (ground) point on the vehicle to be started, at least 18 in (45 cm) from the battery if possible. Ensure that hands and jump leads are clear of any moving parts, and that the two vehicles do not touch. Disconnect the leads in the reverse order.

Mains electricity and electrical equipment

When using an electric power tool, inspection light etc, always ensure that the appliance is correctly connected to its plug and that, where necessary, it is properly earthed (grounded). Do not use such appliances in damp conditions and, again, beware of creating a spark or applying excessive heat in the vicinity of fuel or fuel vapour. Also ensure that the appliances meet the relevant national safety standards.

Ignition HT voltage

A severe electric shock can result from touching certain parts of the ignition system, such as the HT leads, when the engine is running or being cranked, particularly if components are damp or the insulation is defective. Where an electronic ignition system is fitted, the HT voltage is much higher and could prove fatal.

Routine maintenance

For modifications, and information applicable to later models, see Supplement at end of manual

Maintenance is essential for ensuring safety and desirable for the purpose of getting the best in terms of performance and economy from the car. Over the years the need for periodic lubrication has been greatly reduced if not totally eliminated. This has unfortunately tended to lead some owners to think that because no such action is required the items either no longer exist or will last forever. This is certainly not the case; it is essential to carry out regular visual examinations as comprehensively as possible in order to spot any possible defects at an early stage before they develop into major and expensive repairs.

It will be noticed that the service intervals specified for later models (cars manufactured in or after 1978) are longer than those for earlier models (up to and including 1977). This follows official Citroen recommendation; no dramatic design changes have been made to enable later cars to run for longer without attention. The DIY mechanic may well consider it prudent to adhere to the shorter intervals, regardless of the age of his car, since he is avoiding the labour charges which are the main part of any garage servicing bill.

Every 250 miles (400 km) or weekly – whichever comes first

Steering
Check the tyre pressures
Examine the tyres for wear or damage

Hydraulic system
Check the fluid level in the reservoir

Lights, wipers and horns
Do all the lights work at the front and rear?
Are the headlamp beams aligned properly?
Check the windscreen washer fluid level

Engine
Check the level of the oil, top-up if necessary
Check the level of the electrolyte in the battery and top-up the level as necessary
Check coolant level and top-up if necessary

At first 600 miles (1000 km) – new vehicles

Adjust the valve clearances (do not re-torque cylinder head bolts)
Check tension of all drivebelts
Check coolant level
Clean filter in hydraulic fluid reservoir
Check and adjust handbrake operation
Check clutch adjustment
Adjust idle speed
Check CO level
Renew engine oil and filter
Renew manual transmission lubricant
Renew automatic transmission lubricant

Every 6000 miles (10 000 km) for early models, 10 000 miles (15 000 km) for later models, or every six months

Engine
Change engine oil and renew filter element
Clean air filter element
Clean and adjust spark plugs
Clean and adjust contact breaker points and lubricate distributor
Check ignition timing (carburettor engines)

Brakes
Check rear disc pads for wear

Check brake hydraulic circuit for leaks, damaged pipes etc
Check handbrake and adjust if necessary

Transmission
Adjust clutch
Check and if necessary top-up gearbox oil level or automatic transmission fluid

Steering
Check front wheel alignment and adjust if necessary
Check for wear in steering gear and balljoints, and condition of rubber bellows and dust excluders

General
Examine exhaust system for corrosion and leakage
Lubricate all controls, linkages, door locks and hinges

Every 15 000 miles (22 500 km) – later models only

Gearbox or 3-speed automatic transmission
Change the oil

Every 12 000 miles (20 000 km) for early models, 20 000 miles (30 000 km) for later models, or annually

Engine
Check antifreeze strength and top-up if necessary
Clean battery terminals
Check drivebelts tension and adjust if necessary
Renew spark plugs
Renew contact breaker points (carburettor engines)
Check and adjust ignition timing
Clean crankcase ventilation hoses
Adjust valve clearances
Adjust carburettor
Renew in-line fuel filter

General
Check wiper blades and renew if necessary
Check seat belts and anchorages
Check front suspension lower balljoints

Every 24 000 miles (40 000 km) for early models, 30 000 miles (45 000 km) for later models, or two yearly

Engine
Drain, flush and refill cooling system with antifreeze

Hydraulic system
Renew LHM fluid in hydraulic system

General
Dismantle, clean and relubricate rear hub bearings
Check headlamp alignment and adjust if necessary
Inspect suspension bearings and bump stops for wear
Tighten all underbody nuts and bolts
Check body for rust and corrosion and repair as necessary

Every three years

Have the suspension spheres checked and re-charged with gas

Windscreen washer reservoir location

Topping-up the engine oil

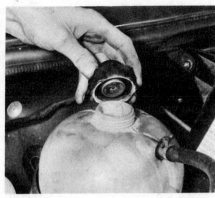

Checking the coolant level in the expansion tank

Removing the engine oil drain plug

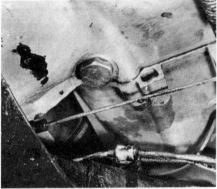

Main gearbox casing drain plug location

Differential casing drain plug location

Gearbox filler plug (manual transmission)

Gearbox oil level dipstick (arrowed)

Fuel tank filler cap

Chapter 1 Engine

For modifications, and information applicable to later models, see Supplement at end of manual

Contents

Specifications

Engine – general

Type .... Transverse, four in-line, overhead valve, inclined 30° towards front

	CX 2000	CX 2200	CX 2400 (carburettor)	CX 2400 (fuel injection)
Displacement	1985 cc	2175 cc	2350 cc	2350 cc
Bore	86.0 mm	90.0 mm	93.5 mm	93.5 mm
	(3.39 in)	(3.54 in)	(3.68 in)	(3.68 in)
Stroke	85.5 mm	85.5 mm	85.5 mm	85.5 mm
	(3.37 in)	(3.37 in)	(3.37 in)	(3.37 in)
Compression ratio	9.0 : 1	9.0 : 1	8.75 : 1	8.75 :1
Maximum power(bhp at rpm)	102	112 at	115 at	128at
	at 5500	5500	5500	4800
Maximum torque (lbf ft/kgf m at rpm)	112/15.5	123/17.0	132/18.2	145/20.1
	at 3000	at 3500	at 3000	at 3600

Firing order .... 1 – 3 – 4 – 2 (No 1 at flywheel end)
Rotation .... Anti-clockwise viewed from flywheel end

Cylinder head

Type .... Aluminium alloy, with hemispherical combustion chambers
Depth .... 90.0 mm (3.54 in)
Maximum distortion .... 0.10 mm (0.004 in)
    Inlet .... 60° with 45° taper
    Exhaust .... 45°

Valves and valve gear

Seat angle:
    Inlet .... 60°
    Exhaust .... 45°

Stem diameter:
    Inlet . . . .   7.965 to 7.980 mm (0.3136 to 0.3142 in)
    Exhaust . . . .   8.945 to 8.960 mm (0.3522 to 0.3528 in)
Head diameter:
    Inlet . . . .   49.0 $\pm$ 0.25 mm (1.9291 $\pm$ 0.0098 in)
    Exhaust . . . .   39.0 $\pm$ 0.25 mm (1.5354 $\pm$ 0.0098 in)
Valve guide internal diameter:
    Inlet . . . .   7.990 to 8.015 mm (0.3146 to 0.3156 in)
    Exhaust . . . .   8.980 to 9.005 mm (0.3535 to 0.3545 in)
Valve spring length . . . .   39.0 mm (1.535 in) under load of 88.2 $\pm$ 6.2 lb 40.0 $\pm$ 2.8 kg
    30.6 mm (1.205 in) under load of 185.2 $\pm$ 4.0 lb 84.0 $\pm$ 1.8 kg
Tappet bore diameter . . . .   23.975 to 24.05 mm (0.9439 to 0.9469 in)
Valve clearance (cold):
    Inlet . . . .   0.15 mm (0.006 in)
    Exhaust . . . .   0.20 mm (0.008 in)
Valve timing (with valve clearance of 1.10 mm (0.043 in):
    Inlet valve opens . . . .   0° 30' BTDC
    Inlet valve closes . . . .   42° 30' ABDC
    Exhaust valve opens . . . .   38° 30' BBDC
    Exhaust valve closes . . . .   4° 30' ATDC
Timing chain to guide clearance . . . .   0.10 to 0.50 mm (0.004 to 0.020 in)
Pushrods:
    Length – inlet . . . .   188.35 to 189.40 mm (7.415 to 7.457 in)
    Length – exhaust . . . .   **212.60 to 213.65 mm (8.370 to 8.411 in)**
    Maximum distortion . . . .   1.0 mm (0.040 in)
Camshaft:
    Type . . . .   Chain driven, three bearing
    Endfloat . . . .   0.05 to 0.30 mm (0.002 to 0.012 in)
    Thrust plate thickness . . . .   5.44 to 5.46 mm (0.214 to 0.215 in)

Cylinder block

Type . . . .   Cast iron with wet liners
Liners:
Base gasket thickness (uncompressed):
    CX 2000 and CX 2200 . . . .   0.085 to 0.115 mm (0.0033 to 0.0045 in)
    CX 2400 . . . .   0.09 to 0.11 mm (0.0035 to 0.0043 in)
Protrusion (uncompressed):
    CX 2000 and CX 2200 . . . .   0.04 to 0.135 mm (0.0016 to 0.0053 in)
    CX 2400 . . . .   0.045 to 0.115 mm (0.0018 to 0.0045 in)
Bore diameter (CX 2000):
    Class 1 . . . .   86.010 to 86.020 mm (3.3862 to 3.3866 in)
    Class 2 . . . .   86.020 to 86.030 mm (3.3866 to 3.3870 in)
    Class 3 . . . .   86.030 to 86.040 mm (3.3870 to 3.3874 in)
Bore diameter (CX 2200):
    Class 1 . . . .   90.010 to 90.020 mm (3.5437 to 3.5441 in)
    Class 2 . . . .   90.020 to 90.030 mm (3.5441 to 3.5445 in)
    Class 3 . . . .   90.030 to 90.040 mm (3.5445 to 3.5449 in)
Bore diameter (CX 2400):
    Class 1 . . . .   93.500 to 93.510 mm (3.6811 to 3.6815 in)
    Class 2 . . . .   93.510 to 93.520 mm (3.6815 to 3.6819 in)
    Class 3 . . . .   93.520 to 93.530 mm (3.6819 to 3.6823 in)

Pistons and connecting rods

Type . . . .   Convex crown, 1 compression ring, 2 oil scraper rings
Gudgeon pin bore:
    CX 2000 and CX 2200 . . . .   25.003 to 25.010 mm (0.9844 to 0.9846 in)
    CX 2400 . . . .   25.001 to 25.006 mm (0.9843 to 0.9845 in)
Gudgeon pin diameter . . . .   24.996 to 25.000 mm (0.9841 to 0.9843 in)
Piston diameter (CX 2000):
    Class 1 . . . .   85.95 to 85.96 mm (3.3839 to 3.3843 in)
    Class 2 . . . .   85.96 to 85.97 mm (3.3843 to 3.3846 in)
    Class 3 . . . .   85.97 to 85.98 mm (3.3846 to 3.850 in)
Piston diameter (CX 2200):
    Class 1 . . . .   89.93 to 89.94 mm (3.5406 to 3.5409 in)
    Class 2 . . . .   89.94 to 89.95 mm (3.5409 to 3.5413 in)
    Class 3 . . . .   89.95 to 89.96 mm (3.5413 to 3.5417 in)
Piston diameter (CX 2400):
    Class 1 . . . .   93.430 to 93.440 mm (3.6783 to 3.6787 in)
    Class 2 . . . .   93.440 to 93.450 mm (3.6787 to 3.6791 in)
    Class 3 . . . .   93.450 to 93.460 mm (3.6791 to 3.6795 in)
Connecting rod endfloat . . . .   0.037 to 0.247 mm (0.0015 to 0.0097 in)

Crankshaft

Type	Forged steel, five bearing
Crankpin diameter:	
Class A	53.990 to 54.005 mm (2.1256 to 2.1262 in)
Class B	53.490 to 53.505 mm (2.1059 to 2.1065 in)
Main journal diameter:	
Class A	64.035 to 64.050 mm (2.5201 to 2.5217 in)
Class B	63.535 to 63.550 mm (2.5014 to 2.5020 in)
Endfloat	0.045 to 0.16 mm (0.0018 to 0.0063 in)

Lubrication system

Oil pressure (at 95 to 105°C/203 to 221°F):	
2000 rpm	3.0 bars (43.5 psi)
4000 rpm	4.0 to 5.0 bars (58.0 to 72.5 psi)
Warning lamp switch operating pressure	475 to 675 mbars (7.0 to 9.8 psi)
Oil temperature switch operating temperature:	
Up to January 1975	147° to 150° C (297° to 302° F)
January 1975 on	135° to 138° C (275° to 280° F)
Oil pump relief valve spring length under load of 24.0 lb (10.9 kg) ...	42.0 mm (1.65 in)
Filter bypass valve pressure	550 mbars (8.0 psi)
Oil capacity (including filter)	5.3 litres (9.3 Imp pts)
Filter capacity	0.65 litres (1.1 Imp pts)
Difference between dipstick 'min' and 'max' marks	1.1 litres (1.9 Imp pts)

Torque wrench settings

	lbf ft	kgf m
4-speed manual gearbox models		
Torque bar nut	59.0	8.2
Flexible mounting to subframe	22.0	3.0
Flexible mounting assembly	72.0	10.0
5-speed manual and torque converter models		
Torque bar nut	72.0	10.0
RH flexible mounting assembly	72.0	10.0
LH flexible mounting assembly	116.0 to 123.0	16.0 to 17.0
All models		
Timing cover	10.0 to 14.0	1.4 to 1.9
Camshaft thrust plate	10.0 to 14.0	1.4 to 1.9
Timing chain guide	10.0 to 14.0	1.4 to 1.9
Timing chain tensioner	6.5 to 8.0	0.9 to 1.1
Oil filter mounting	7.0 to 11.0	1.0 to 1.5
Oil temperature switch	22.0 to 25.0	3.0 to 3.5
Oil filter	8.0 to 11.0	1.1 to 1.5
Sump plug	25.0 to 32.5	3.5 to 4.5
Crankshaft balance weights	52.0 to 57.75	7.2 to 8.0
Cylinder head bolts:		
Initial	21.75	3.0
Final	43.5 to 47.0	6.0 to 6.5
Rocker cover	3.5 to 6.0	0.5 to 0.8
Camshaft pulley nut	58.0	8.0
Oil pressure switch	21.5 to 25.5	3.0 to 3.5
Flywheel	65.0	9.0
Driveplate (torque converter)	58.0 to 65.0	8.0 to 9.0
Big-end cap	52.0 to 58.0	7.2 to 8.0
Main bearing cap	65.0 to 72.0	9.0 to 10.0
Camshaft sprocket:		
7 mm diameter	16.0 to 18.0	2.2 to 2.5
8 mm diameter	22.5 to 24.5	3.1 to 3.4
Exhaust valve rocker pedestal	15.0 to 20.0	2.1 to 2.8
Inlet and exhaust manifold	15.0	2.1
Crankcase to cylinder block	10.0 to 14.0	1.4 to 1.9
Cover to crankcase	8.0	1.1
Engine to gearbox bolts	13.0	1.8

1 General description

The engine is of 4-cylinder, in-line, overhead valve type mounted transversely within the front subframe, and inclined 30° towards the front.

The aluminium alloy cylinder head incorporates hemispherical combustion chambers, and the inclined valves are operated by pushrods and tappets from the camshaft. Independent rocker shafts are provided for the exhaust valve rockers, but the inlet valve rockers pivot on a common shaft.

The crankshaft is of five bearing type, and the centre main bearing incorporates semicircular thrust washers to control crankshaft end-float.

The camshaft is chain driven from the crankshaft and is supported in three bearings; endfloat is controlled by a thrust plate. A hydraulically assisted timing chain tensioner is fitted.

The cylinder block incorporates removable wet liners of cast iron, and the pistons are equipped with one compression ring and two oil control rings.

Crankcase ventilation is provided by a hose from the rocker cover to the air filter housing.

An internally mounted gear type oil pump provides lubrication, and is driven by a skew gear on the camshaft. Engine oil is fed from the oil pump to an externally mounted oil filter canister and then to the engine oil galleries. From the oil galleries, the oil is fed to the crankshaft, camshaft and rocker shafts. A pressure relief valve is incorporated in the oil pump body.

The engine/gearbox assembly is mounted on the front subframe. On four-speed manual gearbox models, two lower mountings are provided, together with two upper torque bars incorporating rubber bushes. On five-speed manual gearbox and torque converter models, one mounting is provided beneath the engine, one vertical mounting on the gearbox, and one upper torque bar incorporating rubber bushes.

2 Major operations possible with engine/gearbox in car

The following operations can be carried out without having to remove the engine/gearbox from the car:

(a) Removal and servicing of the cylinder head
(b) Removal of the timing cover, chain and gears
(c) Removal of the tappets (cam followers)
(d) Renewal of the engine mountings

3 Major operations only possible after removal of engine/gearbox from car

The following operations can only be carried out after removal of the engine/gearbox from the car:

(a) Removal of the camshaft and oil pump
(b) Removal of the piston/connecting rod assemblies and liners
(c) Renewal of the crankshaft main bearings
(d) Renewal of the crankshaft oil seal
(e) Removal of the flywheel or torque converter driveplate

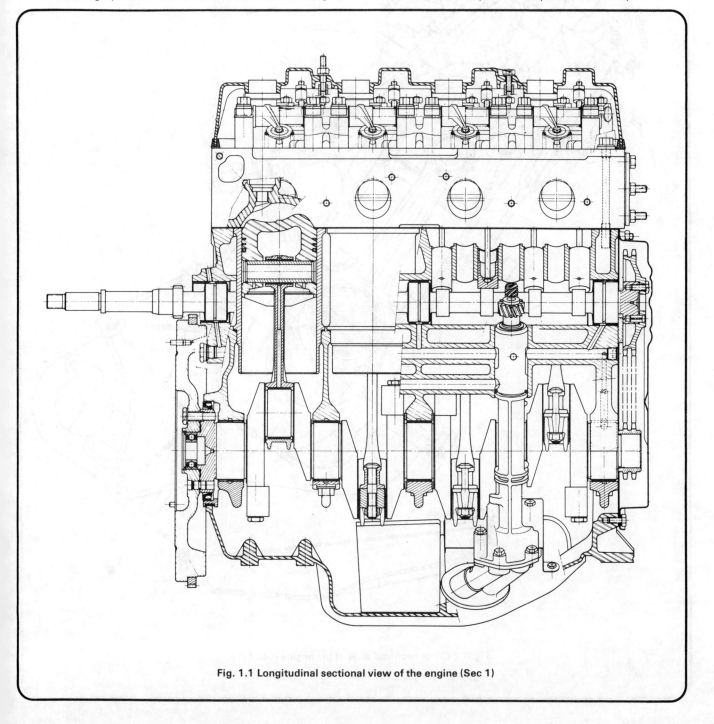

Fig. 1.1 Longitudinal sectional view of the engine (Sec 1)

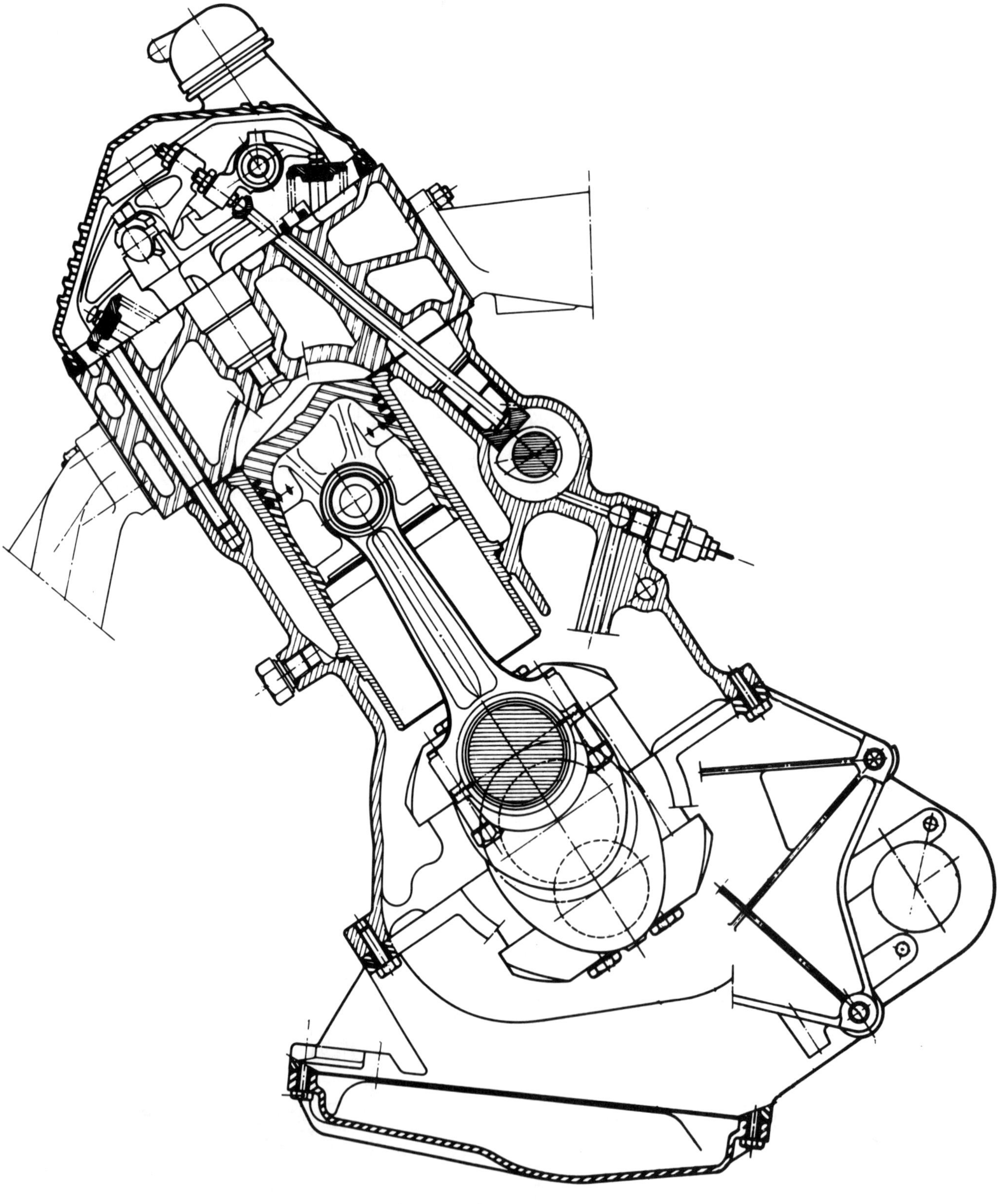

Fig. 1.2 Cross-sectional view of the engine (Sec 1)

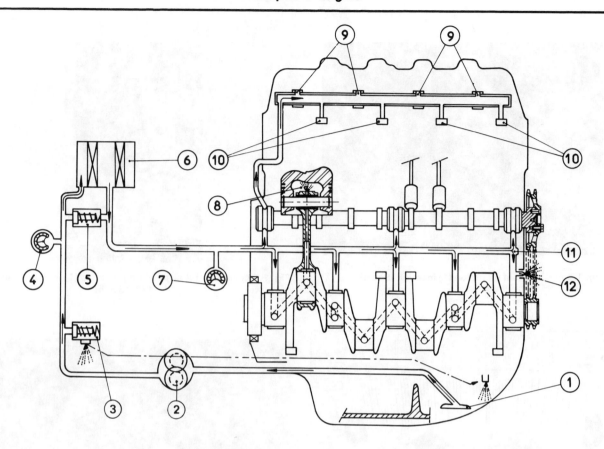

Fig. 1.3 Diagram of the lubrication system (Sec 1)

1 Strainer	5 Filter by-pass valve	8 Piston cooling oil jet	11 Gallery
2 Oil pump	6 Filter	9 Inlet valve rocker arms	12 Timing chain lubrication and
3 Pressure relief valve	7 Oil pressure switch	10 Exhaust valve rocker arms	hydraulic tensioner
4 Oil temperature switch			

---

4 Method of engine removal

The engine and gearbox must be lifted from the car as a complete unit, then separated from each other on the bench.

5 Engine/gearbox assembly – removal

1 Remove the bonnet as described in Chapter 12.
2 Apply the handbrake and remove the front wheel embellishers.
3 Extract the split-pin and loosen the driveshaft nuts on both sides of the car.
4 Jack-up the front of the car, check the rear wheels, and remove the front roadwheels.
5 Disconnect and remove the battery.
6 Unscrew the hydraulic system pressure regulator bleed screw 1 to 1½ turns, and on models equipped with power steering depress the brake pedal several times to release the pressure.
7 Remove the spare wheel from the engine compartment.
8 Drain the cooling system as described in Chapter 2.
9 Remove the driveshafts as described in Chapter 7.
10 Drain the engine oil into a suitable container.
11 Remove the radiator as described in Chapter 2.
12 *Models equipped with air conditioning.* Whenever overhaul of a major nature is being undertaken to the engine, components of the air conditioning system may obstruct the work. Such items of the system may not have room to be unbolted and moved aside sufficiently within the limits of their flexible connecting pipes to avoid such obstruction. The system should therefore be discharged by your dealer or a competent refrigeration engineer. As the system must be completely evacuated before re-charging, the necessary vacuum equipment to do this is only likely to be available at the specialists. The refrigerant fluid

is Freon 12 and although harmless under normal circumstances, contact with the eyes or skin must be avoided. If Freon comes into contact with a naked flame then a poisonous gas will be created which is injurious to health.
13 Unbolt the earth lead from the gearbox, and disconnect the wiring from the reversing lamp switch.
14 On models equipped with a torque converter, disconnect the two supply wires from the clutch control switch and the electro-valve.
15 Disconnect the multiplug connector located near the battery, and the fusible link.
16 Detach the air cleaner hose from the carburettor, and the ventilation hose from the rocker cover.
17 Disconnect the supply wire from the radiator temperature switch.
18 Remove the air cleaner assembly as described in Chapter 3.
19 Disconnect the wires from the coil after noting their position.
20 Remove the diagnostic plug from the support.
21 Remove the pressure regulator from the gearbox as described in Chapter 8.
22 On models fitted with the single cylinder hydraulic pump, disconnect and plug the hoses. On models fitted with the seven piston hydraulic pump, remove the pump *without disconnecting the supply hose* (refer to Chapter 8) and place it on the bulkhead.
23 Disconnect the multiplug connector by the subframe crossmember.
24 Prise the spring clips from the gearchange balljoints and disconnect them from the selector levers.
25 On manual gearbox models, remove the bolt from the gearbox end cover, and remove the speedometer cable; refit the bush and bolt and hand tighten it (photo).
26 On torque converter models, separate the front and rear sections of the speedometer cable.
27 On models with power steering, unscrew the bolt and remove the

Fig. 1.4 Engine loom multiplug (1) location (Sec 5)

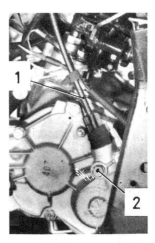

Fig. 1.5 Location of the speedometer cable (1) and bush retaining bolt (2) (Sec 5)

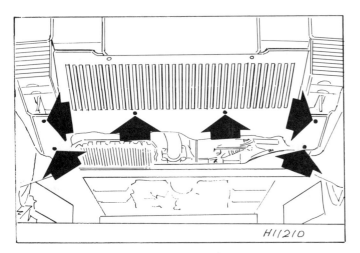

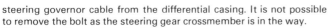

Fig. 1.6 Stone guard securing bolt locations (arrowed) (Sec 5)

Fig. 1.7 Location of the gearbox mounting bolt (1) on five speed and torque converter gearbox models (Sec 5)

steering governor cable from the differential casing. It is not possible to remove the bolt as the steering gear crossmember is in the way.
28 Remove the gearbox dipstick.
29 On torque converter models, drain the fluid as described in Chapter 6 and disconnect the supply and return hoses from the gearbox.
30 Disconnect the accelerator and choke cables from the carburettor with reference to Chapter 3.
31 Disconnect the hoses from the expansion bottle, three-way union, and inlet manifold.
32 Disconnect the heater hoses at the bulkhead.
33 Disconnect the supply pipe from the fuel pump and the return pipe from the carburettor. Detach the wire from the cut-off valve on the carburettor.
34 Where fitted, disconnect the pneumatic oil gauge hoses.
35 On manual gearbox models, unscrew the securing bolts and remove the stone guard from beneath the front subframe. Disconnect the clutch cable from the release arm with reference to Chapter 5.
36 On models with power steering, remove the brake accumulator as described in Chapter 8.
37 Unscrew the retaining nuts and detach the exhaust downpipe from the exhaust manifold.
38 Position a suitable hoist over the engine/gearbox and attach it to the lifting brackets provided. Take the weight of the assembly.
39 On four-speed manual gearbox models unscrew and remove the lower mounting bolts, noting that the longer bolt is located on the right-hand side. Unscrew and remove the two pivot bolts securing the

upper torque bars to the subframe (photos).
40 On torque converter and five-speed manual gearbox models, unscrew and remove the lower engine mounting bolt, the gearbox mounting bolt, and the pivot bolt securing the upper torque bar to the subframe.
41 Check that all wires, cables and hoses have been disconnected, then lift the engine/gearbox assembly from the car (photo). Take care not to damage any of the components mounted on the subframe and bulkhead. Lower the unit onto a workbench or a large piece of wood. On torque converter and five-speed manual gearbox models, recover the shims located between the gearbox and the vertical mounting.

6 Engine – separation from gearbox

1 Remove the starter motor as described in Chapter 10.
2 Loosen the retaining bolt and remove the drivebelt cover.
3 Remove the TDC sensor (photo) and disconnect the wire from the reversing lamp switch.
4 Remove the alternator as described in Chapter 10.
5 Loosen the tensioner bolt and remove the water pump drivebelt.
6 Unscrew the retaining nut and withdraw the camshaft pulley(s) (photo).
7 Disconnect the return hose from the water pump.
8 Remove the rubber cap from the end of the camshaft, unscrew the nut, and remove the pulley and shims. Note the quantity of shims for correct reassembly.

5.25 Removing the speedometer cable

5.39A An upper torque bar engine mounting

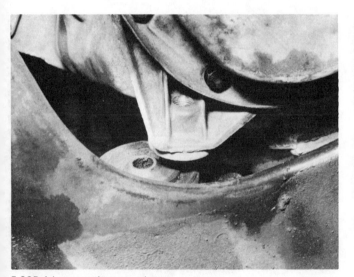
5.39B A lower engine mounting

5.41 Removing the engine/gearbox assembly

9   Unbolt the flywheel cover plate (photo).
10   On torque converter models, unscrew and remove the bolts retaining the driveplate to the torque converter. Bolt a piece of angled iron to the bottom of the gearbox to restrain the torque converter in subsequent operations.
11   Unscrew and remove the bolts retaining the gearbox bellhousing to the engine.
12   With the help of an assistant, withdraw the gearbox from the engine in a straight line (photo).

7   Engine dismantling – general

1   When the engine is removed from the car it, and particularly its accessories, are more vulnerable to damage. If possible mount the engine on a stand, or failing this, make sure it is supported in such a manner that it will not topple over whilst undoing tight nuts and bolts.
2   Cleanliness is important when dismantling the engine to prevent exposed parts from contamination. Before starting the dismantling operations clean the outside of the engine with paraffin, or a good grease solvent if it is particularly dirty. Carry out this cleaning away from the area in which the dismantling is to take place.
3   If a stand is not available carry out the work on a bench or wooden platform. Avoid working with the engine directly on a concrete floor, as

grit presents as real source of trouble.
4   As parts are removed clean them in a paraffin bath. However, do not immerse parts with internal oilways in paraffin as it is difficult to remove, usually requiring a high pressure hose. Clean oilways with nylon pipe cleaners.
5   It is advisable to have suitable containers to hold small items by their groups as this will help when reassembling the engine and also prevent possible losses.
6   Always obtain complete sets of gaskets when the engine is being dismantled. It is always a good policy to fit new gaskets in view of the relatively small cost involved. Retain the old gaskets when dismantling the engine with a view to using them as a pattern to make a replacement if a new one is not available.
7   When possible refit nuts, bolts and washers in their location as this helps to protect the threads and will also be helpful when the engine is being reassembled as it establishes their location.
8   Retain unserviceable items until the replacement parts are obtained so that the replacement parts can be checked against the old part to ensure that the correct item has been supplied.

8   Ancillary components – removal

1   With the engine separated from the gearbox, the externally

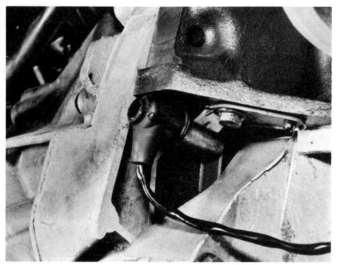

6.3 TDC sensor location

6.6 The camshaft pulley

6.9 Flywheel cover plate location

6.12 Separating the gearbox from the engine

mounted ancillary components can be removed.

2   The components are given in the following list together with the relevant Chapter where detailed descriptions may be found. The removal sequence need not necessarily follow the order given:

> Clutch assembly (Chapter 5)
> Manifolds and carburettor (Chapter 3)
> Fuel pump (Chapter 3)
> Water pump (Chapter 2)
> HT leads and spark plugs (Chapter 4)
> Oil filter canister (Section 14 of this Chapter)
> Engine mountings and torque bars
> Distributor (Chapter 4)
> Coil from cylinder head (2 bolts)
> Dipstick and oil gauge hoses
> Engine wiring loom (noting wire locations)
> Crankcase ventilation cover and hoses
> Oil pressure switch (photo)
> Oil temperature switch

9   Cylinder head – removal

If the engine is still in the car, first carry out the following opera-

tions:

> (a) Drain the cooling system
> (b) Remove the manifolds complete with carburettor
> (c) Remove the water pump
> (d) Disconnect the battery negative lead
> (e) Remove the spare wheel
> (f) Disconnect the ventilation hose from the rocker cover
> (g) Disconnect the HT leads from the spark plugs

1   Unbolt and remove the rocker cover. Remove the rubber seals.
2   Unscrew and remove the nuts retaining the exhaust rocker shafts and rockers (photos). Remove the rockers and identify them for refitting in the same positions.
3   Unscrew the unions and remove the oil transfer pipe from the cylinder head and block.
4   Unbolt the cover from the end of the cylinder head.
5   Unscrew each of the cylinder head bolts half a turn at a time in the reverse order to that shown in Fig. 1.16.
6   Remove the inlet rocker shaft complete (photo). Remove the O-ring seals.
7   Shake the pushrods free from the cam followers, then withdraw them from the cylinder head keeping them in strict order to ensure correct refitting (photo).
8   Lift the cylinder head from the block. If it is stuck, tap it free with a

Fig. 1.8 Using the special Citroën bolts to retain the liners in the cylinder block (Sec 9)

Fig. 1.9 Timing chain guide (1) and Brampton type tensioner (2) showing timing mark locations (A and B) (Sec 11)

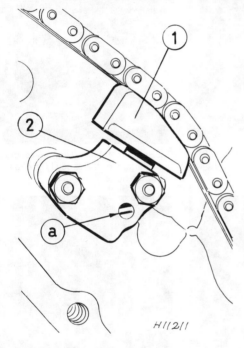

Fig. 1.10 Sedis type timing chain tensioner (Sec 11)

1 Pressure pad
2 Body
a Locking key

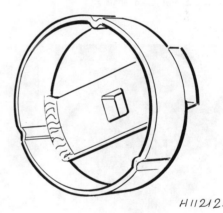

Fig. 1.11 Special Citroën tool for removing oil filter. A strap wrench can be used instead (Sec 14)

wooden mallet. **Do not** insert a lever into the gasket joint – you may damage the mating faces.
9   Remove the cylinder head gasket. If the engine is to be tuned before refitting the head, the liners **must** be clamped firmly in the block (see Fig. 1.8) (photo).

10 Cylinder head – dismantling

1   Unbolt the water outlet elbow from the head.
2   Using a valve spring compressor, compress each spring in turn until the split collets can be removed. Release the compressor and remove the retainer, spring, washer and oil seal (photos). If the retainers are difficult to release, do not continue to tighten the compressor, but gently tap the top of the tool with a hammer. Always make sure that the compressor is held firmly over the retainer.
3   Remove each valve from the combustion chambers, keeping all the components in their correct sequence unless they are to be renewed (photo). When numbering the valves, remember that No 1 cylinder is at the flywheel or water pump end of the cylinder head.

11 Timing cover, gears, and chain – removal

If the engine is still in the car, jack-up the right-hand front of the car and support it on an axle stand. Remove the roadwheel and the rubber cover from the wheel arch.
1   Unscrew the retaining nuts and bolts and remove the timing cover and gasket (photos).
2   Turn the crankshaft until No 1 piston (flywheel end) is at top dead centre (TDC) on the compression stroke. If the cylinder head is already removed, temporarily insert No 1 cylinder pushrods to check that the cam followers are positioned on the backs of the cams. The TDC line on the flywheel must also be positioned opposite the lug on the gearbox bellhousings.
3   If not already apparent, mask the timing gears in relation to each other using a straight edge between their centres.
4   If the engine is removed, mark the flywheel ring gear and cylinder block in relation to each other as a further precaution.
5   Unbolt and remove the timing chain guard (photo).
6   Two types of chain tensioner are fitted. Where a hole is drilled on

8.2 Removing the oil pressure switch

9.2A Removing the exhaust rocker shafts and rockers

9.2B Exhaust rocker components

9.6 Removing the inlet rocker shaft

9.7 Location of the pushrods

9.9 Suitable bolts, nuts and washers can be used instead of the special Citroën liner clamping bolts

10.2A Using a valve spring compressor

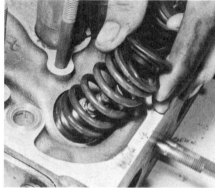
10.2B Removing a valve spring and retainer

10.2C Removing a valve spring seat

10.2D Valve oil seal location

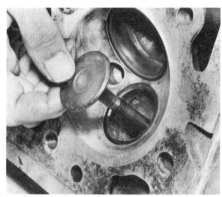
10.3 Removing an exhaust valve

11.1A Showing access to the timing cover with the engine in the car

11.1B Removing the timing cover

11.5 Timing chain guide location

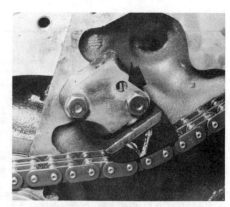

11.6A Timing chain tensioner with key (arrowed) in normal position

11.6B Timing chain tensioner with key (arrowed) in locked position

11.8 Removing the camshaft sprocket and timing chain

13.1 Removing the crankcase bottom cover

13.2 Location of metal gauze screen in the lower crankcase

13.4A Removing the oil gauge pipe

13.4B Removing the dipstick tube

13.5A Removing the oil pump lower retaining bolt

13.5B Removing the oil pump upper retaining bolt

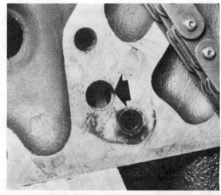

13.6 Showing the timing chain tensioner fitted (arrowed)

the tensioner, insert a small screwdriver and turn it so that the tensioner pad is retracted, then turn the screwdriver in the opposite direction to lock the pad (photos). If there is no hole drilled on the tensioner, the pad must be kept retracted by hand while removing the tensioner.

7   Unbolt and remove the tensioner.

8   Unscrew the camshaft sprocket bolts, then remove the sprocket and timing chain (photo).

12 Flywheel/torque converter driveplate – removal

1   Have an assistant hold the flywheel or torque converter driveplate stationary. On manual gearbox models, a wide blade screwdriver can be held against a starter ring gear tooth.

2   Unscrew and remove the retaining bolts and withdraw the flywheel or driveplate from the end of the crankshaft.

13 Oil pump – removal

1   Unbolt and remove the crankcase between cover and gasket (photo).

2   Unscrew the retaining bolts and remove the metal gauze screen (photo).

3   Unbolt and remove the lower crankcase.

4   Remove the oil gauge pipe and dipstick tube from the cylinder block (photos).

5   Unscrew and remove the oil pump retaining bolts at the base and side of the cylinder block, then withdraw the oil pump (photos).

6   Unscrew the retaining plug and remove the timing chain tensioner filter from the block (photo).

14 Oil filter and housing – removal

1   Using a strap wrench, or the special Citroen tool No 6002-T, unscrew the oil filter canister from the housing and discard it (photo).

2   Unbolt and remove the oil filter housing and recover the spring (photo).

15 Camshaft and tappets – removal

1   Unbolt the distributor housing from the cylinder block and withdraw it over the end of the camshaft (photo).

2   Lift the tappets (cam followers) from the cylinder block and identify them for position (photo).

3   Unbolt and remove the thrust plate from the timing chain end of the cylinder block (photo).

4   Withdraw the camshaft from the timing chain end of the cylinder block, taking care not to damage the three camshaft bearings as the lobes of the cams pass through them (photo).

16 Pistons and liners – removal

1   Using a centre punch, mark the liners in relation to the cylinder block. Remember that No 1 cylinder is nearest the flywheel end of the engine.

2   Check the big-end caps for identification marks. If necessary, use a centre punch on the caps and connecting rods to identify them also.

3   Turn the crankshaft so that No 1 crankpin is facing across the crankcase (ie half way down).

4   Using a 15 mm socket, unscrew No 1 big-end bearing cap nuts

14.1 View of the oil filter from below

14.2 Removing the oil filter housing

15.1 Removing the distributor housing

15.2 Removing the tappets (cam followers)

15.3 Camshaft thrust plate location

15.4 Removing the camshaft

and withdraw the cap complete with bearing shell (photo).

5   Remove the bolts retaining the liners, if fitted in Section 9.

6   Using a block of wood, tap No 1 liner from the cylinder block and withdraw it complete with No 1 piston.

7   Remove the piston from the liner, then refit the big-end bearing cap and nut.

8   Repeat the procedure given in paragraphs 4 to 7 on liner No 4, then turn the crankshaft through half a turn and repeat the procedure on liners 2 and 3.

9   If the big-end bearing shells are to be refitted, use masking tape to identify them for location.

17 Crankshaft and main bearings – removal

1   Check the main bearing caps for identification marks. If necessary, use a centre punch on the caps and cylinder block to identify them.

2   Before removing the crankshaft, check that the endfloat is within the specified limits by inserting a feeler blade between the centre crankshaft web and the thrust washers. This will indicate whether the thrust washers require renewal or not (photo).

3   Unscrew and remove the main bearing cap bolts and withdraw the caps complete with bearing shells. Identify the shells for location if they are to be refitted (photos).

4   Remove the oil seal from the flywheel end of the crankshaft, then carefully lift the crankshaft from the crankcase (photo).

5   Extract the bearing shells from the crankcase recesses and identify them for location with masking tape (photo).

18 Examination and renovation – general

With the engine completely stripped, clean all the components and examine them for wear. Each part should be checked and where necessary renewed or renovated as described in the following Sections. Renew main and big-end shell bearings as a matter of course unless you know that they have had little wear and are in perfect condition.

19 Oil pump – examination and renovation

1   Unscrew and remove the five retaining bolts and remove the cover and bracket from the oil pump.

2   Bend back the lip and remove the metal base (photo).

3   Using an Allen key, unscrew the relief valve plug and remove the spring and plunger (photo).

4   Examine the gear teeth and relief valve faces for wear and pitting; if evident, renew the oil pump complete (photo). Check the relief valve spring gasket against the specified length and renew it if necessary.

5   Reassemble the oil pump in the reverse order to dismantling and prime it by operating it in clean engine oil.

20 Crankcase ventilation system – description

1   The crankcase ventilation system comprises a hose connected between the rocker cover and air cleaner, and a further hose connected between a cover on the timing chain end of the cylinder block and the carburettor intake hose.

2   Periodically the hoses should be examined for security and condition.

3   At the intervals specified in Routine Maintenance, remove the hoses and clean away any sludge with paraffin (photo).

21 Crankshaft and main bearings – examination and renovation

1   Examine the bearing surfaces of the crankshaft for scratches or scoring and, using a micrometer, check each journal and crankpin for ovality. Where this is found to be in excess of 0.0254 mm (0.001 in) the crankshaft will have to be reground and undersize bearings fitted.

2   Crankshaft regrinding can be carried out at a Citroen garage or a suitable engineering works who will normally supply the matching undersize main and big-end shell bearings.

3   Crankshaft endfloat with the main bearing caps fully tightened

should be as specified. If necessary new centre bearing thrust washers may be fitted; these are usually supplied together with the main and big-end bearings on a reground crankshaft.

4   On torque converter models, check that the location bush in the end of the crankshaft is serviceable. If necessary fit the torque converter in the bush and check for any excessive movement.

22 Pistons and liners – examination and renovation

1   Examine the liners for taper, ovality, scoring and scratches. If they are worn, a ridge will be found near the top face indicating the upper limit of travel of the top piston ring. Excessive liner wear will normally be apparent before dismantling the engine, usual symptoms being excessive oil consumption and piston slap.

2   If the liners are only slightly worn, special rings can be fitted to the pistons to restore compression and reduce the oil consumption. A motor factor will be able to advise which rings to fit. The top ring must be stepped, or it may break on the wear ridge on the liner.

3   Examine the pistons for ovality, scoring and scratches. If new pistons are to be fitted, first mark the piston crown in relation to the connecting rod. Remove the gudgeon pin retaining circlips (photo), then increase the complete piston in boiling water and drive out the gudgeon pin with a suitable diameter shaft metal punch. Heat the new piston and fit it to the connecting rod so that the crown contours are in the same position as the old piston. Make sure that the circlips are fully inserted.

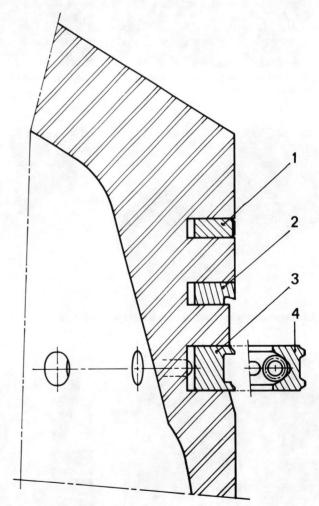

Fig. 1.12 Cross-sectional view of piston to show piston rings (Sec 22)

1 Compression ring
2 Oil scraper ring (Conical on later CX 2000 models)
3 Oil control ring
4 Alternative oil control ring

16.4 Removing a big-end bearing cap

17.2 Checking the crankshaft endfloat with a feeler gauge

17.3A Removing the centre main bearing cap

17.3B Removing the flywheel and main bearing cap

17.4 Crankshaft oil seal location (flywheel end)

17.5 Removing a main bearing shell

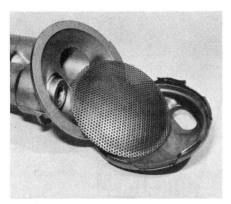

19.2 Oil pump strainer and retaining metal base

19.3 Oil pump relief valve spring and plunger

19.4 The oil pump gears

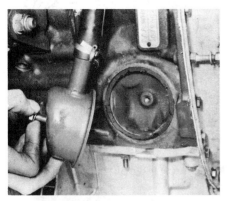

20.3 Removing the crankcase ventilation system cover

22.3 Gudgeon pin retaining circlip location

23.2 Liner supporting shoulder (arrowed) in the cylinder block

25.2 A badly worn tappet (cam follower) – note the pitting (arrowed)

25.3 Removing the oil seal from the distributor housing

26.2 Timing chain tensioner components (Brampton type)

4   If new piston rings are to be fitted to the original pistons, remove the old rings by expanding them over the top of the piston. The use of some old feeler blades or sheet tin will prevent the rings dropping into the ring grooves.

5   Fit the new rings by reversing the removal procedure, but make sure that the faces marked 'Top' are towards the piston crown. The oil control ring is fitted to the bottom groove, the scraper ring to the middle groove, and the compression ring to the top groove. The compression ring may be fitted either way round unless it is stepped.

23 Cylinder block and crankcase – examination and renovation

1   Examine the cylinder block and crankcase for damage and cracks.
2   Clean away all traces of gasket from the liner supporting shoulders (photo).
3   Check that the oil galleries and waterways are clear by probing with a piece of wire.

24 Flywheel – examination and renovation

1   Examine the clutch driven plate surface of the flywheel. If this is scored, the flywheel must either be renewed or refaced by an engineering works.
2   Examine the teeth of the starter ring gear; if they are chipped or worn, the ring must be renewed. To do this, drill the ring and split it with a cold chisel (*take care* to protect your eyes from flying fragments) and remove it.
3   Heat the new ring to 200° C (392° F) in an electric oven, then quickly fit it to the flywheel with its non-machined face against the flywheel shoulder.
4   Allow the ring to cool naturally without quenching.
5   Check the gearbox spigot bearing for excessive wear. If it requires renewal, remove the circlip and drive it out of the flywheel with a suitable diameter tube located on the outer track. Fit the new bearing in the same manner, making sure that it is located firmly against the retaining circlip.

25 Camshaft and tappets – examination and renovation

1   Examine the camshaft bearing journals, cam lobes, gear teeth and bearings for wear or scoring. If evident, renew the shaft and bearings. This work is best carried out by a suitable engineering works who will have the necessary tools.
2   Examine the tappets (cam followers) for wear, particularly on the surface which contacts the cam lobe. Renew them if necessary (photo).
3   Prise the oil seal from the distributor housing and drive the new seal into position (photo).

26 Timing cover, gears and chain – examination and renovation

1   Examine the teeth on the camshaft and crankshaft sprockets and renew them if they are at all hooked in appearance. The use of a press

will be required for the crankshaft sprocket. Renew the chain also if new sprockets are fitted.
2   Examine the chain tensioner and, if the rubber pad is worn or hardened, renew the tensioner (photo).
3   Examine the timing chain guide for wear and renew it if necessary.
4   Examine the timing chain for wear and renew it if necessary. A worn chain will bend in an arc when held horizontally. If a high mileage has been covered it is a sensible precaution to renew the chain as a matter of course.
5   Check the timing cover for damage and if necessary renew it.

27 Cylinder head – decarbonising and valve grinding

1   This operation will normally only be required at comparatively high mileages. However, if persistent pinking occurs and performance has deteriorated even though the engine adjustments are correct, decarbonising and valve grinding may be required.
2   With the cylinder head removed, use a scraper to remove the carbon from the combustion chambers and ports. Be careful not to damage the head, it is made of aluminium. Remove all traces of gasket or jointing compound from the cylinder head surface, then wash it thoroughly with paraffin. Take particular care to clean the ports and cylinder head bolt holes.
3   Using a straight edge and feeler gauge, check the cylinder head surface for distortion. If this is in excess of the specified maximum, the head will have to be resurfaced by a specialist engineering works.
4   If the engine is still in the car, clean the piston crowns and upper edges of the liners. Make sure that no carbon finds it way between the pistons and liners otherwise damage may occur. To do this, locate two of the pistons at the top of their liners and seal off the remaining liners with paper and masking tape. Press a little grease between the two pistons and the liners, then clean away the carbon. Lower the two pistons and wipe away the grease which will now contain carbon particles.
5   The remaining piston crowns should be cleaned in a similar manner. To prevent carbon build-up, polish the piston crowns with metal polish, removing all traces afterwards.
6   Examine the heads of the valve for pitting and burring, especially the exhaust valve heads. Renew any valve which is badly burnt. Examine the valve seats at the same time. If the pitting is very slight it can be removed by grinding the valve heads and seats together with coarse and then fine grinding paste.
7   Where excessive pitting has occurred, the valve seats must be recut and the valves renewed. Recutting the valve seats is a job for a Citroen garage or specialist engineering works.
8   Valve grinding is carried out as follows. Place the cylinder head upside down on a bench with a block of wood at each end to give clearance for the valve stems.
9   Smear a trace of coarse carborundum paste on the seat face and apply a suction grinding tool to the valve head. With a semi-rotary action, grind the valve head to its seat, lifting the valve occasionally to redistribute the grinding paste. When a dull matt even surface is produced on both the valve seat and the valve, then wipe off the paste and repeat the process with fine carborundum paste as before. A light spring placed under the valve head will greatly ease this operation. When a smooth unbroken ring of light grey matt finish is produced, on

both valve and valve seat faces, the grinding operation is complete.

10 Scrape away all carbon from the valve head and the valve stem. Carefully clean away every trace of grinding compound, taking great care to leave none in the ports or in the valve guides. Clean the valves and valve seats with a paraffin soaked rag then wipe with clean rag. (If an air line is available blow clean).

11 If the valve guides are worn, the valve stem will exhibit excessive side movement. If this is the case, new guides must be fitted by a Citroen garage or engineering works.

12 If theoriginal valve springs have been in use for 20 000 miles (32 000 km) or more, renew them. The valve stem oil seals should also be renewed whenever the cylinder head is dismantled.

13 Make sure that the cylinder head oilways and waterways are clear by probing them with a piece of wire.

28 Engine reassembly – general

1 To ensure maximum life with minimum trouble from a rebuilt engine, not only must everything be correctly assembled, but it must also be spotlessly clean. All oilways must be clear, locking washers and spring washers must be fitted where indicated. Oil all bearings and other working surfaces thoroughly with engine oil during assembly.

2 Before assembly begins, renew any bolts or studs with damaged threads.

3 Gather together a torque wrench, oil can, clean rag, and a set of engine gaskets and oil seals together with a new oil filter canister.

29 Crankshaft and main bearings – refitting

1 Clean the backs of the bearing shells and the bearing recesses in both the crankcase and the caps.

2 Press the main bearing shells into the crankcase and caps and oil them liberally (photo).

3 Stick the centre bearing thrust washers into the crankcase and cap using a little grease (photos).

4 Lower the crankshaft into position, then fit the main bearing caps (photos). Coat the flywheel end cap with sealing compound in the area shown in Fig. 1.13 before fitting it.

5 Insert and tighten the main bearing cap bolts to the specified torque (photo).

6 Check that the crankshaft rotates smoothly, then check that the endfloat is within the specified limits by inserting a feeler blade between the centre crankshaft web and the thrust washers.

7 Using a tube of suitable diameter, push the crankshaft oil seal over the flywheel end of the crankshaft with its open end facing into the engine. Take care not to damage the seal.

30 Pistons and liners – refitting

1 Position the piston ring gaps at 120° intervals, then apply engine oil liberally to the pistons and liners.

2 Clean the backs of the bearing shells and the recesses in the connecting rods and big-end caps.

3 Press the big-end bearing shells into the connecting rods and caps in their correct positions and oil them liberally (photo).

4 Fit a ring compressor to No 1 piston, then insert the piston in No 1 liner. Drive the piston into the liner with the wooden handle of a hammer (photo).

5 Locate a base gasket on the liner shoulder and coat it with sealing compound (photo).

6 With No 1 crankpin facing across the crankcase, insert the piston and liner into the flywheel end of the cylinder block. Check that the arrow on the piston is facing the flywheel end, then locate the liner and

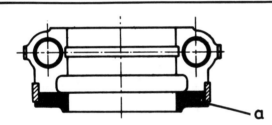

Fig. 1.13 Flywheel end main bearing cap sealing compound area (a) (Sec 29)

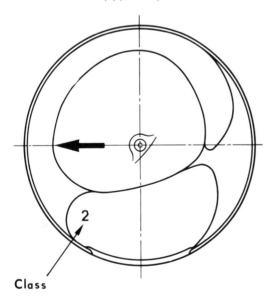

Fig. 1.14 Piston crown location arrow and class identification mark (Sec 30)

Fig. 1.15 Correct assembly of timing chain (Sec 34)

a Camshaft timing mark   *c Crankshaft timing mark*
b Timing chain

29.2 Main bearing shells fitted in the crankcase

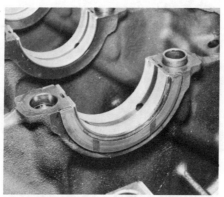
29.3A Correct location of the centre bearing thrust washers

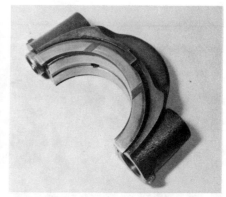
29.3B Centre main bearing cap with thrust washers fitted

29.4A Crankshaft positioned in the main bearings

29.4B Main bearing caps fitted over the crankshaft

29.5 Tightening the main bearing cap bolts

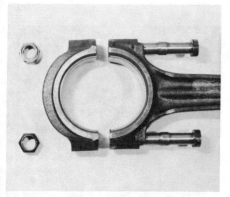
30.3 Connecting rod and cap components

30.4 Using a ring compressor to fit the pistons

30.5 Base gasket location on the liner shoulder

30.6A Fitting the liner assembly

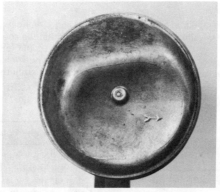
30.6B Assembly arrow on the piston crown must point to flywheel end

30.6C Locating the connecting rod on the crankpin

30.7A Fit the connecting rod bolts ...

30.7B ... and tighten the big-end bearing nuts to the specified torque

31.1 The camshaft fitted in the cylinder block

33.1 Location of the O-ring seal on the oil pump

33.2 Inserting the oil pump lower mounting bolt

33.3 Fitting the lower crankcase cork seal

33.4 Fitting the lower crankcase

34.2 Fitting the timing chain and camshaft sprocket

34.7 Spacer locations on the timing cover

tap the piston to position the connecting rod on the crankpin (photos).

7   Fit the big-end bearing cap in its correct position, then tighten the nuts evenly to the specified torque (photos).

8   Using a straight edge and feeler blade, check that the liner protrusion above the face of the cylinder block is within the specified limits.

9   Check that the crankshaft turns smoothly.

10   Repeat the procedure given in paragraphs 4 to 9 for the remaining three piston and liner assemblies and retain them in position with bolts as described in Section 9.

31 Camshaft and tappets – refitting

1   Oil the camshaft bearings and carefully insert the camshaft from the timing chain end of the cylinder block (photo).

2   Fit the thrust plate and tighten the retaining bolt to the specified torque.

3   Using a dial gauge or feeler blades, check that the camshaft endfloat is within the specified limits. If not, renew the thrust plate.

4   Oil the tappet (cam followers) and fit them in the cylinder block in their original positions.

5   Fit the distributor housing, with a new gasket, and tighten the retaining bolts.

32 Oil filter and housing – refitting

1   Refit the oil filter housing complete with spring and a new gasket. Tighten the retaining bolts to the specified torque.

2   Smear the sealing rubber with engine oil, then fit and tighten the oil filter canister to the specified torque using a strap wrench or the special Citroen tool No 6002-T. Alternatively, tighten the canister by hand.

33 Oil pump – refitting

1 Locate a new O-ring seal in the oil pump groove, then insert the oil pump into the cylinder block (photo).

2 Insert and tighten the oil pump retaining bolts on the main bearing and on the side of the block (photo).

3 Place a new cork seal in the flywheel end main bearing cap (photo). Coat the seal and the lower crankcase mating surface with jointing compound. Refit the timing chain tensioner filter and tighten the retaining plug.

4 Fit the lower crankcase and tighten the retaining bolts finger-tight; locate the two studs by the driveshaft mounting (photo).

5 Refit the dipstick tube and oil gauge pipe to the cylinder block.

6 Refit the metal gauze screen to the lower crankcase and tighten the retaining bolts.

34 Timing cover, gears and chain – refitting

1 Rotate the crankshaft and the camshaft (with sprocket temporarily fitted) until the timing marks are adjacent to each other. Remove the camshaft sprocket.

2 Loop the timing chain over the two sprockets and fit the camshaft sprocket to the camshaft (photo). Refer to Fig. 1.15 and check that with length (b) taut, the timing marks (a) and (c) are located on a line between the sprocket centres. Check also that No 1 piston is at TDC.

3 When the timing chain is located correctly, remove the camshaft sprocket retaining bolts one at a time and coat their threads with a locking agent. Tighten the bolts to the specified torque whilst holding the crankshaft stationary with a lever between the (temporarily refitted) flywheel bolts.

4 Lock the timing chain tensioner in its retracted position. To do this on the type with a drilled hole, press the rubber pad in whilst turning a screwdriver inserted through the hole; when fully retracted, turn the screwdriver in the opposite direction to lock it. To lock the other type, press the rubber pad in and turn it clockwise.

5 Refit the tensioner and tighten the retaining bolts to the specified torque. Unlock the tensioner by turning a screwdriver inserted in the hole, or by depressing the pressure pad, as appropriate.

6 Fit the timing chain guide so that the specified chain to guide clearance is within limits. Tighten the retaining bolts to the specified torque.

7 Refit the timing cover with a new gasket. Fit the retaining bolts and nuts (with thrust washers) and tighten them finger-tight to align the lower crankcase (photo).

8 Tighten the lower crankcase bolts evenly and in diagonal sequence to the specified torque.

9 Tighten the timing cover bolts and nuts evenly and in diagonal sequence to the specified torque.

10 If the engine is in the car, paragraph 8 does not apply. Reverse the procedure given in the preliminary note in Section 11.

11 Refit the crankcase bottom cover with a new gasket.

35 Flywheel/torque converter driveplate – refitting

1 Locate the flywheel or torque converter driveplate on the crankshaft.

2 Coat the threads of the retaining bolts with a locking agent, then insert them into the crankshaft.

3 Tighten the retaining bolts evenly to the specified torque whilst an assistant holds the flywheel or torque converter driveplate stationary (photo).

36 Cylinder head – reassembly and refitting

1 Fit the valves in their original sequence or, if new valves have been obtained, to the seats to which they have been ground.

2 Oil the valve stems liberally, then fit the oil seal, washer, spring, and retainer over the first valve. Compress the spring with the valve spring compressor, insert the split collets and release the compressor.

3 Repeat the procedure given in paragraph 2 on the remaining valves. Tap the end of each valve stem with a non-metallic mallet to settle the collets.

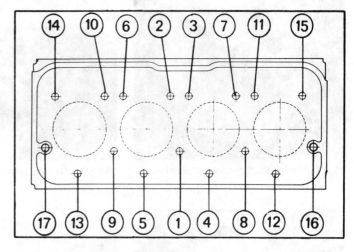

Fig. 1.16 Cylinder head bolt tightening sequence (Sec (36)

Fig. 1.17 Engine/gearbox mounting alignment tool (Sec 39)

A Pins   B Beam

Fig. 1.18 Aligning the engine/gearbox lower mountings (Sec 39)

A Pin   B Beam

35.3 Tightening the flywheel retaining bolts

36.5 Cylinder head gasket located on the block

36.6 Refitting the cylinder head

36.8A Seal location (arrowed) in the rocker assembly

36.8B Inserting the head bolts through the rocker shaft

36.9 Tightening the cylinder head bolts

36.10A Fitting the exhaust rocker shafts

36.10B Showing the complete assembled rocker gear

36.12 Oil transfer pipe location

39.1 Right-hand engine mounting

41.7A Adjusting an inlet valve clearance

41.7B Adjusting an exhaust valve clearance

4 Refit the water outlet elbow to the cylinder head and tighten the retaining bolts.
5 Make sure that the faces of the cylinder head and block are perfectly clean. Remove the liner retaining bolts (if fitted), then place the new gasket on the cylinder block with the word 'Cefilac' or 'Coopers' uppermost (photo). **Do not** use jointing compound.
6 Lower the cylinder head into position and insert the head bolts adjacent to the exhaust valves (photo).
7 Insert the pushrods in their original locations.
8 Locate the new O-ring seals, then refit the inlet rocker shaft complete (photos). Insert the remaining head bolts. Make sure that the pushrods are engaged with the inlet valve rockers.
9 Tighten the cylinder head bolts in two stages to the specified torque using the sequence shown in Fig. 1.16 (photo).
10 Refit the exhaust rocker shafts and rockers. Make sure that the pushrods are engaged with the exhaust valve rockers, then tighten the retaining nuts to the specified torque (photos).
11 Refit the cover to the end of the cylinder head and tighten the bolts.
12 Refit the oil transfer pipe to the cylinder head and block with new washers, and tighten the unions (photo).
13 Adjust the valve clearances as described in Section 41.
14 Locate the rocker cover on the cylinder head together with the rubber gasket and seals, then tighten the retaining bolts to the specified torque.
15 If the engine is still in the car, reverse the procedure given in Section 9 with reference to the relevant Chapters of this manual.

37 Ancillary components – refitting

1 Refer to Section 8, and refit the listed components with reference to the Chapters indicated.

38 Engine – refitting to gearbox

1 Refer to Section 6 and reverse the separation procedure.
2 Adjust the water pump drivebelt tension as described in Chapter 2, and the alternator drivebelt tension as described in Chapter 10.

39 Engine/gearbox assembly – refitting

1 Reverse the removal procedure given in Section 5, but before starting work, the engine/gearbox mountings must be aligned with each other to avoid strain which would lead to their early deterioration (photo). To do this, obtain Citroen tool No 6003-T as shown in Fig. 1.17, or fabricate a similar tool out of a length of wood. Adjust mounting positions on the engine/gearbox and subframe so that the mounting centres are an identical distance apart. On four-speed manual gearbox models, the left-hand subframe mounting is adjustable; on five-speed and torque converter models, the right-hand subframe mounting is adjustable.
2 Tighten the mounting bolts to the specified torque after adjusting them.
3 The upper torque bar and gearbox mountings (where fitted) must be adjusted after the engine/gearbox is fitted, with the lower mounting bolts tightened to the specified torque. 1.0 mm (0.04 in) thick shims must be inserted as necessary so that the mounting bolts can be tightened without loading the rubber bushes.
4 After refitting the engine, adjust the clutch cable (where fitted) as described in Chapter 5, adjust the accelerator and choke cables as described in Chapter 3, refill the torque converter (if fitted) as described in Chapter 6, and tighten the front driveshaft nuts as described in Chapter 7.
5 Refill the cooling system as described in Chapter 2.
6 Refill the engine with oil.
7 Check and top-up the gearbox oil level on manual gearbox models.
8 Refit the roadwheels and lower the car to the ground.

40 Engine – adjustment after major overhaul

1 With the engine refitted to the vehicle, make a final check to make sure that everything has been reconnected and that no rags or tools

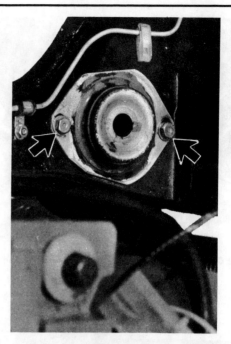

Fig. 1.19 Engine/gearbox lower mounting retaining bolts – arrowed (Sec 39)

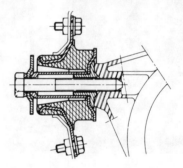

Fig. 1.20 Cross-sectional view of an engine/gearbox lower mounting (Sec 39)

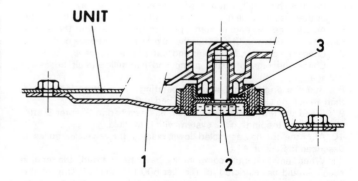

Fig. 1.21 Cross-sectional view of a gearbox mounting on a five-speed or torque converter gearbox (Sec 39)

1 Plate
2 Bolt
3 Shims

Fig. 1.22 Camshaft extension bearing retaining bolt locations (1)
(Sec 41)

Fig. 1.23 Pneumatic oil level gauge filling orifice (a) and adjustment
hole (arrowed) (Sec 43)

Fig. 1.24 Pneumatic oil level gauge knob (1), level indicator (a),
and adjustment hole (arrowed) (Sec 43)

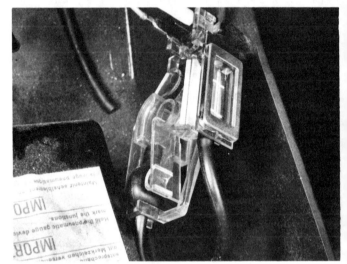

43.2 The pneumatic oil level gauge

have been left in the engine compartment.

2   Prime the high pressure pump as described in Chapter 8.

3   Turn the carburettor slow running screw in about half a turn; this will be necessary to compensate for the tightness of the new engine components.

4   Pull the choke fully out and start the engine. This may take a little longer than usual as the fuel pump and carburettor bowl will be empty.

5   As soon as the engine starts, push in the choke unitl the engine runs at a fast tickover. Check that the oil pressure light goes out.

6   Check the oil filter, fuel hoses and water hoses for leaks.

7   Check the high pressure pump and hydraulic circuit hoses for leakage.

8   Run the engine until normal operating temperature is reached, then adjust the slow running as described in Chapter 3.

9   Bleed the brake hydraulic system as described in Chapter 9 after checking and topping-up the system with LHM fluid.

10   After the engine has cooled down, readjust the valve clearances as described in Section 41.

11   When new internal components have been fitted, the engine speed should be restricted for the first 600 miles (1000 km). At this mileage, renew the engine oil, tighten the cylinder head bolts to the specified torque, and then adjust the valve clearances.

41 Valve clearances – adjustment

1   The valve clearances must be adjusted with the engine cold.

2   If the engine is in the car, jack-up a front wheel and engage top gear on manual gearbox models in order to turn the engine. On torque converter models, remove the plate on the bellhousing and use a wide blade screwdriver on the starter ring gear to turn the engine.

3   On fuel injection engines, remove the injection manifold.

4   Remove the rocker cover and its gasket.

5   Turn the engine until No 1 exhaust valve is fully open. (No 1 exhaust valve is at the flywheel end of the engine. Exhaust valve rockers are on the four separate shafts; inlet valve rockers are on the single long shaft).

6   Insert a feeler blade of the correct thickness between the rocker arm and valve stem of No 3 inlet valve. If the blade is not a firm sliding fit, loosen the locknut on the rocker arm with a ring spanner and turn the bell pin with a screwdriver. Tighten the locknut whilst holding the ball pin stationary and recheck the adjustment.

7   Check and adjust the remaining valve clearances with the relevant exhaust valve fully open in accordance with the following table (photos):

Exhaust valve open	Adjust valves
1	3 (inlet), 4 (exhaust)
3	4 (inlet), 2 (exhaust)
4	2 (inlet), 1 (exhaust)
2	1 (inlet), 3 (exhaust)

8   Refit the rocker cover and gasket, and the injection manifold where applicable.

9   Refit the plate on the bellhousing on torque converter models.

10   Lower the car to the ground if it was jacked-up.

11   If the rocker arms are still noisy after making the previous adjust-

ments, the camshaft extension bearing may be in need of adjustment. First remove the drivebelt cover, release the tensioner, and remove the water pump drivebelt.

12 Unscrew the retaining nut and remove the pulley from the camshaft.

13 Loosen the three bearing housing bolts.

14 Turn the engine until No 4 exhaust valve is fully open, then tighten the bearing housing bolts.

15 Refit the pulley, drivebelt and cover as described in Chapter 2.

16 Adjust the valve clearance again as previously described.

42 Valve timing – checking

1 The following method may be used to check the valve timing with the engine in the car. First remove the spare wheel.

2 Remove the injection manifold on fuel injection engines.

3 Remove the rocker cover and gasket.

4 Turn the engine until No 4 piston is at top dead centre (TDC) with both valves rocking. The exact point of TDC can be ascertained by aligning the mark on the flywheel with the lug on the bellhousing.

5 Adjust the clearance of No 1 inlet valve to 1.10 mm (0.043 in).

6 Rotate the crankshaft exactly 1 turn in the normal direction of rotation of the engine, then check the clearance of No 1 inlet valve. If it is between (0.05 and 0.25 mm) (0.002 and 0.010 in), the valve timing is correct.

7 Release No 1 inlet valve to its normal clearance as described in Section 41, then refit the rocker cover, injection manifold (where applicable) and the spare wheel.

43 Pneumatic oil level gauge – filling and adjusting

1 Remove the map pocket and oil gauge bracket.

2 Disconnect the tube from the top of the gauge (photo).

3 Fully unscrew the adjustment screw on the front of the gauge.

4 With the gauge horizontal, pour LHM fluid through the filler orifice until it reaches the minimum mark on the indicator.

5 Connect the tube to the top of the gauge, then refit the gauge and map pocket.

6 Check the oil level using the engine dipstick. The car must be parked on level ground.

7 Fully depress the gauge knob and adjust the screw so that the indicated level is identical to the actual level on the engine dipstick.

8 Release the knob and check that the LHM fluid falls below the minimum mark.

44 Fault diagnosis – engine

Symptom	Reason/s
Engine fails to start	Discharged battery
	Loose battery connection
	Loose or broken ignition leads
	Moisture on spark plugs, distributor cap or HT leads
	Incorrect spark plug or contact points gap
	Cracked distributor cap or rotor
	Dirt or water in carburettor
	Empty fuel tank
	Faulty fuel pump
	Faulty starter motor
	Faulty choke mechanism
Engine idles erratically	Intake manifold air leak
	Leaking cylinder head gasket
	Worn timing sprockets
	Worn camshaft lobes
	Faulty fuel pump
	Incorrect valve clearances
Engine misfires	Incorrect spark plug or contact points gap
	Uneven compressions
	Faulty coil or condenser
	Dirt or water in carburettor
	Incorrect carburettor adjustment
	Burnt out valve
Engine stalls	Incorrect carburettor adjustment
	Sticking choke mechanism
	Air leak in inlet manifold
	Incorrect ignition timing
Excessive oil consumption	Worn pistons and liners
	Crankshaft oil seal leaking
	Valve guides and valve stem seals worn

Chapter 2 Cooling system

For modifications, and information applicable to later models, see Supplement at end of manual

Contents

Specifications

System type .... Thermosyphon, water pump assisted, pressurized, self-bleeding. Thermostatically controlled radiator cooling fan(s)

Header tank cap pressure .... 1.0 bar (14.5 lbf/in^2)

Thermostat opening temperature .... 84° C (183° F)

Warning lamp switch operating temperature
248 sq in radiator .... 113° to 117° C (235° to 243° F)
310 and 356.5 sq in radiators .... 110° to 114° C (230° to 236° F)

Electric fan thermal switch
Cut-in temperature:
    248 sq in radiator .... 101° to 104° C (214° to 219° F)
    310 and 356.5 sq in radiators .... 95° to 100° C (203° to 212° F)
Cut-out temperature:
    248 sq in radiator .... 95° to 92° C (203° to 198° F)
    310 and 356.5 sq in radiators .... 95° to 90° C (203° to 194° F)

Radiator and fan applications

	Radiator area (sq in)	No of blades	No of fans
CX 2000 (pre-1975, except towing equipment)	248	10	1
CX 2000 (post-1975) and CX 2200 (except towing equipment, air conditioning or torque converter)	310	5	1
CX 2000 and CX 2200 (with towing equipment or torque converter)	310	5	2
CX 2200 (with air conditioning)	310	10	2
CX Prestige (except torque converter or air conditioning)	310	10	2
CX 2400 (except towing equipment, air conditioning or torque converter)	310	10	1
CX 2400 (with any one of the above)	310	10	2
CX 2400 GTi (except towing equipment)	356.5	10	1
CX 2400 GTi (with towing equipment), CX Prestige and CX 2400 (with torque converter and air conditioning)	356.5	10	2

System capacity

CX 2000 and CX 2200 Saloons:
    248 sq in radiator .... 11.0 litres (19.3 pints)
    310 sq in radiator .... 10.6 litres (18.6 pints)
CX 2000 Estate .... 10.6 litres (18.6 pints)
CX Prestige and CX 2400 Saloons:
    310 sq in radiator .... 10.6 litres (18.6 pints)
    356 sq in radiator .... 12.5 litres (22.0 pints)
CX 2400 Estate .... 10.6 litres (18.6 pints)
CX 2400 GTi .... 12.3 litres (21.6 pints)
CX 2400 Ambulance .... 11.8 litres (20.8 pints)

Drivebelt tensions
Water pump, alternator and air conditioning compressor (if fitted):
  New .... 40 to 45 kgf (88 to 99 lbf)
  Used .... 25 to 30 kgf (55 to 66 lbf)
Power steering pump (if fitted):
  New .... 35 to 40 kgf (77 to 88 lbf)
  Used .... 20 to 22.5 kgf (44 to 50 lbf)
Toothed drivebelt for water pump (if air conditioning fitted) .... 15 to 18 kgf (33 to 40 lbf)

Torque wrench settings
	lbf ft	kgf m
Drain plug (cylinder block)	21.5 to 29.0	3.0 to 4.0
Thermal switch (cylinder head)	18.0 to 21.5	2.5 to 3.0
Thermal switch (radiator)	13.0 to 14.5	1.8 to 2.0
Camshaft pulley nut	58.0	8.0
Alternator pulley nut	29.0	4.0
Alternator retaining bolt	44.0	6.1
Seven piston pump retaining nut	29.0	4.0

1 Cooling system – general description

1   The cooling system is of the pressurized type and comprises a front mounted radiator, a water pump belt-driven from the camshaft pulley, and an electric fan (or fans) fitted to the front of the radiator. A thermostat is located in the water pump spacer housing. The thermal switch for the temperature warning lamp is located on the cylinder head (photo) and the thermal switch which controls the electric cooling fan is located either on the right-hand lower side or the left-hand upper side of the radiator.
2   Bleed screws are provided on the water pump. An expansion tank is located on the right-hand side of the bulkhead (photo). Some later models are equipped with a de-aeration chamber which prevents the circulation of coolant through the header tank.
3   The cooling system functions as follows. Cold water in the bottom of the radiator circulates through the radiator bottom hose to the water pump, where it is forced by the impeller into the cylinder block and head along the internal waterways. The water cools the cylinder liners, combustion surfaces and valve seats, and is then circulated through the inlet manifold and returned to the water pump (photo). On fuel injection models, and on CX 2400 models with air conditioning and a torque converter the water is returned to the water pump via the car interior heater unit when in operation.
4   When the water has absorbed sufficient heat from the engine, the thermostat begins to open and water is then circulated to the top of the radiator through the top hose. On passing through the radiator tubes, the water cools, assisted by the inrush of air when the car is in motion. Additionally, when the water in the radiator reaches a specified temperature, the electric fan (or fans) are energised by a thermal switch to provide extra cooling. When the water reaches the bottom of the radiator, the cycle is repeated. Another thermal switch operates a warning lamp if the coolant temperature becomes dangerously high.
5   When starting from cold, the thermostat remains closed and the circulation of water is restricted in order to allow the engine to reach its normal operating temperature as quickly as possible.
6   As the coolant expands with increasing temperature, excess flows into the expansion tank, whence it is returned to the main system when cooling reduces the volume again. A safety valve is fitted in the expansion tank cap.

2 Cooling system – draining

1   It is preferable to drain the cooling system when the engine is cold. If this is not possible, *take care to avoid scalding*. Place a cloth over the filler cap on the expansion tank and turn it slowly in an anti-clockwise direction until the safety notch is reached. Wait a minute or two with the cap in this position to allow the pressure to escape from the system, then continue turning the cap anti-clockwise and remove it.
2   If the coolant is to be retained for further use, place a suitable container beneath the radiator and front of the engine.
3   Unscrew the radiator drain tap located at the bottom right or bottom left of the radiator (photo), then unscrew and remove the cylinder block drain plug located beneath the exhaust manifold.
4   Move the interior heater controls to maximum heat.

3 Cooling system – flushing

1   After considerable time, the radiator and engine waterways may become restricted or even blocked with scale or sediment which will reduce the efficiency of the cooling system. To prevent this condition occurring, the coolant should be drained and the system flushed every 2 years. Where the system has been neglected and severe restriction has occurred, reverse flushing may be required.
2   Normal flushing is carried out by inserting a hose in the header tank filler neck and allowing water to run through the system until it flows from the radiator drain tap and cylinder block drain plug without any discoloration.
3   Where reverse flushing is necessary, remove the radiator as

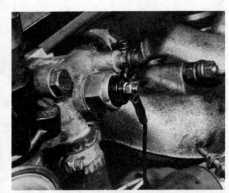
1.1 Temperature warning lamp thermal switch location

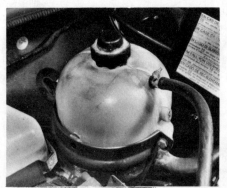
1.2 Expansion tank location

1.3 Cylinder head outlet housing, showing heater and inlet manifold supply hoses

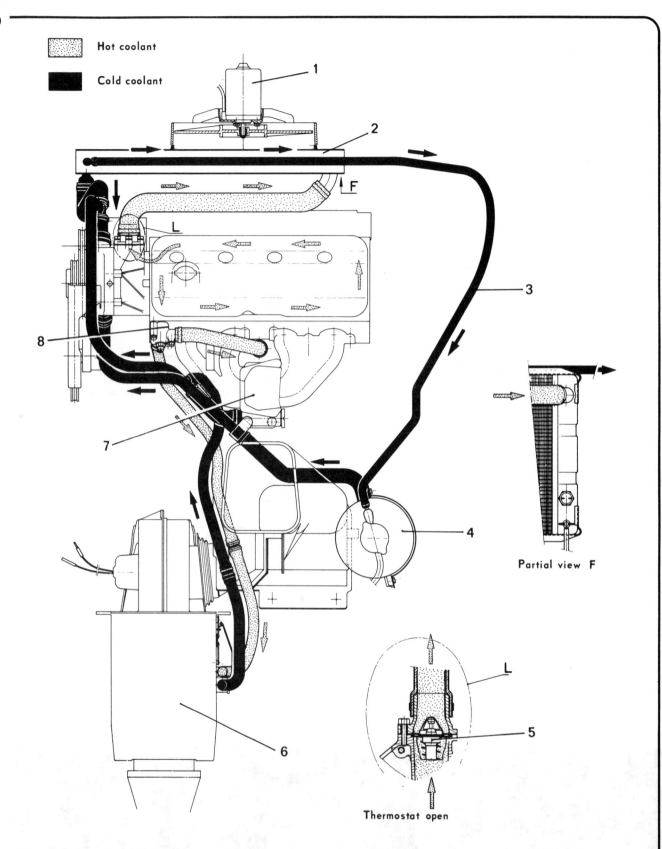

Hot coolant

Cold coolant

F

L

3

8

7

4

Partial view F

6

L

5

Thermostat open

Fig. 2.1 Diagrammatic view of the cooling system fitted to CX 2000 models up to January 1975, without towing equipment (Sec 1)

1 Electric fan	3 De-aeration pipe	5 Thermostat	7 Inlet manifold
2 Radiator	4 Expansion tank	6 Heater	8 Cylinder head outlet housing

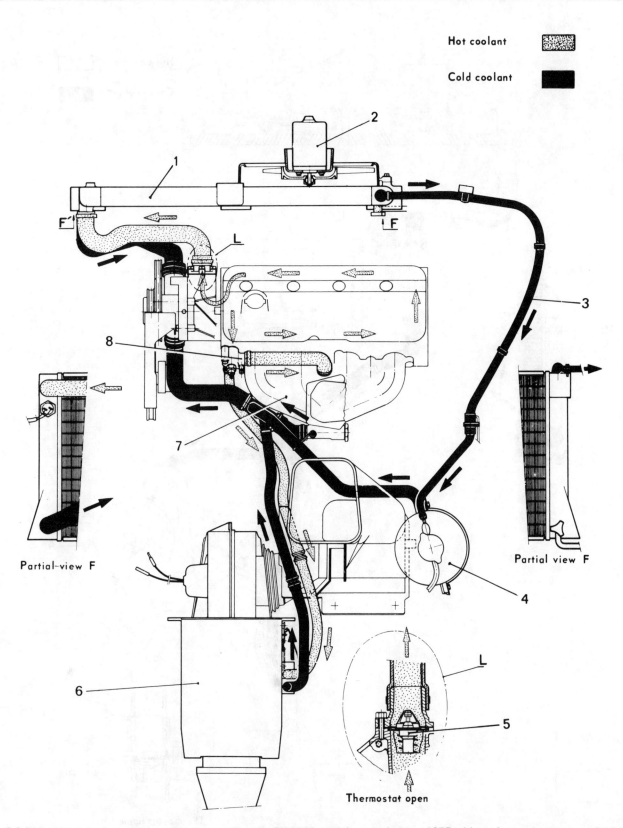

Hot coolant

Cold coolant

Partial-view F

Partial view F

Thermostat open

Fig. 2.2 Diagrammatic view of the cooling system fitted to CX 2000 models up to January 1975 with towing equipment, and CX 2200 and CX 2400 models from January 1975 on without air conditioning, fuel injection or torque converter (Sec 1)

1 Radiator
2 Electric fan motor
3 De-aeration pipe
4 Expansion tank
5 Thermostat
6 Heater
7 Inlet manifold
8 Cylinder head outlet housing

42

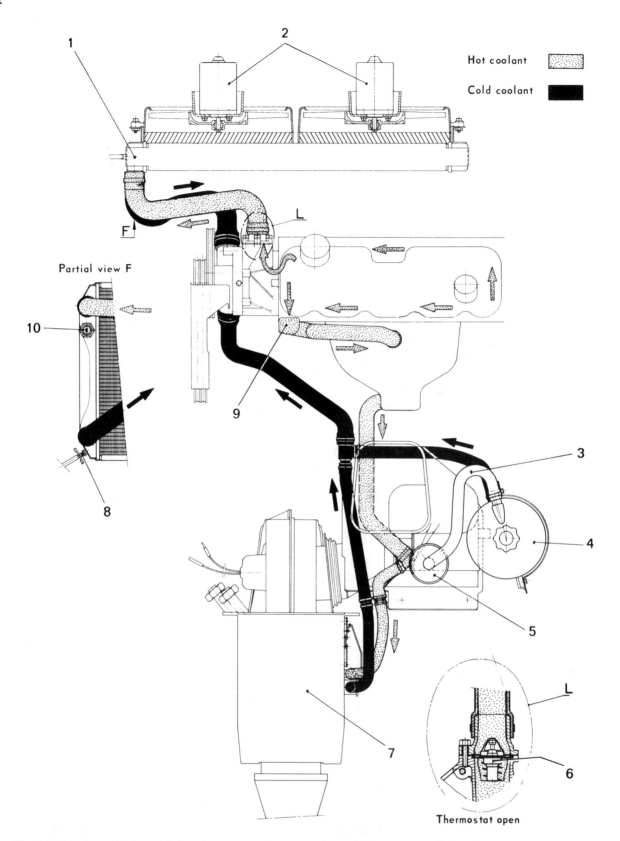

Hot coolant

Cold coolant

Partial view F

Thermostat open

Fig. 2.3 Diagrammatic view of the cooling system fitted to CX 2400 models with torque converter and air conditioning (Sec 1)

1 Radiator
2 Electric fan motors
3 De-aeration pipe
4 Expansion tank
5 De-aeration chamber
6 Thermostat
7 Heater
8 Drain tap
9 Cylinder head outlet housing
10 Electric fan thermal switch

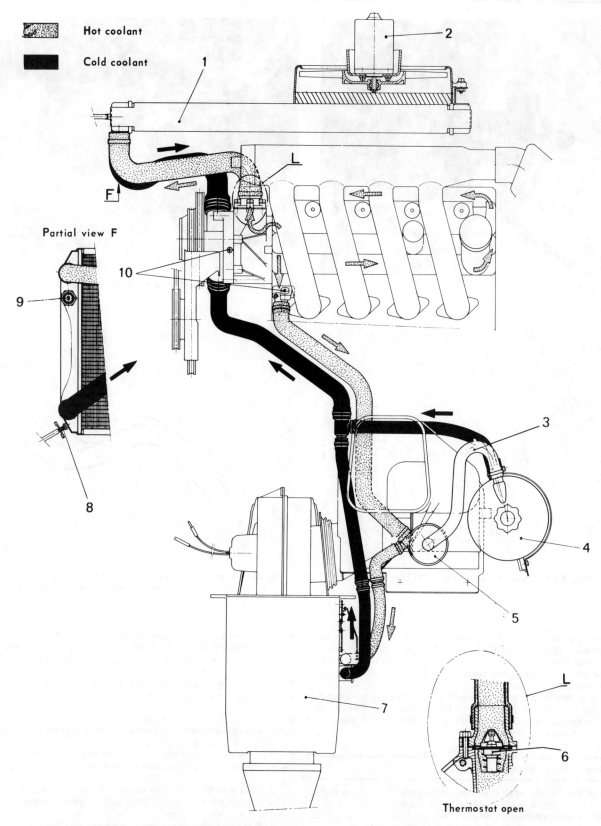

Hot coolant

Cold coolant

Partial view F

L

Thermostat open

Fig. 2.4 Diagrammatic view of the cooling system fitted to CX 2400 models with fuel injection (Sec 1)

1 Radiator
2 Electric fan motors
3 De-aeration pipe
4 Expansion tank
5 De-aeration chamber
6 Thermostat
7 Heater
8 Drain tap
9 Electric fan thermal switch
10 Bleed screws

2.3 Radiator drain tap location

4.6 Bleed screw (arrowed) on the cylinder head outlet housing

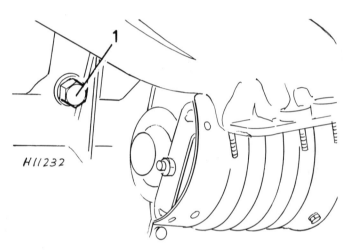

Fig. 2.5 Cylinder block drain plug (1) (Sec 2)

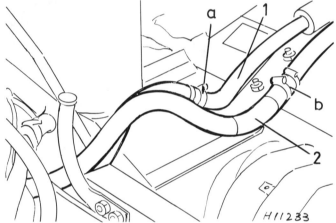

Fig. 2.6 Heater inlet hose (1) and outlet hose (2) showing the intermediate connecting pipes (a) and (b) (Sec 4)

described in Section 6, invert it, and insert a hose in the bottom water outlet. Continue flushing until clear water flows from the top water inlet. Similarly, insert a hose in the engine top hose and reverse flush the engine waterways until clear water flows from the cylinder block drain plug and bottom hose.

4   If all else fails, a proprietary de-scaling and flushing compound may be used in accordance with the maker's instructions. Make sure that any compound used is suitable for use in engines containing both aluminium and cast iron components.

4   Cooling system – filling

1   Tighten the radiator drain tap, and the cylinder block drain plug after making sure that the copper washer is serviceable.
2   Move the interior heater controls to maximum heat.
3   Remove the spare wheel from the engine compartment.
4   Loosen the hose clip and disconnect the heater inlet hose near the bulkhead. (The outlet hose has a white band round it). Using a funnel, pour 0.6 litre (1 pt) of coolant into the hose in order to prime the heater, then reconnect the hose and tighten the clip.
5   Pour coolant of the correct mixture (see Section 5) into the expansion tank until it reaches the minimum level plate.
6   Loosen the bleed screw on the cylinder head outlet located by the

inlet manifold, allow the trapped air to escape, then tighten the screw (photo). Similarly, loosen the bleed screw located on the top of the water pump and allow the air to escape. Tighten the screw when coolant flows from it.
7   Top-up the expansion tank until the coolant level is between the minimum level plate and the bottom of the filler neck, then refit the cap.
8   Run the engine at 2000 rpm until it reaches the normal operating temperature (indicated by the electric fan or fans cutting in), then allow it to idle for approximately 10 minutes.
9   Stop the engine and open each bleed screw in turn to release any trapped air, tightening the screws afterwards. Take care to avoid scalding.
10 Without removing the filler cap, check that the coolant level is at the bottom of the filler neck. If necessary, allow the engine to cool down then add more coolant.
11 Refit the bleed screw rubber covers and the spare wheel.
12 If the system has been only partially drained without disturbing the coolant in the heater, it may not be necessary to fill the heater as described in paragraph 4. If air is trapped in the heater matrix, it will not operate efficiently.
13 On CX Ambulance models fitted with an auxiliary heater, it will be necessary to fill the auxiliary heater with 1.6 litres (2.8 pts) of coolant before carrying out the procedure given in the previous paragraphs.

Fig. 2.7 Cylinder head outlet bleed screw (1) and water pump bleed screw (2) (Sec 4)

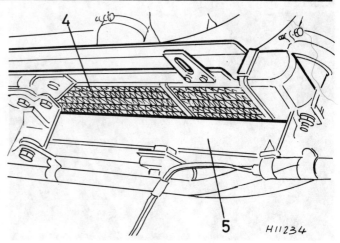

Fig. 2.8 Radiator (4) and condenser (5) fitted to models equipped with air conditioning (Sec 6)

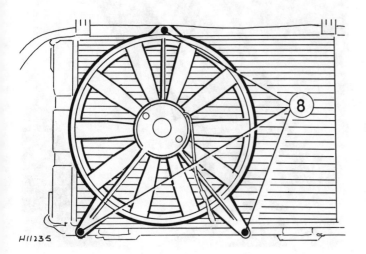

Fig. 2.9 Single fan retaining bolt locations (8) on the radiator (Sec 6)

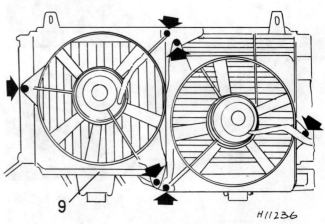

Fig. 2.10 Radiator and oil cooler (9) fitted to models with a torque converter, showing the fan retaining bolts (arrowed) (Sec 6)

5 Antifreeze mixture

1   The coolant should be renewed every two years not only to maintain the anti-freeze properties, but also to prevent corrosion which would otherwise occur as the strength of the inhibitors is progressively reduced.

2   Before adding antifreeze to the system, check all hose connections and the condition of the hoses, otherwise the searching action of the mixture may cause a leak.

3   The cooling system must be drained and flushed as described in Section 2 and 3, and the antifreeze solution mixed in a suitable container before filling the system as described in Section 4.

4   The quality of antifreeze which should be used is given in the table below, expressed as a percentage of the system capacity given in the Specifications.

Antifreeze solution	Protection to
28%	-15°C (5°F)
50%	-30°C (-22°F)

5   Whenever the cooling system requires topping-up, it is advisable to use the identical antifreeze solution in order to avoid dilution.

6 Radiator – removal, inspection, cleaning and refitting

1   Drain the cooling system as described in Section 2.

2   Disconnect the battery negative terminal, and the radiator thermal switch leads (photo).

3   To prevent water entering the alternator, either remove it as described in Chapter 10 or cover it with polythene sheeting.

4   Unbolt the front grille and retaining clamp, and release the clip along its bottom edge. On models equipped with air conditioning, detach the condenser from the radiator.

5   Disconnect the electric fan (or fans) wiring at the plug (photo).

6   Unscrew the retaining bolts and withdraw the fan assembly from the radiator (and oil cooler if fitted).

7   On models fitted with a torque converter, detach the oil cooler from the radiator.

8   *Pre-1975 models.* Unscrew the retaining bolt and detach the bracket holding the heater/inlet manifold return pipe. Loosen the hose clips and detach the water pipe and radiator bottom hose from the intermediate elbow. Loosen the hose clips and detach the radiator top hose from the cylinder head outlet, and the short hose from the water pump.

9   *1975 models onwards.* Loosen the jubilee clips and detach the top and bottom hoses from the radiator.

6.2 Thermal switch is located below radiator top hose on this model

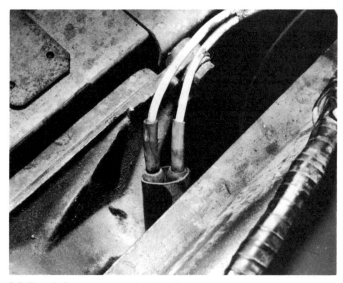
6.5 Electric fan connector plug location

6.10 De-aeration hose connection to the radiator

6.11A A radiator upper mounting

6.11B Removing the radiator

8.4A Remove the thermostat outlet flange ...

8.4B ... to reveal the thermostat and gasket

9.4 The drivebelt guard plate

9.8 Radiator top and bottom hose connections to the water pump and spacer

9.11 Removing the water pump

9.12A Water pump spacer inner retaining nut (arrowed)

9.12B Removing the water pump spacer

10.9A Water pump and alternator drivebelts

10.9B Tensioning the water pump drivebelt by levering the tensioner with a screwdriver

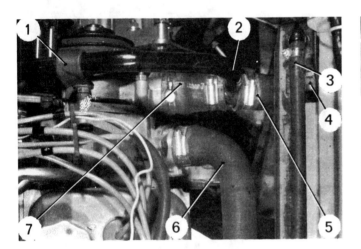

Fig. 2.11 Radiator hose location on models before January 1975 (Sec 6)

1 Bracket   5 Bottom hose
2 Water return pipe   6 Top hose
3 De-aeration hose   7 Intermediate hose
4 Radiator retaining bolt

Fig. 2.12 Using the special tool 3085-T to check the pulley alignment (Sec 10)

2 Camshaft pulley retaining nut

10 On all models except CX 2400 with fuel injection , a torque converter, or air conditioning, disconnect the de-aeration hose from the top of the radiator (photo).

11 Unscrew the two upper retaining bolts and lift out the radiator, taking care not to damage the cooling fins (photos). Do not allow antifreeze to drop onto the bodywork, otherwise damage to the paint will result.

12 Radiator repair is best left to a specialist; applying heat with a soldering iron is not always successful and may easily result in further leaks. Filler paste can sometimes be used for emergency repairs.

13 Clean the radiator matrix of flies by brushing with a soft brush or hosing with water.

14 Flush the radiator as described in Section 3 and check it thoroughly for signs of leaking and damage. Renew any hoses or clips which are unserviceable.

15 Refitting is a reversal of removal, but the cooling system must be filled as described in Section 4.

7 Pressure cap – description and testing

1 The cooling system is pressurized by a spring tensioned valve in the expansion tank filler cap. If escaping pressure can be heard from the cap, or if the system requires constant topping-up and no other leaks are located, it can be assumed that the pressure cap is faulty.

2 Most garages are equipped to test pressure caps, but if a new one is fitted, make sure that it is of the correct rating as given in the Specifications.

8 Thermostat – removal, testing and refitting

1 A faulty thermostat can cause overheating or slow engine warm up, and can also affect the performance of the heater.

2 Drain off approximately half of the coolant so that the level is below the water pump spacer at the flywheel end of the engine.

3 Disconnect the radiator top hose from the pump spacer and tie it to one side.

4 Unscrew the retaining bolts and withdraw the outlet flange. Remove the gasket (photos).

5 Withdraw the thermostat from its location in the spacer.

6 To test whether the unit is serviceable, suspend the thermostat by a piece of string in a pan of water being heated. Using a thermometer, check that the thermostat commenses to open at the specified

temperature. Remove the thermostat and check that when it has been cooled it is completely closed. Renew the thermostat if it fails to open or close correctly.

7 Refitting is a reversal of removal, but check that the mating surfaces are clean, and always fit a new flange gasket. Refill the system as described in Section 4. Note that the thermostat must always be fitted with the spring facing into the spacer.

9 Water pump – removal and refitting

1 Drain the cooling system as described in Section 2.
2 Disconnect the battery negative terminal.
3 Remove the alternator as described in Chapter 10, leaving the drive belt still attached to the water pump.
4 Unscrew the retaining nut and bolt and withdraw the guard plate from the drivebelts (photo).
5 On models equipped with air conditioning, loosen the tensioner, remove the toothed drivebelt, unscrew the retaining nuts and place the compressor on one side. **Do not** unscrew the refrigerant pipe unions.
6 On all other models, loosen the tensioner and remove the drivebelt from the water pump pulley and camshaft pulley. Where a seven-piston hydraulic pump is fitted, it will also be necessary to slacken the pivot and tension bolts in order to remove the drivebelt.
7 Remove the alternator drivebelt from the water pump pulley.
8 Disconnect the hoses from the water pump inlet ports and spacer port (photo).
9 Detach the water pipe bracket and the distributor guard bracket from the water pump and cylinder head bracket.
10 Remove the upper support bracket on models equipped with air conditioning; also disconnect the lead from the temperature sensor on the water pump spacer (where fitted).
11 Unscrew the retaining nuts and withdraw the water pump over the studs (photo). Remove the gasket.
12 The spacer can now be removed from the cylinder head after removing the retaining nuts (photos). Remove the gasket.
13 Examine the water pump impeller and body for damage and wear. If this is evident, obtain a new unit. Clean all traces of gasket from the mating surfaces of the water pump, spacer and cylinder head.
14 Refitting is a reversal of removal, but always use new gaskets, and refill the cooling system as described in Section 4. To ensure long drivebelt life, the pulleys must be correctly aligned with each other and the belts tensioned as described in Section 10.

10 Pulleys and drivebelts – adjustment and tensioning

1 Correct alignment of the pulleys is best achieved by using the special Citroen tool No 3085-T as shown in Fig. 2.12. However, a length of copper tube bent to the contour of the pulley then checked for straightness can be used just as effectively.
2 Remove the drivebelts as described in Section 9, then check that the camshaft pulley is aligned with the water pump pulley outer groove. If not, unscrew the camshaft pulley retaining nut, remove the pulley, and add shims behind the pulley as necessary.
3 Refit the pulley and tighten the nut to the specified torque.
4 Check that the alternator pulley is aligned with the water pump inner groove. If not, unscrew the nut, remove the alternator pulley, and add shims as necessary.
5 Refit the pulley and tighten the nut to the specified torque.
6 On models equipped with a seven-piston hydraulic pump, first check that it is firmly secured to the support plate, then check that the pump pulley is aligned with the outer groove of the camshaft pulley. If necessary, add shims between the pump housing and the support plate to correct the alignment.
7 Tighten the pump retaining nuts to the specified torque when the adjustment is completed.
8 On models equipped with air conditioning, note that no alignment is necessary between the camshaft pulley and water pump pulley. Alignment of the toothed belt tensioner, water pump pulley and compressor pulley must be within 0.5 mm (0.02 in) of each other. To align the toothed belt tensioner with the water pump pulley, add shims between the tensioner and its mounting plate. To align the compressor with the water pump, add shims between the compressor with the water pump, add shims between the compressor mounting plate and the clutch housing. To align the tensioner with the compressor, move the mounting plate within the slots.
9 If a belt tensioner tool is available, the drivebelts should be refitted and tensioned to the amounts given in the Specifications. If not, tension the belts so that they can be moved approximately 6.4 mm (0.25 in) when firmly pressed by the thumb half way between the pulleys (photos).
10 On models equipped with air conditioning it is important to tension the toothed belt correctly; if it is too loose the belt will wear rapidly, and if it is too tight the belt will whistle in operation. The correct tension can be achieved by tightening the belt until it whistles in operation, then loosening it until the noise stops.

11 Fault diagnosis – cooling system

Symptom	Reason/s
Overheating	Low coolant level
	Faulty heater tank pressure cap
	Faulty thermostat
	Drivebelt slipping
	Clogged radiator matrix
	Incorrect engine timing
	Corroded or clogged system
	Faulty electric fan(s) or thermal switch
	Brakes binding
Cool running	Faulty or missing thermostat
	Faulty electric fan (s) or thermal switch
Loss of coolant	Faulty header tank pressure cap
	Leaking hose or radiator
	Leaking water pump gaskets
	Blown cylinder head gasket

Chapter 3 Fuel and exhaust systems

For modifications, and information applicable to later models, see Supplement at end of manual

Contents

Specifications

Fuel pump
Type .... Mechanical, pushrod operated from eccentric on camshaft
Pressure .... 325 mbars (4.7 lbf/in^2)

Air cleaner .... Dry, long life cartridge or metal gauze

Carburettor
Type .... Weber, dual barrel, tamperproofed from October 1976
Identification:
    CX 2000 (to July 1976) – standard .... 34 DMTR 25/200
    CX 2000 (to July 1976) – air conditioning .... 34 DMTR 25/100
    CX 2000 (July 1976 on) – standard .... 34 DMTR 25/250
    CX 2000 (July 1976 on) – air conditioning .... 34 DMTR 25/150
    CX 2200 – standard .... 34 DMTR 28/200
    CX 2200 – air conditioning .... 34 DMTR 28/100
    CX 2200 – torque converter .... 34 DMTR 28/300
    CX 2400 Prestige (to July 1976) .... 34 DMTR 35/300
    CX 2400 (July 1976 on) – basic .... 34 DMTR 35/250
    CX 2400 (July 1976 on) – Prestige, air conditioning, or
    torque converter .... 34 DMTR 35/350

Calibration:

	Primary choke	Secondary choke
CX 2000		
Venturi	22	26
Main jet	115	135
Air correction jet	AD1 (195)	AD2 (180)
Emulsion tube	F30	F25
Idling jet	50	70
Air bleed	110	70
Pump jet	40	—
Econostart jet	110	—
Econostart orifice	100	—
Needle valve	1.75	1.75
CX 2200		
Venturi	23	26
Main jet	120	135
Air correction jet	AD1 (195)	AD2 (180)
Emulsion tube	F30	F25
Idling jet	50	70
Air bleed	110	70

	Primary choke	Secondary choke
Pump jet	40	—
Econostart jet	—	110
Econostart orifice	—	100
Needle valve	1.75	1.75
CX 2400		
Venturi	23	27
Main jet	115	130
Air correction jet	225	190
Emulsion tube	F21	F25
Idling jet	50	50
Air bleed	100	70
Pump jet	45	—
Needle valve	1.75	1.75
Float level setting (all models)	7.0 ± 0.25 mm (0.276 in ± 0.010 in)	
Primary throttle fast idle opening (all models)	1.25 ± 0.05 mm (0.049 ± 0.002 in)	
Maximum vacuum choke opening:		
CX 2000, CX 2200 and CX 2400 Prestige (to July 1976)	3.25 to 3.75 mm (0.128 to 0.148 in)	
CX 2400 (all other models)	3.75 to 4.25 mm (0.148 to 0167 in)	
Idling speed:		
CX 2000, CX 2200, CX 2400, carburettor engines without torque converter	850 to 900 rpm	
CX 2200, CX 2400 carburettor engines with torque converter	700 to 750 rpm	
Exhaust CO content (all carburettor engines)	1.5 to 2.5%	
Minimum exhaust CO_2 content (all carburettor engines)	8.7%	

Fuel injection system

Type	Bosch L-Jetronic electronic
Idling speed	850 to 900 rpm
Exhaust CO content (maximum)	4.5%

Fuel tank capacity

68.0 litres (15.0 Imp galls)

Fuel octane rating

99 (UK 4 star, France Super)

Torque wrench settings

	lbf ft	kgf m
Exhaust flange	10 to 13	1.4 to 1.8
Fuel pump	15	2.1
Fuel tank	11	1.5
Inlet manifold	15	2.1
Exhaust manifold	15	2.1

1 General description

The fuel tank is mounted at the rear of the car. Carburettor engines are equipped with a camshaft operated fuel pump and Weber or Solex dual barrel carburettor; fuel injection engines are equipped with an electric fuel pump and a Bosch low pressure electronic injection system.

The air cleaner element is of the long life type. Some models have temperature-controlled air cleaner intake.

The exhaust system incorporates an expansion chamber beneath the centre of the car, and a silencer located at the rear of the system. It is supported at the rear by rubber mountings and at the front subframe by a swivel bracket; a flexible section is located beneath the engine/gearbox assembly.

2 Air cleaner element – removal, cleaning and refitting

1 The air cleaner element should be removed and cleaned at the intervals specified in Routine Maintenance. More frequent cleaning may be required if the car is operated in very dusty conditions. Removal of the right-hand headlamp will facilitate access to the air cleaner.
2 On CX 2000 and CX2200 models, release the spring clips and withdraw the cover and element. On CX 2400 models, unbolt the air cleaner top section from the right-hand side engine compartment panel and withdraw the square metal element from the lower section after removing the wing nuts (photo).
3 Clean the element and the interior of the air cleaner body. At the same time, check the inlet and crankcase hoses for deterioration and clean them.
4 Refitting is a reversal of removal, but on CX 2400 models, lightly oil the element with clean engine oil.

3 Fuel pump (mechanical type) – description and testing

1 The fuel pump is located below the inlet manifold and is operated by a pushrod in contact with an eccentric on the camshaft.
2 The pump is of sealed construction and cannot be dismantled. In the event of a fault developing, the pump must be renewed.
3 To test the operation of the pump, disconnect the return line from the carburettor and plug the carburettor outlet. Insert a pressure gauge with a tee connection into the hose circuit from the pump to the carburettor.
4 Start the engine and check that the gauge registers the specified pressure.
5 Stop the engine and make sure that there is no sudden drop in pressure; if there is, either the carburettor needle valve or the pump return valve is not seating correctly.
6 To check the pump for leakage, first remove it and plug the outlet part. Connect the inlet port to compressed air at a pressure of 11.6 psi (800 mbars), then immerse the pump in petrol. A leak will be indicated by a stream of air bubbles.

4 Fuel pump (mechanical type) – removal and refitting

1 Remove the spare wheel from the engine compartment.
2 Note the location of the inlet and outlet hoses, then disconnect them from the fuel pump.
3 Unscrew the two retaining nuts and withdraw the pump from the crankcase (photo).
4 Remove the spacer and two paper gaskets from the mounting studs.

2.2 Air cleaner element on CX 2400 models

4.3 Removing the fuel pump

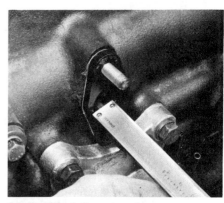

4.5 Checking fuel pump gasket to cam dimension

Fig. 3.1 Checking the fuel pump gasket to camshaft dimension with a depth gauge (A) (Sec 4)

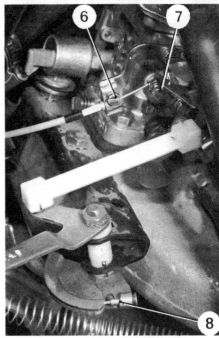

Fig. 3.3 Location of choke cable clamp screws (6 and 7), and accelerator cable (8) (Sec 6)

Fig. 3.2 Fuel pump pushrod protrusion dimension (a) (Sec 4)

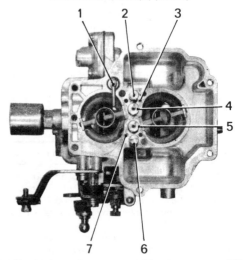

Fig. 3.4 View of carburettor jets with cover removed (Sec 7)

1 Accelerator pump jet
2 Primary idling fuel jet
3 Primary idling air bleed
4 Primary air correction jet, emulsion tube and main jet
5 Secondary air correction jet, emulsion tube and main jet
6 Secondary idling fuel jet
7 Secondary idling air bleed

5   Refitting is a reversal of removal, but the following additional points should be noted:

(a) *Clean away all traces of gasket from the mating surfaces, and always use two new gaskets fitted either side of the spacer*

(b) *Before refitting the fuel pump use vernier calipers to check the distance from the outer face of the assembled gasket to the upper and lower sections of the camshaft eccentric (photo). The dimension with the eccentric in the upper position should be 27.4 ± 0.35 mm (1.079 ± 0.014 in); with the eccentric in the lower position it should be 32.4 ± 0.35 mm (1.276 ± 0.014 in). The pump pushrod protrusion (see Fig. 3.2) must be a minimum of 4.5 mm (0.177 in)*

(c) *Tighten the nuts to the specified torque*

5   Fuel tank – removal, servicing and refitting

1   Unscrew and remove the fuel tank filler cap, unscrew the drain plug, and drain the contents into a suitable sealed container.
2   Disconnect the battery negative terminal.
3   The fuel tank is located at the rear of the car and is retained by two metal straps. Locate the strap nuts on the rear floor panel, and unscrew them whilst supporting the fuel tank.
4   Disconnect the fuel supply, breather and return pipes, and the wires from the fuel gauge sender unit.
5   Withdraw the fuel tank from under the car.
6   If the tank is leaking, it should be repaired by a specialist or alternatively a new tank fitted. Never be tempted to solder or weld a leaking fuel tank.
7   If the tank is contaminated with sediment or water, it can be swilled out using several changes of fuel, but if any vigorous shaking is required to dislodge accumulations of dirt, the fuel gauge sender unit should first be removed.
8   Refitting is a reversal of removal.

6   Accelerator and choke cables – removal, refitting and adjustment

1   The accelerator cable is attached to a grooved quadrant and lever assembly located at the right-hand side of the inlet manifold at one end, and to the accelerator pedal at the other end (photos). To remove it, unhook the return spring from the lever and detach the cable stop from the bracket and quadrant. Disconnect the cable from the accelerator pedal and remove it from the bulkhead by removing the circlip and turning the plastic bush through 90° (photo).
2   Refitting the accelerator cable is a reversal of removal, but it must be adjusted so that the carburettor throttle valves are fully open with the accelerator pedal fully depressed, and fully shut with the pedal released.
3   The choke cable is attached to the carburettor by a clamp and screw. To remove it, loosen the clamp screw and inner cable retaining screw, and remove the cable from the carburettor. Release the cable at the facia and withdraw it after lowering the facia panel (photos).
4   Refitting the choke cable is a reversal of removal, but before tightening the inner cable screw, depress the choke knob fully then pull it out approximately 3.2 mm ($\frac{1}{8}$ in).

7   Carburettor – general description

1   The carburettor is a Weber 34 DMTR dual barrel type incorporating an accelerator pump in the primary choke, and a vacuum-assisted choke valve also in the primary choke.
2   The secondary choke throttle valve commences to open only when the primary throttle valve is approximately $\frac{2}{3}$rds open.
3   A solenoid operated cut-off valve stops the supply of fuel to the idling circuit when the ignition is switched off.
4   On models equipped with a torque converter or air conditioning, the carburettor incorporates a step-up valve to compensate for the additional lead on the engine.
5   On carburettors fitted to cars manufactured from October 1976 on, the adjustments are sealed with plastic 'tamperproof' plugs or caps. These can only be removed and new ones fitted with a special

tool, and the plugs and caps are also colour coded to indicate previous adjustments. Before removing the plugs or caps, it is advisable to check that current legislation permits this action.

8   Carburettor – idling speed adjustment

1   Run the engine until it reaches its normal operating temperature, indicated by the electric cooling fan (or fans) cutting in.
2   Check that the lights and all electrical components are switched off, and (where fitted) that the air conditioning compressor is switched off.
3   On models fitted with a torque converter, select neutral or Part (P).
4   Adjust the idle speed screw on the carburettor until the engine is running at the specified idling speed. The tachometer on the instrument panel will indicate the speed, but if this is suspected of being inaccurate, connect an independent tachometer to the engine.
5   Turn the mixture screw on the carburettor in each direction until a point is reached where the engine speed is highest.
6   Adjust the idle speed screw to bring the engine speed within the specified limits.
7   If an exhaust gas analyser is available, adjust the idling speed and mixture screws until the quantities of CO and CO_2 are within the specified limits.
8   Make any final adjustments with the mixture screw.
9   On models equipped with air conditioning, switch on the compressor, then adjust the step-up valve screw so that the engine speed is 1000 to 1050 rpm.
10   On models equipped with a torque converter, apply the handbrake and engage a gear, then adjust the step-up valve screw so that the engine speed is 725 to 775 rpm.
11   Switch off the engine. Where it is not possible to achieve smooth idling, check the inlet manifold, vacuum pipes and crankcase ventilation hoses for leaks. The ignition timing and valve clearances must also be correct.

9   Carburettor – removal and refitting

1   Remove the spare wheel from the engine compartment.
2   Loosen the clamp and adjustment screws and remove the choke cable from the carburettor.
3   Pull the linkage rod from the throttle lever balljoint.
4   Disconnect the supply lead from the cut-off solenoid (photo).
5   Unscrew the nuts securing the air cleaner hose to the top of the carburettor and detach the support bracket. Lift the hose assembly from the carburettor.
6   Disconnect the supply and return pipes from the carburettor (photo).
7   Disconnect the vacuum pipes from the carburettor.
8   Unscrew the retaining nuts in diagonal sequence, and withdraw the carburettor from the inlet manifold.
9   Refitting is a reversal of removal, but always use new gaskets. Adjust the idling speed as described in Section 8.

10   Carburettor – float level adjustment

1   Remove the carburettor as described in Section 9.
2   Clean the exterior with petrol.
3   Detach the pipe from the choke vacuum capsule, and unscrew the screws securing the capsule to the carburettor.
4   Lift the rimmed collar and disconnect the choke operating rod from the lever.
5   Unscrew and remove the screws securing the cover to the main body. Lift the cover away, making sure that the gasket is not damaged.
6   Check that the return hook is correctly located on the needle valve and float arm, then hold the cover vertical with the floats hanging from the fulcrum pin; the float arm must just contact the spring tensioned ball in the end of the needle without pushing it into the needle.
7   Using vernier calipers, check that the distance from the gasket on the cover to the nearest surface of the floats is as given in Specifications. If not, bend the tab which contacts the needle as necessary.
8   The dimension checked in paragraph 7 must be the same for each float. If necessary, bend the connecting bar.
9   Locate the cover and gasket on the carburettor, insert the retaining

6.1A Accelerator cable attachment to the grooved quadrant (arrowed)

6.1B Showing the accelerator pedal and bracket

6.1C Removing the accelerator cable from the bulkhead

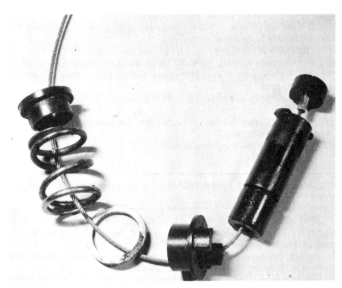

6.1D Accelerator cable mounting components

6.1E Fitting the accelerator cable quadrant pivot bush

6.1F Accelerator cable bracket and adjustment ferrule

6.3A Choke cable attachment to the carburettor

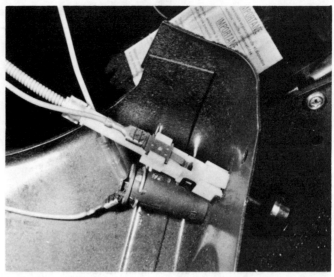

6.3B Choke cable connection to the facia panel

9.4 Carburettor cut-off solenoid (arrowed)

9.6 Carburettor supply and return pipes

Fig. 3.5 Idle mixture screw (2) and idle speed screw (3) on standard Weber carburettor (Sec 8)

Fig. 3.6 Step-up valve screw (4), idle mixture screw (2) and idle speed screw (3) on Weber carburettor fitted to models with air conditioning or a torque converter (Sec 8)

Fig. 3.7 Carburettor components (Sec 10)

1 Cover retaining screw
2 Vacuum tube
3 Capsule retaining screws
4 Choke lever
5 Choke rod
a Rimmed collar

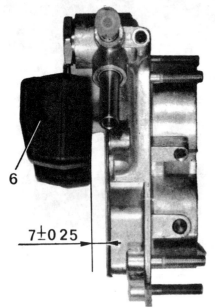

7 ± 0.25

Fig. 3.8 Float level adjustment dimension in mm (Sec 10)

6 Float

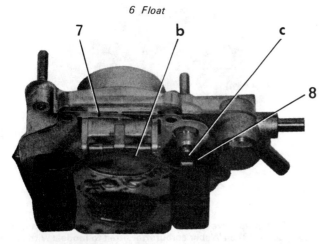

Fig. 3.9 Carburettor cover components (Sec 10)

7 Gasket
b Connecting bar
c Adjustment tab
8 Return hook

screws and washers, and tighten them evenly and in diagonal sequence.
10 Connect the choke operating rod to the lever, and refit the choke vacuum capsule and pipe.
11 Refit the carburettor as described in Section 9 and adjust the idling speed as described in Section 8.

11 Carburettor – choke valve fast idle and vacuum capsule adjustment

1 With the carburettor removed, fully close the choke valve by turning the operating lever.
2 With the throttle lever in the closed position, use a small drill to measure the distance between the edge of the primary throttle valve and the barrel wall. If this is not within the limits given in Specifications, loosen the locknut on the throttle lever, adjust the stop screw and retighten the nut.
3 Hold the choke valve fully closed with the operating lever, and connect a vacuum pump and gauge to the vacuum capsule. With a vacuum of 400 mm Hg or more, the capsule lever should contact the adjustment stop; it not, the capsule is faulty and must be renewed.
4 With the capsule lever in contact with the adjustment stop, use a drill to measure the distance between the straight edge of the choke valve and the barrel wall. If this is not within the limits given in Specifications, adjust the stop screw as necessary.
5 Release the choke lever and reconnect the vacuum pipe.

12 Fuel injection system – description

1 The Bosch L-Jetronic fuel injection system is of low pressure intermittent type, and the main components are an electric fuel pump, filter, electronic control unit (ECU), injectors and an air-flow sensor.
2 The throttle valve is located in the air inlet chamber. Two air by-pass circuits are provided, one for cold starting supplementary air, and the other for idling speed adjustment.
3 The air-flow sensor is located adjacent to the air filter, and supplies the ECU with a voltage signal which varies in strength according to the amount of air entering the engine.
4 The fuel pump operating switch and the air temperature sensor are incorporated into the air flow sensor.
5 The electronic control unit (ECU) is not always located in the same place – in the workshop it was found behind the panel in the nearside footwell under the glovebox (Turbo) and behind the panel to the right of the accelerator pedal (non-turbo). The ECU supplies an impulse to the injection which varies in length according to the quantity of air being drawn into the engine. Other factors affecting the duration of injection are the engine temperature and air temperature, and separate sensors supply the ECU with this information. The ECU is triggered by the low tension circuit of the electronic ignition system. Injection occurs twice for each rotation of the camshaft.
6 The injectors are connected in parallel and inject fuel simultaneously twice for each engine cycle; they are located in the inlet manifold branches, close to the inlet valves. There are four injectors, one for each cylinder. Each injector incorporates an electromagnetically controlled needle which lifts off its seat when the solenoid is energised. The quantity of fuel injected is determined by the duration of injection and this function is controlled by the ECU. Fuel pressure at the injectors is kept constant by a pressure regulator in the return line to the fuel tank. The regulator is also connected to inlet manifold vacuum and, since the injectors are also subject to the same vacuum, the fuel pressure is modulated in order to limit the quantity of fuel injected to the injection period only.
7 A separate cold start injector is located in the inlet chamber for providing additional fuel for cold starting; it operates in a similar manner to the injectors described in paragraph 6 but incorporates a valve and seat instead of a needle. The cold start injector only operates when the starter motor is energised and when the engine temperature is below 35°C (95°F). At -20°C (-4°F) the cold start injector operates for 7.5 seconds, but as the temperature increases, the duration of operation is reduced.
8 The throttle valve spindle incorporates a switch with two contacts, one for idling speed, the other for full load. The switch supplies the ECU with either one of these impulses in order to alter the injection period when required.
9 The pressure regulator maintains the fuel pressure in the system at 29.0 lbf/in^2 (2 bars) when the engine is idling.

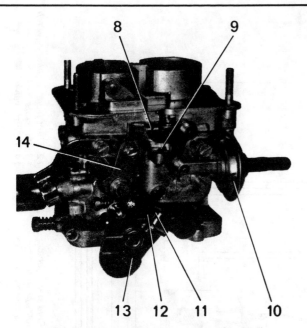

Fig. 3.10 Carburettor components (Sec 11)

8   Capsule lever
9   Adjustable stop
10 Vacuum capsule
11 Locknut

12 Fast idle adjustment
13 Throttle lever
14 Choke lever

Fig. 3.11 Vacuum movement dimension (a) of the choke valve (Sec 11)

10 Vacuum capsule

15 Choke valve

13 Fuel injection system – precautions

1   The electronic components of the fuel injection system incorporate semi-conductors, and therefore the following precautions must always be taken before working on the system.
2   **Do not** disconnect the ECU with the ignition on, nor disconnect the battery with the engine running.
3   Always disconnect the battery before charging it from a mains charger.
4   When checking the engine compression, disconnect the coil positive terminal to prevent fuel being injected.
5   If using an ohmmeter on the system, use only the battery powered type.

14 Fuel injection components – testing

1   Before testing any component, check that the circuit is being supplied with current. First disconnect the ECU, then use a voltmeter to trace the current from the relay, located beneath the left-hand headlamp, to each component.

Fuel pump
2   With the ECU disconnected, operate the starter and check that the fuel pump, located by the right-hand rear wheel, is heard to operate. Make sure that it is properly earthed.
3   Remove the air hose from the air sensor, and switch on the ignition.
4   When the air flow sensor flap is moved manually from rest, the fuel pump should operate; if not, the sensor switch contact may be faulty.

Supplementary air control
5   Disconnect the ECU, and check that the arrow on the air control is facing the correct way.
6   Disconnect the air control hoses; with the engine temperature below 60°C (140°F) the quadrant must be open and vice versa.
7   With the hoses connected and the ECU wiring connected, allow the engine to idle. With the engine temperature below 60°C (140°F), compress the control unit supply hose with the hand; the engine speed should decrease. With the temperature above 60°C (140°F) disconnect the outlet hose; the engine speed should increase.

Air flow sensor
8   Disconnect the air hoses and check that the control flap moves freely. It is not necessary to lubricate the flap.

Injectors
9   With the engine idling, disconnect the supply wire to each injector in turn; the engine speed should decrease by equal amounts provided the engine mechanical condition is good.
10 The delivery of each injector can be checked with a calibrated container. Remove the injector and energise the solenoid after having disconnected the ECU. With the ignition switched on, each injector should deliver approximately 200 cc/min.

Water temperature sensor
11 With the engine at normal operating temperature, disconnect the sensor supply lead; the engine should stall.

Air temperature sensor
12 Disconnect the ECU, then measure the resistance between terminals 6 and 27 with a battery operated ohmmeter; the reading should be in accordance with the following table:

Air temperature	Resistance
- 10°C (14°F)	8 to 11 k ohms
+ 20° C (68°F)	2 to 3 k ohms
+ 50°C (122°F)	750 to 900 ohms

Cold start injector
13 Disconnect the ECU, remove the cold start injector, and locate it over a calibrated container.
14 Connect terminal 46 to earth, switch on the ignition and operate the starter. The quantity of fuel delivered must be 135 cc/min.
15 If the cold start injector is in good working order, reconnect it to the thermal switch, and check that it operates in accordance with the following table:

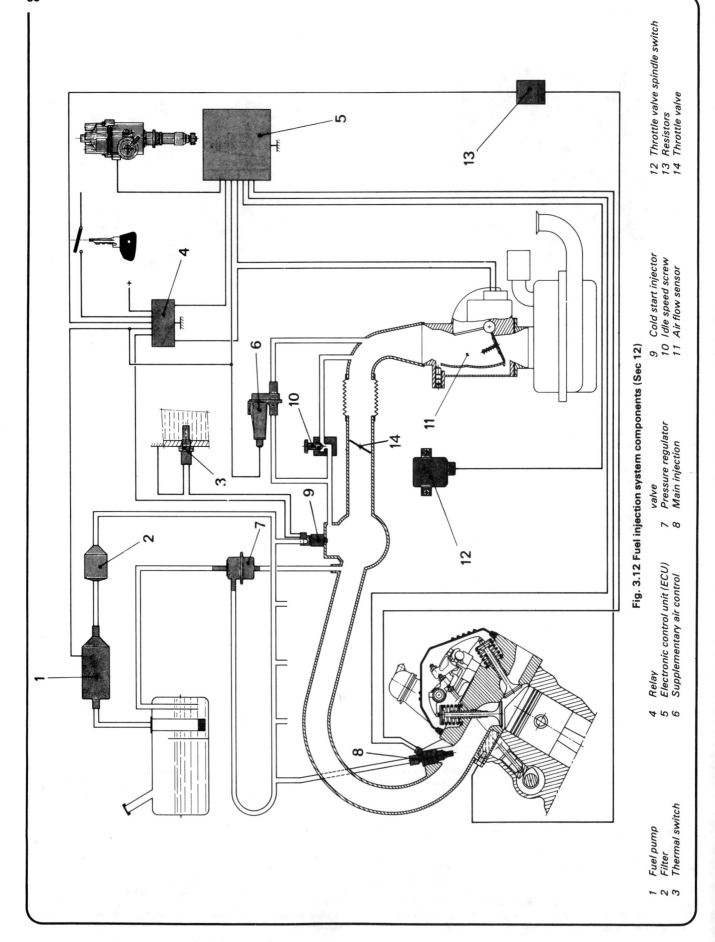

Fig. 3.12 Fuel injection system components (Sec 12)

1	Fuel pump	4	Relay
2	Filter	5	Electronic control unit (ECU)
3	Thermal switch	6	Supplementary air control

	valve	9	Cold start injector
7	Pressure regulator	10	Idle speed screw
8	Main injection	11	Air flow sensor

12	Throttle valve spindle switch
13	Resistors
14	Throttle valve

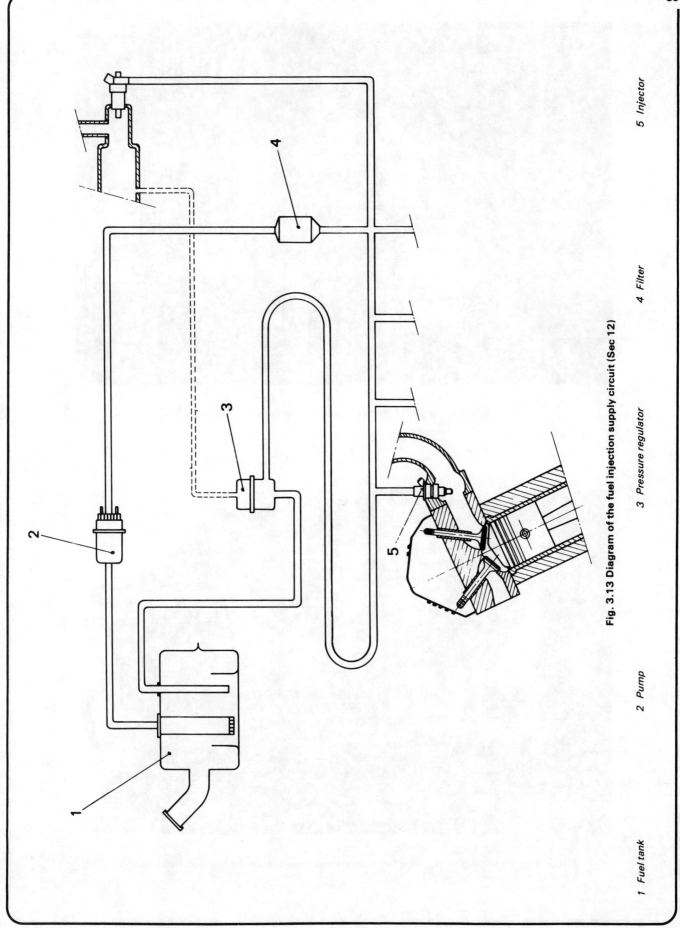

Fig. 3.13 Diagram of the fuel injection supply circuit (Sec 12)

1 Fuel tank   2 Pump   3 Pressure regulator   4 Filter   5 Injector

Fig. 3.14 Location of the fuel system air flow sensor (1) (Sec 14)

Fig. 3.15 Location of the injectors (1) and water temperature sensor (2) on the fuel injection system (Sec 14)

Fig. 3.16 Location of the fuel injection system cold start injector (1) (Sec 14)

Fig. 3.17 Location of the fuel injection system cold start thermal switch (2) (Sec 14)

Fig. 3.18 Checking the fuel injection system pressure (Sec 15)

    1 Cold start injector   2 Pressure gauge

Fig. 3.19 Location of the fuel injection system idle speed screw (1) (Sec 16)

Fig. 3.20 Exhaust downpipe flange nut locations – arrowed (Sec 17)

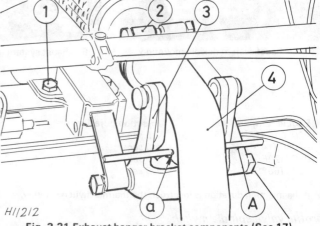

H11212

Fig. 3.21 Exhaust hanger bracket components (Sec 17)

1 Bolt   4 Exhaust pipe
2 Clamp   a Drilling
3 Lever   A Adjustment rod

17.1A Removing the inlet manifold

17.1B An inlet manifold gasket

17.2A Removing the exhaust manifold

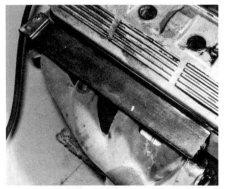

17.2B Exhaust manifold heat shield location

17.3 Disconnecting the exhaust downpipe from the manifold

17.4 Exhaust downpipe clamp

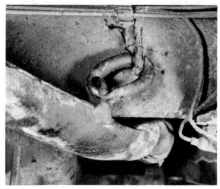

17.5 An exhaust system flexible mounting

17.6 Exhaust system front hanger location

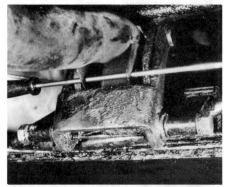

17.7 Adjusting the exhaust system front hanger

Engine temperature	Injection duration
- 20°C (- 4°F)	7.5 sec
- 10°C (14°F)	5.0 sec
0°C (32°F)	3.0 sec
20°C (68°F)	1.0 sec

If the injection duration is incorrect, the thermal switch is faulty.

Throttle valve spindle switch
16 Disconnect the ECU.
17 Using a battery operated ohmmeter, check that the resistance between the multiple connector terminals 2 and 18 is nil, with the accelerator pedal fully released.
18 Fully depress the accelerator pedal, and check that the resistance between the multiple terminals 3 and 18 is nil.

Electronic control unit (ECU)
19 Check that all connections and terminals are in good condition.
20 Start the engine and allow it to idle, then tap the ECU lightly; if the engine falters as a result, the internal soldered joints may be defective.

15 Fuel injection system – testing pressure

1 Disconnect the fuel pipe from the cold start injector, and connect a pressure gauge and tee piece between the injector and pipe.
2 Start the engine and allow it to idle; the pressure should be 2 bars (29.0 lbf/in^2).
3 Disconnect the vacuum pipe from the pressure regulator; the fuel pressure should increase to 2.5 bars (36.25 lbf/in^2).
4 If the readings obtained in paragraphs 2 and 3 are incorrect, check

that the vacuum pipe is fitted correctly and is not blocked. If the pipe is in order but the pressure is incorrect, renew the pressure regulator.
5 Switch off the engine and check that the pressure remains at 2 bars (29.0 lbf/in²). If not, leakage is occurring from the circuit; the most likely places are the cold start injector, main injector, or pressure regulator diaphragm.

16 Fuel injection system – idling speed adjustment

1 Run the engine until it reaches its normal operating temperature, indicated by the electric cooling fan (or fans) cutting in.
2 Check that the lights and all electrical components are switched off, and (where fitted) that the air conditioning compressor is switched off.
3 Adjust the idle speed screw, located near the engine oil filler cap, until the engine is running at the specified idling speed. The tachometer on the instrument panel will indicate the speed, but if this is suspected of being inaccurate, connect an independent tachometer of a type which may be used with electronic ignition.
4 If an exhaust gas analyser is available, check that the CO content does not exceed the specified limit. If this is not correct, check all air hoses for leakage and make sure that the ignition and valve clearance adjustments on the engine are correct.
5 On models equipped with air conditioning, switch on the compressor and adjust the screw located on the auxiliary box next to the

electro-valve until the engine idles at 1000 to 1050 rpm.
6 Switch off the engine and remove the tachometer and exhaust gas analyser.

17 Manifolds and exhaust system – general

1 The inlet manifold is attached to the rear (bulkhead) side of the cylinder head. When refitting, always use new gaskets and tighten the securing nuts to the specified torque (photos).
2 The exhaust manifold is attached to the front side of the cylinder head. Whenever it has been removed, use a new gasket when refitting and make sure that the head shield is fitted to the top (photos).
3 To remove the exhaust system, first unscrew the bolts or nuts securing the downpipe to the exhaust manifold (photo).
4 Loosen the clamp and remove the downpipe from the exhaust system (photo).
5 Release the flexible mountings from the rear subframe (photo). Remove the support washer and detach the rear silencer mounting.
6 Unscrew the front exhaust hanger mounting bolts and withdraw the exhaust system to the rear (photo).
7 Refitting is a reversal of removal, but before tightening the nuts and bolts, make sure that the rear flexible mountings are vertical and not strained. Also adjust the position of the front hanger as follows. Insert a 6.0 mm (0.236 in) diameter rod through the special drilling, then move the hanger until its arms touch the rod. Tighten the clamp and mounting bolts, then remove the rod (photo).

18 Fault diagnosis – fuel and exhaust systems

Symptom	Reason/s
Excessive fuel consumption	Air cleaner element choked
	Leak in the fuel circuit
	Carburettor float level too high
	Carburettor flooding (needle valve stuck)
	Carburettor mixture adjustment incorrect
	Valve clearance adjustment incorrect
	Fuel injection ECU faulty
	Fuel injection cold start injector faulty
	Fuel injection air leak
	Sticking air flow sensor (fuel injection)
	Fuel injection injector faulty
Insufficient fuel delivery or weak mixture	Carburettor needle valve sticking
	Fuel pump faulty
	Air leak on inlet manifold
	Carburettor mixture adjustment incorrect
	Fuel injection pump faulty
	Sticking air flow sensor (fuel injection)
	Fuel injection injector faulty
	Fuel injection ECU faulty

Chapter 4 Ignition system

For modifications, and information applicable to later models, see Supplement at end of manual

Contents

Specifications

System type
Carburettor engines	Contact breaker and coil
Fuel injection engines	Transistorised ignition module, coil, distributor with magnetic impulse generator
Firing order	1 – 3 – 4 – 2 (No 1 at flywheel end)

Distributor
Make	Ducellier or Magneti-Marelli
Direction of rotation (viewed from cap end)	Clockwise
Dwell angle (carburettor engines)	55° ± 2° 30' (61% ± 3%)
Maximum dwell angle variation	1°
Condenser capacity (carburettor engines)	0.30 ± 0.03µF
Contact breaker gap (carburettor engines)	0.40 mm (0.016 in)
Star to sensor gap (fuel injection engines)	0.3 to 0.5 mm (0.012 to 0.020 in)
Centrifugal advance curve:	
CX 2000 and CX 2200	LA2
CX 2400 (carburettor engines)	LA4
CX 2400 (fuel injection engines)	LA5
Vacuum advance curve:	
CX 2400 (carburettor engines)	LD2
CX 2400 (fuel injection engines)	LD3

Ignition timing
Static timing (all models)	10° BTDC
Dynamic timing:	
Carburettor engines	10° BTDC ± 1° at idling speed
Fuel injection engines	25° BTDC at 2500 rpm

Spark plugs
Type	Short reach
Make:	
CX 2000 and CX 2200	AC 42FS, Bosch W225 T35, Eyquem 705 S, Marchal 35/1B, Champion L87Y, Marelli CW7N, or equivalent
CX 2400	AC 43FS, Bosch W175 T35, Marchal 35/36, Marelli CW6N, or equivalent
Gap (all models)	0.6 to 0.7 mm (0.024 to 0.028 in)

Coil
Type:	
Carburettor engines	External ballast resistor
Fuel injection engines	High output, incorporating transistorised ignition module
Transistorised module resistance	960 to 1140 ohms

Torque wrench settings
	lbf ft	kgf m
Spark plugs (engine cold)	14.5 to 18.0	2.0 to 2.5
Distributor clamp nut	13.5 to 15.0	1.9 to 2.1

1 General description

The ignition system fitted to engines with a carburettor is of the conventional type and comprises a 12 volt battery, coil contact breaker points, distributor and spark plugs. The ignition system fitted to engines with fuel injection is of the electronic type and comprises a 12 volt battery, high output coil, a transistorised module, a distributor with a magnetic impulse generator and spark plugs. The distributor in both systems is driven by a skew gear near the flywheel end of the camshaft.

In order to enable the engine to run correctly, an electrical spark must be produced at the spark plug to ignite the fuel/air mixture in the combustion chamber at exactly the right moment in relation to engine speed and load.

In the conventional system, low tension (LT) voltage is fed from the battery to the coil primary windings and then to the distributor contact breaker points. With the points closed, an electromagnetic field is produced around the secondary, high tension (HT) windings in the coil. When the points open, a high tension current is induced in the coil secondary windings, which is fed via the distributor cap and rotor arm to each spark plug. The capacitor or condenser in the distributor serves as a buffer for the surge of low tension current and also prevents excessive arcing across the contact breaker points.

In the electronic ignition system the secondary high tension (HT) circuit operates in an identical way to the conventional system, however the primary low tension (LT) circuit is operated electronically instead of by the contact breaker points. The distributor contains a star plate, with four arms, which is attached to the spindle. As the plate turns, the arms pass close to a sensor containing a permanent magnet and coil, and an impulse is created in the coil. This impulse switches off the transistor in the module which in turn causes a collapse of the voltage in the coil primary windings. HT current is this induced in the coil secondary windings.

Both conventional and electronic systems incorporate ignition advance mechanisms. Centrifugal advance is governed by weights attached to the distributor shaft which move outwards as the engine speed increases. The upper part of the shaft is rotated by the weights and the ignition timing is thus advanced. During part throttle operation, performance and fuel economy can be improved by advancing the ignition further than that provided by the centrifugal weights. To do this, a vacuum capsule connected to the distributor baseplate advances the ignition timing when the carburettor throttle valve is only partly open. At all other times the centrifugal weights provide the only advance.

2 Contact breaker points – adjustment and lubrication

1   To check the contact breaker points gap using a feeler gauge, first remove the distributor cap and the rotor arm.
2   Jack-up the left-hand front of the car until the roadwheel is just clear of the ground, then engage top gear. On C-matic models, remove the torque converter housing cover.
3   Turn the engine by rotating the wheel, or with a screwdriver (C-matic), until the heel of the moving contact is on a high point of the cam.
4   Insert a clean feeler gauge of the specified thickness between the two points; the feeler gauge should be a firm sliding fit without forcing the points apart (photo). If adjustment is necessary, loosen the fixed contact retaining screw and move the contact as necessary. Always recheck the gap after retightening the retaining screw. Take care not to contaminate the contact faces with oil from the feeler gauge.
5   Periodically, inject two or three drops of oil through the distributor baseplate to lubricate the centrifugal weights and the driveshafts. Do not get oil on the contact breaker points.
6   Smear a little multi-purpose grease on the cam lobes to lubricate the heel of the moving contact.
7   Refit the motor arm and distributor cap.
8   To check the contact breaker points adjustment with a dwell meter or oscilloscope, do not remove the distributor cap and rotor. Connect the instrument in accordance with the manufacturer's instructions and start the engine; the dwell angle or ratio must be within the specified limits. If adjustment is necessary, remove the distributor cap and rotor and reduce the points gap to increase the dwell angle, and vice versa.
9   If the method described in paragraph 8 is used, do not forget the periodic lubrication as described in paragraphs 5 and 6.

3 Contact breaker points – renovation or renewal

1   Remove the distributor cap and rotor (photo).
2   Open the contact breaker points and examine the contact faces for deterioration. If they are discoloured or pitted, remove the points assembly as follows.
3   Remove the spring clip, detach the LT lead, and remove the moving contact point complete with insulating washers.
4   Unscrew the fixed contact retaining screw and withdraw the fixed contact point (photo).
5   Dress each contact with an oilstone or emery tape until the pits or craters have been removed. Make sure that the finished face is smooth and retains its original contour. If the points are severely pitted, or if refacing them removes the hardened metal, they must be renewed.
6   After refacing the points, reassemble them and check that they make good contact with each other when closed.
7   Clean the points with a methylated spirit moistened cloth, and apply a small drop of oil to the moving contact pivot.
8   Refit the assembly to the distributor baseplate using a reversal of the removal procedure.
9   Readjust the points gap using a feeler gauge as described in Section 2, and if possible check the adjustment with a dwell meter.

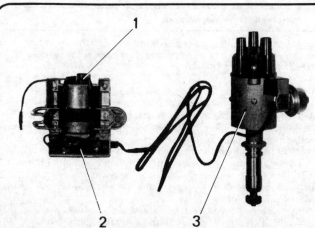

Fig. 4.1 Components of the electronic transistorized ignition system (Sec 1)

1   High output coil
2   Transistorized module
3   Distributor

Fig. 4.2 Location of the electronic ignition star plate (5) and magnetic pick up sensor (4) (Sec 5)

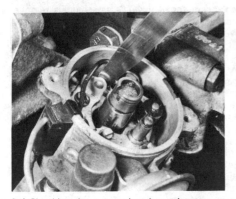

2.4 Checking the contact breaker points gap with a feeler gauge

3.1 View of the contact breaker points with distributor cap and rotor removed

3.4 The fixed contact point and retaining screw (arrowed)

4 Capacitor – testing, removal and refitting

1 The capacitor (or condenser) is fitted in parallel with the contact breaker points. As previously mentioned, it acts as an electrical buffer, absorbing the surge of voltage which occurs when the points open and releasing it when they close again.
2 Failure of the capacitor may result in it presenting either a short circuit or an open circuit. If it fails in the short circuit mode, total failure of the ignition system will result as the contact breaker points will be unable to interrupt the low tension circuit. If it fails in the open circuit mode, the spark at the plugs will be seriously weakened or completely absent, and arcing will occur at the contact breaker points.
3 Accurate testing of the capacitor can only be carried out with special equipment. A rough check can be carried out by removing the distributor cap, making sure that the points are closed, switching on the ignition and separating the points with a screwdriver. A strong blue flash would suggest capacitor failure in the open circuit mode; no spark at all suggests failure in the short circuit mode, or some other fault. The simplest test is by substitution of a new capacitor. It is not an expensive item.
4 To remove the capacitor, detach the lead from the LT rubber block and remove the retaining screw.
5 Refitting is a reversal of removal.

5 Electronic ignition – star to sensor gap adjustment

1 Remove the distributor cap and rotor arm.
2 On manual gearbox models, jack-up the left-hand front of the car and engage top gear. On C-matic models, remove the cover from under the torque converter housing.
3 Turn the engine by the roadwheel (manual gearbox) or with a screwdriver in the starter ring gear (C-matic), until one arm of the rotor plate is facing the magnetic pick-up of the sensor.
4 Using a *non-magnetic* (eg brass) feeler gauge, check that the gap between the star plate and pick-up is as given in the Specifications.
5 If necessary, loosen the retaining screws and adjust the sensor.
6 Tighten the screws, then refit the rotor arm and distributor cap.
7 Refit the torque converter cover on C-matic models, or lower the car to the ground on manual gearbox models.

6 Distributor – removal and refitting

1 Disconnect the HT leads from the coil and spark plugs. Detach the HT leads from the support bracket.
2 Remove the guard bracket from around the distributor.
3 Disconnect the pipe from the vacuum advance capsule.
4 Disconnect the low tension and diagnostic wiring from the distributor.
5 On manual gearbox models, jack-up the left-hand front of the car and engage top gear. On C-matic models remove the torque converter housing cover. Remove all four spark plugs to facilitate turning the engine in subsequent operations.

6 Place the palm of the hand over No 1 spark plug hole, noting that this is at the flywheel end of the engine, ie left-hand side viewed from the driver's seat.
7 Turn the engine in a forward direction until pressure is felt through No 1 spark plug hole, then continue to turn the engine until the 10° BTDC line on the flywheel is exactly opposite the fixed pointer visible through the timing hole (see Fig. 4.3).
8 Remove the distributor cap and check that the rotor arm is pointing in the direction B shown in Figs. 4.4, 4.5 or 4.6. Mark the distributor body and housing positions with a centre punch.
9 Unscrew and remove the nut and lift away the distributor clamp (photo).
10 Withdraw the distributor from the housing (photo).
11 To refit the distributor, first check that the 10° BTDC timing line is aligned with the fixed pointer.
12 Position the rotor arm as shown by the dotted lines A 'in Figs. 4.4, 4.5 or 4.6, then hold the distributor over the location housing also as shown in the figures in relation to the longitudinal axis of the engine.
13 Lower the distributor into the housing. When the drivegear is fully meshed with the camshaft skew gear, the rotor arm should move to the original position B shown in the figures.
14 Refit the clamp and tighten the nut with the fingers, then align the punch marks made previously.
15 Refit the low tension and diagnostic wiring, the vacuum hose and guard bracket.
16 Refit the HT leads to the coil, spark plugs and support bracket, and the distributor cap.
17 Adjust the ignition timing as described in Section 7 after refitting the spark plugs.
18 Refit the torque converter housing cover if the ignition timing is to be checked using a stroboscope.

7 Ignition timing – adjustment

Note: *On the fuel injection engine fitted with electronic ignition adjust the ignition timing with a stroboscope; on carburettor engines, either of the following methods may be used.*

Test lamp
1 Jack-up the left-hand front of the car and engage top gear (manual gearbox) or remove the torque converter housing cover (C-matic).
2 Remove No 1 spark plug from the flywheel end of the cylinder head, place the palm of the hand over the plug hole, and turn the engine by hand until pressure is felt from No 1 cylinder.
3 Continue turning the engine in a forward direction until the 10° BTDC (before top dead centre) line on the flywheel is exactly opposite the fixed pointer visible through the timing hole on the gearbox bellhousing) (photo).
4 Connect a 12 volt test lamp and leads between the contact breaker (RUP) terminal on the coil and a suitable earth.
5 Disconnect the HT lead from the centre of the coil and switch on the ignition.
6 If the test lamp is already glowing, turn the distributor body clockwise (viewed from the top) until the lamp goes out.
7 Turn the distributor body anti-clockwise until the test lamp lights

Are your plugs trying to tell you something?

Normal.
Grey-brown deposits, lightly coated core nose. Plugs ideally suited to engine, and engine in good condition.

Heavy Deposits.
A build up of crusty deposits, light-grey sandy colour in appearance.
Fault: Often caused by worn valve guides, excessive use of upper cylinder lubricant, or idling for long periods.

Lead Glazing.
Plug insulator firing tip appears yellow or green/yellow and shiny in appearance.
Fault: Often caused by incorrect carburation, excessive idling followed by sharp acceleration. Also check ignition timing.

Carbon fouling.
Dry, black, sooty deposits.
Fault: over-rich fuel mixture.
Check: carburettor mixture settings, float level, choke operation, air filter.

Oil fouling.
Wet, oily deposits. Fault: worn bores/piston rings or valve guides; sometimes occurs (temporarily) during running-in period.

Overheating.
Electrodes have glazed appearance, core nose very white - few deposits. Fault: plug overheating. Check: plug value, ignition timing, fuel octane rating (too low) and fuel mixture (too weak).

Electrode damage.
Electrodes burned away; core nose has burned, glazed appearance. Fault: pre-ignition. Check: for correct heat range and as for 'overheating'.

Split core nose.
(May appear initially as a crack). Fault: detonation or wrong gap-setting technique. Check: ignition timing, cooling system, fuel mixture (too weak).

WHY DOUBLE COPPER IS BETTER FOR YOUR ENGINE.

Unique Trapezoidal Copper Cored Earth Electrode — 50% Larger Spark Area — Copper Cored Centre Electrode

Champion Double Copper plugs are the first in the world to have copper core in both centre _and_ earth electrode. This innovative design means that they run cooler by up to 100°C – giving greater efficiency and longer life. These double copper cores transfer heat away from the tip of the plug faster and more efficiently. Therefore, Double Copper runs at cooler temperatures than conventional plugs giving improved acceleration response and high speed performance with no fear of pre-ignition.

Champion Double Copper plugs also feature a unique trapezoidal earth electrode giving a 50% increase in spark area. This, together with the double copper cores, offers greatly reduced electrode wear, so the spark stays stronger for longer.

 FASTER COLD STARTING

 FOR UNLEADED OR LEADED FUEL

 ELECTRODES UP TO 100°C COOLER

 BETTER ACCELERATION RESPONSE

 LOWER EMISSIONS

 50% BIGGER SPARK AREA

 THE LONGER LIFE PLUG

Plug Tips/Hot and Cold.
Spark plugs must operate within well-defined temperature limits to avoid cold fouling at one extreme and overheating at the other.
Champion and the car manufacturers work out the best plugs for an engine to give optimum performance under all conditions, from freezing cold starts to sustained high speed motorway cruising.
Plugs are often referred to as hot or cold. With Champion, the higher the number on its body, the hotter the plug, and the lower the number the cooler the plug. For the correct plug for your car refer to the specifications at the beginning of this chapter.

Plug Cleaning
Modern plug design and materials mean that Champion no longer recommends periodic plug cleaning. Certainly don't clean your plugs with a wire brush as this can cause metal conductive paths across the nose of the insulator so impairing its performance and resulting in loss of acceleration and reduced m.p.g.
However, if plugs are removed, always carefully clean the area where the plug seats in the cylinder head as grit and dirt can sometimes cause gas leakage.
Also wipe any traces of oil or grease from plug leads as this may lead to arcing.

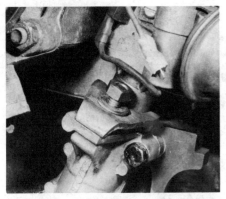
6.9 Removing the distributor clamp

6.10 Removing the distributor

7.3 Timing hole and pointer on the gearbox bellhousing

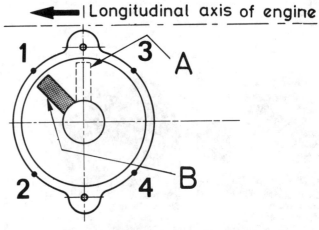

Fig. 4.4 Rotor arm positions – conventional ignition without vacuum capsule (Sec 6)

A *Before inserting distributor*
B *After inserting distributor*

Fig. 4.3 Location of the ignition timing hole (a) and fixed pointer (b) (Sec 6)

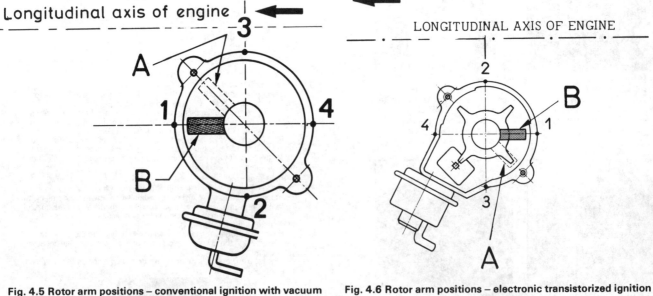

Fig. 4.5 Rotor arm positions – conventional ignition with vacuum capsule (Sec 6)

A *Before inserting distributor*
B *After inserting distributor*

Fig. 4.6 Rotor arm positions – electronic transistorized ignition (Sec 6)

A *Before inserting distributor*
B *After inserting distributor*

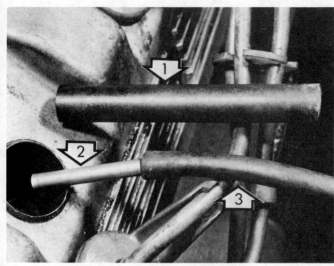

9.12A Using a rubber tube (3) to fit the spark plug extension rods (2). Also shown is the insulator (1)

9.12B Fitting a spark plug lead and seal

Fig. 4.7 Location of the distributor clamp nut (2) (Sec 6)

Fig. 4.8 Timing marks on the flywheel (Sec 7)

1   *Flywheel*
C   *10° BTDC timing mark (yellow on carburettor engines)*

up. At this point the contact points have just separated.
8   Tighten the clamp nut to the specified torque and switch off the ignition.
9   Remove the test lamp, and refit the coil HT lead and No 1 spark plug.
10 Lower the car to the ground, or refit the housing cover.

Stroboscope
11 If the distributor has just been refitted, lower the car to the ground and select neutral (manual gearbox).
12 On CX 2400 models, disconnect the vacuum advance pipe from the distributor and plug its end.
13 Connect the stroboscope in accordance with the manufacturer's instructions (usually to No 1 HT lead at the distributor cap).
14 On carburettor engines, start the engine and allow it to run at

idling speed (see Chapter 3). On fuel injection engines, start the engine and run it at 2500 rpm; an assistant can do this from inside the car whilst observing the tachometer. Take care not to get anything caught in the moving parts of the engine, and keep clear of the cooling fan(s).
15 Point the stroboscope through the timing hole on the clutch bellhousing; the timing marks on the flywheel will appear to be stationary and the fixed pointer should be aligned with the specified dynamic advance.
16 If adjustment is necessary, loosen the distributor clamp nut and turn the distributor body anti-clockwise (viewed from the top) to advance the ignition and clockwise to retard the ignition. Tighten the clamp nut when the setting is correct.
17 With the stroboscope still connected, a check can be made on the operation of the centrifugal advance mechanism. To do this, gradually increase the engine speed by moving the throttle lever, at the same

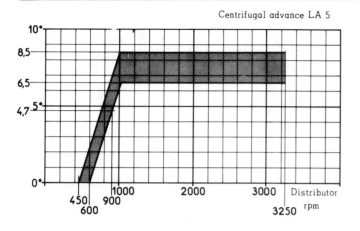

Centrifugal advance LA 5

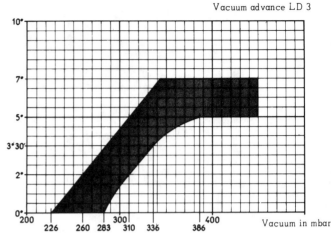

Vacuum advance LD 3

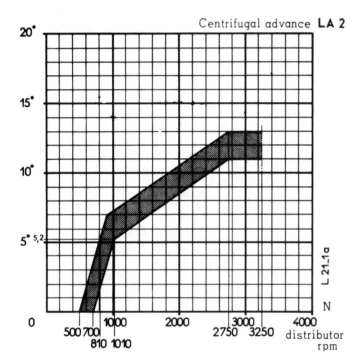

Centrifugal advance **LA 2**

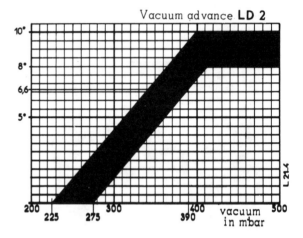

Vacuum advance **LD 2**

Fig. 4.10 Distributor vacuum advance curves (Sec 7)

time pointing the stroboscope at the timing marks on the flywheel. The timing should gradually advance in accordance with the graphs shown in Fig. 4.9. If this is not the case, it is possible to alter the advance curve by changing the tension of the centrifugal weight return springs, but this can prove to be a delicate procedure and should not be undertaken lightly.

18 Where a vacuum advance pipe is fitted, the operation of the capsule can be checked by running the engine at a fast tickover whilst observing the timing marks on the flywheel. Connect the pipe to the capsule and check that the timing advances in addition to the centrifugal advance. A further check can be made by moving the distributor cap, sucking on the vacuum pipe, and checking that the distributor baseplate moves anti-clockwise.

19 Remove the stroboscope and make sure that the vacuum pipe is firmly attached to the capsule.

8 Coil – description

1   The coil is located on the right-hand side of the cylinder head or on the engine compartment front panel. It has an externally mounted ballast resistor which is bypassed when the starter motor is in operation, to compensate for the reduced battery voltage and thus give a good spark when starting.

2   Always make sure that the coil leads are fitted to the correct terminals. If they are reversed, misfiring and loss of power may result.

3   Testing of the coil requires an ohmmeter and special equipment, and is best left to a suitably equipped automobile electrician. However, if a coil is suspected of being faulty, substitution with a known good unit will determine whether a fault is present.

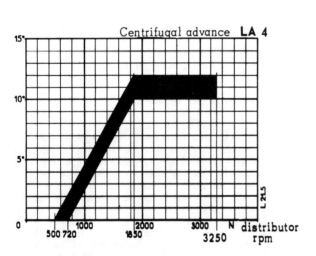

Centrifugal advance **LA 4**

Fig. 4.9 Distributor centrifugal advance curves (Sec 7)

9 Spark plugs and HT leads – general

1   The correct functioning of the spark plugs is vital for the correct running and efficient operation of the engine. The spark plugs fitted as standard are as listed in the Specifications at the beginning of this Chapter.

2   At the intervals specified in Routine Maintenance, the plugs should be removed, examined and cleaned. If worn excessively, they must be renewed. The condition of the spark plugs can give more indication of the overall condition of the engine – refer to the illustrations.

3   If the insulator nose of the spark plug is clean and white, with no deposits, it is an indication that the mixture is too weak, or that too hot a plug is fitted. (A hot plug transfers heat away from the electrode slowly – a cold plug transfers it away quickly).

4   If the tip and insulator nose are covered with sooty black deposits, then this is indicative that the mixture is too rich. Should the plug be black and oily, then it is likely that the engine cylinders and piston rings are worn, as well as the mixture being rich.

5   A properly tuned engine, under normal running conditions, will have a light deposit of a greyish brown colour on the electrodes.

6   If there are traces of long brown tapering stains on the outside of the white portion of the spark plug, then the plug will have to be renewed, as this shows that there is a faulty joint between the plug body and the insulator, and that pressure is being allowed to leak past.

7   If possible clean the spark plug in a sand blasting machine as this will remove carbon deposits more thoroughly than cleaning by hand. The machine will also test the condition of the spark plugs under pressure conditions. Any plug that fails to spark at the recommended pressure should be discarded.

8   The spark plug gap is of considerable importance as its efficiency will be seriously affected if the gap is too large or too small. Refer to the Specifications for the correct gap.

9   Set the gap by measuring it with a feeler gauge, and then bend open, or close, the outer electrode until the correct gap is obtained. Never bend the centre electrode as this will probably crack the insulation and cause plug failure.

10   To help get the spark plug thread correctly seated in the cylinder head when replacing the plugs, push a rubber tube over the insulator and screw the plug in as far as possible with the tube. Finish tightening the plug to the specific torque with a torque wrench.

11   No routine maintenance is required for the plug leads other than being kept clean by wiping them regularly and checking for deterioration of the insulation and loose connections.

12   Always make sure that the spark plug extension rods are tightened, and that the insulators and seals are correctly located (photos).

10 Fault diagnosis – ignition system

1   With the exception of timing maladjustment or advance-retard defects, both of which will be evident as lack of performance and possibly pinking (pre-ignition) or overheating, ignition faults can be divided into two types: total failure (engine fails to start, or cuts out completely, perhaps intermittently) and partial failure (misfiring, regular or otherwise, on one or more cylinder).

2   Electronic ignition, where fitted, is normally very reliable. Fault diagnosis should be confined to checking the star to sensor gap, the continuity of leads and the security of connections, and the dryness and condition of insulation on the HT side. In particular, it is not advisable to remove HT leads when the engine is running, as the voltage present is considerably higher than that in a conventional ignition system, and there is a risk both of personal injury and of damage to the coil insulation. The checks below apply only to contact breaker ignition systems.

3   The commonest cause of difficulty in starting, especially in winter, is a slow engine cranking speed combined with a poor spark at the plugs. Before commencing the checks below, ensure that the battery is fully charged, that the HT leads and distributor cap are clean and dry, that the points and plugs are in good condition and correctly gapped, and that all LT connections (including the battery terminals) are clean and tight.

Engine will not start

4   Remove the plug cap and hold the metal end of the lead about 6

mm ($\frac{1}{4}$ in) away from the block. *Hold the lead with insulating material – eg a rubber glove, a dry cloth, or insulated pliers – to avoid electric shocks.* Have an assistant crank the engine on the starter motor: a fat blue spark should be seen and heard to jump from the end of the lead to the block. If it does, this suggests that HT current is reaching the plugs, and that either the plugs themselves are defective, the timing is grossly maladjusted, or the fault is not in the ignition system. If the spark is weak or absent although the cranking speed is good, proceed with the checks below. If the cranking speed is low check the battery and starter motor.

5   Remove the HT lead which enters the centre of the distributor cap, hold the end near the block and repeat the check described above. A good spark now, if there was none at the plug lead, indicates that HT current is not being transmitted to the plug lead. Check the carbon brush and the plug lead terminals inside the distributor cap, the inside of the cap itself for dampness, cracks or tracking marks (black lines formed where insulation defects allow the passage of current), and the rotor arm for cracks or tracking. If tracking is evident on the distributor cap or rotor arm, the component must be renewed, although in an emergency it may be possible to interrupt the track by scraping or filing. If there is no spark at the HT lead from the coil, carry on to the next check.

6   The HT system has now been checked, with the exception of the HT lead from the coil to the distributor and the HT terminal on the coil itself. If these seem to be in order, start checking the LT system. With the distributor cap and rotor arm removed, turn the engine if necessary until the points are closed, then switch on the ignition and separate the points with an insulated screwdriver. A strong blue spark suggests condenser failure in the open circuit mode: fit a new one and the engine should run. No spark at all when the points are separated could be due to condenser failure in the short circuit mode: temporarily disconnect it and check again. If there is still no spark, either the point faces are contaminated – clean them with methylated spirit – or the fault is elsewhere in the LT system. For further checking a 12 volt test lamp or a voltmeter will be required.

7   Connect the test lamp or voltmeter between the coil contact breaker (RUP) terminal and earth. Turn on the ignition and separate the points with a piece of cardboard. A reading suggests that the fault is either a broken lead between the coil and distributor or an internal fault in the coil. No reading indicates a fault further up the line, or a short circuit to earth in the distributor. Disconnect the distributor-to-coil LT lead, leaving the test lamp connected to the coil: a reading now where there was none before indicates a short circuit to earth somewhere between the lead and the fixed contact. Check the insulating washers on the moving contact pivot, the lead from the distributors LT terminal to the moving contact and the contact itself. No reading still means that further checking is required.

8   Connect the test lamp or voltmeter to the other coil LT terminal, separate the points and turn on the ignition. A reading here with none at the RUP terminal confirms an internal fault in the coil, which will have to be renewed. (A reading at *both* terminals suggests an internal short circuit, but if everything else is in order this would probably blow a fuse). No reading indicates a defective ballast resistor (see below), or a break in supply from the battery to the coil via the ignition switch. The fuse which protects the ignition circuit also protects a number of other items (see Chapter 10), and presumably it will be noticed if these are not working either. As a 'get-you-home' measure it may be possible to connect a wire directly from the ballast resistor terminal (*not* from the coil itself) to the battery live (+) terminal, but check the wiring from the resistor to the ignition switch and from the switch to the battery first.

Engine fires but will not run

9   If the coil ballast resistor is defective the ignition system will function normally whilst the starter motor is operating, but will cut out as soon as the ignition key returns to its normal position. This condition is confirmed if voltage is present at the supply (ignition switch) side of the resistor but not at the coil side. It is inadvisable to by-pass the resistor, as this could lead to overheating of the coil and subsequent damage.

Engine misfires

10   Uneven running and misfiring should first be checked by seeing that all leads, particularly HT, are dry and connected properly. See that they are not shorting to earth through broken or cracked insulation. If they are, you should be able to see and hear it. If not, then check the

plugs, contact points and condenser just as you would in a case of total failure to start. A regular misfire can be isolated by removing each plug lead in turn *(not with electronic ignition)*; removing a good lead will accentuate the misfire, whilst removing the defective lead will make no difference.

11 If misfiring occurs at high speed check the points gap, which may be too small, and the plugs. Check also that the spring tension on the points is not too light thus causing them to bounce. This requires a special pull balance so if in doubt it will be cheaper to buy a new set of contacts rather than go to a garage and get them to check it. If the trouble is still not cured then the fault lies in the carburation or engine itself.

12 If misfiring or stalling occurs only at low speeds the points gap is possibly too big. If not, then the slow running adjustment on the carburettor may need attention.

Chapter 5 Clutch

For modifications, and information applicable to later models, see Supplement at end of manual

Contents

Specifications

Clutch type . . . .   Single dry plate, diaphragm spring, cable actuated

Disc diameter
CX 2000, CX 2200 (up to Jan 1976), CX 2400 (fuel injection) . . . . .   225.0 mm (8.86 in)
CX 2200 (later models), CX 2400 (carburettor) . . . .   228.6 mm (9.00 in)

Thrust bearing
Bearing type . . . .   Self-centering
Bearing to diaphragm free play . . . .   1.0 to 1.5 mm (0.04 to 0.06 in)

Torque wrench settings

	lbf ft	kgf m
Clutch to flywheel bolts	17.0	2.3

1 General description

The clutch is of single dry plate type and incorporates a diaphragm spring. Actuation is by means of a cable through a pendant mounted pedal.

The cover unit comprises a pressed steel casing which is dowelled to the flywheel and retained by bolts. The pressure plate, diaphragm spring and fulcrum rings are incorporated into the cover unit.

The clutch driven plate is free to slide along the splined gearbox primary shaft, and is held in position between the flywheel and the pressure plate by the diaphragm spring. Friction lining material is rivetted to the clutch driven plate, which incorporates a spring cushioned hub to absorb transmission shocks and assist in smooth clutch engagement.

When the clutch pedal is depressed, the cable moves the release arm which presses the release bearing against the centre of the diaphragm spring. As the centre of the spring is pushed in, the periphery moves outward and the pressure plate is disengaged from the clutch driven plate.

When the clutch pedal is released, the diaphragm spring forces the pressure plate into contact with the driven plate which is then firmly sandwiched between the pressure plate and the flywheel.

As the friction linings on the driven plate wear, the pressure plate will gradually move closer to the flywheel and the clutch release arm free play will increase. Periodic adjustment must therefore be carried out as described in Section 2.

2 Clutch – adjustment

1   The clutch free play should be adjusted at 10 000 mile (15 000 km) intervals. First jack-up the front of the car and support it on axle stands. Check the rear wheels.
2   Locate the clutch release arm beneath the gearbox bellhousing and unhook the return spring from the support plate (photo).
3   Loosen the adjustment locknut, then tighten the adjustment nut until resistance is felt, indicating that the thrust bearing is in contact with the diaphragm spring. Stop turning as soon as resistance is felt.
4   From inside the car, check that the cable end is seated correctly in the clutch pedal and that the clutch pedal is in contact with its return stop.
5   Unscrew the adjustment nut $2\frac{1}{2}$ turns exactly and tighten the locknut; the thrust bearing to diaphragm spring free play will now be correct.
6   Hook the return spring onto the support plate, and lower the car to the ground.

3 Clutch cable – renewal

1   Jack-up the front of the car and support it on axle stands. Chock the rear wheels.
2   Unhook the return spring from its support plate beneath the gearbox.

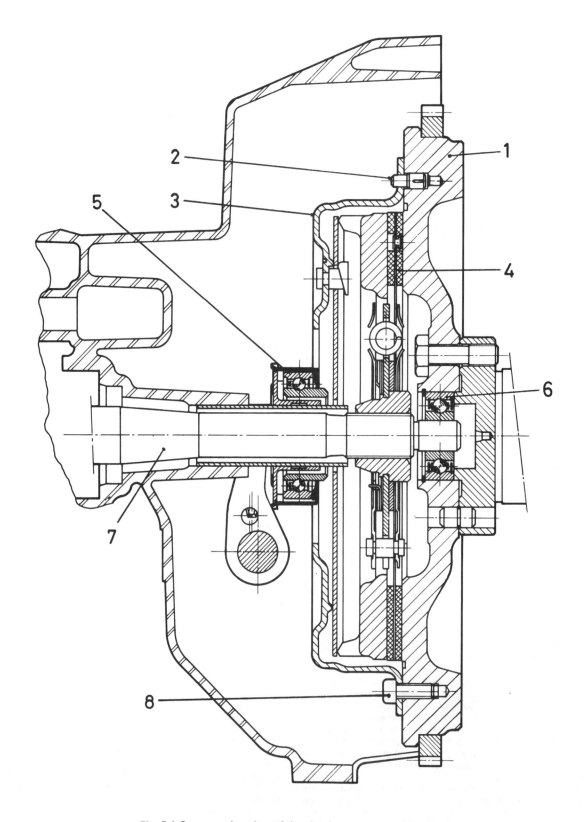

Fig. 5.1 Cross-section view of the clutch components (Sec 1)

1	Flywheel	4	Driven plate and friction linings	6	Spigot bearing	
2	Location dowel			7	Primary shaft	
3	Clutch cover	5	Release bearing	8	Retaining bolt	

2.2 Clutch release arm location

3.5 Remove the support from the bulkhead and detach the cable

5.3 Removing the clutch cover and driven plate

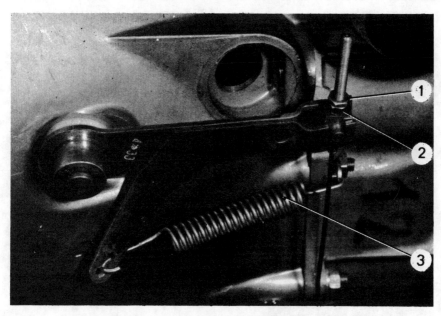

Fig. 5.2 Clutch release arm and cable adjustment (Sec 2)

1 Locknut   3 Return spring
2 Adjustment nut

3   Loosen the clutch locknut and adjustment nut enough to allow the stop pin to be disengaged from the release arm.
4   Withdraw the cable sleeve from the gearbox housing.
5   Working in the engine compartment, detach the cable from the clutch pedal after removing the support from the bulkhead (photo).
6   Remove the spare wheel from the engine compartment, and withdraw the clutch cable complete with the support.
7   Fitting the new cable is a reversal of removal, but it will be necessary to adjust the free play as described in Section 2.

4 Clutch pedal – removal and refitting

1   Working inside the car, unhook the return spring from the clutch pedal.
2   Jack-up the front of the car and support it on axle stands, then detach the return spring from the release lever and loosen the cable locknut and adjustment nut.
3   Detach the cable from the clutch pedal. On early models a pin must be removed but on later models the cable can simply be unhooked.
4   Unscrew and remove the pivot bolt and withdraw the clutch pedal.
5   Examine the pedal and bolt for damage and deterioration and renew the components as necessary.
6   Refitting is a reversal of removal, but apply a little grease to the

pivoting surfaces and when completely assembled, adjust the free play as described in Section 2.

5 Clutch – removal

1   Access to the clutch can only be gained by removing the engine and transmission unit as described in Chapter 1, and withdrawing the gearbox from the engine. With the engine on a workbench, first mark the clutch cover in relation to the flywheel in order to ensure correct refitting should the original clutch be serviceable.
2   Hold the flywheel stationary with a screwdriver or similar tool engaged in the teeth of the ring gear, then unscrew the socket head retaining bolts a turn at a time until the pressure of the diaphragm spring is relieved. A suitable key will be necessary to engage the bolts, and the square drive type is to be preferred so that a torque wrench can be used for refitting.
3   With all the bolts removed, withdraw the cover assembly and driven plate from the flywheel (photo).

6 Clutch – inspection and renovation

1   Examine the cover unit and driven plate for wear and deterioration. If oil is present on the friction lining, the gearbox primary shaft oil seal

7.2A Clutch release bearing retaining spring location

7.2B Removing the clutch release bearing

7.3A Release arm retaining circlip location

7.3B Removing the bush ...

7.3C ... and release fork

7.4 Correct fitted location of the release bearing spring

Fig. 5.3 Clutch pedal return stop (a) location (Sec 2)

8.4 Using a gearbox primary shaft to centralise the clutch driven plate

or crankshaft rear oil seal may be faulty requiring renewal. If light scoring is apparent on the pressure plate or flywheel it may be ignored, but if the scoring is very deep the components must be renewed. In the case of the flywheel, it may be possible to machine the surface, but this should only be carried out by a specialist engineering firm.

2   Renew the driven plate if the linings are worn down to the rivets or within 0.5 mm (0.02 in) of them, or if the splines, hub and cushion springs show signs of wear.

3   Examine the pressure plate and cover assembly and if there are signs of excessive wear or of cracking, renew the unit complete.

4   With the clutch removed from the flywheel it is well worth while to check the spigot bearing in the centre of the flywheel. If the bearing requires renewal, refer to Chapter 1 for the procedure.

7   Release bearing and fork – removal and refitting

1   The release bearing is of ball bearing, grease sealed type although it is designed for long life, it is worth renewing it whenever the driven plate requires renewal. If the bearing is excessively worn, there will be signs of grease leakage and the bearing will sound rough when spun.

2   To remove the bearing, the engine must be separated from the gearbox and clutch bellhousing. Using a screwdriver, prise off the

retaining spring and withdraw the bearing from the location sleeve (photo).

3   To remove the release fork and shaft, extract the circlip and remove the release arm (photo). Lever out the bush and withdraw the release fork and shaft from inside the clutch bellhousing (photos).

4   Refitting is a reversal of removal, but lubricate the shaft bushes with a little multi-purpose grease (photo).

8   Clutch – refitting

1   Before refitting the clutch, it will be necessary to obtain a tool for centralising the driven plate. An old primary shaft or a suitable piece of dowel with a step at one end to engage the spigot bearing and driven plate may be used.

2   Locate the driven plate against the face of the flywheel with the projecting part of the hub facing outward (ie away from the flywheel).

3   Place the cover unit over the driven plate and onto the locating dowels; if the original unit is being refitted, make sure that the previously made marks are aligned.

4   Insert the guide tool through the splined hub of the driven plate so that the end of the tool locates in the flywheel spigot bearing, then insert the cover retaining bolts and lightly tighten them (photo).

5   Move the guide tool from side to side and up and down several times until the driven plate is in a central position, then tighten the retaining bolts a turn at a time in diagonal sequence to the specified torque, using a torque wrench.

6   Remove the guide tool and make sure that the splines of the driven plate are clean.

7   Assemble the gearbox to the engine and refit the unit to the car as described in Chapter 1; the clutch cable will of course require adjustment as described in Section 2.

See overleaf for 'Fault diagnosis – clutch'

9 Fault diagnosis – clutch

Symptom	Reason/s
Judder when taking up drive	Loose engine/gearbox mountings Friction linings worn or contaminated with oil Worn splines on gearbox primary shaft or driven plate hub Worn flywheel spigot bearing
Clutch fails to disengage	Incorrect cable adjustment Driven plate sticking on primary shaft splines (may be due to rust if vehicle off road for long period) Damaged or misaligned cover/pressure plate assembly
Clutch slips	Incorrect cable adjustment Friction linings worn or contaminated with oil
Noise when depressing clutch pedal	Worn or damaged release bearing Worn splines on gearbox primary shaft or driven plate hub
Noise when releasing clutch pedal	Distorted driven plate Broken or weak driven plate cushions springs Loose engine/gearbox mountings

Chapter 6 Manual and semi-automatic gearbox

For modifications, and information applicable to later models, see Supplement at end of manual

Contents

Specifications

Four-speed manual gearbox

Type . . . . Four forward speeds, all with synchromesh and one reverse

Ratios:	Standard	Economy CX 2000
1st	3.166 : 1	3.1666 : 1
2nd	1.8333 : 1	1.8333 : 1
3rd	1.1333:1	1.1333 : 1
4th	0.8 : 1	0.75 : 1
Reverse	3.1538 : 1	3.1538 : 1
Final drive	4.769 : 1	4.357 : 1

1st/2nd synchro hub endfloat (max) . . . . 0.05 mm (0.002 in)
2nd to 3rd gear halfring endfloat (max) . . . . 0.05 mm (0.002 in)
Bearing outer race to casing clearance (max) . . . . 0.05 mm (0.002 in)
Differential bearing preload . . . . 0.15 mm (0.006 in)
Oil capacity . . . . 1.6 litres (2.8 Imp pints)

Five-speed manual gearbox

Type . . . . Five forward speeds, all with synchromesh and one reverse

Ratios:
1st . . . . 3.1666 : 1
2nd . . . . 1.8333 : 1
3rd . . . . 1.25 : 1
4th . . . . 0.9393 : 1
5th . . . . 0.7333 : 1
Reverse . . . . 3.1538 : 1
Final drive . . . . 4.769 : 1
Oil capacity . . . . 1.7 litres (3.0 Imp pints)
Other specifications as four-speed gearbox

Semi-automatic (C-matic) gearbox

Type . . . . Three forward speeds, all with synchromesh, and reverse. Torque
converter. Safety locking device with parking pawl

Ratios:
1st . . . . 1.944 : 1
2nd . . . . 1.133 : 1
3rd . . . . 0.800 : 1
Reverse . . . . 2.388 : 1
Final drive . . . . 4.789 : 1
1st/Reverse synchro hub endfloat (max) . . . . 0.05 mm (0.002 in)
1st to 2nd gear halfring endfloat (max) . . . . 0.05 mm (0.002 in)

Bearing outer race to casing clearance (max) .... 0.05 mm (0.002 in)
Differential bearing preload .... 0.15 mm (0.006 in)

Torque converter
Fluid pressure:
    At 700 rpm .... 3.5 bars (51 lbf/in^2)
    At 2000 rpm .... 5.5 bars (80 lbf/in^2)
    At maximum rpm .... 10.0 bars (145 lbf/in^2)
Warning lamp switch operating temperature .... 132° to 138° C (269° to 280° F)
Fluid capacity:
    Total .... 5.5 litres (9.7 Imp pints)
    Drain and refill .... 2.0 to 3.0 litres (3.5 to 5.3 Imp pints)

Torque wrench settings

	lbf ft	kgf m
4-speed manual gearbox		
Drain and filler plugs	25.5 to 32.5	3.5 to 4.5
Final drive casing nuts:		
8 mm	20.5	2.8
10 mm	36.0	5.0
Selector shaft bush nut	79.5 to 87.0	11.0 to 12.0
Dipstick guide bush nut	21.5 to 29.0	3.0 to 4.0
Final drive gear	58.5 to 65.0	8.1 to 9.0
Primary shaft bolt	97.5 to 108.5	13.5 to 15.0
Secondary shaft nut	141.0 to 155.5	19.5 to 21.5
Selector fork bolts	20.5	2.8
Reversing lamp switch	8.75 to 10.0	1.2 to 1.4
Differential bearing side plate	20.5	2.8
Gearchange lever selector bush	79.5 to 94.0	11.0 to 13.0
End cover bolt	20.5	2.8
5-speed manual gearbox – as 4-speed except:		
Secondary shaft nut	130.0 to 145.0	18.0 to 20.0
Primary shaft nut	130.0 to 145.0	18.0 to 20.0
End cover bolt	14.5 to 16.0	2.0 to 2.2
Semi-automatic gearbox – as 4-speed except:		
Main casing screws and nuts (8 mm)	20.5	2.8
Selector shaft bush nut	79.5 to 94.0	11.0 to 13.0
Filter	25.5 to 29.0	3.5 to 4.0
Electro valve union screw	21.5 to 25.5	3.0 to 3.5
Oil pump	20.5	2.8
Electro valve	20.5	2.8
Contact retaining bolts	1.5 to 2.0	0.2 to 0.3
Parking pawl selector dog	20.5	2.8
Reverse idler gear shaft	5.3 to 7.25	0.8 to 1.0
Clutch control switch	7.25 to 8.0	1.0 to 1.1
Detent plate	10.75 to 11.5	1.5 to 1.6

1 General description

Three types of gearbox are fitted to the CX models, namely, the four-speed manual gearbox, the five-speed manual gearbox, and the three-speed semi-automatic (C-matic) gearbox. All three types have synchromesh on the forward speeds, and the semi-automatic gearbox also has synchromesh on reverse.

Gear selection is by means of a short floor-mounted remote control lever, which is connected to two gearchange levers on the gearbox by adjustable links and balljoints.

The gearbox casing is attached to the flywheel end of the engine and incorporates the final drive and differential gears.

Drive from the engine flywheel is transmitted to the gearbox primary shaft via the clutch or torque converter. Constant mesh gears and synchro units transmit the drive to the secondary shaft which incorporates a pinion in mesh with the final drive gear. The drive is then transmitted through the differential gears and driveshafts to the front wheels.

2 Gearbox – removal and refitting

The complete gearbox including the clutch bellhousing cannot be removed with the engine in situ, therefore where removal of the complete gearbox is required, the engine and gearbox must be removed as described in Chapter 1. Separation of the gearbox from the engine is also described in Chapter 1, together with the refitting procedures.

On manual gearboxes (ie not equipped with torque converter) it is possible to dismantle the gearbox components without removing the engine from the car. However, it should be noted that it is not possible to dismantle the final drive with this method.

3 Four-speed manual gearbox (complete) – dismantling and inspection

1   With the complete gearbox removed from the car, wash off all external dirt with paraffin or a grease solvent and wipe dry.
2   Remove the drain plugs and drain the oil, then refit and tighten the plugs.
3   Remove the clutch release bearing and fork from the bellhousing as described in Chapter 5.
4   Unbolt the tensioner mounting and drive out the camshaft support bearing with a suitable diameter tube (photo).
5   Remove the dust seal from the bellhousing (photo).
6   Unscrew the nuts and remove the gearchange bracket and arm assembly (photo).
7   Unscrew the bolt and remove the gearchange arm from the selector shaft.
8   Unbolt and remove the engine mounting (photo).
9   Unscrew and remove the reversing lamp switch (photo).
10 Unbolt the end cover and remove it (photo).
11 Prise out the circlips retaining the primary and secondary shaft bearings (photo).
12 Unbolt and remove the reverse gear shaft retaining plate (photo).

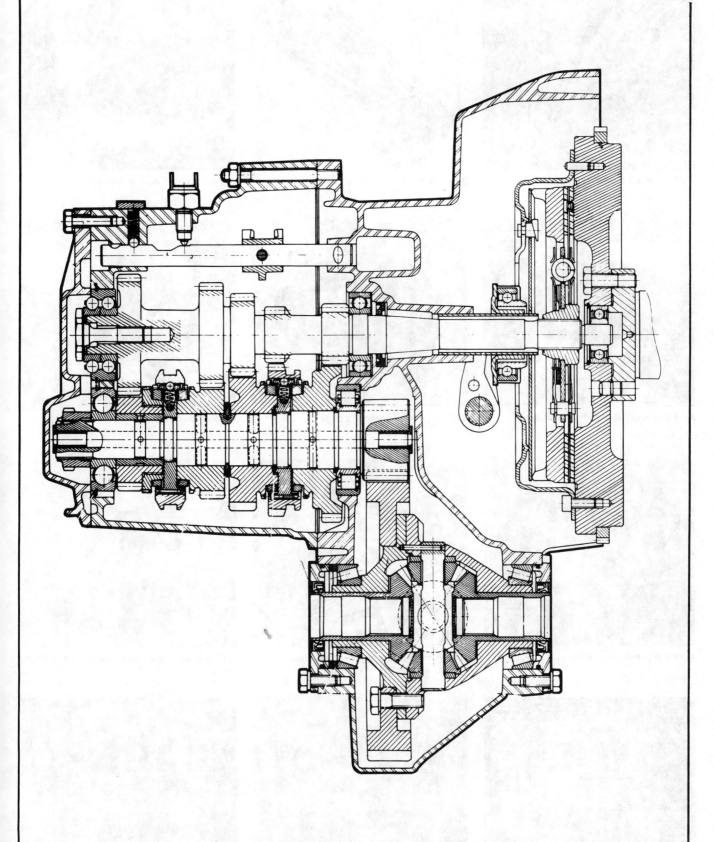

Fig. 6.1 Cross-section view of the four-speed manual gearbox (Sec 3)

3.4A Drivebelt tensioner location

3.4B View of the drivebelt tensioner

3.5 Bellhousing dust seal location

3.6 Removing the gearchange bracket

3.8 The gearbox mounting plate

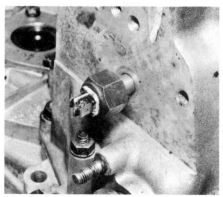

3.9 Removing the reversing lamp switch

3.10 The gearbox end cover

3.11 Primary and secondary shaft bearing circlips (arrowed)

3.12 Removing the reverse gear shaft retaining plate

3.13A Detent plate location

3.13B Removing the detent springs

3.13C Removing the detent balls

3.16 Selector finger components

3.17 Primary shaft end bolt

3.18 Removing the reverse gear selector rod and dog

3.19 Removing the 1st/2nd and 3rd/4th selector rods, fork and dog

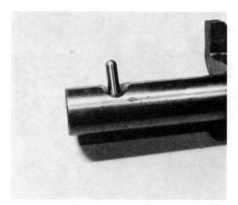

3.20 Removing the 3rd/4th selector rod interlock plunger

3.22 Location of the reverse selector lever and bracket

3.23 Reverse idler gear, shaft and seal

3.25 Location of the primary shaft oil seal

3.26A A differential side plate

3.26B The differential side plate oil seal and O-ring (arrowed)

3.27 Removing the differential cover

3.29 Location of the speedometer drive bush and pinion

3.35A Remove the 4th gear ...

3.35B ... the 4th gear bush ...

3.35C ... the 3rd/4th synchro unit ...

3.35D ... the 3rd gear synchro ring ...

3.35E ... and the 3rd gear

3.36A Removing the 2nd gear retaining ring (arrowed) ...

3.36B ... and thrust washers

3.37A Removing the 2nd gear ...

3.37B ... and synchro ring

3.38 1st/2nd synchro unit retaining circlip location

3.39A Removing the 1st/2nd synchro unit ...

3.39B ... synchro ring ...

3.39C ... and 1st gear

3.40 Location of the secondary shaft bearing and circlip

Fig. 6.2 Selector shaft components on the four-speed manual gearbox (Sec 3)

1	Spring	3	Selector shaft
2	Nut	4	Studs

13 Unbolt the plate from the side of the casing and remove the three springs and detent balls, using a pen magnet (photos).
14 Unscrew the retaining nuts and withdraw the main casing, using a wooden mallet to tap it free; at the same time turn the selector shaft to disengage the finger. Remove the gasket.
15 Lock the gearbox shafts by selecting two gears at the same time.
16 Unscrew the selector shaft nut from the main casing and remove the shaft, springs and finger (photo).
17 Temporarily refit the casing and loosen the bolt on the end of the primary shaft (photo). Remove the casing.
18 Unscrew the reverse gear selector dog retaining bolt, after reselecting neutral, pull out the selector rod and remove the dog (photo).
19 Unscrew the bolts retaining the 1st/2nd and 3rd/4th selector forks and dog, pull out the selector rods, and remove the forks and dog; the 1st/2nd selector fork must be withdrawn over the casing studs (photo).
20 Remove the interlock plunger from the 3rd/4th selector rod (photo).
21 Remove the two interlock plungers from the main casing using a pen magnet.
22 Unbolt and remove the reverse selector lever and bracket assembly (photo).
23 Pull out the reverse idler gear shaft and reverse idler gear together with the oil seal (photo).
24 Remove the primary and secondary shaft assemblies together from the bellhousing casing.

25 Using a soft metal punch, drive the primary shaft oil seal from the bellhousing casing (photo).
26 Mark the differential side plates side for side, then unbolt and remove them. Remove the oil seals and O-rings (photos).
27 Unscrew the securing nuts and withdraw the differential cover (photo).
28 Mark the bearing outer races side for side, then lift out the differential unit.
29 Remove the speedometer drive bush and pinion from the end cover (photo).
30 Unscrew the bolt from the end of the primary shaft.
31 Remove the bearings from the primary shaft using a suitable puller or by mounting the outer races on a vice. Take care not to lose the balls from the double track bearing.
32 Mount the secondary shaft in a vice by gripping the first gear between two blocks of wood. Engage first gear.
33 Unscrew the speedometer drive nut (*left-hand thread*). If the correct size spanner is not available, place two bolts on the flats of the nut and use an adjustable spanner to unscrew the nut.
34 Remove the bearing from the secondary shaft with a puller.
35 Remove the 4th gear and bush, 3rd/4th synchro unit and rings and 3rd gear (photo). Mark the synchro unit and rings for location.
36 Remove the retaining ring and the halfring thrust washers (photos).
37 Remove the 2nd gear and synchro ring (photos). Mark the ring for location.
38 Prise out the circlip retaining the 1st/2nd synchro unit (photo). To do this, wrap some thin metal foil around the shaft and lever the circlip onto it, then slide the circlip and foil off the shaft.
39 Remove the 1st/2nd synchro unit from the shaft, followed by the synchro ring and 1st gear (photo). Mark the synchro unit and ring for location.
40 Prise out the circlip retaining the bearing and remove the circlip as described in paragraph 38 (photo).
41 Remove the bearing from the secondary shaft with a puller or by locating it on a vice and tapping the shaft through.
42 If necessary, the differential may be dismantled. First mark the final drive gear and differential flanges in relation to each other.
43 Unscrew the gear retaining bolts evenly and in diagonal sequence. Remove the gear and left-hand flange.
44 Remove the sun gear and fibre washer and the shaft locating roll pins.
45 Drive out the shafts and remove the planet gears and thrust pads. Mark each component for location.
46 Remove the remaining sun gear and fibre washer. Mark them for location.
47 Using a puller, remove the taper roller bearings and inner races; mark them side for side.
48 Clean all components with paraffin and wipe dry with lint-free cloth. Examine the gears for worn or chipped teeth, and check the

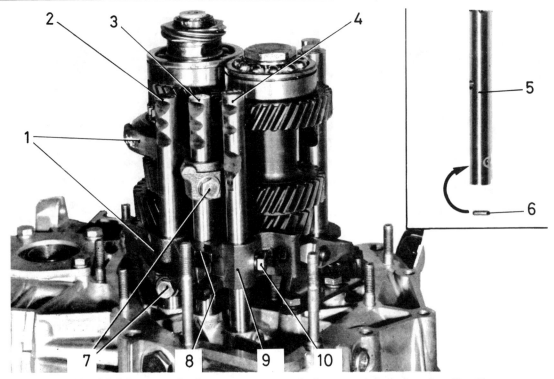

Fig. 6.3 Selector mechanism components on the four-speed manual gearbox (Sec 3)

1	Forks	6	Interlock plunger
2	1st/2nd selector rod	7	Bolts
3	3rd/4th selector rod	8	Control dog
4	Reverse selector rod	9	Control dog
5	3rd/4th selector rod	10	Bolt

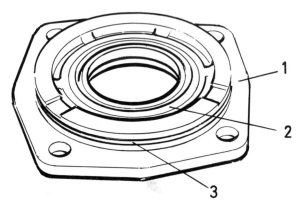

Fig. 6.4 Differential side plate (1), oil seal (2), and O-ring seal (3) (Sec 3)

bearings for wear; spin the single track type in the hand and check them for any excessive play or rough running. Examine the selector mechanism and detent grooves in the rods for wear. Check the casing studs for thread wear and damage. Check the synchro units and rings for wear which will be evident if gear changing is not smooth. Renew all components as necessary and obtain a set of new oil seals and gaskets.

---

4 Four speed manual gearbox (complete) – reassembly

---

1   Press the taper roller bearings onto the respective ends of the differential halves.
2   Insert the sun gear and fibre washer into the right-hand differential half.

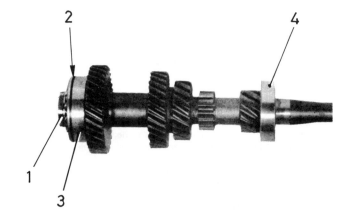

Fig. 6.5 Primary shaft components on the four-speed manual gearbox (Sec 3)

1	Bolt	3	Double track bearing
2	Circlip groove	4	Single track bearing

3   Locate one thrust pad and planet gear in the differential, then insert the crosshead and shaft, and the planet gear shaft. Check that the sun gear turns smoothly and has approximately 0.1 mm (0.004 in) endplay; check the endplay with a dial gauge.
4   If necessary, fit a fibre washer of different thickness until the endplay is correct, then remove the shaft and refit all the planet gears in their respective positions together with the thrust pads and shafts.
5   Locate the shaft locating rollpins in the flange.
6   Refit the remaining sun gear together with the fibre washer.
7   Locate the left-hand flange over the sun gear in its previously

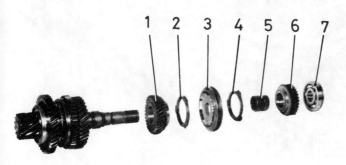

Fig. 6.6 Secondary shaft components on the four-speed manual gearbox (Sec 3)

1	3rd gear	5	Bush
2	Synchro ring	6	4th gear
3	3rd/4th synchro unit	7	Bearing
4	Synchro ring		

Fig. 6.7 Secondary shaft components on the four-speed manual gearbox (Sec 3)

1   Synchro ring   2   2nd gear

Fig. 6.9 Differential unit flange (1) (Sec 3)

Fig. 6.8 Secondary shaft components on the four-speed manual gearbox (Sec)

1	1st gear	3	1st/2nd synchro unit
2	Synchro ring		

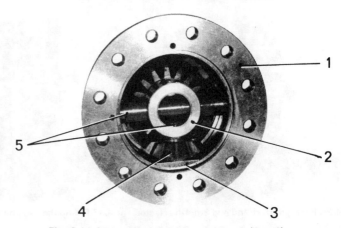

Fig. 6.10 Differential unit fibre washer (1) and sun gear (2) (Sec 3)

Fig. 6.11 Assembling the differential unit (Sec 4)

1	Housing	4	Planet gear
2	Crosshead	5	Shafts
3	Thrust pad		

noted position, then locate the final drive gear on the flange and tighten four retaining bolts inserted at equidistant intervals.

8   Check that the left-hand sun gear turns smoothly and has approximately 0.1 mm (0.004 in) endplay measured with a dial gauge. If not, the thickness of the fibre washer must be changed.

9   Insert all the final drive gear retaining bolts and tighten them evenly to the specified torque. Note that the recessed side of the gear must be on the same side as the bolt heads.

10 Check that the differential gears turn smoothly.

11 Locate the outer races on their respective tapered rollers, then lower the differential assembly into the bellhousing casing (photo).

12 Smear the mating faces with sealing compound, then refit the differential cover and tighten the securing nuts by hand.

13 Fit a new oil seal in the right-hand side plate with its closed end 3.0 mm (0.118 in) from the outer surface of the plate; smear its lip with a little grease.

14 Fit a new O-ring seal, then locate the plate on the casing and tighten the retaining bolts by hand.

15 Using a tube and mallet, tap the left-hand bearing outer race in as far as possible, then tighten the differential cover nuts and right-hand side plate bolts in diagonal sequence to the specified torque.

16 Using vernier calipers or a dial gauge, note the distance between the mating flange of the left-hand side plate and its inner face. Note also the distance from the casing mating face to the left-hand bearing outer race. The difference between these readings plus a further 0.15 mm (0.006 in) represents the thickness of shims to be fitted in order to achieve the correct bearing preload. Locate the shims next to the outer race of the left-hand taper roller bearing (photo).

17 Fit a new oil seal in the left-hand side plate with its closed end 3.0 mm (0.118 in) from the outer face of the plate; smear its lip with a little grease.

18 Fit a new O-ring seal, then locate the plate on the casing and

4.11 Fitting the differential assembly

4.16 Differential left-hand side bearing shim location

4.19 Secondary shaft with bearing fitted

4.28A Lock the speedometer drive nut by peening into the notch

4.28B The complete secondary shaft assembly

4.35 Primary and secondary shaft assemblies fitted in the bellhousing

4.36 Fitting the 1st/2nd and 3rd/4th selector forks

4.37 Fitting the 1st/2nd selector rod

4.38 Fitting an interlock plunger

4.40 Fitting the 3rd/4th selector rod

4.42 Reverse idler gear and shaft

4.48 Engaging the selector finger with selector dogs and fork

tighten the retaining bolts in diagonal sequence to the specified torque.

19 Using a long tube, drive the bearing onto the secondary shaft. Fit the circlip with the chamfered side against the bearing to facilitate future removal; use metal foil to slide it into position (photo).

20 Locate the 1st gear, synchro ring and 1st/2nd synchro unit on the secondary shaft. Make sure that the synchro unit sleeve groove is facing the 1st gear.

21 Using metal foil, slide the circlip into its groove. Check that the 1st/2nd synchro hub endfloat does not exceed the maximum specified. To do this, push the circlip against the hub and check that a feeler blade of the specified maximum thickness cannot be inserted between the circlip and the visible end of its groove. If necessary, fit a thicker circlip.

22 Refit the synchro ring and 2nd gear.

23 Fit the halfring thrust washers and retaining ring.

24 Push the halfring thrust washers against the 2nd gear, and check that a feeler blade of the specified maximum thickness cannot be inserted between the washers and the visible end of the groove. If necessary, fit thicker washers but make sure that each half is of identical thickness.

25 Refit the 3rd gear and 3rd/4th synchro unit with synchro rings.

26 Refit the bush and 4th gear.

27 Tap the bearing into the secondary shaft using a tube, then screw on the speedometer drive nut (left-hand thread) with the flats facing the bearing. Make sure that the bearing circlip groove is outermost.

28 Mount the secondary shaft between blocks of wood in a vice by gripping the first gear, then engage first gear. Tighten the speedometer drive nut to the specified torque and lock it by peening into the notch with a centre punch (photos).

29 Using a suitable tube, drive the bearing inner tracks onto the primary shaft. Make sure that the circlip groove in the outer track of the end bearing is furthest from the gear.

30 Grip the primary shaft in a vice between blocks of wood, then insert and tighten the retaining bolt to the specified torque.

31 Grease the speedometer drive pinion, then locate it together with the bush in the end cover. Make sure that the bush is aligned with the bolt hole, and that the end cover locating dowels are in position.

32 Drive the primary shaft oil seal into the bell housing casing with its open end facing towards the bearing bore. Smear a little grease on the sealing lips.

33 Temporarily fit the primary shaft and bearing in the gearbox casing, fit the circlip and tap the bearing so that the circlip is resting on the casing shoulder. Using a straight-edge and feeler blades, check that the face of the bearing outer race in relation to the casing face is not recessed by more than 0.05 mm (0.002 in) or protruding by more than 0.02 mm (0.0008 in). If necessary, select a circlip which will position the outer race within the limits. Remove the circlip and primary shaft from the casing.

34 Using the same procedure, check the secondary shaft outer race protrusion.

35 With the synchro sleeves in neutral, mesh the primary shaft gears with the secondary shaft gears and insert them into the bellhousing casing (photo). Tap both shafts with a wooden mallet to ensure that the bearings are fully home.

36 Locate the 1st/2nd and 3rd/4th selector forks on their respective synchro hub sleeves with the retaining bolt holes towards the bellhousing casing (photo).

37 Insert the 1st/2nd selector rod through the fork and into the casing, align the holes, and tighten the selector fork bolt to the specified torque (photo).

38 Position the interlock plunger in the 1st/2nd selector rod hole by inserting it through the 3rd/4th selector rod bore (photo).

39 Insert the small diameter interlock plunger into the 3rd/4th selector rod.

40 Locate the dog, then insert the 3rd/4th selector rod through the fork and dog and into the casing. Align the holes and tighten the selector fork and dog bolts to the specified torque (photo).

41 Position the interlock plunger against the 3rd/4th selector rod by inserting it through the reverse selector rod bore.

42 Fit the reverse idler gear with the groove facing away from the bellhousing casing, then insert the shaft through it and into the casing. Make sure that the oil seal is located correctly (photo).

43 Refit the reverse selector lever and bracket assembly with the lever located in the reverse gear groove, then insert and tighten the retaining bolts.

44 Locate the dog, then insert the reverse selector rod through the dog and into the casing. Align the holes and tighten the selector dog belt to the specified torque.

45 Select each gear in turn and check that only one gear can be engaged at a time. After the check, move the selector rods to neutral with the dogs and fork aligned.

46 Refit the selector shaft, springs and finger in the main casing. Fit the bush nut, complete with copper washer, and tighten it to the specified torque.

47 Clean the mating faces of the main casing and bellhousing casing and fit the new gasket, dry.

48 Locate the main casing over the gearbox shafts and onto the bellhousing casing. At the same time, locate the selector finger with the selector dogs and fork (photo).

49 Refit and tighten the casing retaining nuts in diagonal sequence to the specified torque. Refit the clutch return spring lug.

50 Spring the circlips into their grooves on the shaft bearing outer races.

51 Engage the retaining plate with the reverse gear shaft and tighten the bolt.

52 Insert the detent balls and springs into the casing, then refit the retaining plate with a new gasket and tighten the bolts.

53 Coat the mating faces of the end cover and main casing with sealing compound. Refit the end cover and tighten the retaining bolts in diagonal sequence to the specified torque.

54 Insert and tighten the reversing lamp switch to the specified torque.

55 Locate the engine mounting on the casing and tighten the retaining bolts.

56 Locate the gearchange arm on the selector shaft and tighten the retaining bolt.

57 Refit the gearchange bracket and arm assembly and tighten the retaining nuts.

58 Using suitable adhesive, stick the dust seal onto the bellhousing.

59 Using a tube, drive the camshaft support bearing into the tensioner mounting, then refit the mounting and tighten the retaining bolts.

60 Fit the clutch release bearing and fork as described in Chapter 5.

61 Remove the filler plug and fill the gearbox with the specified quantity of oil. Tighten the plug with a key.

62 Adjust the selector rods as described in Section 12.

5 Five-speed manual gearbox (complete) – dismantling, inspection and reassembly

1 The procedure is basically the same as that described in Sections 3 and 4. However, before the main casing can be removed, the 5th gear selector mechanism must be detached from the 5th synchro unit sleeve and the 5th/reverse selector rod.

2 The primary and secondary shaft nuts must also be removed. To do this, engage 5th gear by moving the synchro unit sleeve, then engage reverse gear by turning the selector shaft. With the gearbox locked, unscrew and remove the nuts.

3 Remove the 5th synchro unit, synchro ring, 5th gear and bush from the secondary shaft and mark the synchro unit and ring for location.

4 Remove the gear from the primary shaft with a suitable puller.

5 Using an Allen key, unscrew the countersunk screws and remove the shaft bearing retaining plate.

6 The remaining procedure is identical with that described in Section 3 and 4, except that the reverse selector fork is different.

7 Before refitting the end cover, adjust the selector rods as described in Section 12.

8 Refit the end cover and fill the gearbox with the specified quantity of oil.

6 Four or five-speed manual gearbox (in situ) – dismantling, inspection and reassembly

1 This method may be used to dismantle the primary and secondary shafts and selector mechanism of the gearbox. However, if the clutch or final drive components require dismantling, the complete gearbox must be removed as described in Section 2.

2 After the following preliminary procedures, reference should be

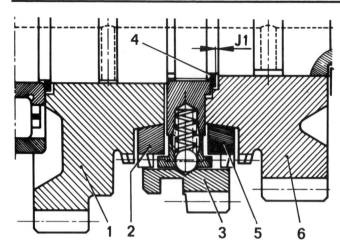

Fig. 6.12 Cross-sectional view of part of the secondary shaft (Sec 4)

1	1st gear	5	Synchro ring
2	Synchro ring	6	2nd gear
3	Synchro unit sleeve		J1 = endfloat
4	Circlip		

INTERLOCKING OF SELECTOR RODS

Fig. 6.13 Cross-sectional view of the selector rod interlock plungers (Sec 4)

made to Sections 3, 4 and 5.

3   Jack-up the left-hand front of the car and support it on an axle stand. Apply the handbrake and remove the roadwheel.

4   Remove the gearbox drain plug and drain the oil into a suitable container.

5   Unfasten the rubber cover from the wheel arch.

6   Disconnect the battery earth lead from the gearbox.

7   Loosen the right-hand engine mounting bolt, leaving a few threads engaged.

8   Unscrew and remove the left-hand engine mounting bolt.

9   Place a trolley jack and block of wood beneath the clutch bellhousing casing and take the weight of the engine.

10   Unscrew and remove the engine/gearbox upper mounting bolts from the subframe.

11   Remove the retaining bolt and disconnect the speedometer cable from the end cover.

12   Jack-up the engine/gearbox assembly until the gearbox casing is in line with the wheel arch aperture.

13   As an extra precaution, disconnect the clutch cable from the release arm (see Chapter 5).

14   Unbolt and remove the engine mounting.

15   Disconnect the gearchange and balljoints, and detach the gearchange bracket and arms.

16   Refer to Section 3, paragraphs 9 to 25. Use a lever to remove the primary shaft oil seal from the bellhousing casing. Refer also to Section 5 for the five-speed version.

17   Refer to Section 3, paragraphs 29 to 41 and 48.

18   *On no account* operate the clutch release arm with the primary shaft removed, otherwise the clutch disc will be displaced.

19   For reassembly, refer to Section 4, paragraphs 19 to 54, with reference also to Section 5 where necessary. Reverse the procedure given in paragraphs 3 to 15 of this Section.

20   Adjust the engine mountings as described in Chapter 1.

21   Adjust the 4th gear selector rod stop as described in Section 12.

22   Fill the gearbox with the specified quantity of oil.

23   Adjust the clutch cable as described in Chapter 5.

---

7   Semi-automatic (C-matic) gearbox – dismantling and inspection

1   With the gearbox removed from the car, wash off all external dirt with paraffin and wipe dry.

2   Remove the torque converter retaining bracket, withdraw the torque converter and allow it to drain into a suitable container for several hours.

3   Remove the three drain plugs, drain the fluid into a suitable container, then refit and tighten the plugs.

4   Unbolt the retaining plate and remove the camshaft bearing from the bellhousing casing.

5   Unbolt and remove the tensioner mounting.

6   Unscrew the nuts and remove the gearchange bracket and arm assembly.

7   Unscrew the bolt and remove the gearchange arm from the selector shaft.

8   Unbolt and remove the engine mounting.

9   Unscrew and remove the reversing lamp switch.

10   Using an Allen key, remove the clutch control switch and detent plate.

11   Remove the three springs and detent balls using a pen magnet.

12   Unbolt the end cover and remove it; note the location of the stud.

13   Prise out the circlips retaining the primary and secondary shaft bearings.

14   Unscrew the retaining nuts and withdraw the main casing, using a wooden mallet to tap it free. Take care not to damage the selector rod roll pins which operate the clutch switch. Remove the gasket.

15   Unhook the parking pawl return spring and unscrew the shaft retaining screw and locknut. Lift out the reverse idler gear shaft and remove the washer, spring and parking pawl.

16   Withdraw the reverse idler gear.

17   Remove the parking pawl selector rod and spring.

18   Unscrew the 1st/reverse and 2nd/3rd selector fork and dog retaining bolts and remove the selector rods, forks and dog.

19   Remove the interlock plunger from the 2nd/3rd selector rod, and recover the two remaining interlock plungers from the selector rod bores using a pen magnet.

20   Remove the primary and secondary shaft assemblies together from the bellhousing casing.

21   Withdraw the spring and mainshaft from the bellhousing casing.

22   Mark the differential side plates side for side, then unbolt and remove them. Remove the oil seals and O-rings.

23   Unscrew the securing nuts and withdraw the differential cover.

24   Mark the bearing outer races side for side, then lift out the differential unit.

25   Remove the speedometer drive bush and pinion from the end cover.

26   Unbolt the oil pump, remove the stop screw, and withdraw the oil pump casing, pinions and O-ring seal from the bellhousing casing. *Do not* attempt to remove the reaction tube.

27   Unbolt the electro-valve assembly and remove the gasket.

28   Unscrew the return hose union, then unbolt the bottom cover and remove the gasket.

29   Unscrew and remove the filter from the casing.

30   Unscrew the selector shaft nut from the main casing and remove

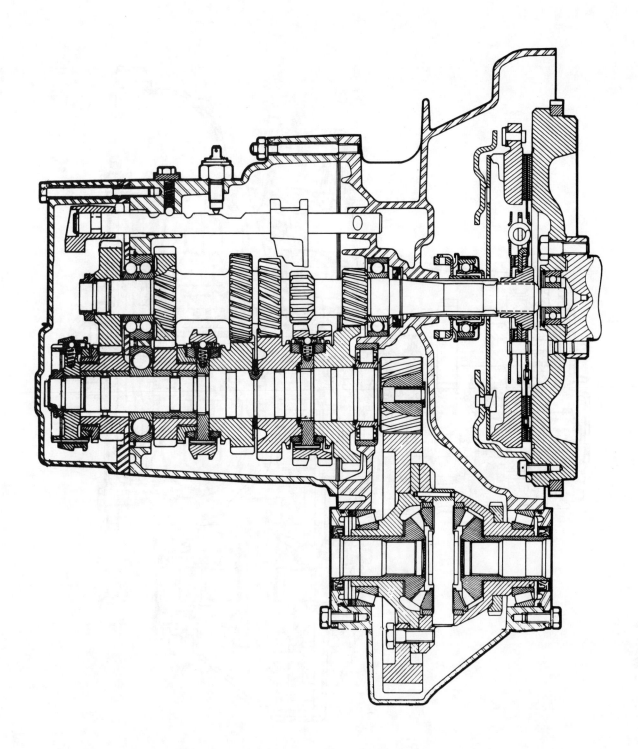

Fig. 6.14 Cross-sectional view of the five-speed manual gearbox (Sec 5)

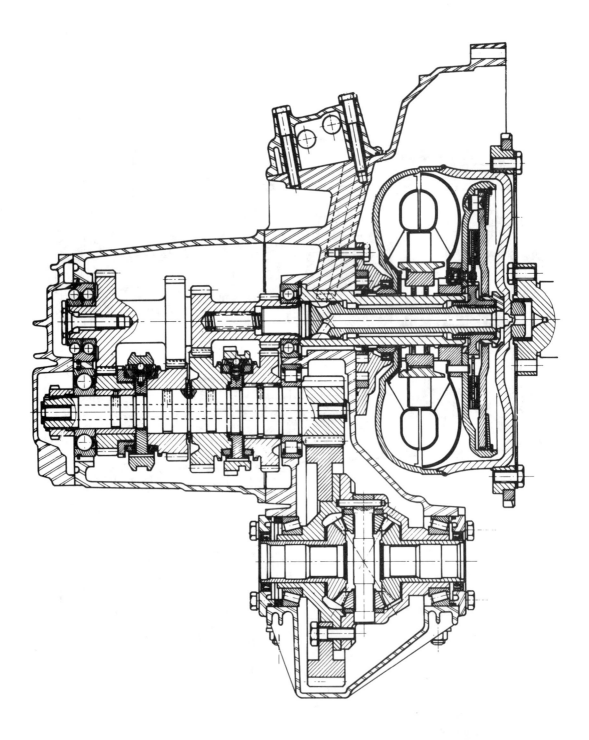

Fig. 6.15 Cross-sectional view of the semi-automatic (C-matic) gearbox (Sec 7)

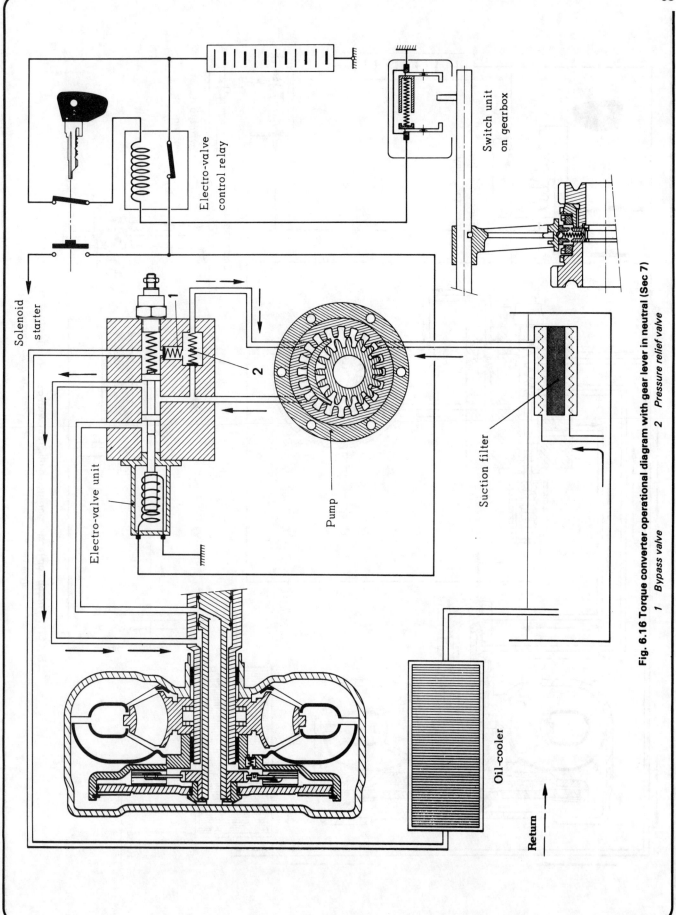

Fig. 6.16 Torque converter operational diagram with gear lever in neutral (Sec 7)

1   *Bypass valve*   2   *Pressure relief valve*

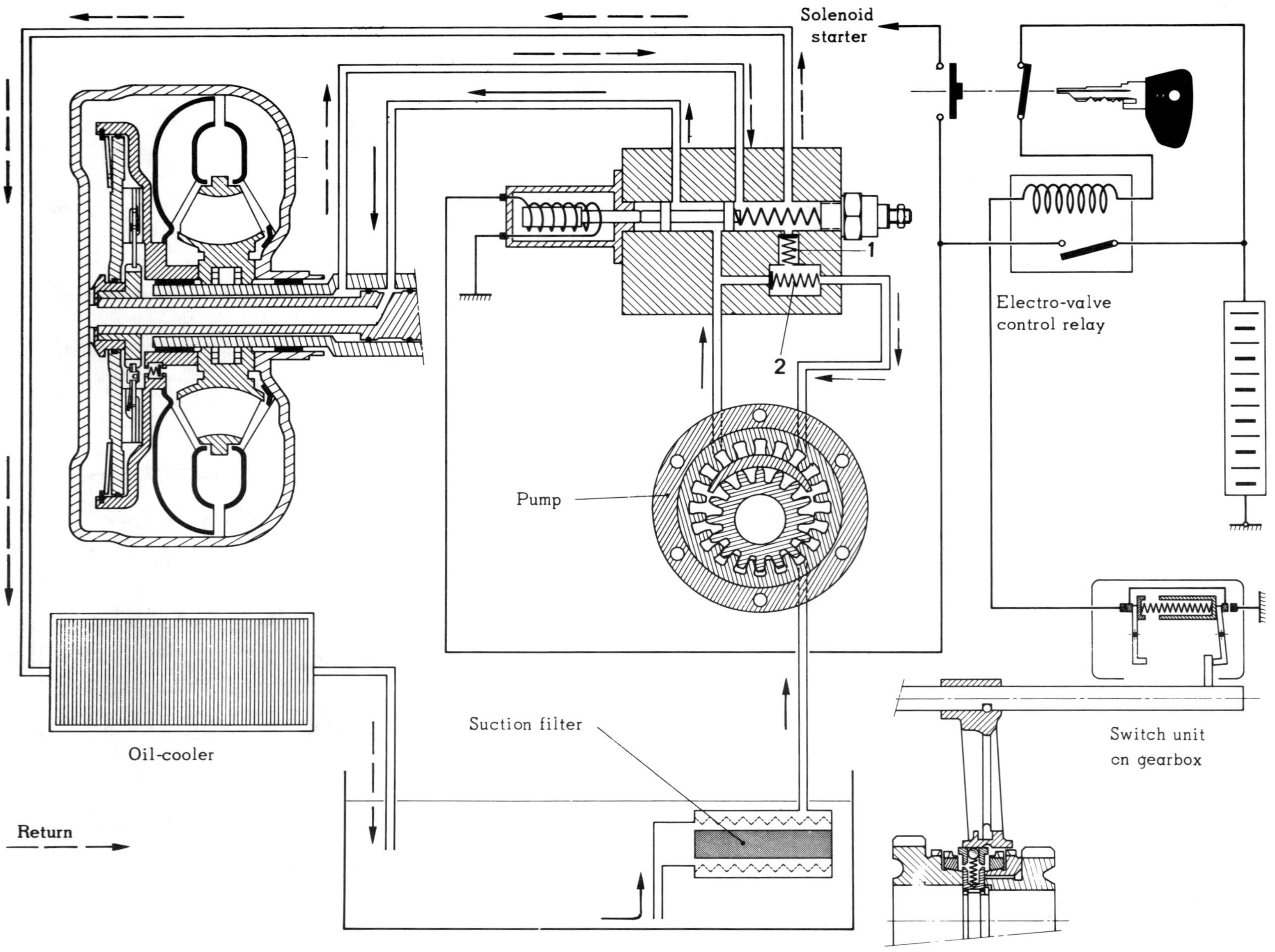

Fig. 6.17 Torque converter operational diagram with gear engaged (Sec 7)

1   Bypass valve   2   Pressure relief valve

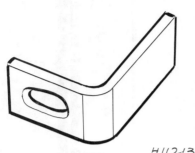

Fig. 6.18 Bracket for retaining torque converter during gearbox removal (Sec 7)

Fig. 6.19 Torque converter (1) and retaining bracket (2) (Sec 7)

Fig. 6.20 Drain plug location (1, 2 and 3) on the semi-automatic (C-matic) gearbox (Sec 7)

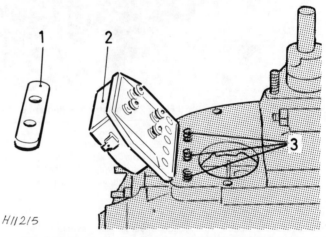

Fig. 6.21 Removing the clutch control switch on the semi-automatic (C-matic) gearbox (Sec 7)

1 Detent plate
2 Switch
3 Springs

the shaft, springs and finger.

31 Mount the primary shaft between blocks of wood in a vice, and unscrew the bearing retaining bolt.

32 Remove the bearings from the primary shaft using a suitable puller or by mounting the outer races on a vice. Take care not to lose the balls from the double track bearing.

33 Mount the secondary shaft between blocks of wood in a vice by gripping the reverse gear. Engage reverse gear.

34 Unscrew the speedometer drive nut (left-hand thread). If the correct size spanner is not available, place two bolts on the flats of the nut and use an adjustable spanner to unscrew the nut.

35 Remove the bearing from the secondary shaft with a puller.

36 Remove the 3rd gear and bush, 2nd/3rd synchro unit and rings and 2nd gear. Mark the synchro unit and rings for location.

37 Remove the retaining ring and the halfring thrust washers.

38 Remove the 1st gear and synchro ring. Mark the ring for location.

39 Prise out the circlip retaining the 1st/reverse synchro unit.

40 Remove the 1st/reverse synchro unit from the shaft, followed by the synchro ring, reverse gear and the needle roller cage. Mark the synchro unit and ring for location.

41 Prise out the circlip retaining the bearing, and remove the circlip as described in paragraph 39.

42 Remove the bearing from the secondary shaft with a puller, or by locating it on a vice and tapping the shaft through.

43 Remove the pinions from the oil pump, then lever out the oil seal with a screwdriver.

44 If necessary, the differential may be dismantled. Refer to Section 3, paragraphs 42 to 47.

45 Clean and inspect the components as described in Section 3, paragraph 48. In addition check the casing internal channels, preferably using compressed air.

46 Using a straight-edge (eg a metal ruler) and feeler blades, check

that the clearance between the oil pump mounting face and the face of the pinions is 0·03 to 0·06 mm (0·001 to 0·002 in). If not, renew the oil pump.

8 Semi-automatic (C-matic) gearbox – reassembly

1 If the differential unit has been dismantled, reassemble it as described in Section 4, paragraphs 1 to 18.

2 Refit the electro-valve assembly together with a new gasket to the bellhousing casing. Tighten the retaining bolts to the specified torque.

3 Locate the upper washer, flexible washer, new filter and gasket on the filter plug, then tighten it into the casing to the specified torque.

4 Refit the bottom cover with a new gasket and tighten the bolts evenly in diagonal sequence.

5 Insert the return hose union with a new washer and tighten it.

6 Remove the old oil seals from the mainshaft and fit new ones after soaking them in torque converter fluid. Wrap masking tape around the mainshaft splines to prevent damage to the seals and compress the two adjacent seals using Citroën tool No 6316-TB.

7 Smear the reaction tube in the bellhousing casing with torque converter fluid, then insert the mainshaft and remove the tool.

8 Using a long tube, drive the bearing onto the secondary shaft. Fit the circlip with the chamfered side against the bearing to facilitate future removal; use metal foil to slide it into position.

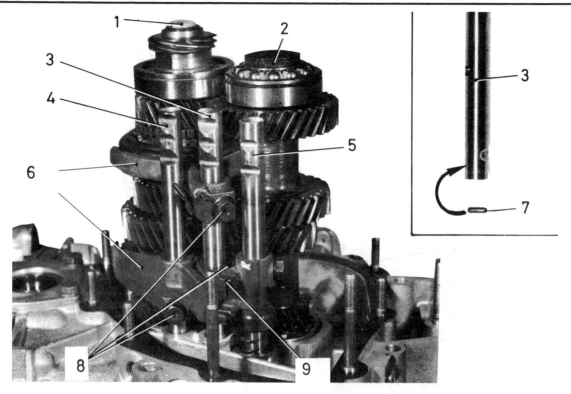

Fig. 6.22 Selector mechanism on the semi-automatic (C-matic) gearbox (Sec 7)

1 Secondary shaft	6 Selector forks
2 Primary shaft	7 Interlock plunger
3 2nd/3rd selector rod	8 Bolts
4 1st/reverse selector rod	9 Control dog
5 Parking pawl selector rod	

9 Locate the needle roller cage, reverse gear, synchro ring and 1st/reverse synchro unit on the secondary shaft. Make sure that the synchro unit sleeve groove is facing the reverse gear.
10 Using old feeler blades, slide the circlip into its groove, then check that the 1st/reverse synchro hub endfloat does not exceed the maximum specified. To do this, push the circlip against the hub and check that a feeler blade of the specified maximum thickness cannot be inserted between the circlip and the visible end of its groove. If necessary, fit a thicker circlip.
11 Refit the synchro ring and 1st gear.
12 Fit the halfring thrust washers and retaining ring.
13 Push the halfring thrust washers against the 1st gear, and check that a feeler blade of the specified maximum thickness cannot be inserted between the washers and the visible end of the groove. If necessary, fit thicker washers, but make sure that each half is of identical thickness.
14 Refit the 2nd gear and 2nd/3rd gear synchro unit with synchro rings.
15 Refit the bush and 3rd gear.
16 Tap the bearing onto the secondary shaft using a tube; make sure that the circlip groove is towards the end of the shaft.
17 Screw on the speedometer drive nut (left-hand thread) with the flats facing the bearing.
18 Mount the secondary shaft between blocks of wood in a vice by gripping the reverse gear, then engage reverse gear. Tighten the speedometer drive nut to the specified torque and lock it by peening into the notch with a centre punch.
19 Using a suitable tube, drive the bearing inner tracks onto the primary shaft. Make sure that the circlip groove in the outer track of the end bearing is towards the end of the shaft.
20 Grip the primary shaft in a vice between blocks of wood, then insert and tighten the retaining bolt to the specified torque.
21 Lubricate the spring with torque converter fluid, then insert it into the primary shaft bore.

22 Grease the speedometer drive pinion, then locate it together with the bush in the end cover. Make sure that the bush is aligned with the bolt hole, and that the end cover locating dowels are in position.
23 Temporarily fit the primary shaft and bearing in the gearbox casing, fit the circlip and tap the bearing so that the circlip is resting on the casing shoulder. Using a straight-edge and feeler blades, check that the face of the bearing outer race in relation to the casing face is not recessed by more than 0·05 mm (0·002 in) or protruding by more than 0·02 mm (0·0008 in). If necessary, select a circlip which will position the outer race within these limits. Remove the circlip and primary shaft from the casing.
24 Using the same procedure, check the secondary shaft outer race protrusion.
25 With the synchro sleeves in neutral, mesh the primary shaft gears with the secondary shaft gears and insert them into the bellhousing casing. Tap both shafts with a wooden mallet to ensure that the bearings are fully home.
26 Refit the selector shaft, springs and finger in the main casing. Fit the bush nut complete with copper washer, and tighten it to the specified torque.
27 Check that the protrusion of the roll pin on the 1st/reverse selector rod is 26·0 ± 1·0 mm (0·984 ± 0·04 in).
28 Check that the protrusion of the roll pin on the 2nd/3rd selector fork is 11·0 ± 1·0 mm (0·433 ± 0·04 in).
29 Check that the parking pawl selector rod components (3, 4, 5, 8 and 10 in Fig. 6.32) are assembled in the order shown. Make sure that the selector dog retaining bolt is tightened to the specified torque.
30 Locate the 1st/reverse and 2nd/3rd selector forks on their respective synchro hub sleeves with the retaining bolt holes towards the bellhousing casing.
31 Insert the 1st/reverse selector rod through the fork and into the casing. Align the holes and tighten the selector fork bolt to the specified torque.
32 Position the interlock plunger in the 1st/reverse selector rod hole

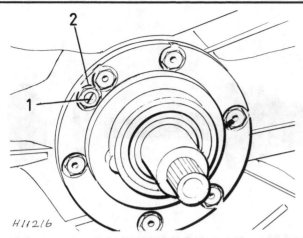

Fig. 6.23 Semi-automatic (C-matic) gearbox oil pump, showing location of 2nd gear selector rod stop screw (1) and locknut (2) (Sec 7)

Fig. 6.24 Semi-automatic (C-matic) gearbox bellhousing casing (Sec 7)

1 Electro valve	3 Fluid return union
2 Filter	4 Cover

Fig. 6.25 Semi-automatic (C-matic) gearbox filter plug (1) location (Sec 7)

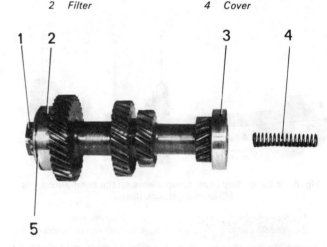

Fig. 6.26 Primary shaft components on the semi-automatic (C-matic) gearbox (Sec 7)

1 Bolt	4 Spring
2 Double track bearing	5 Circlip groove
3 Single track bearing	

by inserting it through the 2nd/3rd selector rod bore.

33 Insert the small diameter interlock plunger into the 2nd/3rd selector rod.

34 Locate the dog, then insert the 2nd/3rd selector rod through the fork and dog and into the casing. Align the holes and tighten the selector fork and dog bolts to the specified torque.

35 Position the interlock plunger against the 2nd/3rd selector rod by inserting it through the parking pawl selector rod bore.

36 Insert the parking pawl selector rod complete with dog and spring into the casing and position it in neutral.

37 Check that the protrusion of the roll pin on the reverse idler gear shaft is 20·0 to 21·0 mm (0·787 to 0·827 in), then fit the washer, spring parking pawl and reverse idler gear onto the shaft. Hook the spring over the roll pin.

38 Insert the reverse idler gear shaft into the casing with the parking pawl located on the selector dog.

39 Coat the threads with sealing compound, then tighten the reverse idler gear shaft locking screw into the casing to the specified torque and tighten the locknut.

40 Using a feeler gauge, check that the clearance between the parking pawl and the washer is 0·05 to 0·4 mm (0·002 to 0·016 in). If not, a washer of different thickness must be fitted after removing the shaft again.

41 Select each gear in turn and check that only one gear can be engaged at a time. After the check, move the selector rods to neutral with the dogs and fork aligned. Do not check the parking pawl operation at this stage, otherwise the selector rod may be displaced.

42 Clean the mating faces of the main casing and bellhousing csing, and fit the new gasket, dry.

43 Locate the main casing over the gearbox shafts and onto the bellhousing casing. At the same time, locate the selector finger with the selector dogs and fork.

44 Refit and tighten the casing retaining nuts in diagaonal sequence to the specified torque.

45 Spring the circlips into their grooves on the shaft bearing outer races.

46 Coat the mating faces of the end cover and main casing with sealing compound. Refit the end cover and tighten the retaining bolts in diagonal sequence to the specified torque. Locate the stud in the previously noted position.

47 Insert the detent balls and springs into the casing, then locate the clutch control switch with a new gasket on the casing. Refit the detent plate and, using an Allen key, tighten the retaining bolts to the specified torque.

48 Insert and tighten the reversing lamp switch to the specified torque.

49 Locate the oil pump inside the bellhousing and centralise it with Citroën tool No 6315-T. Tighten the bolts in diagonal sequence to the specified torque.

50 Using Citroën tool No 6315-T again, drive the new oil seal into the oil pump casing. Remove the tool and smear torque converter fluid on the oil seal lip.

51 Locate the engine mounting on the casing and tighten the retaining bolts.

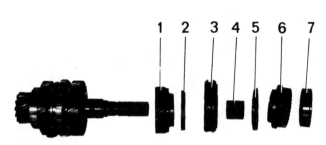

Fig. 6.27 Secondary shaft components on the semi-automatic (C-matic) gearbox (Sec 7)

1	2nd gear	5	Synchro ring
2	Synchro ring	6	3rd gear
3	2nd/3rd synchro unit	7	Bearing
4	Bush		

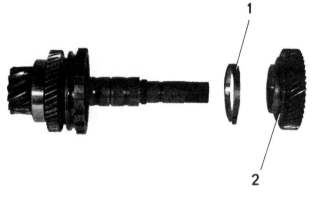

Fig. 6.28 Secondary shaft components on the semi-automatic (C-matic) gearbox (Sec 7)

1	Synchro ring	2	lst gear

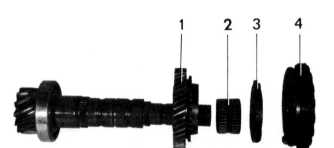

Fig. 6.29 Secondary shaft components on the semi-automatic (C-matic) gearbox (Sec 7)

1	Reverse gear	3	Synchro ring
2	Needle cage	4	1st/reverse synchro unit

Fig. 6.30 Oil pump components on the semi-automatic (C-matic) gearbox (Sec 7)

1	Inner rotor	3	O-ring seal
2	Outer rotor	4	Oil seal

52 Locate the gearchange arm on the selector shaft and tighten the retaining bolt.
53 Refit the gearchange bracket and arm assembly and tighten the retaining nuts.
54 Refit the tensioner mounting and tighten the retaining bolts.
55 Coat the threads with sealing compound, then insert the 2nd gear selector rod stop through the oil pump casing and into the bellhousing casing. Engage 2nd gear, then screw in the stop until it just contacts the rod. Screw the stop in a further half turn and tighten the locknut.
56 Using the same procedure, adjust the 3rd gear stop on the end cover.
57 Using a tube, drive the camshaft bearing outer race into the bellhousing casing. Refit the retaining plate and tighten the retaining bolts.
58 Locate the torque converter on the mainshaft splines, making sure that the two pegs engage with the oil pump. Fit the retaining bracket to hold the torque converter in the bellhousing until fitted to the engine.
59 Remove the filler plug and fill the gearbox with the specified torque converter fluid to the upper mark on the level dipstick with the gearbox in its normal attitude. Check and top-up the level as described in Section 9 when the gearbox is fitted in the car.
60 Adjust the clutch control switch contacts as described in Section 11.
61 Check the torque converter fluid pressure when the gearbox is fitted in the car, as described in Section 10.

---

9 Semi-automatic (C-matic) gearbox – checking fluid level

1 Remove the spare wheel from the engine compartment.
2 Run the engine until it reaches its normal operating temperature.
3 With the car on level ground and the engine running, remove the

dipstick from the differential cover and check the fluid level against the 'warm' mark. If necessary, remove the filler plug with a square drive key and top-up the level with the specified torque converter fluid. Refit the filler plug.
4 Apply the handbrake and chock the front wheels. With the engine idling, engage any gear (not Park – P), then disengage the gear. Repeat this 10 to 12 times, then place the gear lever in Park (P).
5 Check the fluid level with the engine running again and if necessary, top it up; the difference between the 'cold' and 'warm' marks is approximately 0·2 litres (0·4 Imp pt).
6 Stop the engine and refit the filler plug and spare wheel.

---

10 Semi-automatic (C-matic) gearbox – checking fluid pressure

1 Run the engine until it reaches its normal operating temperature, then switch it off.
2 Unscrew the pressure take-off plug on the electro-valve and tighten a pressure gauge into the hole.
3 With the gear lever in the parking (P) position, run the engine at 700 rpm and check that the pressure is as specified. Increase the engine speed to 2000 rpm and check that the fluid pressure is as specified.
4 If the fluid pressure is incorrect, check the fluid level and filter condition before suspecting any major component.
5 Stop the engine and remove the pressure gauge. Tighten the plug together with its copper washer.

---

11 Semi-automatic (C-matic) gearbox – adjusting the control switch

1 Remove the spare wheel from the engine compartment.

Fig. 6.31 Bellhousing casing components on the semi-automatic
(C-matic) gearbox (Sec 7)

1   Electro-valve   4   Flexible washer
2   Plug   5   Filter element
3   Washer   6   Gasket

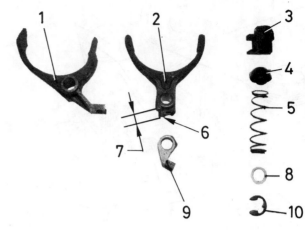

Fig. 6.32 Semi-automatic (C-matic) gearbox selector components
(Sec 8)

1   1st/reverse selector fork   6   Roll pin
2   2nd/3rd selector fork   7   Roll pin protrusion
3   Control dog   8   Washer
4   Cam   9   Control dog
5   Spring   10   E-clip

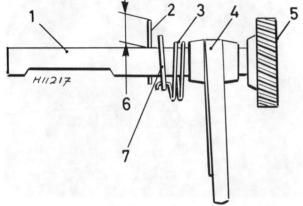

Fig. 6.33 Semi-automatic (C-matic) gearbox selector components
(Sec 8)

1   Reverse idler gear shaft   5   Reverse idler gear
2   Roll pin   6   Roll pin protrusion
3   Spring   7   Washer
4   Parking pawl

Fig. 6.34 3rd gear selector rod adjustment screw (2) and locknut
(1) on the semi-automatic (C-matic) gearbox (Sec 8)

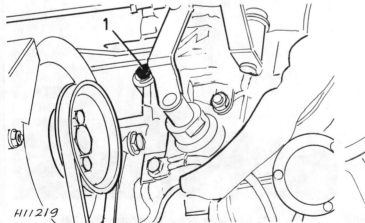

Fig. 6.35 Semi-automatic (C-matic) gearbox fluid filler plug (1)
location (Sec 8)

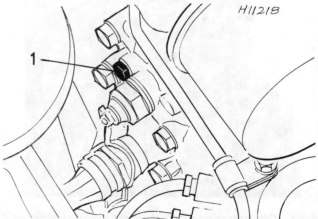

Fig. 6.36 Pressure take-off plug (1) location on the semi-automatic
(C-matic) gearbox (Sec 10)

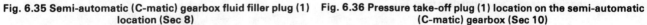

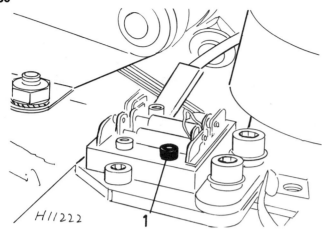

H11222

Fig. 6.37 Clutch control switch location with cover removed
(Sec 11)

1   Adjusting bolt

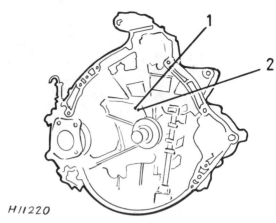

H11220

Fig. 6.38 3rd gear selector rod adjustment screw (1) and locknut
(2) on the four-speed manual gearbox (Sec 12)

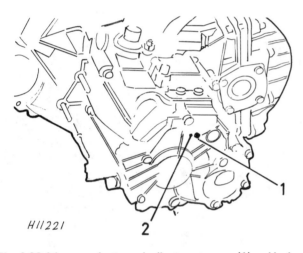

H11221

Fig. 6.39 4th gear selector rod adjustment screw (1) and locknut
(2) on the four-speed manual gearbox (Sec 12)

Fig. 6.40 3rd (1) and 5th (2) gear selector rod adjustment screw
locations on the five-speed manual gearbox (Sec 12)

Fig. 6.41 4th gear selector rod adjustment scew (1) location on
the five-speed manual gearbox (Sec 12)

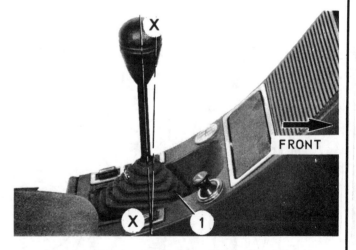

Fig. 6.42 Gear lever inclination diagram (Sec 13)

1   Rubber gaiter
X-X Vertical

Fig. 6.43 Gear lever cover (2) and retaining bolt (1) location (Sec 13)

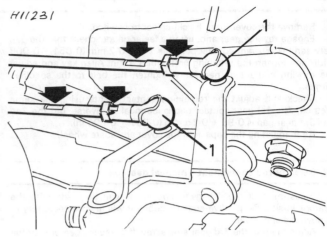

H11231

Fig. 6.44 Gearchange rod location, showing flats - arrowed (Sec 13)

1   Balljoints

13.3A Gearchange shaft

13.3B Gearchange intermediate levers

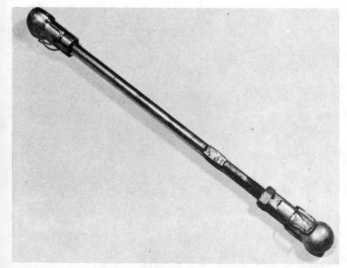

13.4A A gearchange rod assembly

13.4B Gearchange levers on the gearbox

2   Remove the cover from the clutch control switch.
3   Engage reverse gear and, using a feeler gauge, check that the gap between the relevant contact points is $1\cdot3 \pm 0\cdot2$ mm ($0\cdot051 \pm 0\cdot008$ in). If not, loosen the retaining bolt with a 4 mm Allen key and adjust the moving contact as necessary. Tighten the bolt to the specified torque.
4   Check and adjust the remaining contact points using the same method. The 1st gear contact gap is identical to reverse, but the 2nd and 3rd gear gap is $0\cdot95 \pm 0\cdot15$ mm ($0\cdot037 \pm 0\cdot006$ in).
5   After adjusting the gaps, refit the cover and spare wheel.

12 Selector rod adjustment – manual gearbox

1   Adjustment of the 4th gear stop screw can be made with the gearbox in situ. On the five-speed gearbox it will first be necessary to remove the end cover.
2   Adjustment of the 3rd gear stop screw (four-speed gearbox) or the 3rd and 5th gear stop screws (five-speed gearbox) is only possible after removing the gearbox.
3   Adjustment of each stop screw is identical. First remove the stop screw and coat its threads with a sealing compound. Insert the screw

and engage a few threads, then engage the relevant gear and turn the stop screw until it just touchés the selector rod. Screw in the stop screw one further turn and tighten the locknut.
4   Refit the end cover on the five-speed gearbox.

13 Gear lever – adjustment

1   Move the gear lever into the neutral position.
2   When viewed from the side, the gear lever should be inclined to the rear by approximately 3° from the vertical (see Fig. 6.42). If not, remove the rubber gaiter, loosen the cover retaining bolts and adjust the position of the cover. If the movement of the cover is insufficient, adjust the length of the gearchange rod at the horizontal arm on the gearbox.
3   When viewed from the rear, the gear lever should be in the vertical plane. If not, adjust the length of the gearchange rod at the vertical arm on the gearbox (photos).
4   When adjusting the gearchange rods, make sure that the flats on the rods and balljoints are aligned (photos, Fig. 6.44).
5   Tighten all nuts and bolts and refit the rubber gaiter.

14 Fault diagnosis – manual and semi-automatic gearbox

Symptom	Reason/s
Ineffective synchromesh	Worn synchro rings
Jumps out of gear	Weak detent springs
	Worn selector mechanism
	Incorrect selector road adjustment
	Worn gears or synchro units
Noisy, rough, whining, or vibration	Worn bearings or gears
	Lack of oil or incorrect grade (manual gearbox)
	Incorrect bearing preload adjustments
Difficult gear changing (semi-automatic gearbox)	Clutch control switch points gap incorrect
	Faulty electro-valve
Clutch slip on steep hills (semi-automatic gearbox)	Low fluid pressure
	Faulty torque converter
	Filter blocked
Gearbox overheats (semi-automatic gearbox)	Blocked oil cooler
	Faulty torque converter

Chapter 7 Driveshafts

For modifications, and information applicable to later models, see Supplement at end of manual

Contents

Specifications

Driveshaft joints
Outer . . . .   Constant velocity balljoints
Inner . . . .   Tri-axe

Driveshaft length (between joints)
4-speed gearbox:
  Left-hand side . . . .   343.5 mm (13.52 in)
  Right-hand side . . . .   423.0 mm (16.65 in)
5-speed gearbox:
  Left-hand side . . . .   378.5 mm (14.90 in)
  Right-hand side . . . .   388.0 mm (15.28 in)

Lubricant type . . . .   Multi-purpose grease

Torque wrench settings

	lbf ft	kgf m
Driveshaft nut	253 to 290	35 to 40
RH shaft bearer nut	5.0	0.7
Lower balljoint nut	36.0	5.0
Anti-roll bar link nut	21.5	3.0

1 General description

The driveshafts incorporate constant velocity balljoints at their outer ends next to the front wheel hubs. The inner, gearbox, ends are fitted with tri-axle sliding bush type joints.

The driveshafts are secured to the front wheel hubs by nuts locked with split-pins. The left-hand driveshaft is secured to the differential planet gear by an internally expanding snap-ring. The right-hand driveshaft is a sliding fit in the differential planet gear and is retained in position by eccentric head bolts holding the outer ball bearing race to the engine lower crankcase.

2 Driveshafts – removal and refitting

1 Apply the handbrake firmly or have an assistant depress the brake pedal. Remove the wheel embellisher.
2 Extract the split-pin, remove the retainer, then unscrew the driveshaft nut (photo). Make sure that the correct size socket is used as the nut is very tight.
3 Jack-up the front of the car and support it on axle stands. Remove the roadwheel and chock the rear wheels.
4 Loosen the pressure release screw on the hydraulic circuit pressure regulator.

5 Unscrew and remove the nut securing the anti-roll bar link to the upper suspension arm.
6 In order to attach the extractor to the suspension arm, remove the split-pin and withdraw the suspension unit from the upper suspension arm. Using the extractor disconnect the anti-roll bar link from the suspension arm.
7 Detach the disc brake cooling deflector from the steering knuckle.
8 Unscrew and remove the lower balljoint nut from the lower suspension arm.
9 Using a universal balljoint remover, detach the lower balljoint from the suspension arm (photo).
10 To remove the left-hand driveshaft follow paragraphs 11 to 13.
11 Turn the steering wheel fully anti-clockwise, then withdraw the driveshaft from the hub, using a hide hammer if necessary to tap the end of the shaft.
12 Support the weight of the steering knuckle with a trolley jack or axle stand.
13 The driveshaft can now be removed from the differential planet gear by forcing it against the tension of the retaining snap-ring (photo). If difficulty is experienced it will be necessary to obtain Citroen tool No 6351-T (see Fig. 7.6) which consists of a clamp and slide hammer.
14 Removal of the right-hand driveshaft is described in paragraphs 15 to 18.
15 Turn the steering wheel fully clockwise then withdraw the driveshaft from the hub, using a hide hammer if necessary to release it.

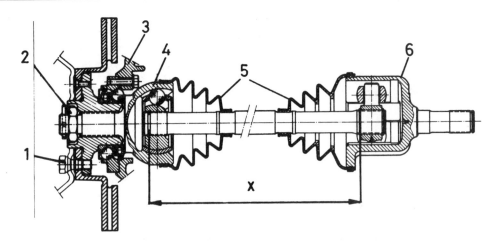

Fig. 7.1 Cross-sectional view of the left-hand driveshaft (Sec 1)

1   Wheel bolt   5   Rubber bellows
2   Nut   6   Tri-axe joint
3   Steering knuckle   X = length
4   CV joint

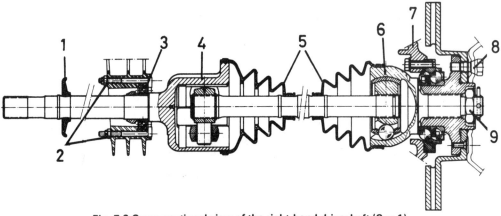

Fig. 7.2 Cross-sectional view of the right-hand driveshaft (Sec 1)

1   Dust cover   5   Rubber bellows
2   Eccentric head bearing   6   CV joint
    retaining bolts   7   Steering knuckle
3   Intermediate bearing   8   Wheel bolt
4   Tri-axe joint   9   Nut

Fig. 7.3 Loosening the driveshaft nut using the special Citroën tool to stop the wheel rotating (Sec 2)

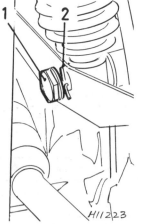

Fig. 7.4 Location of the anti-roll bar link retaining nut (1) and suspension retaining split-pin (2) (Sec 2)

Fig. 7.5 Using an extractor (6304-T) to remove the anti-roll bar link (3) (Sec 2)

Fig. 7.6 Showing special tool for removing the driveshafts (Sec 2)

1	Tri-axe joint	3	Tool clamp nuts
2	Driveshaft	a	Tool location

Fig. 7.7 Right hand driveshaft intermediate bearing (Sec 2)

4	Self-locking nuts	5	Eccentric head bolts

Fig. 7.8 Location of the rubber O-ring (1) on the left-hand driveshaft (Sec 2)

Fig. 7.9 Inserting the right-hand driveshaft into the differential planet gear (Sec 2)

1	Driveshaft	3	Bush
2	O-ring	4	Dust cover

2.2 Removing the driveshaft nut retainer split-pin

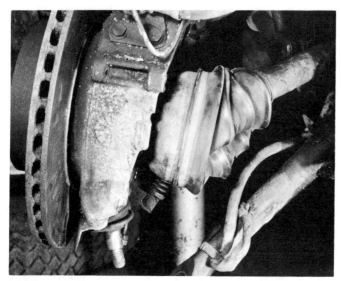

2.9 Disconnecting the suspension lower balljoint

2.13 Removing the left-hand driveshaft

2.17A Location of the right-hand driveshaft intermediate bearing in the lower crankcase

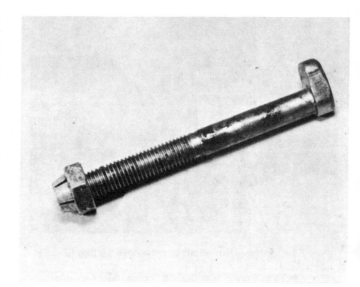

2.17B Right-hand driveshaft intermediate bearing retaining bolt

2.18A Right-hand driveshaft intermediate bearing

2.18B Right-hand driveshaft dust cover and seal location

16 Support the weight of the steering knuckle with a trolley jack or axle stand.
17 Loosen the two nuts retaining the bearing outer race in the engine lower crankcase, and turn the bolt heads through 180° to release them from the bearing (photos).
18 The driveshaft can now be removed from the differential planet gear together with the intermediate supporting ball bearing (photo). If it is tight, use the tool described in paragraph 13. Recover the seal and dust cover (photo).
19 Remove the snap-ring, O-ring, and on the right-hand driveshaft, the shaft bush.
20 Clean the driveshaft and examine it for damage and deterioration. If either joint is worn internally, the complete driveshaft must be renewed. If the rubber bellows are torn, new ones may be fitted if available, but remember to pack the joints with the specified grease.
21 Always fit new snap-rings and rubber O-rings together with a new bush on the right-hand driveshaft if this is required.
22 Refitting is a reversal of removal, but the following additional points should be noted:

(a) After inserting the driveshaft into the left-hand differential planet gear, check that the snap-ring is fully engaged by pulling on the driveshaft
(b) When fitting the right-hand driveshaft, turn the eccentric head bolts to retain the intermediate bearing outer race, then tighten the nuts to the specified torque

(c) Smear the splines and the contact area of the seal before inserting the driveshaft into the hub
(d) Fit a new self-locking nut to the lower suspension balljoint
(e) Smear the face and threads of the driveshaft nut with grease before fitting it
(f) Tighten all nuts to the specified torque
(g) Tighten the pressure release screw on the hydraulic circuit pressure regulator

3 Driveshafts – testing for wear

1 Wear in the driveshafts is characterized by vibration and knocking on taking up the drive. If the intermediate shaft bearing is worn, there may be a rumbling noise emanating from the engine lower crankcase and increasing in intensity as the road speed increases.
2 To test the outer constant velocity balljoints, drive the car from rest of full left and then right lock; a knocking noise indicates that the joints are worn.
3 Testing the inner joints is best accomplished by jacking up the front of the car, supporting it on axle stands, and then attempting to move the driveshafts up, down and sideways. Any excessive movement indicates wear; minimal movement may be the result of lack of lubrication in which case new grease should be packed into the joints.

4 Fault diagnosis – driveshafts

Symptom	Reason/s
Vibration	Worn joints Worn intermediate bearing Loose driveshaft nut or worn hub splines
Knock when taking up drive	Worn joints Worn hub splines Excessive backlash in differential gears Loose roadwheel nuts

Chapter 8 Hydraulic system

Contents

Specifications

Hydraulic pump
Type:
    Manual steering saloon models .... Single cylinder reciprocating, driven by camshaft eccentric
    All other models .... Seven piston oscillating, belt-driven from camshaft pulley
Output:
    Single cylinder .... 1.07 cc/cycle
    Seven piston .... 2.80 cc/rev

Pressure regulator
Cut-out pressure .... 170 ± 5 bars (2466 ± 73 lbf/in²)
Cut-in pressure .... 145 ± 5 bars (2103 ± 73 lbf/in²)

Main accumulator
Capacity .... 0.4 litres (0.7 pint)

Air inflation pressure .... $62 \pm^{2}_{10}$ bars ($899 \pm^{29}_{145}$ lbf/in²)

Brake accumulator
Capacity .... 0.4 litres (0.7 pint)

Air inflation pressure .... $62 \pm^{2}_{32}$ bars ($899 \pm^{29}_{464}$ lbf/in²)

Safety valve
Slide valve seal checking pressure .... 175 bars (2538 lbf/in²)
Slide valve operating pressure .... 110 to 130 bars (1585 to 1885 lbf/in³)
Pressure switch operating pressure .... 75 to 95 bars (1088 to 1378 lbf/in²)

Hydraulic fluid type .... Mineral-based LHM (green colour)

Refill capacity (approx) .... 4.0 litres (7.0 pints)

Torque wrench settings
Hydraulic pipe union nuts:

	lbf ft	kgf m
3.5 and 4.5 mm pipe	5.8 to 6.6	0.8 to 0.9

	lbf ft	kgf m
6.0 mm pipe	6.6 to 8.0	0.9 to 1.1
Hydraulic pump:		
Single piston type	14.0	1.9
Seven piston type	29.0	4.0
Pressure regulator	13.0	1.8
Main accumulator	18.0 to 32.5	2.5 to 4.5
Brake accumulator	21.5	3.0

1 General description

The hydraulic system comprises a fluid reservoir, high pressure pump, pressure regulator and main accumulator, safety valve, brake valve, suspension height correctors and suspension cylinders.

Models fitted with power steering have a brake accumulator, steering governor, and control unit in addition to the previous components; estate models also have a brake pressure limiter.

The hydraulic circuits are shown in diagram form in Figs. 8.21 to 8.26 inclusive.

Hydraulic fluid is drawn from the reservoir, located in the engine compartment on the left-hand side, to the high pressure pump. On saloon models with manual steering the pump is of the reciprocating type driven by an eccentric on the engine camshaft; on all other models the pump incorporates seven pistons and is belt-driven from a pulley on the end of the camshaft.

The pressurised fluid is fed to the pressure regulator which maintains a pressure in the hydraulic circuit in excess of 2000 lbf/in², excess fluid being returned to the reservoir. Incorporated in the pressure regulator is the main accumulator which consists of an air chamber and fluid area separated by a rubber membrane. When the hydraulic circuit is fully pressurised, the membrane is forced into the air chamber, and a reserve of pressurised fluid is maintained within the accumulator.

On saloon models with manual steering, the fluid is fed from the pressure regulator to a safety valve (or priority valve) which incorporates outlets for the front brake circuit, front suspension circuit and rear suspension circuit. The front brake circuit runs through the pedal-operated brake valve to the front brake calipers. The front suspension circuit runs through the front height corrector to the front suspension cylinders. The rear suspension circuit runs through the rear height corrector to the rear suspension cylinders. The rear brake calipers are supplied with hydraulic fluid from the rear suspension circuit via the pedal-operated brake valve. This arrangement results in more braking effort at the rear wheels when increased loads are carried by the rear suspension.

On saloon models with power steering, the fluid is fed from the pressure regulator to the front brake accumulator which incorporates a one-way ball valve and a pneumatic accumulator similar to the main accumulator. The unit maintains a reserve of pressurised fluid exclusively for the front brake which is then controlled by the pedal-operated brake valve. The body of the accumulator also incorporates an outlet from the regulator circuit to a three-way union. The union outlets feed fluid to the steering governor (for stiffening the steering during increasing road speeds), and to the safety valve (or priority valve). The safety valve incorporates outlets for the power steering circuit, the front suspension circuit and the rear suspension circuit. The power steering circuit runs through the control unit to the ram. The front suspension circuit runs through the front height corrector to the front suspension cylinders. The rear suspension circuit runs through the rear height corrector to the rear suspension cylinders. The rear brake calipers are supplied with fluid from the rear suspension circuit when the brake valve is operated, thus ensuring that the rear brake effort is varied in direct proportion to the weight being carried by the rear suspension.

The hydraulic circuits for estate models are identical with those for saloon models except for the operation of the rear brakes. On the circuits already described, the rear brake circuit pressure is limited to the rear suspension pressure. However, with the greater variation of loads carried by estate models, a more satisfactory arrangement is to vary the rear brake circuit pressure in relation both to the front brake circuit pressure and to the rear suspension pressure. This function is carried out by a brake pressure limiter with an internal slide valve. The limiter has inlets for the front brake circuit, the rear brake circuit, and the rear suspension circuit, and its operation is more fully described in Chapter 9.

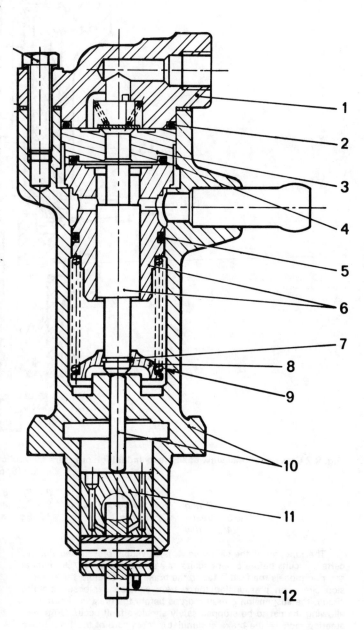

Fig. 8.1 Cross-sectional view of single cylinder high pressure hydraulic pump fitted to manual steering saloon models up to October 1976 (Sec 1)

1	Cover	7	Circlip
2	O-ring	8	Spring seat
3	Seat	9	Spring
4	O-ring	10	Body and intermediate piston
5	O-ring	11	Plunger
6	Sleeve and piston	12	Roller

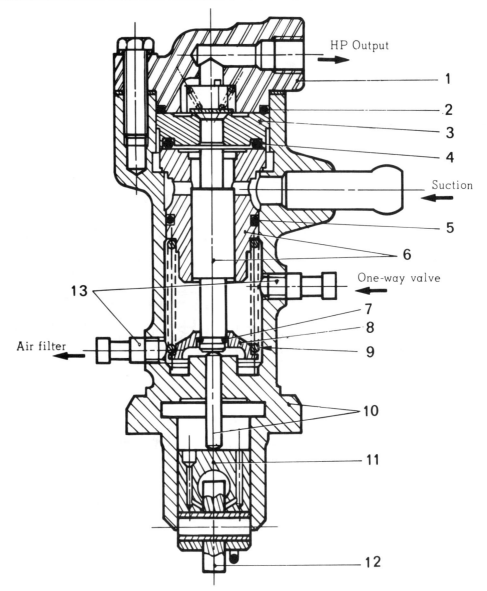

Fig. 8.2 Cross-sectional view of single cylinder high pressure hydraulic pump fitted to manual steering saloon models from October 1976 on (Sec 1)

1	Cover	5	O-ring	8	Spring seat	11	Plunger
2	O-ring	6	Sleeve and piston	9	Spring	12	Roller
3	Seat	7	Circlip	10	Body and intermediate piston	13	Breather unions
4	O-ring						

The function of the safety valve is to supply pressurised fluid to certain circuits before other circuits as a safety precaution. On manual steering models the fluid is fed to the brake circuit before the suspension circuit on pressurising the system and, on depressurising the circuit, the suspension pressure drops before the braking circuit, thus allowing the car to be stopped safely should a fault occur. On power steering models, the brake accumulator takes care of the front brake circuit, and the safety valve supplies pressurised fluid to the power steering control unit before the suspension and rear brake circuits on pressurising the system. On depressurising the system, the suspension and rear brake circuit pressure drops before the power steering circuit pressure.

The safety valve also incorporates a pressure switch which operates the hydraulic system warning lamp located on the instrument panel inside the car. With the ignition switch on, the lamp glows until normal hydraulic circuit pressure is reached.

The brake valve, suspension height correctors, suspension cylinders, steering governor and control unit and brake pressure limiter are described more fully in Chapters 9 and 11.

2 Hydraulic system and components – precautions

1 Cleanliness is of the utmost importance when working on the hydraulic system and its components. Clean the surrounding area thoroughly before disconnecting the unions and, when removed, plug the pipes and component parts to prevent the entry of dirt and dust.

2 Hydraulic units must be cleaned with petrol or white spirit and preferably dried with compressed air. Steel pipes, rubber components and unions must be cleaned in a similar manner and thoroughly dried with compressed air.

3 Use only LHM mineral hydraulic fluid in the hydraulic system, otherwise the rubber components will be damaged. (Refer to Chapter 9 for rinsing procedures if incorrect fluid is used.) LHM fluid is green in colour and must be stored in the original sealed container; storage in unsealed containers will affect the characteristics of the fluid.

4 Use only Citroën approved spare parts. Components have a green marking and rubber items have either a green or white marking.

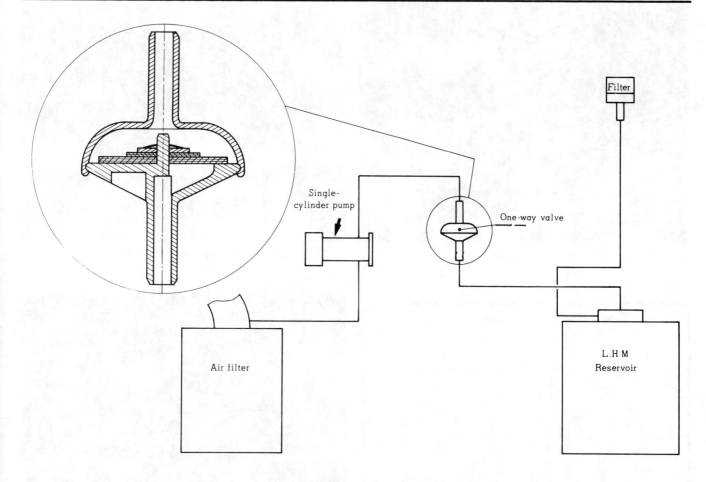

Fig. 8.3 Diagram of the single cylinder high pressure hydraulic pump breather circuit fitted to manual steering saloon models from October 76 on (Sec 1)

5   All rubber components should be renewed as a matter of routine whenever a component is dismantled, and all internal parts must be lubricated with LHM fluid before assembly. Where grease is necessary for lubrication, only mineral grease may be used.

6   Hydraulic system pipes must not touch each other or any other component which may stress or chafe the pipes.

3   Hydraulic system – preliminary checks

1   If a fault occurs in the hydraulic system, the following preliminary checks should be made before checking the individual components.

2   Make sure that the mechanical linkages of all the components move freely and are not seized.

3   With the engine idling, loosen the bleed screw on the pressure regulator located on the clutch housing 1 to $1\frac{1}{2}$ turns (photo). The noise of fluid leakage should be heard.

4   Tighten the bleed screw and check that the noise from the high pressure pump ceases, indicating that the pressure regulator has cut out.

5   If the results of the checks described in paragraphs 3 and 4 are unsatisfactory, first check that the fluid level in the reservoir is correct as described in Section 4, then check that the filter is clean and the high pressure pump primed as described in Section 5. Always make sure that the pressure regulator bleed screw is tightened correctly.

4   Hydraulic fluid level – checking

1   With the engine idling, open the bonnet and locate the hydraulic fluid sight level indicator on the top of the reservoir located on the left-hand side of the bulkhead. The yellow indicator float must be between the maximum and minimum red rings on the transparent dome, with

the ground clearance lever inside the car fully forward in the maximum height position.

2   The difference between the minimum and maximum rings is approximately 0·45 litres (0·8 Imp pt) for saloons and 0·48 litres (0·84 Imp pt) for estate models, and this will give some indication of the quantity of fluid required to top-up the reservoir.

3   Note that the fluid level indication is accurate only after the car has stabilised at the maximum height.

4   If topping-up is necessary, first clean the filler cap and the surrounding area, then remove the cap (photo).

5   Using genuine green LHM fluid, top-up the reservoir until the indicator reaches the upper red mark, then refit the cap and switch off the engine.

6   In an emergency, automatic transmission fluid (ATF), or SAE 10 or 20 engine oil, may be used *provided that the system is completely drained and fresh LHM fluid is substituted at the earliest opportunity.* However, care must be taken not to use an oil with any properties which would damage the rubber components of the system.

5   Hydraulic system – fluid renewal and filter cleaning

1   The LHM hydraulic fluid must be renewed at 30 000 mile (48 000 km) intervals. The reservoir and filters must be cleaned at the same time.

2   Move the ground clearance control lever inside the car fully to the rear in the minimum height position.

3   Loosen the pressure regulator bleed screw 1 to $1\frac{1}{2}$ turn.

4   Spring back the reservoir cover retaining clip and release the cover and central block from the reservoir (photos).

5   Remove the overflow and return filter and the supply filter from the central block.

6   Carefully lift the reservoir from the bulkhead and discard the fluid;

3.3 Loosening the pressure regulator bleed screw

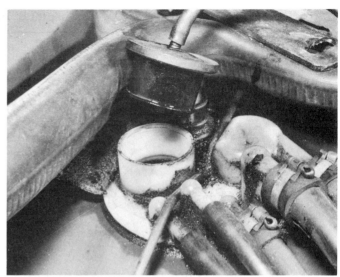
4.4 Removing the filler cap from the hydraulic fluid reservoir

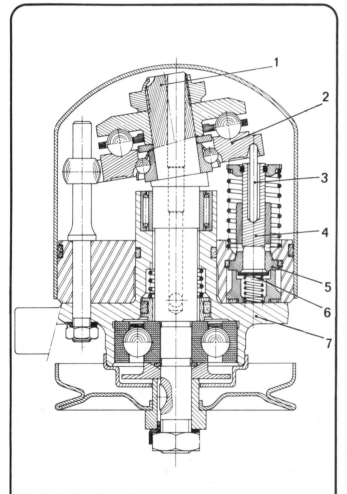
Fig. 8.4 Cross-sectional view of the seven piston high pressure
hydraulic pump (Sec 1)

1	Control shaft	5	Sleeve
2	Oscillating plate	6	Valve
3	Operating rod	7	Body
4	Piston		

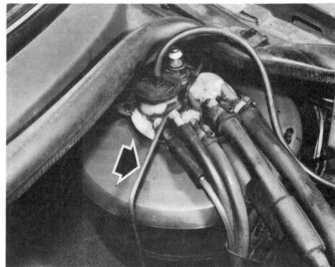
5.4A Location of the hydraulic fluid reservoir cover retaining clip
(arrowed)

5.4B Removing the central block from the hydraulic fluid reservoir

113

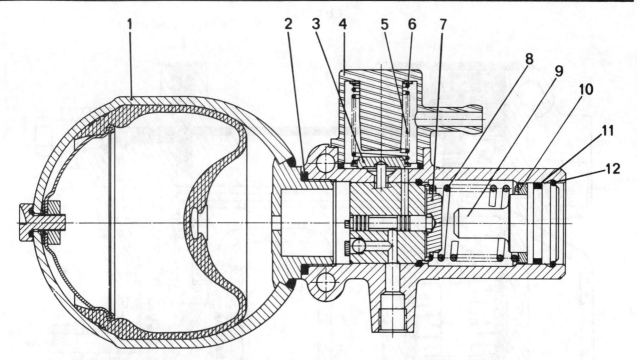

Fig. 8.5 Cross-sectional view of the pressure regulator and main accumulator assembly (Sec 1)

1	Main accumulator	4	Housing	7	Spring plate	10 Shims
2	O-ring	5	Cut-out spring	8	Cut-in spring	11 O-ring
3	Spring plate	6	Shims	9	Stop pillar	12 Circlip

CUT-IN

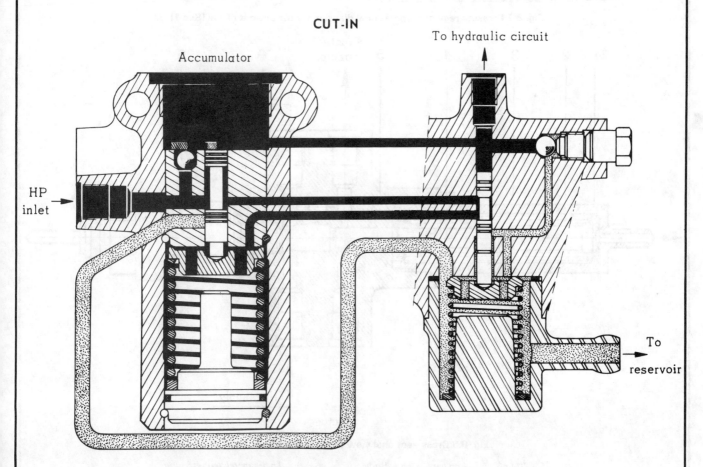

Fig. 8.6 Pressure regulator operational diagram for the cut-in phase (Sec 1)

CUT-OUT

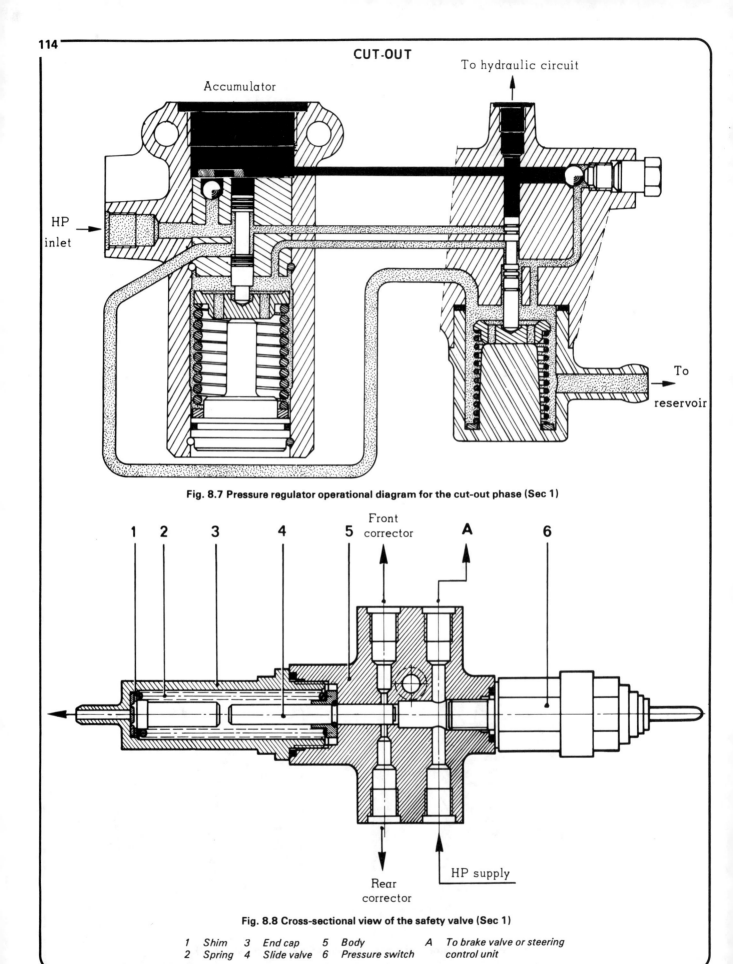

Fig. 8.7 Pressure regulator operational diagram for the cut-out phase (Sec 1)

Fig. 8.8 Cross-sectional view of the safety valve (Sec 1)

1	Shim	3	End cap	5	Body	A To brake valve or steering
2	Spring	4	Slide valve	6	Pressure switch	control unit

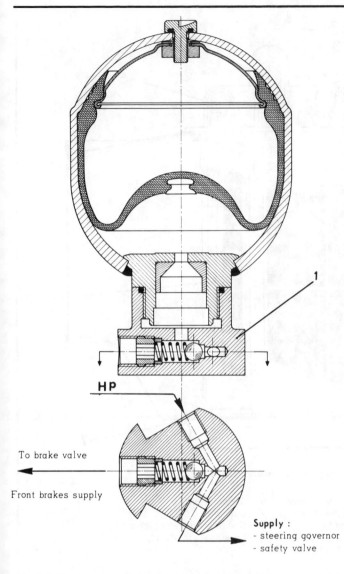

Fig. 8.9 Cross-sectional view of the brake accumulator on models with power steering (Sec 1)

1 Body

HP

To brake valve

Front brakes supply

Supply :
- steering governor
- safety valve

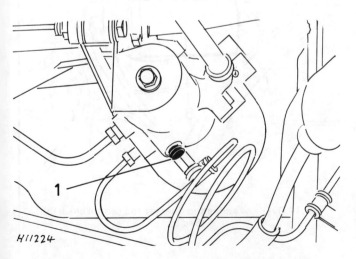

H11224

Fig. 8.10 Location of the pressure regulator bleed screw (1) (Sec 3)

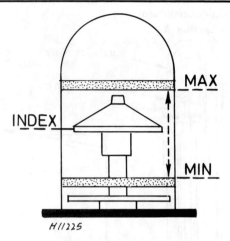

Fig. 8.11 LHM fluid sight level indicator located on the reservoir (Sec 4)

also drain the high pressure pump supply pipe.

7 Remove the deflector plate from the bottom of the reservoir.

8 Clean the filters and reservoir with petrol and blow them dry with compressed air.

9 Refit the reservoir and deflector plate and fill it with the specified quantity of LHM hydraulic fluid. Reassemble the filters and clip the cover assembly onto the reservoir.

10 Disconnect the high pressure pump supply pipe from the reservoir cover central block and, using a small funnel, prime the pump with LHM hydraulic fluid.

11 Refit the supply pipe and move the ground clearance lever fully forwards to the maximum height position.

12 Tighten the pressure regulator bleed screw and top-up the hydraulic fluid level as described in Section 4.

6 Hydraulic pipe joints – assembly

1 To ensure that a perfect seal exists when hydraulic pipe joints are assembled, the following procedure must be carried out.

2 Clean the component port, hydraulic pipe, union nut and sealing rubber and lightly lubricate them with LHM fluid.

3 Slide the sealing rubber onto the end of the pipe until the pipe protrudes from it (photo).

4 Insert the pipe into the component so that the pipe end enters the central hole of the component port. The sealing rubber must enter its location hole fully. Check that the visible part of the pipe is located centrally in the component port.

5 Screw in the union nut by hand whilst keeping the hydraulic pipe stationary, then tighten it to the specified torque.

6 The pipe union is designed to provide increased sealing with increased fluid pressure. Tightening the nut more than the specified amount will not improve the seal, and may easily damage the pipe.

7 Hydraulic system – checking (general)

1 In order to carry out a complete check of the hydraulic system, the tools shown in Fig. 8.17 must be obtained. The pressure gauge must be capable of measuring pressure from 0 to 250 bars (0 to 3650 lbf/in^2); a gauge used to check injection pressures on diesel engines may be suitable.

2 The checking procedure consists of tracing the fluid pressure from the source to the hydraulic component furthest from source, and therefore it is recommended that a complete check is always made even if a particular component is suspected of being faulty. Once the high pressure pump and main accumulator/pressure regulator have been checked, the procedure follows the supply diagrams shown in Figs. 8.21 to 8.26. Check the main circuit shown on the left of these diagrams first (ie downward facing arrows), then check the secondary circuits starting at the top of the diagrams.

3 The procedure described in Sections 11 to 15 applies to saloon models with manual steering, but the method is identical for all other

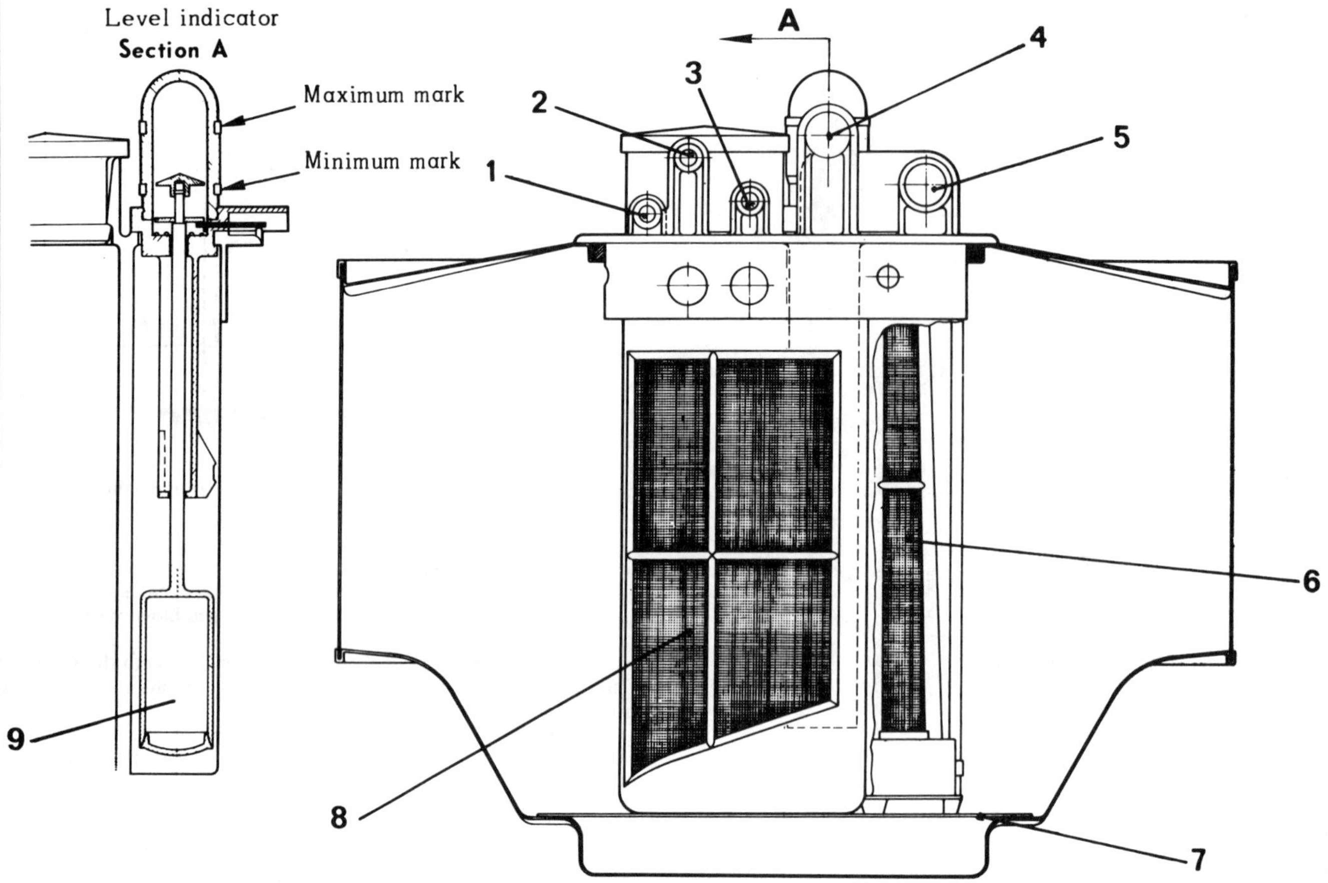

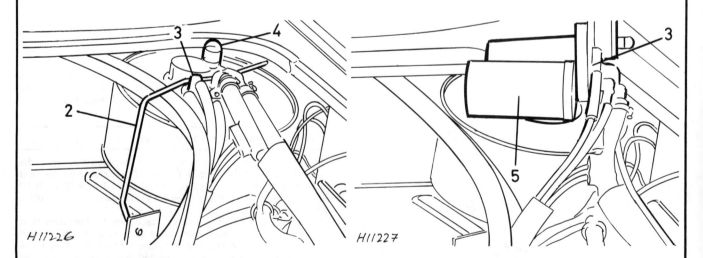

Level indicator
Section A
Maximum mark
Minimum mark
A
1
2
3
4
5
6
7
8
9

Fig. 8.12 Cross-sectional view of the LHM fluid reservoir (Sec 5)

1 Overflow from suspension cylinders
2 Overflow from brake valve, safety valve, and height correctors
3 Return from brake valve
4 Return from pressure regulator and height correctors
5 Pump supply hose
6 Supply filter
7 Deflector
8 Overflow and return filter
9 Level indicator float

2
3
4
H11226

Fig. 8.13 LHM fluid reservoir (Sec 5)

2 Retaining clip 3 Central block 4 Level indicator

3
5
H11227

Fig. 8.14 Overflow and return filter (5) and central block (3) (Sec 5)

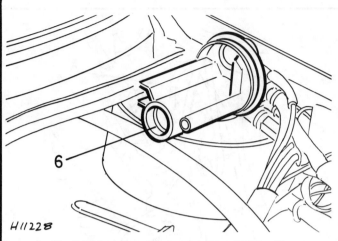

Fig. 8.15 Location of the supply filter (6) (Sec 5)

H11228

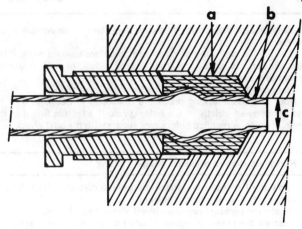

Fig. 8.16 Cross-section through a hydraulic pipe joint (Sec 6)

a Sealing rubber   b Pipe   c Union bore

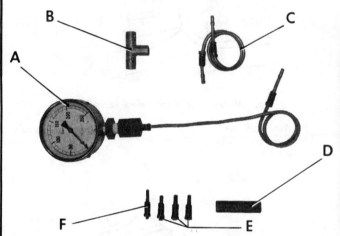

Fig. 8.17 Tools required for checking the hydraulic system (Sec 7)

A Pressure gauge   C Pipe   E Male plugs
B Three-way union   D Female plug   F Male plug

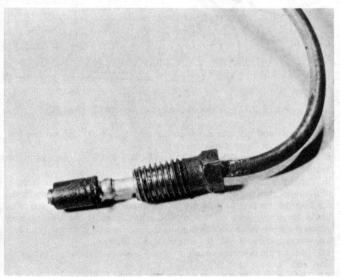

6.3 Hydraulic pipe union and sealing rubber

Fig. 8.18 Pressure gauge connected into the hydraulic system (Sec 8)

A Pressure gauge   2 Pressure regulator outlet
B Three-way union   pipe
C Pipe

11.1 Location of the safety valve

models provided the supply diagrams described in paragraph 2 are followed.

4   Position the car over a pit or on a ramp before starting work; if the hydraulic fluid is cold, first run the car until normal operating temperature is reached.

5   Carry out the preliminary checks described in Section 3.

6   Note that the checking procedure described in Sections 8 to 16 must be followed strictly in the order given. If a fault is found in the system, it must be rectified before proceeding with the next check.

8   Hydraulic system pressure gauge – fitting

1   Apply the handbake and move the ground clearance lever fully to the rear in the minimum height position.

2   Loosen the pressure regulator bleed screw 1 to 1$\frac{1}{2}$ turns.

3   Unscrew the pressure regulator outlet pipe; make sure that you do not unscrew the pump inlet pipe, otherwise the pressure gauge and pump will subsequently be damaged.

4   Using the three-way union and extension pipe, connect the pressure gauge into the circuit as shown in Fig. 8.18.

9   Main accumulator – checking

1   Unscrew the safety valve inlet pipe and plug the pipe using the special adaptors.

2   Tighten the pressure regulator bleed screw and disconnect the distributor to coil lead(s) at the coil (conventional system) or ignition module (electronic system).

3   Spin the engine with the starter; the pressure should gradually rise, then temporarily stabilise at the accumulator air inflation pressure which must be as given in the Specifications.

4   If the air inflation pressure is not within the limits, the main accumulator is faulty.

5   Reconnect the ignition lead when the check has been completed.

10   Pressure regulator – checking

1   Tighten the pressure regulator bleed screw and start the engine.

2   Allow the pressure to rise to its maximum, then let the engine idle for a few minutes for the pressure to stabilize.

3   The regulator cut-out pressure must be as specified.

4   Switch off the engine and note the pressure drop during the next three minutes; if this exceeds 145 psi (10 bars), the regulator is faulty.

5   Start the engine again and allow the pressure to rise to the cut-out pressure.

6   With the engine still running, loosen the pressure regulator bleed screw a little so that the pressure drops slowly. When the cut-in pressure is reached, the pressure will begin to rise as the high pressure pump is brought into the circuit again. The minimum pressure registered on the gauge is the cut-in pressure which must be as specified.

7   If the cut-out or cut-in pressures are incorrect, the regulator is faulty.

8   When the check is finished, switch off the engine and loosen the pressure regulator bleed screw. Remove the plug from the hydraulic pipe and tighten the union into the safety valve.

11   Safety valve (manual steering saloon models) – checking

1   Unscrew and remove the safety valve to bracket retaining bolt (photo).

2   Disconnect the front and rear suspension pipes from the safety valve and plug the ports with the special adaptors.

3   Tighten the pressure regulator bleed screw and start the engine.

4   When the cut-out pressure has been reached, disconnect the rubber overflow return pipe from the end of the valve. If there is a large quantity of fluid leaking from the valve, it is faulty and should be renewed, but if the discharge is minimal, the valve is in good order.

5   Reconnect the return pipe and switch off the engine.

6   Loosen the pressure regulator bleed screw.

7   Unscrew the adaptor plug from the safety valve outlet to the rear

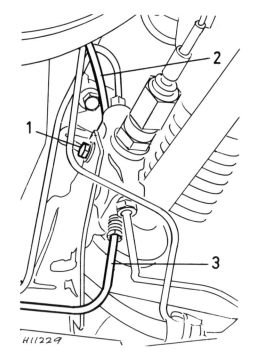

Fig. 8.19 Location of the safety valve (Sec 11)

1   Retaining bolt
2   Front suspension supply pipe
3   Rear suspension supply pipe

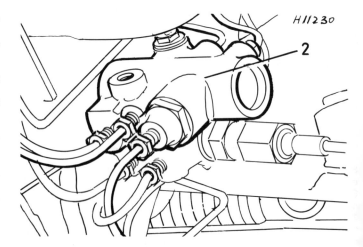

Fig. 8.20 Location of the brake limiter (2) (Sec 20)

suspension and place a small container beneath it. Tighten the pressure regulator bleed screw.

8   Disconnect the distributor to coil lead(s) at the coil (conventional system) or ignition module (electronic system).

9   Spin the engine with the starter whilst observing the safety valve rear suspension outlet. As soon as fluid runs from the outlet, check the reading on the pressure gauge which should be within the specified limits for slide valve operation. The pressure indicates the moment when the slide valve admits fluid to the suspension circuits; if the pressure is not within limits, the safety valve is faulty.

10   Loosen the pressure regulator bleed screw and reconnect the ignition lead.

11   Tighten the adaptor plug into the safety valve rear suspension outlet.

12 Brake control valve (manual steering saloon models) – checking

1   Tighten the pressure regulator bleed screw.
2   Start the engine and allow the fluid pressure to increase to the regulator cut-out pressure.
3   Wait until the pressure has stabilized, then stop the engine and note the pressure drop over the next three minutes. If this exceeds 10 bars (145 lbf/in²), the brake control valve is faulty and the internal slide valves are not sealing correctly; the control valve must be renewed.

13 Safety valve pressure switch (manual steering saloon models) – checking

1   Start the engine and allow the fluid pressure to increase to the regulator cut-out pressure.
2   Switch off the engine and allow it to stop, then switch on the ignition only.
3   Have an assistant depress the brake pedal several times until the hydraulic pressure warning lamp glows on the instrument panel. Immediately check the reading on the pressure gauge; it should be within the limits specified for pressure switch.
4   If the pressure switch does not operate at the correct pressure, it must be renewed.
5   Switch off the ignition and loosen the pressure regulator bleed screw.

14 Front suspension circuit (manual steering saloon models) – checking

1   Unscrew the adaptor plug from the safety valve front suspension outlet port and reconnect the front suspension supply pipe.
2   Tighten the pressure regulator bleed screw.
3   Move the ground clearance lever to the normal running height position, then start the engine.
4   Allow the front of the car to rise, and wait until the pressure gauge reading stabilizes.
5   Switch off the engine and note the pressure drop over the next three minutes. If this exceeds 10 bars (145 lbf/in²), either the front height corrector or front suspension cylinders are leaking. To find the defective component each one must be checked in turn. First loosen the pressure regulator bleed screw and move the ground clearance lever fully to the rear in the minimum height position.

Front height corrector – checking

6   Unscrew the nut securing the supply pipe from the height corrector to the three-way union; the two remaining pipes lead to the front suspension cylinders.
7   Plug the pipe with the special adaptor.
8   Tighten the pressure regulator bleed screw and move the ground clearance lever to the normal running height position.
9   Start the engine and allow it to idle until the regulator cut-out pressure has been reached and stabilized.
10 Switch off the engine and note the pressure drop over the next three minutes. If this exceeds 10 bars (145 lbf/in²), the front height corrector has an internal leak and must be renewed.
11 Unscrew the special adaptor and tighten the supply pipe to the three-way union.

Front suspension cylinders – checking

12 Loosen the pressure regulator bleed screw and move the ground clearance lever fully to the rear in the minimum height position.
13 Unscrew the nut securing the left-hand front suspension cylinder supply pipe to the three-way union, and plug the union with the special adaptor.
14 Tighten the pressure regulator bleed screw and move the ground clearance lever to the normal running height position.
15 Start the engine and allow it to idle until the regulator cut-out pressure has stabilized.
16 Switch off the engine and note the pressure drop over the next three minutes. If this exceeds 10 bars (145 lbf/in²), the right-hand front suspension cylinder has an internal leak and must be renewed.

17 Loosen the pressure regulator bleed screw and move the ground clearance lever fully to the rear in the minimum height position.
18 Unscrew the special adaptor and refit the supply pipe to the three-way union.
19 Tighten the pressure regulator bleed screw and move the ground clearance lever to the normal running height position.
20 Start the engine and allow it to idle until the regulator cut-out pressure has stabilized.
21 Switch off the engine and note the pressure drop over the next three minutes. If this exceeds 10 bars (145 lbf/in²), the left-hand front suspension cylinder has an internal leak and must be renewed.

15 Rear suspension circuit (manual steering saloon models) – checking

1   Loosen the pressure regulator bleed screw, and move the ground clearance lever fully to the rear in the minimum height position.
2   Unscrew the special adaptor from the safety valve rear suspension outlet port and reconnect the rear suspension supply pipe.
3   Insert and tighten the safety valve to bracket retaining bolt.
4   Unscrew the nut securing the hydraulic pipe from the rear suspension to the brake valve and plug the pipe with the special adaptor.
5   The procedure for checking the rear suspension circuit and components is now identical with that for the front suspension, starting at paragraph 2 of Section 14. Note, however, that a four-way union is fitted to the rear suspension; the additional pipe is the supply from the rear suspension circuit to the brake valve for the operation of the rear brakes.

16 Hydraulic system pressure gauge – removal

1   Loosen the pressure regulator bleed screw, then disconnect the three-way union with extension pipe and pressure gauge from the hydraulic system.
2   Insert and tighten the outlet pipe into the regulator.
3   Tighten the pressure regulator bleed screw.

17 Hydraulic pump (single cylinder) – removal and refitting

1   Loosen the pressure regulator bleed screw.
2   Disconnect the pump supply pipe from the inlet port and drain the fluid into a suitable container. If a roll type clip is fitted, remove it and obtain a screw type (worm drive) clip.
3   Unscrew the high pressure output pipe from the pump.
4   On models manufactured after October 1976, disconnect the breather pipes from the pump, having previously noted their location.
5   Unscrew the retaining bolts and withdraw the hydraulic pump from the cylinder block. Clean away any traces of gasket from the mating surfaces.
6   Refitting is a reversal of removal. Always use a new gasket, and prime the pump by disconnecting the supply pipe at the reservoir and filling the pipe with LHM fluid.
7   Reconnect the supply pipe and tighten the pressure regulator bleed screw.

18 Hydraulic pump (seven piston type) – removal and refitting

1   Loosen the pressure regulator bleed screw.
2   Disconnect the pump supply pipe from the inlet port and drain the fluid into a suitable container. If a roll type clip is fitted, remove it and obtain a screw type (worm drive) clip for use when refitting (photo).
3   Unscrew the high pressure output pipe from the pump.
4   Loosen the pump pivot and adjustment nuts, swivel the pump towards the clutch housing, and remove the drivebelt from the pump and camshaft pulleys.
5   Unscrew the pivot and adjustment nuts (photo), remove the bolts, and withdraw the pump from the clutch housing.
6   Refitting is a reversal of removal. Align the camshaft and pump pulleys and adjust the drivebelt tension as described in Chapter 2. Prime the pump by disconnecting the supply pipe at the reservoir and filling the pipe with LHM fluid.
7   Reconnect the supply pipe and tighten the pressure regulator bleed screw.

HP supply
Safety valve
Front suspension
Rear suspension
Brake valve
Rear brakes
Front brakes

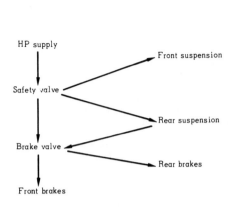

Fig. 8.21 Hydraulic circuit supply diagram for manual steering saloon models

HP supply
Brake accumulator
Brake valve
Supply to front brakes
3-way union
Supply to steering governor
Safety valve
Front suspension
Rear suspension
Brake valve
Supply to rear brakes
Steering (Supply to control slide valve and operating cylinder)

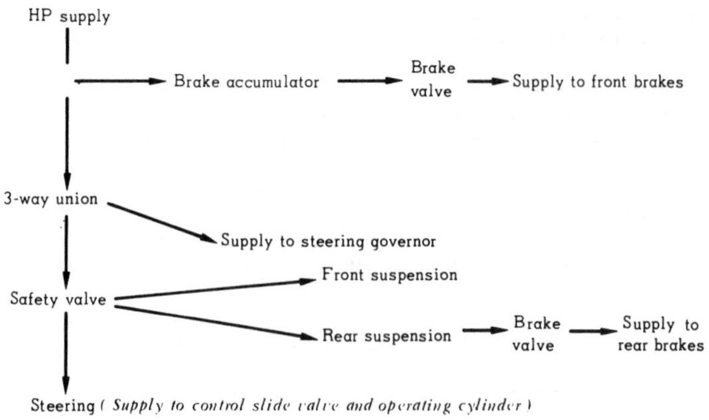

Fig. 8.22 Hydraulic circuit supply diagram for power steering saloon models

Source of pressure
Safety valve
Front suspension
Rear suspension
Brake valve
Brake pressure limiter
Front brakes
Rear brakes

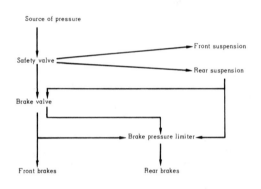

Fig. 8.23 Hydraulic circuit supply diagram for manual steering estate models to September 1976

Source of pressure
Brake accumulator
Brake valve
Front brakes
3-way union
Supply to steering governor
Brake pressure limiter
Safety valve
Front suspension
Rear suspension
Rear brakes
Steering (supply to slide-valve and operating cylinder)

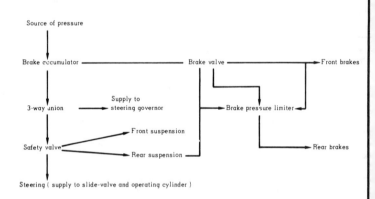

Fig. 8.24 Hydraulic circuit supply diagram for power steering estate models to September 1976

Source of pressure
Safety valve
Front suspension
Rear suspension
Brake valve
Brake pressure limiter
Rear brakes
Front brakes

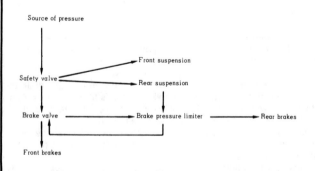

Fig. 8.25 Hydraulic circuit supply diagram for manual steering estate models from September 1976

Source of pressure
Brake accumulator
Brake valve
Front brakes
3-way union
Supply to steering governor
Brake pressure limiter
Safety valve
Front suspension
Rear suspension
Rear brakes
Steering (supply to slide-valve and operating cylinder)

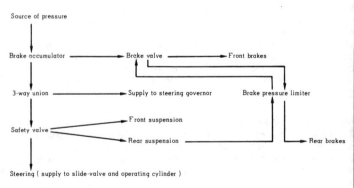

Fig. 8.26 Hydraulic circuit supply diagram for power steering estate models from September 1976

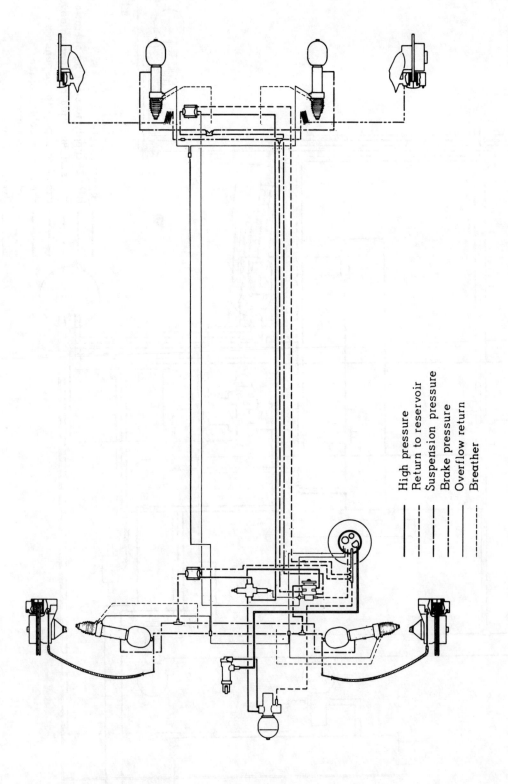

Fig. 8.27 Component hydraulic circuit supply diagram for manual steering saloon models

—— High pressure
----- Return to reservoir
----- Suspension pressure
---- Brake pressure
—— Overflow return
—— Breather

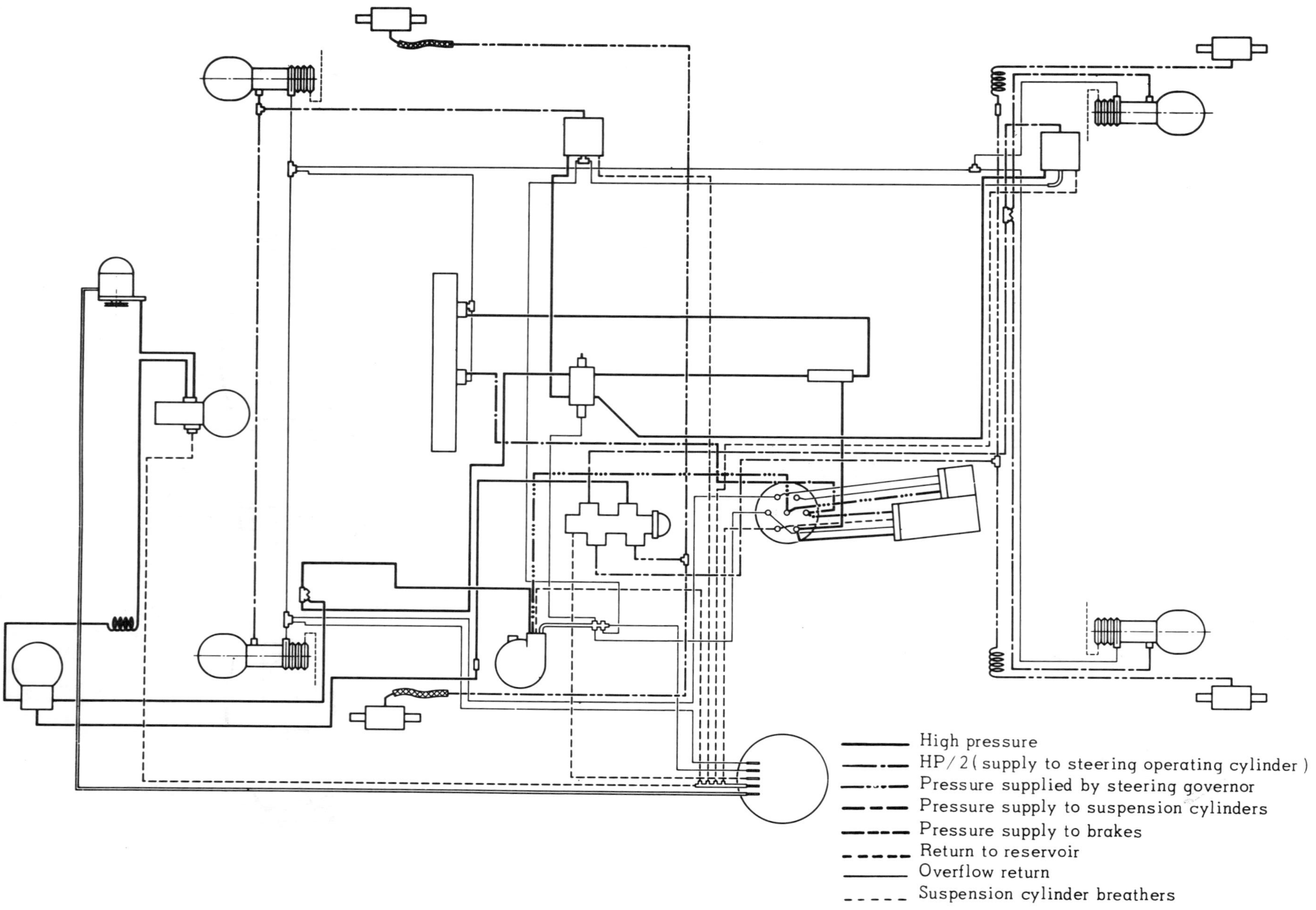

Fig. 8.28 Component hydraulic circuit supply diagram for power steering saloon models

High pressure

HP/2 (supply to steering operating cylinder)

Pressure supplied by steering governor

Pressure supply to suspension cylinders

Pressure supply to brakes

Return to reservoir

Overflow return

Suspension cylinder breathers

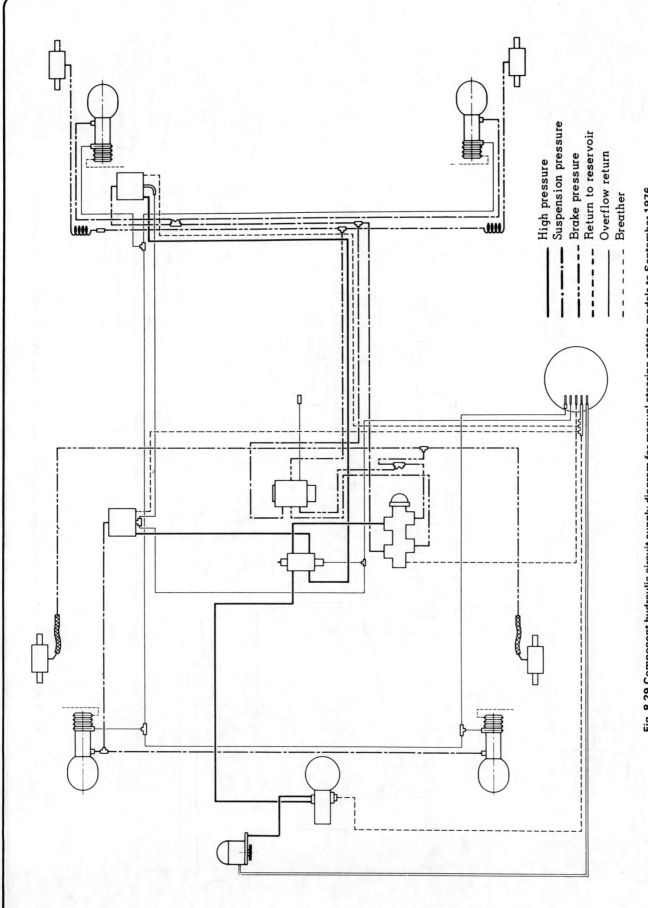

High pressure
Suspension pressure
Brake pressure
Return to reservoir
Overflow return
Breather

Fig. 8.29 Component hydraulic circuit supply diagram for manual steering estate models to September 1976

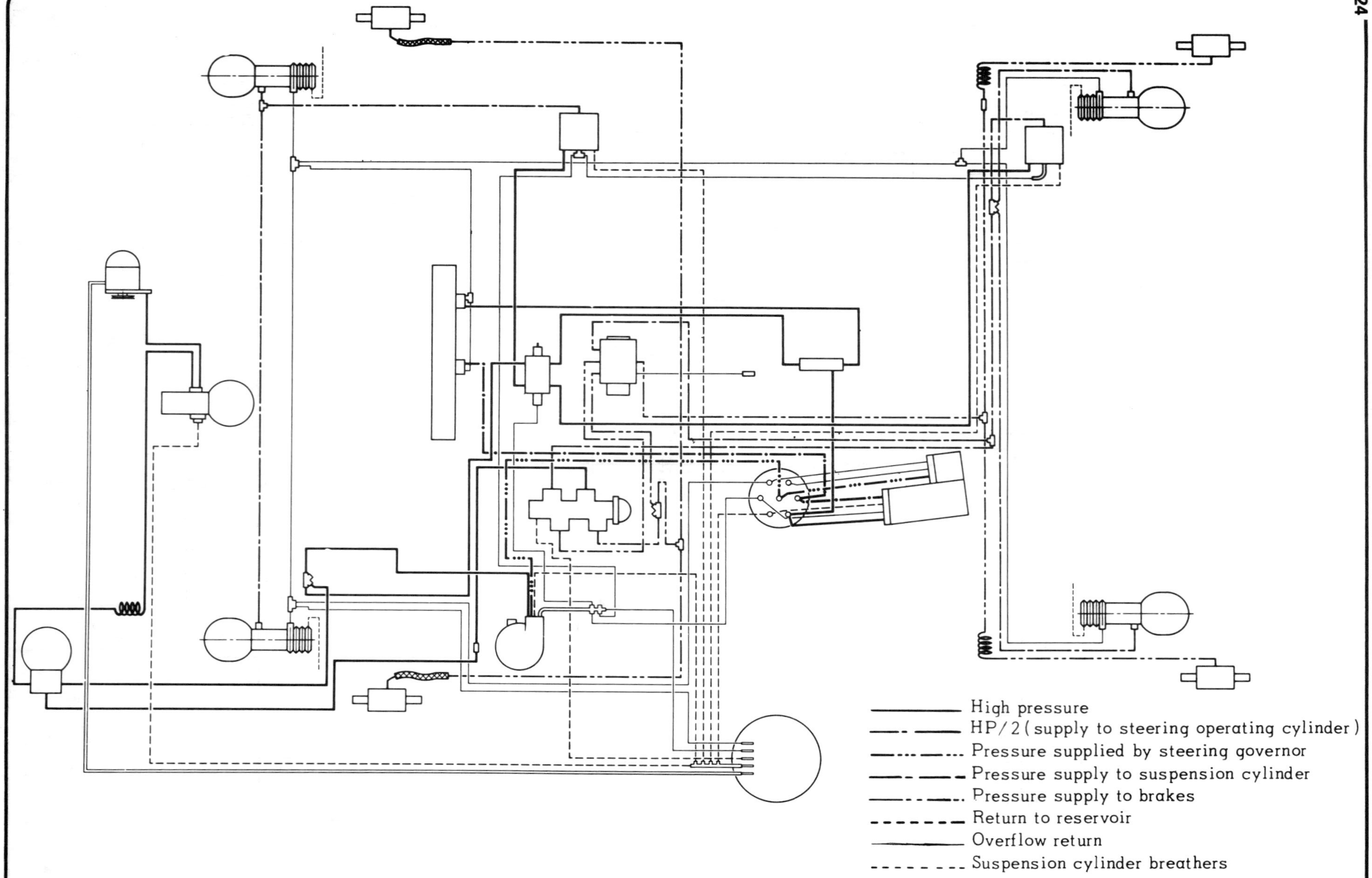

High pressure
HP/2 (supply to steering operating cylinder)
Pressure supplied by steering governor
Pressure supply to suspension cylinder
Pressure supply to brakes
Return to reservoir
Overflow return
Suspension cylinder breathers

Fig. 8.30 Component hydraulic circuit supply diagram for power steering estate models to September 1976

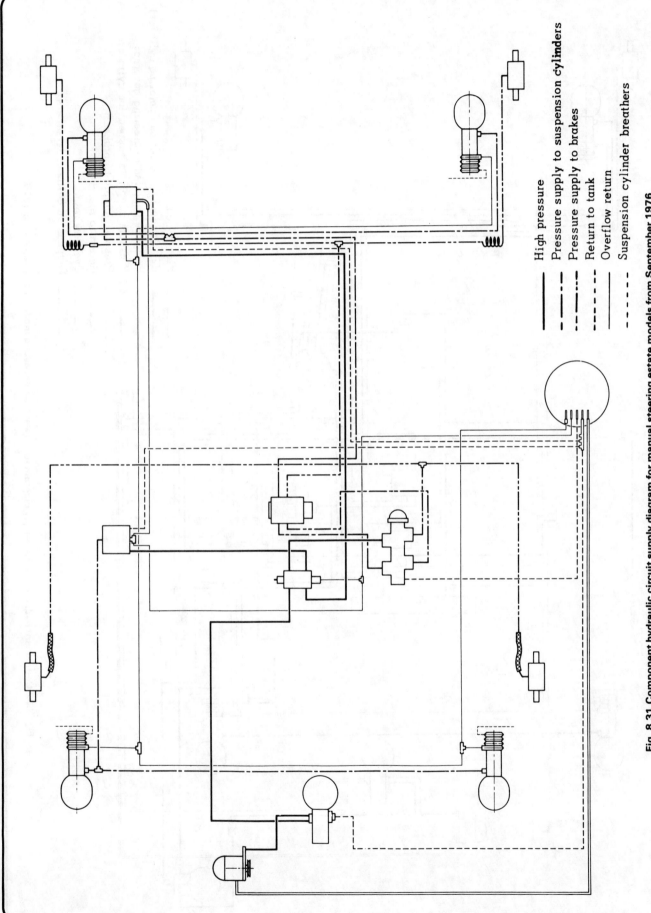

High pressure

Pressure supply to suspension cylinders

Pressure supply to brakes

Return to tank

Overflow return

Suspension cylinder breathers

Fig. 8.31 Component hydraulic circuit supply diagram for manual steering estate models from September 1976

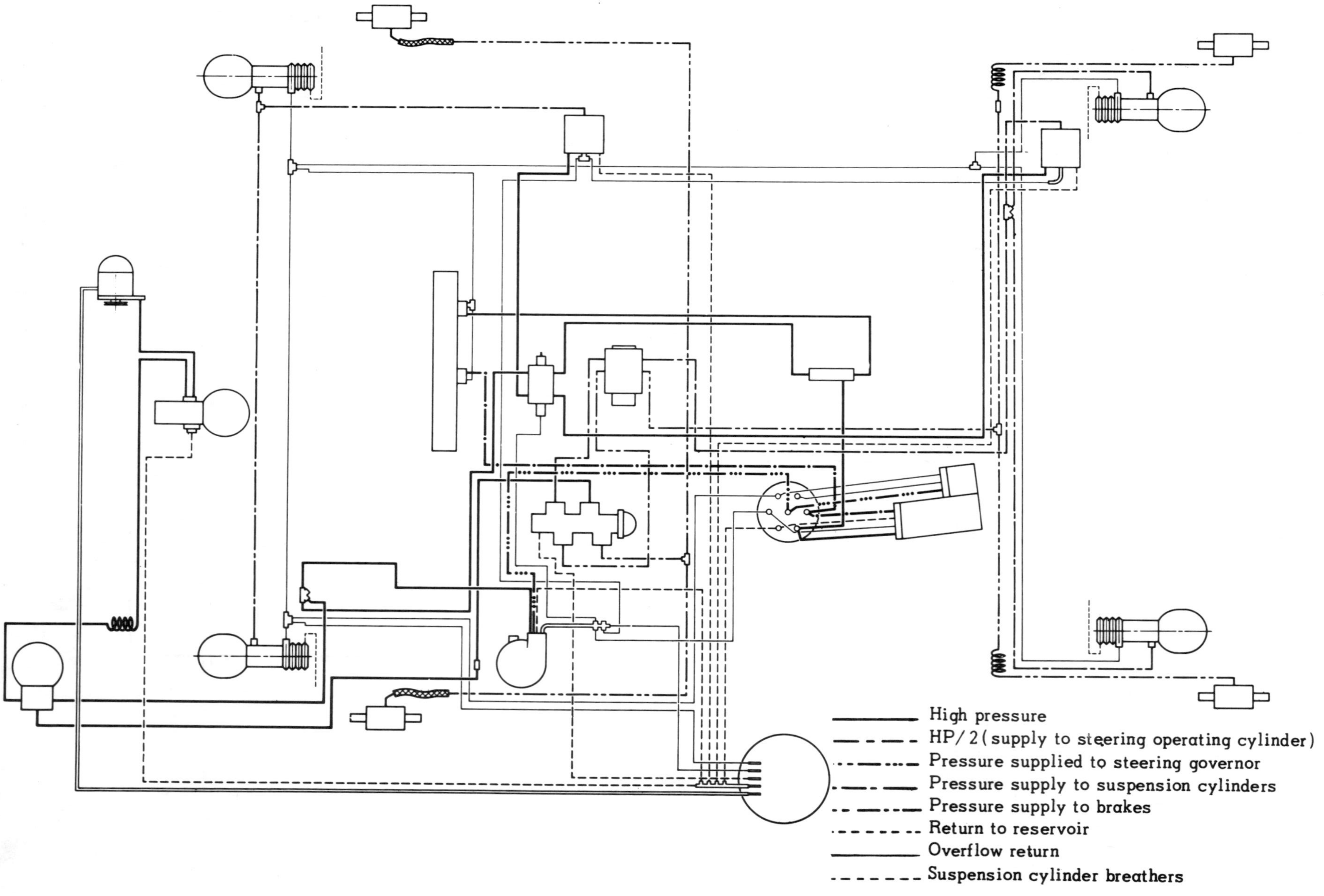

High pressure

HP/2 (supply to steering operating cylinder)

Pressure supplied to steering governor

Pressure supply to suspension cylinders

Pressure supply to brakes

Return to reservoir

Overflow return

Suspension cylinder breathers

Fig. 8.32 Component hydraulic circuit supply diagram for power steering estate models from September 1976

18.2 Location of the hydraulic pump (seven piston type)

18.5 Hydraulic pump mounting and pivot nut locations

19 Pressure regulator and main accumulator – removal and refitting

1   The pressure regulator and main accumulator are located on the front of the gearbox.
2   Loosen the pressure regulator bleed screw.
3   Disconnect the rubber return hose from the regulator and drain the fluid into a suitable container.
4   Unscrew the union nuts securing the inlet and outlet pipes to the regulator.
5   Unscrew the retaining bolts and withdraw the pressure regulator and main accumulator from the gearbox.
6   Refitting is a reversal of removal. Tighten the pressure regulator bleed screw when all the pipes are connected.

20 Safety valve – removal and refitting

1   The safety valve is located on the lower left-hand side of the front subframe, behind the steering gear.
2   Loosen the pressure regulator bleed screw.
3   Disconnect the rubber overflow return pipe from the end of the valve.
4   Unscrew the union nuts securing the inlet and outlet pipes to the safety valve, making a careful note of their location.
5   Disconnect the supply wire from the pressure switch terminal.
6   Unscrew and remove the mounting bolt and withdraw the safety valve. Where a brake limiter is fitted, this is also detached at the same time.
7   Refitting is reversal of removal. Tighten the pressure regulator bleed screw when the pipes and wire are connected.

21 Fault diagnosis – hydraulic system

Symptom	Reason
Loss of hydraulic pressure	Reservoir filters blocked Pump supply pipe leaking Pressure regulator faulty Pump faulty or drivebelt broken Pressure regulator bleed screw loose
Excessive hydraulic pressure	Pressure regulator faulty
Loss of suspension pressure	Safety valve faulty Height corrector faulty Suspension cylinders faulty Height adjustment incorrect (see Chapter 11)
Loss of brake pressure	Brake valve faulty (see also Chapter 9)

Chapter 9 Braking system

For modifications, and information applicable to later models, see Supplement at end of manual

Contents

Specifications

System type
Main brakes	Discs all round, dual hydraulic circuit supplied by main hydraulic system, automatic rear brake limitation. Front pad wear warning system
Handbrake	Cable and rod operation to independent calipers on front discs

Front brakes
Disc diameter	260 mm (10.24 in)
Minimum disc thickness	18.0 mm (0.71 in)
Maximum disc run-out	0.2 mm (0.008 in)
Pad lining thickness:	
Main brake	11.5 mm (0.453 in)
Handbrake	4.15 mm (0.163 in)

Rear brakes
Disc diameter:	
Saloon	233.5 mm (9.19 in)
Estate	235 mm (9.25 in)
Minimum disc thickness:	
Saloon	7.0 mm (0.28 in)
Estate	16.0 mm (0.63 in)
Maximum run-out	0.2 mm (0.008 in)
Pad lining thickness:	
New	12.0 mm (0.472 in)
Minimum	1.5 mm (0.06 in)

Brake hydraulic system
Number of caliper pistons:	
Front	Four
Rear	Two
Pedal to brake valve clearance	0.5 to 3.0 mm (0.020 to 0.118 in)

Torque wrench settings
	lbf ft	kgf m
Front brake pipe to subframe	15.0 to 17.5	2.1 to 2.4
Brake valve bolt	13.0	1.8
Pedal assembly	3.5	0.5
Handbrake eccentric bolt	43.5 to 47.0	6.0 to 6.5
Handbrake cable locknut	11.0	1.5
Brake pipe union nut	16.5 to 18.0	2.3 to 2.5
Front caliper assembly bolts	26.75	3.7
Rear caliper retaining bolts (saloons)	30.5 to 34.0	4.2 to 4.7
Rear caliper retaining bolts (estates)	40.0 to 50.5	6.5 to 7.0

1 General description

The four-wheel braking system is of dual circuit, hydraulic type, with discs fitted to the front and rear brakes. Hydraulic pressure is provided by the high pressure pump in the main hydraulic system, and the rear brakes incorporate automatic limitation according to the load carried by the rear suspension. On saloon models, hydraulic fluid is fed direct from the rear suspension to the rear brake calipers, but on estate models, a brake pressure limiter meters the hydraulic fluid to the calipers.

The front disc pads are equipped with internal electric leads which operate a warning lamp on the instrument panel when the linings are due for renewal.

The front brake calipers comprise outer halves which are removable, and inner halves which are integral with the steering knuckles. The rear disc pads and brake calipers are mounted on the rear suspension arms; these pads do not incorporate a warning system.

The handbrake is mechanically operated by rod and cable to the front discs. The front calipers incorporate disc pads especially for the handbrake, which is independent of the hydraulic system. A handbrake warning system is fitted whereby a warning lamp on the instrument panel flashes with the ignition on and the handbrake applied. The lamp is extinguished when the handbrake is released.

Brake adjustment is fully automatic except on the handbrake.

2 Disc pads (front) – renewal

1   The front disc pads must be renewed when the warning lamp glows on the instrument panel. To do this, first chock the rear wheels, jack-up the front of the car and support it on axle stands.
2   Remove the roadwheel.
3   Turn the steering so that the brake caliper is facing out, then disconnect the pad wear warning lamp wires from the wiring loom (photo).
4   Prise the clip from the location grooves and remove the pad retaining pin from the caliper (photo). If the pin is seized, removal may prove difficult as there is no access from the inner end, but if the pin is moved in each direction several times it can be released gradually.
5   Remove the spring clip and withdraw the pads (photos).
6   The caliper pistons must now be moved outwards to allow room for the new pads. To do this, partially insert the old pads, then lever them apart until the pistons are fully retracted.
7   Brush any dust or dirt from the disc pad recesses in the caliper, taking care not to inhale the dust.

8   Fit the new disc pads with the friction surfaces towards the disc, then refit the spring clip and retaining pin. Make sure that the warning lamp wires are located beneath the inner spring clip.
9   Reconnect the warning lamp wires to the wiring loom.
10 Refit the roadwheel and lower the car to the ground. Note that the front disc pads must always be renewed in sets of four, ie all the front pads must be renewed even if only one is worn to the limit.

3 Disc pads (rear) – inspection and renewal

1   The rear disc pads must be inspected for wear at the intervals specified in Routine Maintenance.
2   Apply the handbrake, jack-up the rear of the car and support it on axle stands. Remove the roadwheel.
3   Unscrew and remove the retaining bolt and withdraw the disc pad cover from the caliper (photo).
4   Remove the spring clip and pull out the two disc pads with a pair of pliers (photo).
5   Brush any accumulated dust and dirt from the disc pads and caliper recesses, taking care not to inhale the dust.
6   Examine the disc pads for wear; if the friction material thickness is less than the specified minimum the pads must be renewed. Note that the rear disc pads must always be renewed in sets of four.
7   If new pads are to be fitted, the caliper pistons must be retracted to accomodate the extra friction material. To do this, partially insert the old pads, then lever them apart to depress the pistons.
8   Fit the new disc pads with the friction surfaces towards the disc.
9   Locate the spring clip with the crossbar at the bottom of the caliper and retain it in position with the through bolt (photo).
10 Refit the disc pad cover and tighten the bolt.
11 Refit the roadwheel and lower the car to the ground.

4 Disc caliper (front) – dismantling, servicing and reassembly

1   Jack-up the front of the car and support it on axle stands. Chock the rear wheels and release the handbrake.
2   Remove the roadwheel.
3   Remove the disc pads as described in Section 2.
4   Disconnect the handbrake intermediate lever from the outer operating arm.
5   Unscrew the four bolts securing the caliper outer half to the steering knuckle and withdraw the outer half.
6   Prise the rubber O-ring from the steering knuckle and caliper inner half assembly.
7   Unscrew the star head screws and remove the brake disc from the hub.
8   Mark each piston in relation to the caliper halves to ensure correct refitting, then remove them. If necessary, a foot pump may be used to remove the piston from the outer half by applying air pressure at the transfer port.

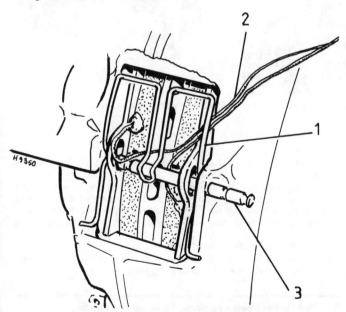

Fig. 9.1 Location of the disc pads (Sec 2)

1 Retaining spring   2 Warning lamp leads   3 Retaining pin

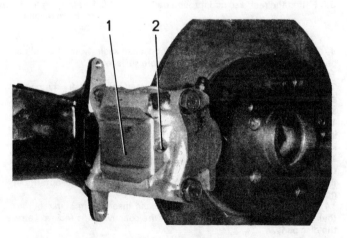

Fig. 9.2 Location of the rear brake disc pad cover (1) and through bolt (2) (Sec 3)

2.3 Disc pad wear warning lamp wire connector

2.4 Removing the disc pad retaining pin

2.5A Removing the front disc pads

2.5B This front disc pad is worn below the minimum limit

3.3 Removing the rear disc pad cover

3.4 Removing the rear disc pads

3.9 Fitting the rear disc pad through bolt

5.4 Removing the hydraulic pipe union nut from the rear caliper

5.6 Showing the two halves of the rear caliper

9   Prise the square section seals and dust seals from the caliper bores, being careful not to scratch the bore surface.

10 Remove the handbrake disc pads.

11 Clean all the components with methylated spirit and dry them with a lint-free cloth. Examine the surfaces of the pistons and bores; if these are scratched or show any bright wear areas, renewal is necessary.

12 If the components are in good order, discard the old seals, including the transfer port seal, and obtain new ones in the form of a repair kit.

13 Fit the new seals using the fingers only to manipulate them into their grooves. Make sure that the square section seals are inserted in the innermost grooves, and the double-lipped seals in the outermost grooves.

14 Dip the pistons in fresh LHM fluid and insert them squarely into their respective bores; make sure that the concave ends face towards the disc pads.

15 Refit the handbrake disc pads.

16 Locate the brake disc on the hub, and tighten the star head

screws.

17 Locate the rubber O-ring in the transfer port on the steering knuckle.

18 Making sure that the mating surfaces of the two caliper halves are scrupulously clean, then locate the outer half and insert the four bolts and lugged washers. Tighten the bolts evenly to the specified torque.

19 Connect the handbrake intermediate lever to the outer operating arm.

20 Refit the disc pads as described in Section 2.

21 Bleed the brake hydraulic system as described in Section 11. Refit the roadwheel and lower the car to the ground.

---

5   Disc caliper (rear) – removal, servicing and refitting

1   Jack-up the rear of the car and support it on axle stands. Chock the front wheels and apply the handbrake.

2   Remove the roadwheel.

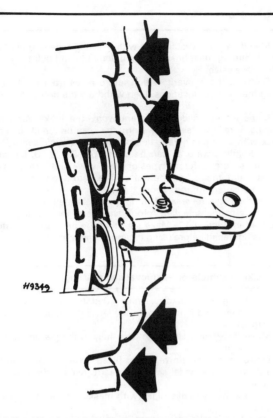

Fig. 9.3 Front brake caliper outer half retaining bolt locations –
arrowed (Sec 4)

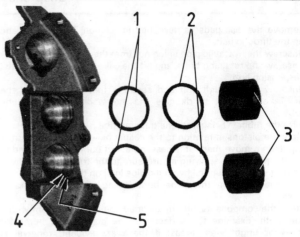

Fig. 9.4 Front brake caliper outer half components (Sec 4)

1 Square section seals   4 Inner groove
2 Dust seals   5 Outer groove
3 Pistons

Fig. 9.6 Location of the rear brake caliper O-ring (1) and transfer
tube (2) (Sec 5)

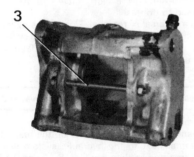

Fig. 9.5 Rear brake caliper through bolt (3) location (Sec 5)

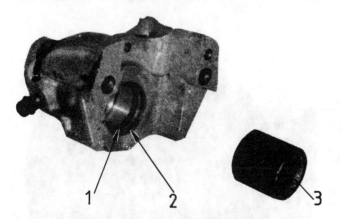

Fig. 9.7 Location of the square section seal (1) and dust seal (2) in
the rear brake caliper. Concave side of piston (3) faces pad (Sec 5)

Fig. 9.8 Checking a front brake disc for run-out, showing extra bolts
inserted – arrowed (Sec 6)

1 Dial gauge   2 Stand

3   Remove the disc pads as described in Section 3, then refit and tighten the through bolt.
4   Unscrew the hydraulic pipe union nut from the caliper (photo).
5   Unscrew the retaining bolts, and lift the caliper assembly from the rear suspension arm.
6   Unscrew the through bolt and separate the two halves of the caliper. Take care not to damage the intermediate transfer tube (photo).
7   Prise the rubber O-ring from the transfer tube.
8   Mark the pistons in relation to the caliper halves to ensure correct refitting, then remove them. If necessary, a foot pump may be used to remove the pistons by applying air pressure to the transfer post. If will also be necessary to plug the hydraulic pipe inlet on the inner half.
9   Prise the seals from the caliper bores, being careful not to scratch the bores.
10 Clean the components with methylated spirit and dry them with a lint-free cloth. Examine the surfaces of the pistons and bores for scratches or bright wear areas; if these are evident, renewal is necessary.
11 If the components are in good order, discard the old seals, including the transfer port seal, and obtain new ones in the form of a repair kit.
12 Fit the new seals using the fingers only to manipulate them into their grooves. The square section seals must be inserted into the innermost grooves of the caliper halves, and the double-lipped seals into the outermost grooves.
13 Dip the piston in fresh LHM fluid, then insert them squarely into their respective bores with the concave ends facing the disc pads.
14 Locate the rubber O-ring over the transfer port tube.
15 Make sure that the mating surfaces of the two caliper halves are scrupulously clean, then locate the outer half on the inner half and retain them together with the through bolt.
16 Refit the caliper to the rear suspension arm, and insert the two retaining bolts with the lugged washers. Tighten the bolts to the specified torque.
17 Unscrew and remove the through bolt.
18 Tighten the hydraulic pipe union nut into the caliper.
19 Refit the disc pads as described in Section 3.
20 Bleed the brake hydraulic system as described in Section 11, then refit the roadwheel and lower the car to the ground.

6   Brake disc – examination, removal and refitting

1   Jack-up the front or rear of the car and support it on axle stands. Remove the roadwheel.
2   Remove the front caliper outer half or rear caliper complete as described in Sections 4 or 5.
3   Examine the disc for deep scoring or grooving. Light scoring is normal but if it is severe, the disc must be removed and either renewed or ground by a suitable engineering works.
4   Check the disc for run-out to determine whether it is distorted or buckled. To do this accurately, a dial gauge will be necessary, but if this is not available, feeler blades can be used against a fixed block as the disc is rotated slowly. Do not confuse wear in the hub bearings with disc run-out.
5   To ensure that the disc is firmly in contact with the hub while checking for run-out, three bolts should be inserted into the wheel bolt holes as shown in Fig. 9.8 and tightened to 7.0 kgf m (5.5 lbf ft). If the specified run-out is exceeded, the disc must be renewed.
6   To remove the disc, unscrew the crosshead retaining screws and withdraw the disc from the hub.
7   Refitting is a reversal of removal, but it will be necessary to bleed the brake hydraulic system as described in Section 11.

7   Brake valve – removal, servicing and refitting

1   Jack-up the front of the car and support it on axle stands. Chock the rear wheels.
2   Move the ground clearance control lever fully to the rear. Unscrew the hydraulic system pressure regulator bleed screw 1 to 1½ turns, and on power steering models operate the brake pedal several times to release the pressure in the brake accumulator.
3   Unscrew the retaining bolts and detach the brake valve from the body (photo).

4   Identify each hydraulic pipe with masking tape in order to ensure correct refitting, then unscrew the union nuts and pull the pipes clear of the brake valve.
5   Disconnect the overflow and return pipes from the brake valve, noting their correct locations, then withdraw the brake valve from the car.
6   If the internal slide valves are worn, the brake valve must be renewed. If only the seals are worn, they can be removed separately. Check with a Citroen garage before removing the old seals. Dismantling is straightforward as can be seen from Fig. 9.10, but note that there are several different types of brake valve and identification is by various paint marks on the valve. The return outlet is located in different positions on the various types.
7   Refitting is a reversal of removal, but tighten the hydraulic pipe union nuts to the specified torque and bleed the braking system as described in Section 11. Make sure that the pressure regulator bleed screw is tightened before using the car on the road.

8   Brake accumulator – removal and refitting

1   The brake accumulator is only fitted to models equipped with power steering, and is located on the left-hand front of the front subframe (photo).
2   Move the ground clearance lever fully to the rear in the minimum height position.
3   Loosen the pressure regulator bleed screw 1 to 1½ turns, then separate the brake pedal several times to release the hydraulic fluid pressure.
4   Identify the hydraulic pipes with masking tape to ensure correct refitting.
5   Detach the brake accumulator from its support plate and withdraw it from the engine compartment.
6   If the accumulator sphere is faulty, it can be unscrewed from the main body after loosening the worm drive clip. An oil filter removal strap may be used to do this.
7   Refitting is a reversal of removal. Tighten the hydraulic pipe union nuts to the specified torque and bleed the braking system as described in Section 11. Check that the pressure regulator bleed screw is tightened before using the car on the road.

9   Brake pressure limiter – description, removal and refitting

1   A brake pressure limiter is fitted in the rear brake circuit on all estate and Prestige models; it is located on the rear left-hand side of the front subframe, next to the hydraulic system safety valve. Two types of limiter are fitted as shown in Figs. 9.13 and 9.14.
2   On models manufactured up to September 1976 the limiter is of the type shown in Fig. 9.13. When the ground clearance lever is in the

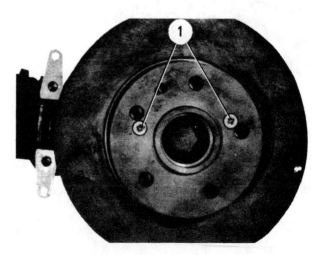

Fig. 9.9 Brake disc retaining screw (1) locations (Sec 6)

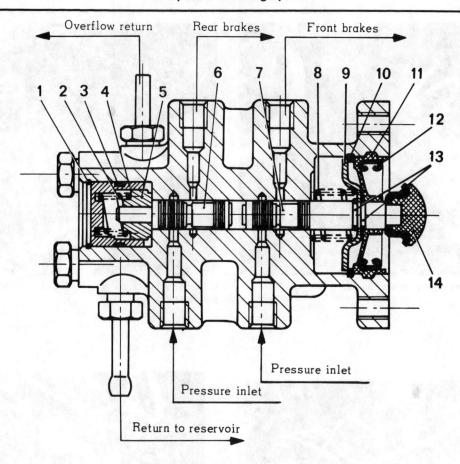

Fig. 9.10 Cross-sectional view of the brake valve (Sec 7)

1	Circlip	5	Thrust cap
2	Spring	6	Rear brake slide valve
3	O-ring	7	Front brake slide valve
4	Plug	8	Spring

9	Thrust cap	12	Bush
10	Circlip	13	Circlips
11	Rubber sleeve	14	Rubber damper

low position there is no pressure in the rear suspension circuit, and the internal slide valve stops any flow of fluid to the rear brakes. With the ground clearance lever in the normal running position, the pressure in the rear suspension circuit forces the slide valve along its bore and allows the rear brakes to be operated. When the front brake pressure reaches a predetermined level, the slide valve is forced back and fluid pressure to the rear brakes ceases. This action is slowed down by an internal ball valve and the compression of air in an air chamber, thus avoiding a sudden decrease of pressure to the rear brakes.

3   On models manufactured from September 1976 on, the limiter is of the type shown in Fig. 9.14. This operates in a similar manner to the limiter described in paragraph 2, but instead of the air chamber, internal drillings and a ball valve prevent the sudden cut-off of pressure to the rear brakes. The limiter does not monitor the front brake fluid pressure, but operates when the rear brake pressure reaches a predetermined level in relation to the pressure in the rear suspension circuit.

4   To remove the limiter, first jack-up the front of the car and support it on stands. Chock the rear wheels.

5   Move the ground clearance lever fully to the rear in the minimum height position.

6   Loosen the hydraulic system pressure regulator bleed screw 1 to 1½ turns.

7   Clean the exterior of the limiter with paraffin and wipe it dry.

8   Identify the position of the hydraulic pipes with masking tape to ensure correct refitting, then unscrew the union nuts.

9   Unscrew and remove the retaining bolt and withdraw the limiter from the car. It is not possible to overhaul the limiter and, if it is proved faulty, it must be renewed.

10   Refitting is a reversal of removal. Tighten the union nuts to the specified torque and bleed the braking system as described in Section

11   Check that the pressure regulator bleed screw is tightened before using the car on the road.

10   Hoses and brake lines – maintenance

1   Regularly inspect the condition of the flexible hydraulic hoses. If they are perished, chafed or swollen they must be renewed.

2   When fitting a flexible hose, make sure that it is not twisted, or touching any other components which may chafe or damage it.

3   The hydraulic brake should be wiped clean regularly and examined for signs of corrosion or denting by flying stones. Examine the support clips to make sure that they are not causing wear to the line surface.

4   Check that the brake lines are not touching any adjacent components or rubbing against any part of the vehicle. Where this is observed, gently bend the line as necessary.

5   If a brake line is damaged or corroded it must be renewed immediately.

6   After fitting a new hose or brake line, the braking system must be bled as described in Section 11.

11   Brake hydraulic system – bleeding

1   The brake hydraulic system must be bled after renewing and refitting any components, brake line, or hose; if this procedure is not carried out, air will be trapped in the circuit and the brakes will not function correctly.

2   Before starting work, check all the brake lines, unions, hoses and connections for possible leakage.

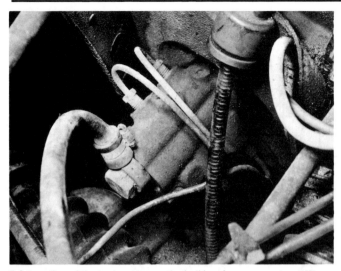

7.3 Location of the brake valve on the bulkhead

8.1 Brake accumulator is on the left of the front subframe (power steering models)

Fig. 9.11 Brake valve (1) detached from the body (Sec 7)

Fig. 9.12 Location of the brake accumulator (1) and support plate (2) (Sec 8)

3   If there is any possibility of fluid other than genuine LHM fluid being in the system, drain the complete hydraulic system as described in Chapter 8 and fill it with the special rinsing solution obtainable from Citroen. Bleed the system and leave the solution in the circuit for approximately 600 miles (1000 km), then drain it out and fill with LHM fluid. If the rubber seals are damaged by the incorrect fluid, it will also be necessary to renew these items at the same time.

4   Collect two clean jars, and a sealed container of LHM fluid. On estate models manufactured before September 1976, a further length of tubing will be required for fitting on the air chamber supply pipe.

5   Carry out the procedure in the order given in this Section.

Front brakes

6   Jack-up the front of the car and support it on axle stands. Chock the rear wheels and remove the front roadwheels.

7   Loosen the pressure regulator bleed screw 1 to 1½ turns.

8   Locate the tubes (preferably transparent) on the front brake caliper bleed screws with their free ends in the jars.

9   Have an assistant fully depress the brake pedal, then loosen the bleed nipples approximately half a turn.

10 On estate models manufactured before September 1976, find the air chamber (on the rear left-hand side of the front subframe) and remove it from the supply pipe. Fit the remaining length of tubing on the supply pipe and support it in a vertical position.

11 With the assistant still holding the brake pedal fully depressed, start the engine and allow it to idle.

12 Tighten the pressure regulator bleed screw and allow the fluid to flow through the bleed nipples until no more air bubbles emerge from the bleed tubes. Immediately tighten the bleed nipples.

13 Release the brake pedal on saloon models, and estate models from September 1976 on. Before doing this on earlier estate models, check that fluid is visible in the tubing fitted to the air chamber supply pipe.

14 Remove the bleed tubes and locate the rubber caps over the bleed nipples.

15 On estate models manufactured before September 1976, remove the air chamber bleed tube. Make sure that the air chamber is free of any sediment by blowing through it with compressed air, then connect the supply pipe and secure the air chamber to the subframe.

16 Check the bleed nipples and air chamber (where fitted) for leakage by fully depressing the brake pedal.

17 Release the foot pedal and switch off the engine.

18 Refit the roadwheels and lower the car to the ground.

19 Check and top-up the hydraulic fluid level in the reservoir as described in Chapter 8.

20 Note that on estate models manufactured before September 1976 it is essential to bleed the front brakes correctly to ensure that the correct amount of air is present in the air chamber. No air in the

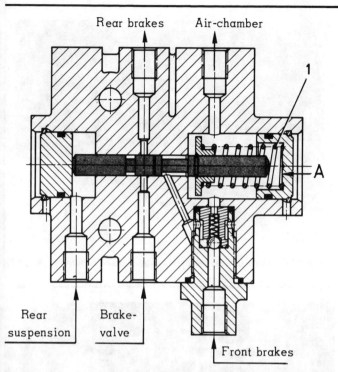

Fig. 9.13 Cross-sectional view of the brake pressure limiter fitted to early estate models (Sec 9)

1 Spring   A Front brake pressure

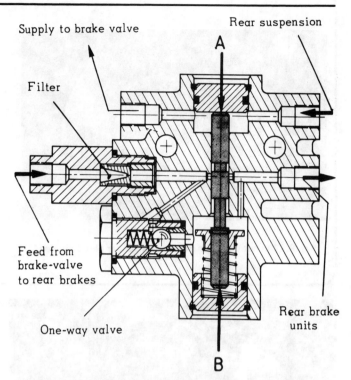

Fig. 9.14 Cross-sectional view of the brake pressure limiter fitted to late estate models (Sec 9)

A Rear suspension pressure   B Rear brake pressure

Fig. 9.15 Location of air chamber (1) and supply pipe (2) on early estate models (Sec 9)

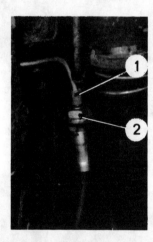

Fig. 9.16 Front brake line connection (Sec 10)

1   Union nut   2   Flexible hose locknut

chamber causes the rear brake pressure cut-out to occur too quickly; too much air causes the cut-out to occur over too long a period.

Rear brakes

21 On estate models manufactured before September 1976 follow paragraphs 22 to 24 inclusive; on all saloon models, and estates manufactured from September 1976 on, follow paragraphs 25 to 30 inclusive. The remaining paragraphs apply to all models.

22 On estate models manufactured before September 1976, jack-up the rear of the car and support it on axle stands. Apply the handbrake.

23 Remove the rear roadwheels.

24 Move the ground clearance lever fully forwards to the maximum height position. The pressure regulator bleed screw must remain tightened throughout the procedure.

25 On all saloon models, and estates manufactured from September 1976 on, move the ground height lever fully to the rear in the

minimum height position.

26 Loosen the pressure regulator bleed screw 1 to 1½ turns, and allow the car to sink to its lowest position.

27 Jack-up the rear of the car and support it on axle stands. Apply the handbrake.

28 Remove the rear roadwheels.

29 Move the ground clearance lever fully forwards to the maximum height position.

30 Tighten the pressure regulator bleed screw.

31 On all models fit bleed tubes on each bleed nipple and place their free ends in the jars (photo).

32 Loosen the bleed nipple approximately half a turn.

33 Have an assistant fully depress the brake pedal, then start the engine and allow it to idle. The fluid will flow through the bleed tubes into the jars.

34 When no more air bubbles emerge from the bleed tubes, tighten

Fig. 9.17 Location of the front brake caliper bleed nipple (1) (Sec 11)

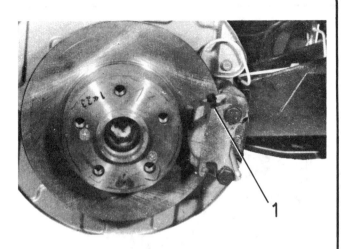

Fig. 9.18 Location of the rear brake caliper bleed nipple (1) (Sec 11)

11.31 Bleeding the rear brakes. Proprietary bleeding kits enable the operation to be carried out single-handed

12.4 Handbrake cable locknut and adjustment nut

12.7 Location of a handbrake eccentric adjuster (arrowed)

12.10 Handbrake cable compensator (heater unit removed for clarity)

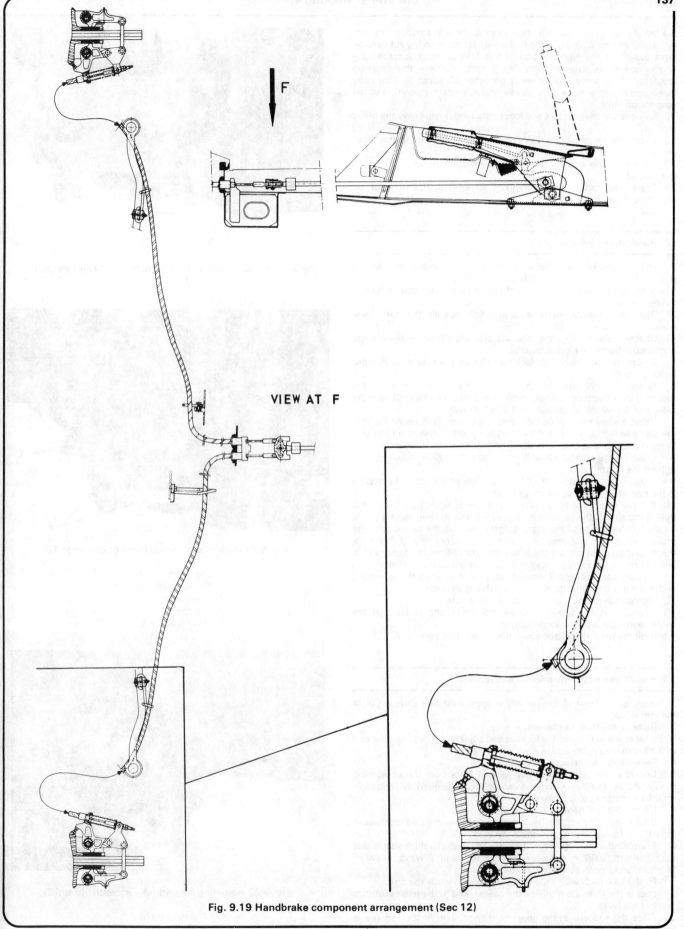

F

VIEW AT F

Fig. 9.19 Handbrake component arrangement (Sec 12)

the bleed nipples immediately, then release the brake pedal. The pressure should now build up in the hydraulic system, with the suspension arms assuming the high position. If this fails to occur, increase the engine speed to approximately 3000 rpm, unscrew the pressure regulator bleed screw and leave it open for 30 seconds. Close the bleed screw, allow the engine to idle and recheck the position of the suspension arms.

35 Remove the bleed tubes and locate the rubber caps over the bleed nipples.

36 Check the bleed nipples for leakage by fully depressing the brake pedal.

37 Switch off the engine, refit the roadwheels and lower the car to the ground.

38 Check and top-up the hydraulic fluid level in the reservoir as described in Chapter 8.

12 Handbrake – adjustment

1 The handbrake must be adjusted at the intervals specified in Routine Maintenance, or after fitting new cables.

2 Jack-up the front of the car and support it on axle stands. Chock the rear wheels.

3 Remove the front roadwheels and fully release the handbrake lever.

4 Unscrew and remove the locknuts and adjustment nuts from the end of each handbrake cable (photo).

5 Loosen the two eccentric locking bolts on the rear of each front brake caliper.

6 Check that the two levers which contact the disc pads are touching the outer stops; if not, loosen the stop screw locknut near the cable and screw the adjustment bolt into the lever.

7 Using a steel plate of suitable thickness, turn each eccentric until the disc pad lightly contacts the disc at the point of maximum run-out. Tighten each locking bolt without turning the eccentric (photo).

8 Unscrew the stop screw until it contacts the caliper housing, then tighten the locknut.

9 Check that the ends of the handbrake cables are located correctly in the operating levers at the caliper end.

10 Pull the end of the handbrake inner cable as far as possible on the right-hand side of the car, and measure its position. Then pull the cable on the left-hand side of the car and again measure the protrusion. The protrusion on one side may be more than the other side; if this is so, the difference must remain the same after the following adjustment in order to retain the cable compensator in a central position (photo).

11 Tighten each cable adjustment nut until it touches the quadrant, and make any final adjustments to the cable protrusion.

12 Tighten the locknuts onto the adjustment nuts.

13 Operate the handbrake lever several times and check that the cables and mechanism operate correctly.

14 Refit the roadwheels and lower the car to the ground.

13 Handbrake pads – inspection and renewal

1 Jack-up the front of the car and support it on axle stands. Chock the rear wheels.

2 Remove the front roadwheel.

3 Unscrew and remove the locknut and adjustment nut from the end of the handbrake cable and remove the cable.

4 Remove the return spring from the levers.

5 Unscrew and remove the two locking bolts from the eccentrics, then withdraw the levers from the caliper. Note the quantity of spacers for the handbrake cable (photos).

6 Lift out the two handbrake pads (photo).

7 Brush away any accumulated dust or dirt from the pad recesses in the caliper, *taking care not to inhale the dust.*

8 Examine the pads for wear; if the friction material thickness is less than 1.0 mm (0.04 in) the pads must be renewed. Always renew all four handbrake pads at the same time.

9 Fit the new pads with the friction surfaces towards the disc.

10 Locate the lever assembly on the caliper, and fit the two eccentrics and locking bolts.

11 Place the spacers on the uppermost lever, then fit the spring and insert the cable (photo).

Fig. 9.20 Handbrake cable adjustment nut (1) and locknut (2) (Sec 12)

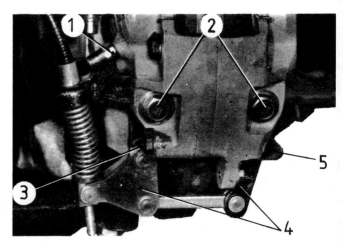

Fig. 9.21 Handbrake linkage components (Sec 12)

1 Stop bolt
2 Eccentric locking bolts
3 Lever stop
4 Linkage
5 Lever stop

Fig. 9.22 Adjusting a handbrake eccentric (Sec 12)

1 Adjusting tool
2 Eccentric

13.5A Removing the handbrake levers from the cable

13.5B Handbrake levers, return spring and adjustment eccentrics

13.6 Location of a handbrake pad

13.11 Fitted position of the handbrake cable and levers

15.2 Location of the stoplamp switch

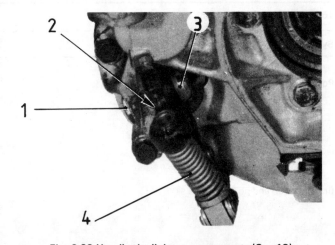

Fig. 9.23 Handbrake linkage components (Sec 13)

1	Locking bolt	3	Eccentric
2	Spacer location	4	Return spring

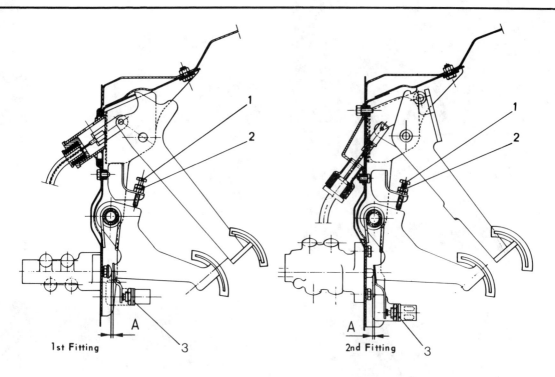

Fig. 9.24 Footbrake pedal clearance dimension (A) (Sec 14)

1 Pedal stop bolt   2 Locknut   3 Stoplamp switch

12 Adjust the handbrake as described in Section 12, then refit the roadwheel and lower the car to the ground.

14 Footbrake pedal – adjustment

1   The clearances between the footbrake pedal and the rubber damper of the brake valve must be as given in the Specifications. If not, loosen the locknut and adjust the stop screw located over the pedal as necessary. Tighten the locknut when the adjustment is completed.
2   The pedal must now be checked for correct operation. First move the ground clearance lever fully to the rear in the minimum height position.
3   Loosen the pressure regulator bleed screw 1 to $1\frac{1}{2}$ turns.
4   On models equipped with power steering, depress the brake pedal several times to release the pressure in the brake accumulator.
5   Fully depress the pedal three or four times, making sure that it returns to its stop freely.
6   Check that the clearance adjusted in paragraph 1 has not altered. The pedal operation is correct if the clearance remains the same.
7   Tighten the pressure regulator bleed screw.

15 Stoplamp switch – adjustment

1   Before adjusting the stoplamp switch, the footbrake pedal must be adjusted as described in Section 14.
2   The stoplamp is located beneath the footbrake pedal and the internal contacts should switch on the stoplamps as soon as the pedal touches the brake valve (photo).
3   If adjustment is necessary, bend the support plate carefully.

16 Fault diagnosis – braking system

Symptom	Reason/s
Poor stopping ability	Brake pads and/or discs badly worn or scored
	Faulty brake valve
	Leak in brake hydraulic system
	Air in brake hydraulic system
	Low main hydraulic system pressure
	Brake pads contaminated with oil
	Faulty rear brake limiter (estate models)
	Faulty brake accumulator (power steering models)
Brake uneven and pulling to one side	Brake pads contaminated with oil
	Worn or distorted disc
	Caliper piston seized
	Different type of linings on disc pads
	Tyre pressures unequal
Inefficient handbrake operation	Worn pads
	Seized cable or levers
	Incorrect adjustment

Chapter 10 Electrical system

For modifications, and information applicable to later models, see Supplement at end of manual

Contents

Specifications

System type .... 12 volt, negative earth

Battery rating
CX 2000 models to June 1975 and
CX 2200 models to January 1976 .... 50 Ah
CX 2000 models from June 1975 and
CX 2200 models from January 1976 .... 45 Ah
CX 2400 models .... 55 Ah
Cold climate countries .... 70 Ah

Alternator
Type and make .... Three phase, 12 volt; Ducellier, Motorola, or Paris-Rhone
Output:
    Standard models (to September 1975) .... 53 amps
    Models with towing equipment (to September 1975) .... 72 amps
    All carburettor models (September 1975 on) .... 72 amps
    All fuel injection models .... 80 amps
    Ambulance models .... 80 amps
Cut-in speed .... 1100 rpm (alternator)
Brush length (new):
    Motorola 510-4 .... 9.4 mm (0.37 in)
    Other models .... 14.5 mm (0.57 in)
Minimum brush length:
    Motorola 510-4 .... 4.0 mm (0.16 in)
    Other models .... 6.0 mm (0.24 in)
Alternator to crankshaft ratio 2.18:1
Field resistance:
    Motorola 510-4 and Paris-Rhone 14R11 .... 4.0 ± 0.2 ohms
    Other models .... 4.5 ± 0.3 ohms

Regulator
Type and make .... Remote location; Paris-Rhone, SEV-Marchal or Ducellier
Voltage at engine speed of 2750 rpm .... 13.0 to 14.2 volts

Starter motor
Type and make .... Pre-engaged, 12 volt; Ducellier or Paris-Rhone

Minimum commutator diameter:
    Ducellier .... 30.25 mm (1.191 in)
    Paris-Rhone .... 35.5 mm (1.398 in)
Armature endfloat:
    Ducellier .... 0.5 mm (0.020 in)
    Paris-Rhone .... 2.2 mm (0.087 in)
Minimum brush length (all models) .... 8.0 mm (0.315 in)

Windscreen wiper motor

Type:
    Front .... Two or three-speed, with automatic stop
    Rear .... Single speed, with automatic stop
Minimum commutator diameter:
    Front .... 23.0 mm (0.906 in)
    Rear .... 12.0 mm (0.472 in)
Minimum brush length:
    Front - Ducellier .... 5.5 mm (0.217 in)
    Front – Bosch .... 7.5 mm (0.295 in)
    Rear .... 3.0 mm (0.118 in)

Fuses

Models manufactured before January 1975:
    White (16 amp) .... Electric window winders
    Mauve (16 amp) .... Heater
    Red (16 amp) .... Stoplamps, accessory terminal, glovebox, direction indicators, instrument panel, windscreen wiper, horns, heater relay, electric window relay
    Green (16 amp) .... Interior lamp, boot, cigar lighter, clock, hazard warning lamp, voltage regulator, reversing lamps, rear window heater
    Yellow (10 amp) .... Ashtray light, cigar lighter light, heater control light, dashboard lighting, side and tail lamp warning, left-hand side and rear lamps
    Blue (10 amp) .... Right-hand side and rear lamps, number plate light
Models manufactured from January 1975 to September 1975:
    Mauve (16 amp) .... Heater
    Red (16 amp) .... Stoplamps, accessory terminal, glovebox, direction indicators, windscreen wipers and washers, horns, heater relay, electric window relay, speedometer light, warning lamp panel
    Green (16 amp) .... Interior lamp, boot, cigar lighter, clock, hazard warning lamp, voltage regulator, reversing lamps, rear window heater, handbrake warning
    White (16 amp) .... Electric window winders
    Yellow (10 amp) .... Ashtray light, cigar light, heater light, clock light, battery motor light, odometer light, sidelamp warning, left-hand front and rear sidelamps
    Blue (10 amp) .... Right-hand front and rear sidelamps, number plate lamp
Pallas models manufactured from September 1975:
    Mauve (16 amp) .... Heater
    Red (16 amp) .... Stoplamps, accessory terminal, glovebox, direction indicators, windscreen washers and wipers, horns, heater relay, electric window relay, speedometer light, instrument panel warning lamps, fuel gauge
    Green (16 amp) .... Interior lamp, bootlamp, cigar lighter, clock, hazard warning, voltage regulator, reversing lamps, heated rear window, handbrake warning
    White (16 amp) .... Electric window winders
    Yellow (10 amp) .... Ashtray light, cigar lighter light, heater light, instrument panel lights, left-hand front and rear sidelamps
    Blue (10 amp) .... Right-hand front and rear sidelamps, number plate lamp
Prestige models manufactured from September 1975:
    Mauve (16 amp) .... Air conditioning relays and controls
    Red (16 amp) .... Clock, hazard warning, stoplamps, idle speed cut-off, voltage regulator, horn, horn relay, windscreen wiper and washers, lighting rheostat, battery meter, oil pressure and temperature, brake pad wear, coolant and oil gauge lights, direction indicators, electric window relay (front), heater relay
    Green (16 amp) .... Electric rear window relay, cigar lighter, exterior mirror, water temperature gauge, reversing lamps, heated rear window, handbrake warning, glovebox, interior lamps, engine compartment light, boot lamp, accessory terminal
    White (16 amp) .... Electric front window switches
    Yellow (10 amp) .... Map reading lamp (plus 5 amp in-line fuse), heater controls light, ashtray and cigar lighter light, instrument panel lights, sidelamp warning, front and rear sidelamps, number plate lamp
    White (10 amp) .... Fog lamp warning, fog lamps
    Yellow (16 amp) .... Rear cigar lighters
    White (16 amp) .... Electric rear window switches
Estate cars manufactured from January 1976:
    Mauve (16amp) .... Heater
    Red (16 amp) .... Stoplamps, accessory terminal, glovebox light, direction indicators, windscreen wipers and washers, horns, heater relay, electric window relay, speedometer light, warning lamps, fuel gauge, tachometer

Green (16 amp) . . . . Interior lamp, boot lamp, cigar lighter, clock, hazard warning lamps, voltage regulator, reversing lamps, heated rear window, handbrake warning, rear screen washers and wiper

White (16 amp) . . . . Electric window winder relay

Yellow (10 amp) . . . . Ashtray light, cigar lighter light, heater controls light, instrument panel lights, sidelamp warning, left-hand front and rear sidelamps

Blue (10 amp) . . . . Right-hand front and rear sidelamps, number plate lamp

Models fitted with electronic fuel injection:

Green (16 amp) . . . . Glovebox, bonnet, boot, interior lamps, accessory terminal, front left-hand mirror, flasher unit, handbrake warning, water temperature gauge, cigar lighter, reversing lamps, heated rear window and warning lamp

Red (16 amp) . . . . Fuel gauge and low fuel warning lamp, speedometer light, tachometer light, battery meter, tachometer, brake pad wear, coolant and engine oil temperature, oil pressure, hydraulic fluid pressure, direction indicators, voltage regulator, windscreen wiper and washers, horn, heater relay, electric front window relay, horn relay, hazard warning lamps, stoplamps, clock

Yellow (10 amp) . . . . Foglamp relay, sidelamps and warning lamp, number plate lamps, instrument panel lights, dashboard lights, map reading lamp (plus 5 amp in-line fuse)

Blue (10 amp) . . . . Rear foglamps and warning lamp

White (16 amp) . . . . Electric front windows

Mauve (16 amp) . . . . Air conditioning relays and controls

Bulbs

	Wattage
Headlamp	55 and 45/40 or 55/60
Side and tail	5
Number plate	5
Direction indicator	21
Stoplamp	21
Reversing lamp	21
Interior lamp (festoon)	7
Boot lamp	5
Ignition key light	2
Cigar lighter (wedge)	1.2
Glovebox	2
Mileometer (wedge)	3
Clock (wedge)	2
Battery meter (wedge)	2
Warning lamps (wedge)	1.2
Speedometer	4
Tachometer	4

Torque wrench settings

	lbf ft	kgf m
Alternator pulley nut	29.0 to 32.5	4.0 to 4.5
Starter motor assembly bolt:		
Ducellier	5.0	0.7
Paris-Rhone	8.0	1.1
Wiper motor mounting	7.2 to 10.8	1.0 to 1.5
Alternator mounting	44.0	6.1
Front wiper arm nut	6.0 to 8.5	0.8 to 1.2
Rear wiper arm nut	4.25	0.6

1 General description

The electrical system is of 12 volt negative earth type. The battery is charged by a belt-driven alternator. A remote two-stage regulator controls the alternator output (photo). The starter motor is of the pre-engaged type.

Although repair procedures are given in this Chapter, it may be more economical over a long period to renew complete components when they develop a fault, especially if they are well worn.

2 Battery – removal and refitting

1 The battery is located in the engine compartment, on the front left-hand side.

2 Disconnect the lead from the negative (–) terminal followed by the lead from the positive (+) terminal.

3 Pull the voltage regulator from its mounting above the battery.

4 Disconnect the battery clamp and lift the battery from its mount-ing platform, taking care not to spill any electrolyte on the bodywork.

5 Refitting is a reversal of removal, but make sure that the polarity is correct before connecting the leads and do not overtighten the clamp.

3 Battery – maintenance

1 Normal weekly battery maintenance consists of checking the electrolyte level of each cell to ensure that the separators are covered by about 6 mm (0·25 in) of electrolyte. If the level has fallen, top-up the battery using distilled water only. Do not overfill. If any electrolyte is spilled, the spillage must be wiped away immediately as electrolyte attacks and corrodes very quickly any metal with which it comes in contact.

2 As well as keeping the terminals clean and covered with petroleum jelly, the top of the battery, and especially the top of the cells, should be kept clean and dry. This helps prevent corrosion and ensures that the battery does not become partially discharged by leakage through dampness and dirt.

3 Once every three months, remove the battery and inspect the

1.1 Location of the regulator unit

7.3A Alternator mounting bolt

7.3B Alternator adjustment strap location

battery tray and battery leads for corrosion (white fluffy deposits on the metal which are brittle to touch). If any corrosion is found, clean off the deposits with ammonia. Paint over the clean metal with an anti-rust/anti-acid paint.

4　At the same time inspect the battery for cracks. If a crack is found, clean and plug it with one of the proprietary compounds marketed for this purpose. If leakage through the crack has been excessive then it will be necessary to refill the appropriate cell with fresh electrolyte as detailed in Section 4. Cracks are frequently caused in the top of the battery cases by topping-up with distilled water in the middle of winter after instead of BEFORE a run. This gives the water no chance to mix with the electrolyte and so the former freezes and splits the battery case.

5　If topping-up the battery becomes excessive and the case has been inspected for cracks that could cause leakage, but none are found, the battery is being over-charged and the voltage regulator will have to be checked.

6　With the battery on the bench at the three monthly check, measure the specific gravity with a hydrometer to determine the state of charge and condition of the electrolyte. There should be very little variation between the different cells and if a variation in excess of 0·025 is present it will be due to either:

(a) Loss of electrolyte from the battery at some time caused by spillage or a leak, resulting in a drop in the specific gravity of the electrolyte when the deficiency was replaced with distilled water instead of fresh electrolyte

(b) An internal short-circuit caused by buckling of the plates or a similar malady pointing to the likelihood of total battery failure in the near future

7　The specific gravity of the electrolyte at different states of charge is given in the following table:

	Ambient temperature over 32°C (90°F)	Ambient temperature under 32°C (90°F)
Fully charged	1·210 to 1·230	1·270 to 1·290
Half discharged	1·130 to 1·150	1·190 to 1·210
Fully discharged	1·050 to 1·070	1·110 to 1·130

4　Electrolyte – replenishment

1　If the battery is in a fully charged state and one of the cells maintains a specific gravity reading which is 0·025 or more lower than the others, and a check of each cell has been made with a voltage meter to check for short circuits (a four to seven seconds test should give a steady reading of between 1·2 and 1·8 volts), then it is likely that electrolyte has been lost from the cell with the low reading.

2　If a significant quantity of electrolyte has been lost through spillage it will not suffice merely to refill with distilled water. Top-up the cell(s) with electrolyte which is a mixture of sulphuric acid and water in the ratio of 2 parts acid to 5 parts water.

3　When mixing the sulphuric acid and water, never add water to sulphuric acid – always pour the acid slowly onto the water in a glass container. If water is added to sulphuric acid, it will explode.

4　Top-up the cell(s) with freshly made electrolyte, then recharge the battery and check the hydrometer readings.

5　Battery – charging

1　In winter when a heavy demand is placed on the battery, such as when starting from cold, and much electrical equipment is continually in use, it is a good idea to occasionally have the battery fully charged from an external source at a rate of 3·5 to 4 amps.

2　Continue to charge the battery at this rate until no further rise in specific gravity is noted over a four hour period.

3　Alternatively, a trickle charger, charging at the rate of 1·5 amps can be safely used overnight.

4　Special rapid 'boost' charges which are claimed to restore the power of the battery in 1 to 2 hours are most dangerous unless they are thermostatically controlled as they can cause serious damage to the battery plates through overheating.

5　While charging the battery ensure that the temperature of the electrolyte never exceeds 37·8°C (100°F).

Caution: If the battery is being charged from an external power source whilst the battery is fitted in the car, both battery leads must be disconnected to prevent damage to the electrical circuits.

6　Alternator – maintenance and special precautions

1　Periodically wipe away any dirt or grease which has accumulated on the outside of the unit and also check the security of the leads. At the same time check the tension of the drivebelt and adjust it if necessary as described in Section 7.

2　Take extreme care when making electrical circuit connections on the car, otherwise damage may occur to the alternator. Always make sure that the battery leads are connected to the correct terminals. Before using electric-arc welding equipment to repair any part of the car, disconnect the battery leads and the alternator output lead. Disconnect the battery leads before using a mains charger. Never run the alternator with the output wire disconnected.

7　Alternator – removal and refitting

1　Disconnect the battery negative terminal.

2　Disconnect the output and regulator leads from the alternator. Note the location of of the anti-interference condenser (where fitted).

3　Slacken the mounting bolt and adjustment strap nut. Push the alternator towards the engine so that the drivebelt can be released from the pulley (photos).

4　Remove the adjustment strap nut and fully unscrew the mounting bolt. Withdraw the alternator from the engine.

5　If the alternator drivebelt requires renewal, the water pump drivebelt must first be removed as described in Chapter 2.

6　Refitting is a reversal of removal. Before tightening the mounting bolt and adjustment strap nut, tension the drivebelt by carefully levering the alternator outwards as near to the pulley end as possible. The

8.5 Alternator brush holder with cover removed (Motorola)

8.6 Alternator brush holder and brushes (Motorola)

10.3 Location of the starter motor and guard plate

10.4 Starter motor mounting bolt locations (arrowed)

tension is correct when the belt deflection under firm thumb pressure is 6·0 mm (0·25 in) midway between the two pulleys.

8 Alternator – testing and brush renewal

1   Accurate testing of the alternator requires the use of a voltmeter, ammeter, and ohmmeter. More information will be found in the Specifications, but if these instruments are not available, it is recommended that a qualified automobile electrician tests the alternator and regulator.
2   The following procedure describes the renewal of the brushes on a Motorola alternator, but the method is similar on the Ducellier or Paris-Rhone.
3   Remove the alternator as described in Section 7.
4   Unscrew the two retaining screws and remove the alternator cover.
5   Unscrew the three crosshead screws and remove the brush holder cover (photo).
6   Unscrew the two retaining screws and withdraw the brush holder (photo).
7   Measure the length of the brushes, and if they are below the

minimum specified dimension, renew them. Clean the slip rings with white spirit.
8   Refitting is a reversal of removal.

9 Starter motor – testing in the car

1   If the starter motor fails to operate, first check the condition of the battery by switching on the headlamps. If they glow brightly, then gradually dim after a few seconds, the battery is in an uncharged condition.
2   If the battery is in good condition, check the terminal connections for security. Also check that the earth lead is making good contact with the bodyframe. Check the security of the main cable and solenoid cable connections on the starter motor.
3   If the starter motor still fails to turn, check that the solenoid is being energised. To do this, connect a 12 volt test lamp and leads between the large solenoid terminal and earth. When the ignition key is turned to the starting position the lamp should glow. If not, either the supply circuit is open due to a broken wire or a faulty ignition switch, or the solenoid is defective. If the solenoid is supplying current to the starter motor, the fault must be in the starter motor.

10 Starter motor – removal and refitting

1 Disconnect the battery negative terminal.
2 Disconnect the lead from the solenoid and the main lead from the starter motor, noting that the alternator output lead is connected to the same terminal.
3 Remove the starter motor guard plate and detach the alternator belt tension strap (photo).
4 Unscrew the through bolts and mounting bolts and withdraw the starter motor from the engine/gearbox assembly (photo).
5 Refitting is a reversal of removal. Tighten the bolts to the specified torque.

11 Starter motor (Ducellier) – dismantling and reassembly

1 Disconnect the field coil supply lead. Remove the three nuts securing the bearing endplate and remove the rear cover. Remove the plastic cover.
2 Drive out the fork hinge pin. Hold the drive gear and remove the bolt and washer from the commutator end of the shaft. Remove the bearing endplate and release the positive brush and its guide.
3 Remove the yoke from the two assembly rods. Remove the solenoid securing nuts and the solenoid. Remove the pinion fork and the armature.
4 Dismantle the solenoid by holding the solenoid core by the two flats and removing the two studs, the bolts, the spring with its washer, the adjustment sleeve and its nut.
5 From the armature assembly remove the celeron washer, the steel washer, the thrust bearing snap ring, the thrust bearing and the driving gear.
6 If necessary, unsolder the positive brush from the yoke and the negative brush from the bearing endplate.
7 Clean all the parts, take care that the cleaning fluid does not get on to the field coils or armature windings. Examine all the parts carefully, if the armature commutator is scored slightly it can be cleaned-up with fine glass paper (never use emery cloth as the carborundum particles will become embedded in the copper surfaces). If necessary undercut the mica insulations using an old hacksaw blade ground to suit. If the commutator is badly worn it will require skimming on a lathe and should be left to an electrical engineer. Check the length of the brushes and renew them if they are below the specified minimum length. Make sure that they slide freely in the brush holders.
8 Using an ohmmeter between the solenoid supply terminal (flat blade) and the terminal marked DEM, check that the insulation resistance of the pull-in coil is approximately 0·37 ohms. With the ohmmeter connected between the solenoid supply terminal and the solenoid body check that the resistance of the hold-in coil is 1·08 ohms. Renew a solenoid which does not satisfy these conditions.

9 If the armature or field coil windings are suspect this is a job best left to an electrical engineer with the necessary test equipment.
10 Assembly is the reversal of the dismantling sequence. When assembling the armature, lightly oil the steel washer, the celeron washer and the splines with a very thin oil. Preset the adjusting sleeve halfway along its travel in the nut.
11 Adjust the travel of the drive pinion as described in Section 12 and fit the plastic cover.

12 Starter motor (Ducellier) – adjusting drive pinion

1 Remove the plastic cover from the solenoid nut, and disconnect the starter motor supply cable.
2 Energise the solenoid with a 12 volt supply, then push in the solenoid case using a 10 mm box spanner until the hold-in winding retains it. The pinion will now be in the engaged position.
3 Using a feeler gauge, check that the distance between the end of the drive pinion and the stop is between 0·5 and 1·0 mm (0·020 and 0·039 in). If necessary, unscrew the three mounting screws, pull out the solenoid as far as possible, and use a screwdriver in the notch on the solenoid core to restrain it whilst the nut is being adjusted. Refit the solenoid and check the clearance again.
4 Disconnect the 12 volt supply from the solenoid and allow the drive pinion to retain to its free position.
5 Using vernier calipers, measure the distance between the end of the drive pinion and the shoulder on the starter flange; this should be a maximum of 30·5 mm (1·2 in).
6 Refit the starter motor supply cable and the plastic cover.

13 Starter motor (Paris-Rhone) – dismantling and reassembly

1 Disconnect the field coil cable from the solenoid. Remove the three retaining nuts, the clamp plate, the fibre seal and the solenoid.
2 Remove the plastic cap. Drive out the hinge pin of the operating lever and its support.
3 Remove the two assembly bolts. Partly separate the endplate, commutator end from the yoke and lift the positive brush from its guide. Remove the driving end starter bearing, the operating lever, the endplate, armature and starter drive assembly and the starter drive.
4 Remove the endplate from the armature by removing the retaining bolt, the thrust washer and the friction washer. Release the endplate, the bakelite coated washer, the steel washer, the flexible washer and the second steel washer.
5 If necessary, unsolder the negative brush from the endplate and the positive brush from the yoke.
6 Cleaning, examination and servicing are identical with the procedures given for the Ducellier starter motor in Section 11. Note that the pull-in coil resistance is 0·21 ohms and the hold-in coil resistance is

Fig. 10.1 Starter motor (Ducellier) drive pinion adjustment dimension (a) (Sec 12)

1 Stop   2 Pinion

a = 0.5 to 1.0 mm

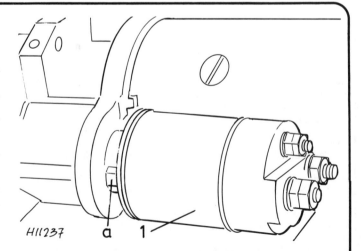

Fig. 10.2 Location of notch (a) on Ducellier solenoid (1) (Sec 12)

1·3 ohms.

7   Reassembly is a reversal of dismantling, but make sure that the bolt with the insulating tape is fitted between the two brush holders.

8   Adjust the travel of the drive pinion as described in Section 14.

14 Starter motor (Paris-Rhone) – adjusting drive pinion

1   The checking procedure is identical with that described in Section 12, except that adjustment is made by turning the adjusting sleeve with a screwdriver.

15 Fuses – general

1   The fuse box is located in the engine compartment on the left-hand front wing inner panel (photo).

2   The circuits protected by the fuses are given in the Specifications. In addition an 80 amp alternator fuse is incorporated in the printed circuit.

3   Always renew a fuse with one of similar rating and never renew it more than once without finding the source of trouble. If necessary, refer to the wiring diagrams at the end of this Chapter. Access to the fuses is gained by pulling the cover off the fuse box.

16 Instrument panel – removal and refitting

1   Disconnect the battery negative terminal.

2   Unscrew the top pad retaining screws located behind the switch clusters and the screws along the top of the instrument panel.

3   Lift off the top pad and release the upper and lower clips (photo). Prise off the tension springs by moving their tabs towards the front of the vehicle.

4   Disconnect the speedometer cable and withdraw the instrument panel so that the multi-plug connectors can be released (photos).

5   Remove the instrument panel (photo).

6   If necessary, the switch clusters can be removed by unscrewing the retaining screws and releasing the covers (photos).

7   Refitting is a reversal of removal. Make sure that the lower spring retaining clips are correctly located and check that the wiring loom is not trapped by the instrument panel.

17 Instruments and gauges – removal and refitting

1   Remove the instrument panel as described in Section 16.

2   To remove the tachometer on the Jaeger instrument panel, first unscrew the three nuts and remove the printed circuit, then unscrew the three crosshead screws and withdraw the tachometer (photo).

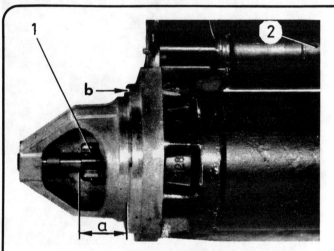

Fig. 10.3 Starter motor (Ducellier) drive pinion for free position dimension (a) (Sec 12)

1 Pinion   2 Solenoid
a = 30.5 mm   b Flange shoulder

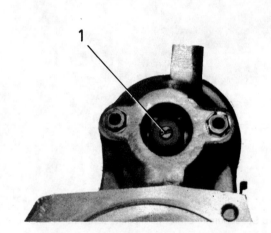

Fig. 10.4 Location of drive pinion adjusting sleeve (1) on the Paris-Rhone starter motor (Sec 14)

Fig. 10.5 Starter motor (Paris-Rhone) drive pinion free position dimension (a) 30.5 mm (Sec 14)

15.1 Fuse box with cover removed

16.3 Instrument panel upper retaining clips

16.4A Speedometer cable connector

16.4B Speedometer cable intermediate connector on the bulkhead

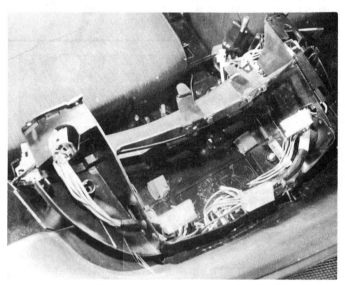

16.5 Facia panel with instrument panel removed (top view)

16.6A Removing the lighting switches

16.6B Removing the direction indicator and horn switches

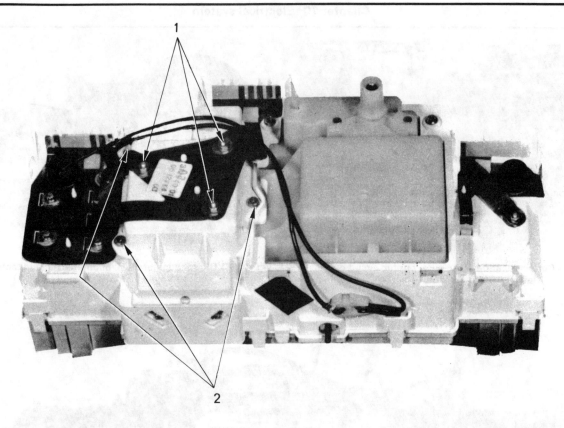

Fig. 10.6 Printed circuit retaining nut (1) and tachometer retaining screw (2) locations on the Jaeger instrument panel (Sec 17)

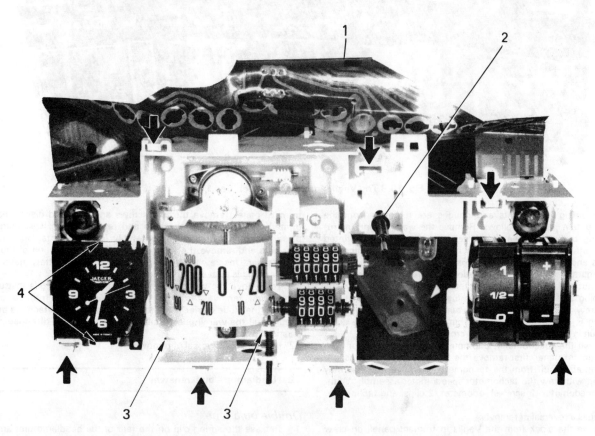

Fig. 10.7 Front cluster retaining clip locations (arrowed) on the Jaeger instrument panel (Sec 17)

1 Printed circuit 2 Warning lamp check button 3 Speedometer location pegs 4 Clock retaining clips

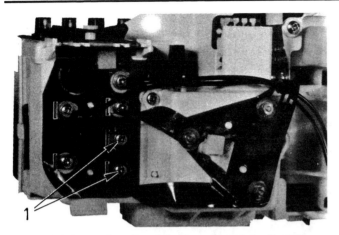

Fig. 10.8 Correct location of the outer printed circuit on the Jaeger instrument panel (Sec 17)

1 Retaining screws

Fig. 10.10 The speedometer (1), odometer (2), and tachometer (3) on the Veglia instrument panel (Sec 17)

Fig. 10.9 The Veglia instrument panel (Sec 17)

3   The remaining instruments and gauges are removed from the Jaeger instrument panel as follows. Remove the warning and instrument lighting bulbs. Remove the three plugs retaining the printed circuit. Pull off the clock knob. Using a screwdriver, disengage the plastic clips and withdraw the front cluster. Remove the two screws and two pegs and withdraw the speedometer.Disconnect the supply plug, earth nut and retaining clips and remove the clock. Unscrew the three retaining screws and remove the fuel gauge. Unscrew the two retaining screws and remove the battery meter (photos).

4   Refitting is a reversal of removal, but make sure that the outer printed circuit is fitted correctly without crossing the two straps.

5   To remove the speedometer, odometer and tachometer from the Veglia instrument panel, first remove the blanking cover and disconnect the printed circuit from the tachometer. Remove the assembly clip pins and withdraw the tachometer/speedometer assembly. Withdraw the speedometer (2 screws), odometer (2 clips) and tachometer (2 screws).

6   Refitting is a reversal of removal.

7   To remove the clock from the Veglia instrument panel, unscrew the screw and two nuts and remove the printed circuit. Remove the bulb and retaining stop, and the adjustment knob. Disengage the plastic clip and withdraw the clock from the slots.

8   Refitting is a reversal of removal.

9   To remove the battery meter and fuel gauge from the Veglia ins-

trument panel, remove the two screws and nuts and disconnect the printed circuit. Remove the bulb and retaining stop. Disengage the plastic clip and withdraw the assembly from the slots. Unscrew the two nuts and remove the fuel gauge, noting the location of the bush and washer. Unscrew the two nuts and remove the battery meter.

10   Refitting is a reversal of removal.

11   To remove the warning lamp cluster from the Veglia instrument panel, first remove the bulbs and disconnect the printed circuit. Remove the diode carrier at the top of the panel and detach the printed circuit. Pull the warning lamp cluster upwards whilst disengaging the plastic clips.

12   Refitting is a reversal of removal.

18 Headlamps – bulb renewal

Double bulb type

1   Release the spring clip on the rear of the headlamp unit and pull out the upper dipped beam bulb (photo).

2   Remove the bulb from the plastic connector (photo).

3   Refitting is a reversal of removal, but make sure that the location pip engages with the cut-out.

4   The lower halogen bulb may be either of Marchal or Cibié type. To

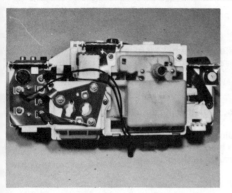

17.2 Rear view of the Jaeger instrument panel

17.3A Front view of the Jaeger instrument panel

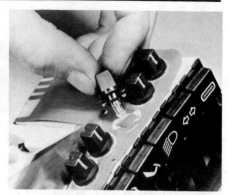

17.3B Removing an instrument panel warning lamp bulb

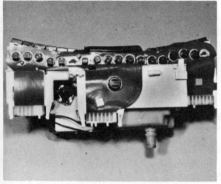

17.3C Top view of the Jaeger instrument panel

18.1 Headlamp upper dipped beam bulb location (double bulb type)

18.2 Removing an upper dipped beam bulb (double bulb type)

18.4A Halogen bulb location in the headlamp (double bulb type)

18.4B Removing a halogen bulb (Marchal) from the headlamp (double bulb type)

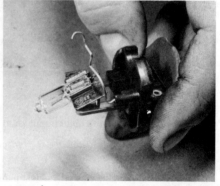

18.4C Removing a halogen bulb (Marchal) from the bulb holder

remove the Marchal type, release the spring clip and remove the bulb holder. Lift the spring and remove the bulb (photos).
5   To remove the Cibié type, turn the cover and release it from the slots, then remove the bulb holder. Lift the spring and remove the bulb.
6   Refitting is a reversal of removal, but make sure that the tab and pip engage with the cut-out and hole.

Single bulb type
7   Pull the connector and cover from the rear of the headlamp.
8   Disengage the retaining clips and withdraw the bulb.
9   Refitting is a reversal of removal, but make sure that the tabs engage with the cut-outs.

All types
10   Note that halogen type bulbs must only be handled when cold, and care should be taken to avoid touching the glass. If the glass is inadvertently touched, clean it with methylated spirit.

19 Headlamps – alignment

1   Accurate headlamp alignment should be carried out by a Citroën garage. However, in an emergency the following procedure will provide an acceptable light pattern.
2   Position the car on a level surface with tyres correctly inflated. Start the engine and allow it to idle, then check that the ground clearance lever is in the normal running position. The car should be positioned approximately 10 metres (33 feet) in front of a wall or garage door.
3   Mark the headlamp bulb centres on the wall.
4   Switch on the main beam and check that the areas of maximum illumination coincide with the marks on the wall. If not, turn the plastic knobs located on the rear of the headlamps; the lower knob controls vertical movement and the side knobs control horizontal movement (photo).

Fig. 10.11 Fuel gauge and battery meter on the Veglia instrument panel (Sec 17)

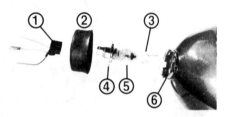

Fig. 10.12 Single bulb headlamp components (Sec 18)

    1 Connector   4 Flange
    2 Cover   5 Bulb
    3 Clips   6 Reflector

Fig. 10.13 Headlamp adjustment knob locations (Sec 19)

    1 Horizontal adjustment   3 Horizontal adjustment
    2 Vertical adjustment

5   Switch off the engine when the adjustment is completed.

20 Headlamps – removal and refitting

1   Remove the headlamp bulbs as described in Section 18.
2   Unscrew the two retaining bolts and remove the clamp and front grille (photos).
3   Turn the plastic retainers on the rear of the headlamps through 90° and remove them.
4   Withdraw the headlamp from the front of the car (photos).
5   Refitting is a reversal of removal, but adjust the beam as described in Section 19.

21 Lamp bulbs – renewal

1   Lamp bulbs should always be renewed with the identical type and rating as listed in the Specifications. Since the lamp circuits are fused it is always worth while checking the relevant fuse before purchasing new bulbs.

Front lamp cluster

2   Press on the transparent cover and move it outwards, then use a screwdriver to disengage the inner end of the cluster.
3   Slide the cluster inwards and withdraw it from the housing as shown in the photograph.
4   Disengage the retaining clips (if fitted), then remove the plastic connector.
5   Push and twist the bulb to remove it (photo).
6   Refitting is a reversal of removal.

Rear lamp cluster

7   Open the boot lid or rear door.
8   On estate models, unscrew the retaining screws and pivot the cluster from the body.
9   Push back the retaining lug and remove the bulbholder (photo).
10   Push and twist the bulb to remove it.
11   Refitting is a reversal of removal.

Rear number plate lamp

12   Open the boot lid or rear door.
13   Pull off the transparent cover (if fitted).
14   Push and twist the bulb to remove it.
15   Refitting is a reversal of removal.

Boot lamp

16   Ease the festoon type bulb from the terminal springs, or push and twist the bayonet type bulb (photo).
17   Refitting is a reversal of removal.

Cigar lighter lamp

18   Rotate the ashtray a quarter of a turn and remove it.
19   Pull down the black lead support and remove the bulb holder.
20   Push and twist the bulb to remove it.
21   Refitting is a reversal of removal.

Glovebox lamp

22   Tilt the bulb slightly and remove it.
23   Refitting is a reversal of removal.

Interior lamp

24   Pull the tab and hinge the cover down.
25   Ease the festoon type bulb from the terminal springs (photo).
26   Refitting is a reversal of removal.

22 Wiper arm – removal, refitting and adjustment

1   Make sure that the wiper motor is stopped in the parked position. Lift the cover from the securing nut (photo).
2   Unscrew the securing nut and prise the arm from the spindle with a wide blade screwdriver. Take care not to damage the paintwork (photo).
3   Refitting is a reversal of removal. With the wiper motor in the parked position, the arm must be positioned as shown in Figs. 10.14 or 10.15. Tighten the wiper arm securing nut to the specified torque.

23 Wiper blade – renewal

1   Lift the wiper arm away from the windscreen.
2   With a small screwdriver, release the plastic lug and withdraw the wiper blade from the arm (photo).
3   Refitting is a reversal of removal.

24 Wiper motor – removal, overhaul and refitting

1   Disconnect the battery negative terminal.
2   Remove the wiper arm as described in Section 22.
3   Unscrew the mounting bolts and disconnect the multiplug (photo).
4   Withdraw the wiper motor (photo).
5   Unscrew the two bolts and withdraw the end cover.
6   Remove the armature (photo).
7   Examine the brushes and renew them if they are less than the minimum specified length (photo).
8   Clean and check the armature commutator; if it is less than the specified minimum diameter, renew it.
9   Reassembly and refitting are a reversal of removal. Make sure that the brushes are located correctly on the commutator.

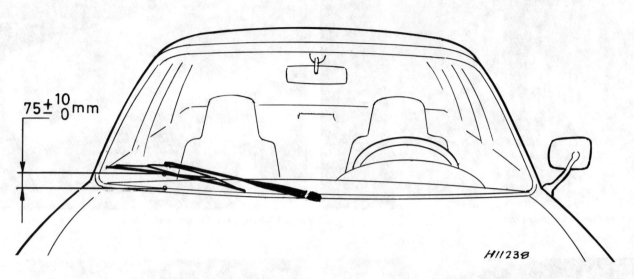

Fig. 10.14 Front windscreen wiper adjustment dimension (Sec 21)

$75 {\pm} {}^{10}_{0}$ mm

H11238

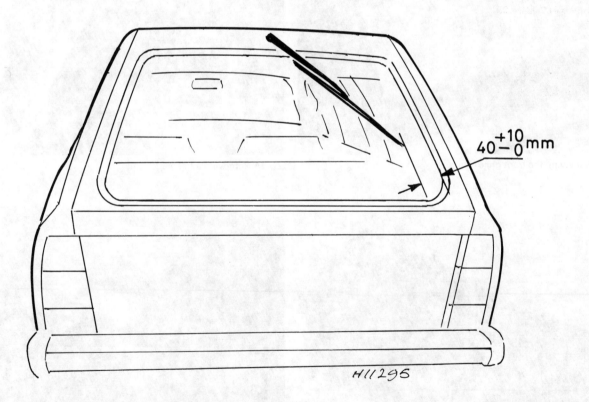

$40 {}^{+10}_{-0}$ mm

H11295

Fig. 10.15 Tailgate wiper adjustment dimension (Sec 21)

19.4 Headlamp adjustment knob

20.2A A front grille clamp retaining bolt

20.2B Removing the front grille clamp

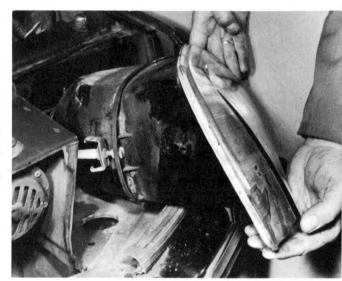

20.4A Removing a headlamp unit

20.4B A headlamp unit (double bulb type)

20.4C Headlamp retaining clip location

21.3 Removing a front lamp cluster

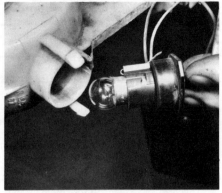
21.5 Removing a bulb from a front lamp cluster

21.9 Removing a bulb holder from a rear lamp cluster

21.16 Boot lamp bulb location

21.25 Interior lamp bulb location

22.1 Wiper arm cover location

22.2 Removing the wiper arm

23.2 Removing the wiper blade from the arm

24.3 Location of the wiper motor and multiplug

24.4 The wiper motor assembly

24.6 Removing the wiper motor armature

24.7 Location of the three wiper motor brushes

25 Fault diagnosis – electrical system

Symptom	Reason/s
Starter fails to turn engine	Battery discharged Battery terminal leads loose or earth lead not securely attached to body Loose or broken connections in starter motor circuit Starter motor switch or solenoid faulty Starter brushes badly worn or sticking, or brush wire connections loose Commutator dirty or worn Starter motor armature faulty Field coils earthed
Starter motor turns engine very slowly	Battery in discharged condition Starter brushes worn or sticking, or brush wires loose Loose wires in starter motor circuit
Starter spins but does not turn engine	Pinion or flywheel gear teeth broken or badly worn
Starter motor noisy or excessively rough engagement	Pinion or flywheel gear teeth broken or badly worn Starter motor retaining bolts loose
Battery will not hold charge for more than a few days	Battery defective internally Electrolyte level too low or electrolyte too weak due to leakage Battery terminal connections loose or corroded Alternator drivebelt slipping Alternator not charging Regulator defective
Lights do not come on	If engine not running, battery discharged Loose, disconnected or broken connections Light switch faulty Bulb filament burnt out or blown fuse
Lights work erratically	Battery terminal or earth connections loose Lights not earthed properly Lights switch faulty
Horn operates all the time	Horn switch faulty
Horn fails to operate	Cable connections loose, broken or disconnected Blown fuse Horn faulty
Horn operates intermittently	Loose connections
Windscreen wipers fail to work	Blown fuse Wiring connections loose, disconnected or broken Wiper motor faulty Wiper mechanism jammed or seized
Wiper arms move sluggishly	Wiper motor faulty Wiper mechanism sticking or worn

Wiring harness code (all wiring diagrams)

No mark/
AV	Front wiring	MC1	Centre console earth (Pallas/Super)
AR	Rear wiring	MC2	Centre console earth (others)
C	Boot harness	P.AR	Interior lamp harness
CFR	Reversing lamp harness	PC	Boot lid harness
CL	Air conditioning	PD	Rear RH door harness
CM	Torque converter	PG	Rear LH door harness
CO	Horn air compressor	PR/H	Rear door harness
D	Diagnostic harness	R	Rear
F	Rear interior lamp switch (Pallas); handbrake (others)	RD	Rear RH side
FV	Flying lead	RG	Rear LH side
H	Tailgate	RT	Rear view exterior mirror
IC	Fuel injection (body)	T	Roof
IM	Fuel injection (engine)	TB	Instrument panel
K	Console	TO	Sunroof
LG	Window winder	VF	Front brake pad wear
M	Engine	V	Electric fan

Wiring diagram colour code

B or Bc	White	N	Black
Bl	Blue	Na	Natural
Gr	Grey	Or	Orange
Ic	Neutral	R	Red
J	Yellow	V or Ve	Green
Mr	Brown	Vi	Violet
Mv	Mauve		

Key to Fig. 10.16 (1975 models)

1	Front RH sidelamp and direction indicator	26	Coolant temperature switch	53	Switch for LH window-winder
2	RH headlamp	27	TDC sensor	54	Flasher unit
3	RH horn	28	Switch for reversing lamps	55	Ignition switch
4	LH horn	30	Relay for window-winder	56	Rheostat for fuel gauge
5	LH headlamp	31	Relay for heater unit	57	Switch for interior lamp
6	Front LH sidelamp and direction indicator	32	Relay for electric fan	58	Switch for heated rear window
8	HT sensor	33	Front RH brake unit	59	Lighting for heater controls
9	Ignition coil	34	Wiper motor	60	Contact for handbrake
10	Blower motor	35	Blower motor	61	RH control unit (lighting) and lighting rheostat
11	Starter motor	36	Hydraulic fluid pressure switch	62	Lighting for instrument panel
12	Alternator	37	Stoplamp switch	63	LH control unit:
13	Distributor	38	Fuse box		Direction indicators and hazard warning switch
14	Electric fan thermal switch	39	Front LH brake unit		Horn switch
15	Compressor for horns	41	Front RH door lighting switch		Windscreen wiper switch
16	Compressor relay	42	RH window-winder motor		Windscreen washer switch
17	Battery	43	Glovebox lighting	64	Rear RH lamp cluster
18	Voltage regulator	44	Accessory terminal	65	Boot lamp
19	Sensor for No 4 cylinder	45	Lighting for pneumatic oil gauge	66	Heated rear window
21	Windscreen washer pump	46	Front LH door lighting switch	67	RH numberplate lamp
22	Socket for fault-finding (diagnostic)	47	LH window-winder motor	68	LH numberplate lamp
23	Oil pressure switch	48	Central interior lamp	69	Contact for boot lamp
24	Idle cut-off	49	Cigar-lighter and lighting	70	Rear LH lamp cluster
25	Oil temperature switch	50	Ashtray lighting		
		51	Handbrake warning lamp flasher unit		
		52	Switch for RH window-winder		

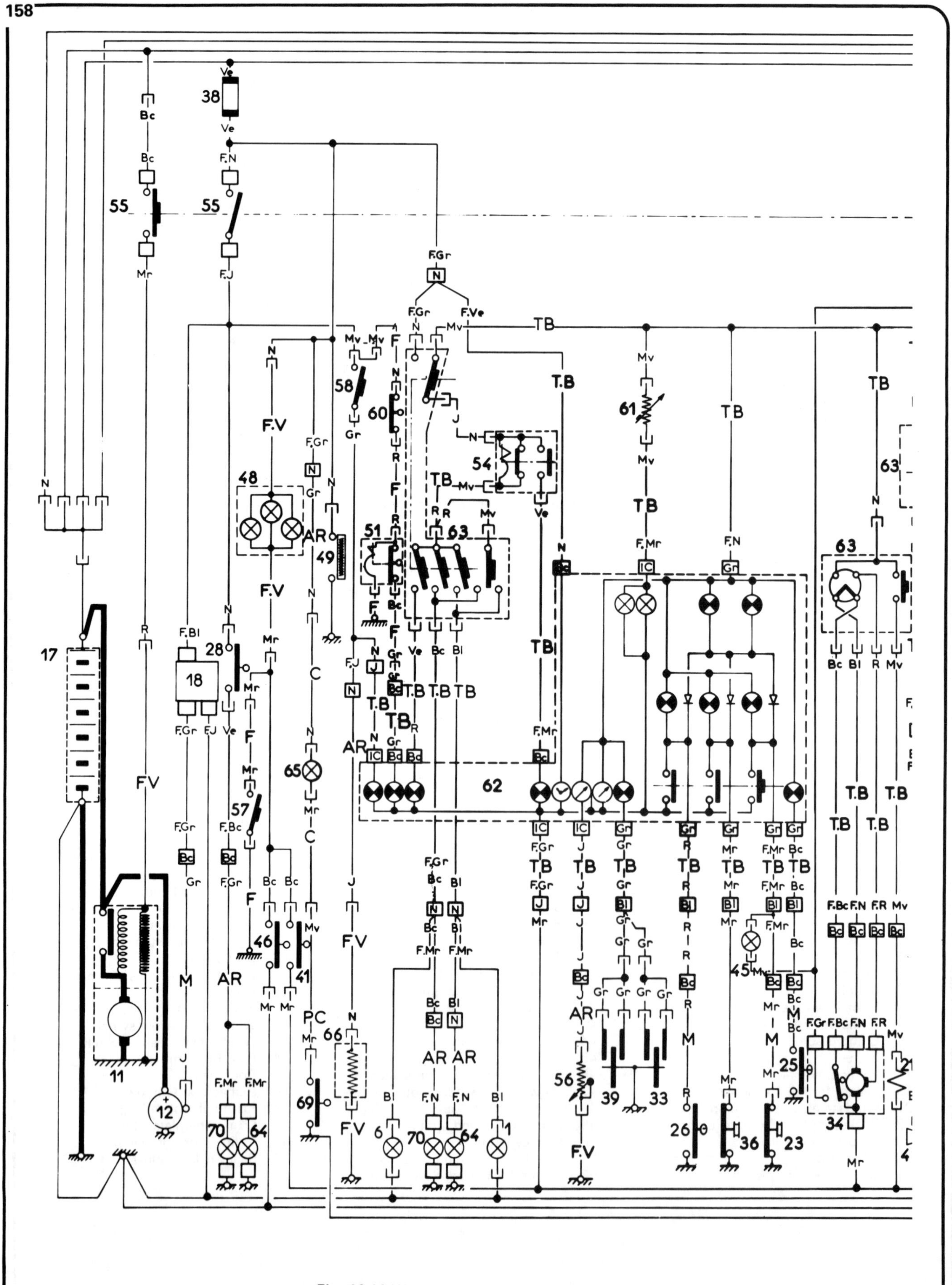

Fig. 10.16 Wiring diagram for 1975 models

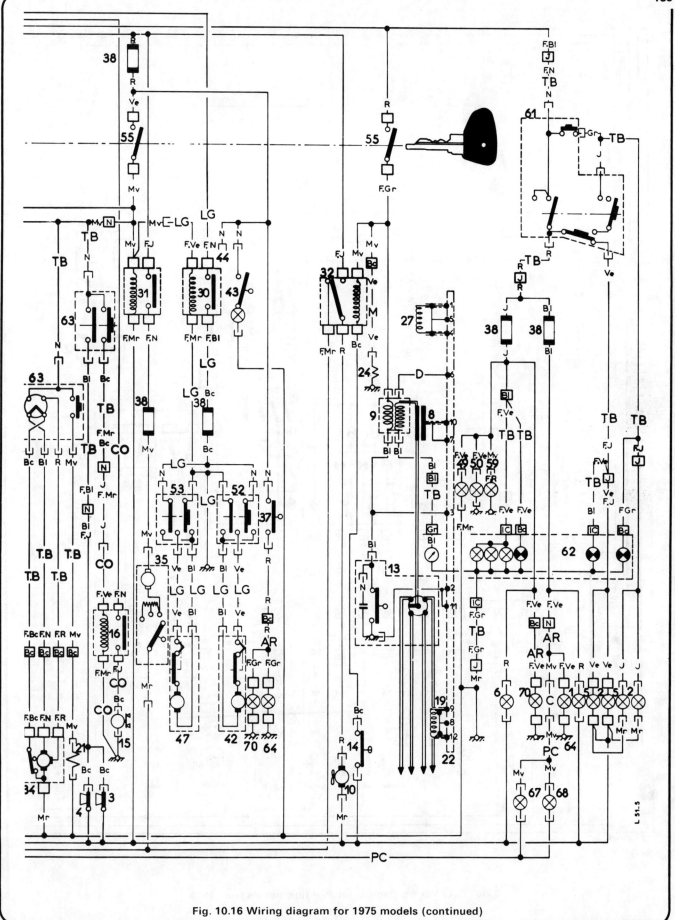

Fig. 10.16 Wiring diagram for 1975 models (continued)

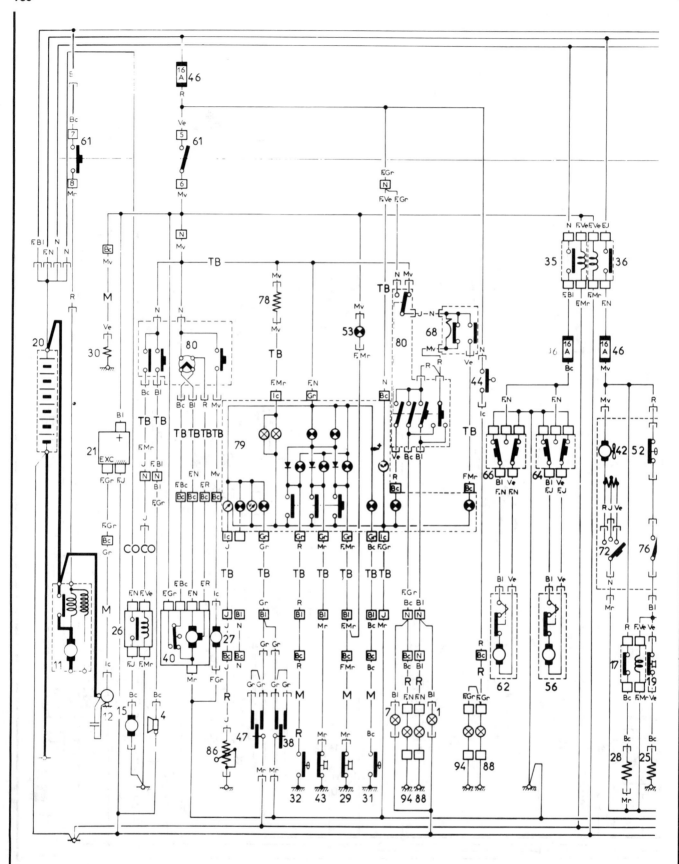

Fig. 10.17 Wiring diagram for Prestige models from 1976

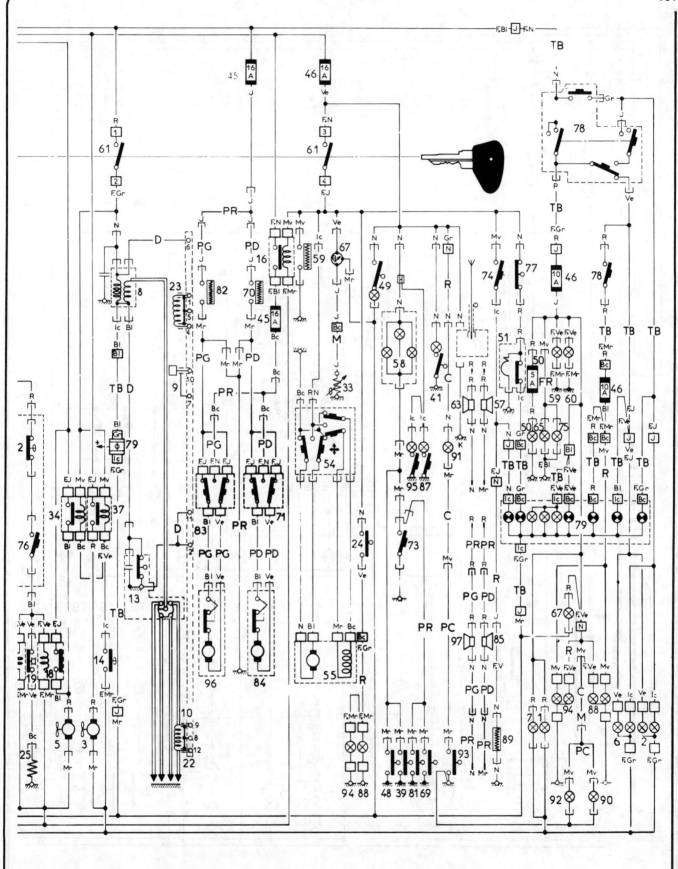

Fig. 10.17 Wiring diagram for Prestige models from 1976 (continued)

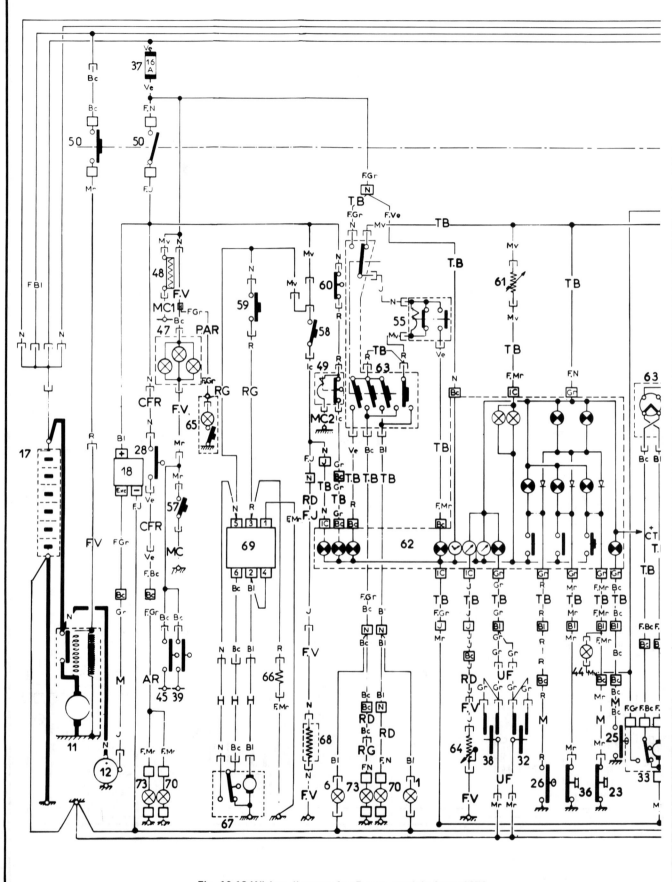

Fig. 10.18 Wiring diagram for Estate models from 1976

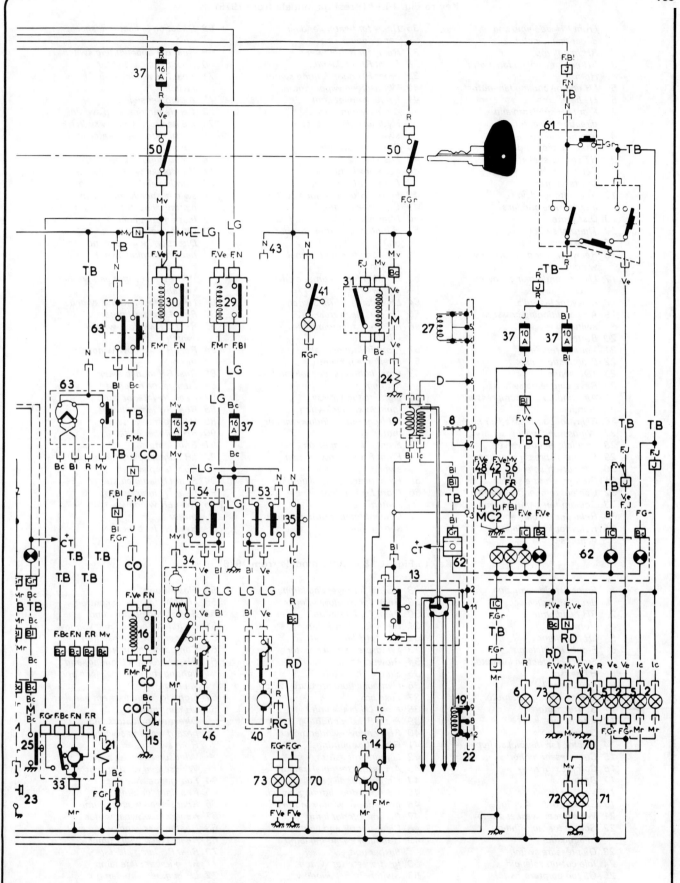

Fig. 10.18 Wiring diagram for Estate models from 1976 (continued)

164

Key to Fig. 10.17 (Prestige models from 1976)

1   Front RH sidelamp and
    direction indicator
2   RH headlamp
3   RH engine cooling fan motor
4   Horn
5   LH engine cooling fan motor
6   LH headlamp
7   Front LH sidelamp and
    direction indicator
8   Ignition coil and anti-
    interference condenser
9   HT sensor socket
10 Sensor for No 4 cylinder
11 Starter motor
12 Alternator and anti-
    interference condenser
13 Distributor
14 Thermal switch
15 Horn compressor
16 Relay for rear door window-
    winder
17 LH air-conditioning blower
    relay
18 Relay for fast-idle
19 Air-conditioning pressure
    switch
20 Battery
21 Voltage regulator
22 Diagnostic socket
23 TDC sensor
24 Reversing lamp switch
25 Air-conditioning compressor
    clutch
26 Relay for compressed air horn
27 Windscreen washer pump
28 Fast idle electro-valve
29 Engine oil pressure switch
30 Idle cut-off solenoid
31 Oil temperature switch
32 Coolant temperature switch
33 Coolant temperature sensor
34 Relay for LH blower
35 Relay for front window-
    winders

36 Relay for heating and air-
    conditioning
37 Relay for RH blower
38 Front RH brake unit
39 Front RH door lighting switch
40 Windscreen wiper motor
41 Under-bonnet light
42 Air blower motor
43 Hydraulic fluid pressure
    switch
44 Stoplamp switch
45 Fuse box (2 fuses)
46 Fuse box (6 fuses)
47 Front LH brake unit
48 Front LH door lighting switch
49 Glovebox lighting
50 Map-reading lamp and fuse
51 Handbrake warning flasher
    unit
52 Air-conditioning thermal
    switch
53 Lighting for pneumatic oil
    gauge
54 LH outside mirror switch
55 LH outside mirror
56 RH front door window-
    winder motor
57 Front RH loudspeaker
58 Interior lamp centre
59 Cigar lighter on console and
    lighting
60 Lighting for ashtray
61 Ignition/starter switch
62 LH front door window-winder
    motor
63 Front LH loudspeaker
64 Front RH window-winder
    switch
65 Front heater control lighting
66 Front LH window-winder
    switch
67 Coolant temperature gauge
    and lighting

68 Direction indicator flasher
    unit
69 Rear RH door lighting switch
70 Rear RH cigar-lighter
71 Rear RH window-winder
    switch
72 Air blower switch
73 Centre interior lamp switch
74 Heated rear window switch
75 Lighting for rear heater
    controls
76 Air conditioning switch
77 Handbrake warning switch
78 Lighting and rear foglamp
    switch, speedo and tacho
    lighting rheostat
79 Instrument panel
80 LH control unit:
    Direction indicators and
    hazard warning switch
    Horn switch
    Windscreen wiper and washer
    switch
81 LH rear door lighting switch
82 Rear LH cigar-lighter
83 Rear LH window-winder
    switch
84 Rear RH window-winder
    motor
85 Rear RH loudspeaker
86 Fuel gauge rheostat
87 Rear RH interior lamp
88 Rear RH lamp cluster
89 Heated rear window
90 RH number plate lamp
91 Boot lamp
92 LH number plate lamp
93 Boot lamp switch
94 Rear LH lamp cluster
95 Rear LH interior lamp
96 Rear LH window-winder
    motor
97 Rear LH loudspeaker

Key to Fig. 10.18 (Estate models from 1976)

1   Front RH sidelamp and
    direction indicator
2   RH headlamp
4   Horn
5   LH headlamp
6   Front LH sidelamp
7   Front LH direction indicator
8   HT sensor
9   Ignition coil
10 Engine cooling fan motor
11 Starter motor
12 Alternator
13 Distributor
14 Electric fan thermal switch
15 Compressor for horns
16 Compressor relay
17 Battery
18 Voltage regulator
19 Sensor for No 4 cylinder
21 Windscreen washer pump
22 Socket for fault-finding
    (diagnostic)
23 Oil pressure switch
24 Idle cut-off solenoid
25 Oil temperature switch
26 Coolant temperature switch
27 TDC sensor

28 Switch for reversing lamps
29 Relay for window-winder
30 Relay for heater unit
31 Relay for electric fan
32 Front RH brake unit
33 Windscreen wiper motor
34 Blower motor
35 Stoplamp switch
36 Hydraulic fluid pressure switch
37 Fuse box
38 Front LH brake unit
39 Front RH door lighting switch
40 RH window-winder motor
41 Glove-box lighting
42 Lighting for ashtray
43 Accessory terminal (radio)
44 Lighting for oil gauge
45 LH front door lighting switch
46 LH window-winder motor
47 Central interior lamp
48 Cigar-lighter and light
49 Handbrake warning lamp
    flasher unit
50 Ignition/starter switch
53 Switch for RH window-
    winder
54 Switch for LH window-
    winder

55 Flasher unit
56 Lighting for heater controls
57 Switch for interior lamp
58 Switch for heated rear window
59 Rear screen wiper switch
60 Contact for handbrake
61 RH control unit (lighting) and
    lighting rheostat for tacho and
    speedo
62 Lighting for instrument panel
63 LH control unit:
    Direction indicators and
    hazard warning switch
    Horn switch
    Windscreen wiper switch
    Windscreen washer switch
64 Fuel gauge rheostat
65 Rear interior lamp
66 Rear screen washer pump
67 Rear screen wiper motor
68 Heated rear window
69 Rear screen wiper timer
70 Rear RH lamp cluster
71 RH number plate lamp
72 LH number plate lamp
73 Rear LH lamp cluster

Key to Fig. 10.19 (Pallas models, 1977/78)

1 RH sidelamp:
  Front RH direction indicator
2 RH headlamp:
  Main beam
  Dipped beam
4 Horn
5 LH headlamp:
  Main beam
  Dipped beam
6 LH sidelamp:
  Front LH direction indicator
8 HT sensor (connector)
9 Ignition coil
10 RH electric fan
11 Starter
12 Alternator
13 Distributor
14 Water temperature switch (fan)
15 Horn compressor
16 Relay for compressor
17 Battery and supply connecting block
18 Voltage regulator
19 Sensor for cylinder No 4
21 Windscreen washer pump
22 Diagnostic socket
23 Engine oil pressure switch
24 Idle cut-off
25 Engine oil thermal switch
26 Engine coolant temperature switch
27 TDC sensor
28 Switch for reversing lamps
30 Relay for window-winder
31 Relay for heater unit
32 Relay for electric fan
33 Front RH brake unit
34 Windscreen wiper motor
35 Air blower
36 Hydraulic fluid pressure switch
37 Stoplamp switch
38 Fuse box
39 Front LH brake unit
40 Switch for hydraulic fluid level
41 Switch for front LH door
42 Switch for front RH door
43 RH window winder motor
44 Loudspeaker on RH door
45 Glove compartment lighting
46 Central interior lamp
47 Map reading lamp
48 Ashtray lighting
49 Cigar lighter
50 Switch for RH window winder
51 Interior lamp switch
52 Heater unit control lighting
53 Handbrake 'on' flasher
54 Switch for LH window winder
55 Heated rear window switch
56 Handbrake switch
57 Choke warning lamp
58 Switch on choke control

59 Radio terminal
61 Lighting control unit:
  Rheostat for tachometer and speedometer lighting
62 Dashboard:
  Lighting for instrument dials
  Lighting for tachometer and speedometer
  Tachometer
  Thermal voltmeter
  Fuel gauge
  Clock
  Warning lamp for handbrake
  Warning lamp for main beam
  Warning lamp for direction indicators
  Warning lamp for side and tail lamps
  Warning lamp for hazard warning device
  Warning lamp for hydraulic fluid (pressure and level)
  Warning lamp for engine oil pressure
  Warning lamp for water temperature
  Warning lamp for engine oil temperature
  Warning lamp for low fuel level in tank
  Warning lamp for front brake wear
  Warning lamp for dipped beam
  Warning lamp for heated rear window
  Warning lamps for emergency 'stop'
  Test-button for 'stop' warning lamps
63 LH control unit:
  Direction indicators
  Hazard warning lamps
  Horns
  Windscreen wiper and washer
64 Lighting for pneumatic gauge
65 Ignition and starter switch
66 LH rear-view mirror
67 Switch for rear-view mirror
68 LH window-winder motor
69 Loudspeaker on LH door
70 Anti-theft lighting
71 Flasher unit
72 Windscreen washer timer
73 Fuel gauge rheostat
74 Switch for rear RH door
75 Rear RH interior lamp
76 Rear RH lamp cluster:
  Tail lamp
  Direction indicator
  Stoplamp
  Reversing lamp
77 Boot lighting
78 Number plate RH lighting
79 Heated rear window
80 Number plate LH lighting
81 Switch for boot lighting
82 Switch for rear LH door
83 Rear LH interior lamp
84 Rear LH lamp cluster:
  Tail lamp
  Direction indicator
  Stoplamp
  Reversing lamp

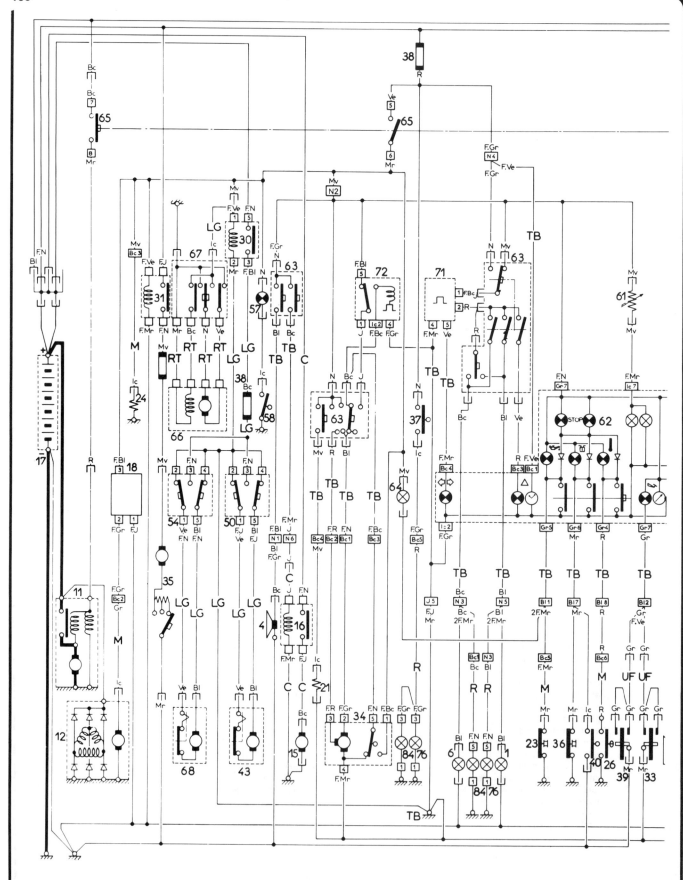

Fig. 10.19 Wiring diagram for Pallas models, 1977/78

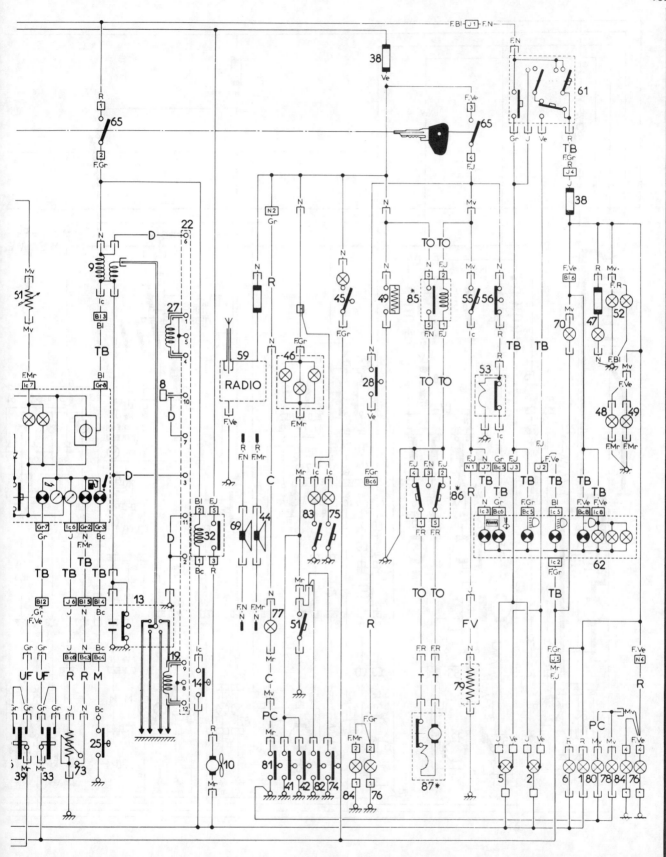

Fig. 10.19 Wiring diagram for Pallas models, 1977/78 (continued)

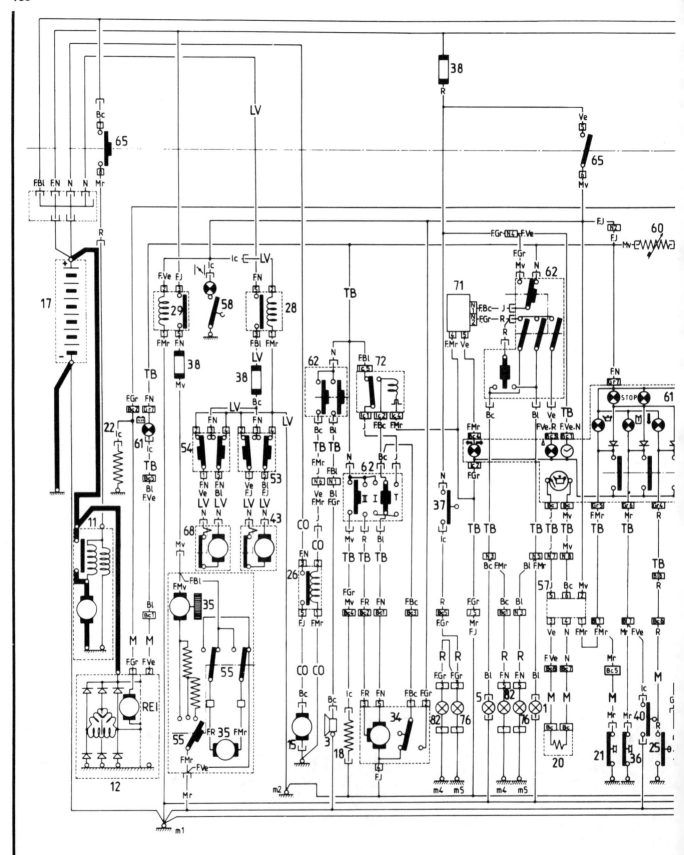

Fig. 10.20 Wiring diagram for CX 2400 (carburettor model), 1978 to 1980

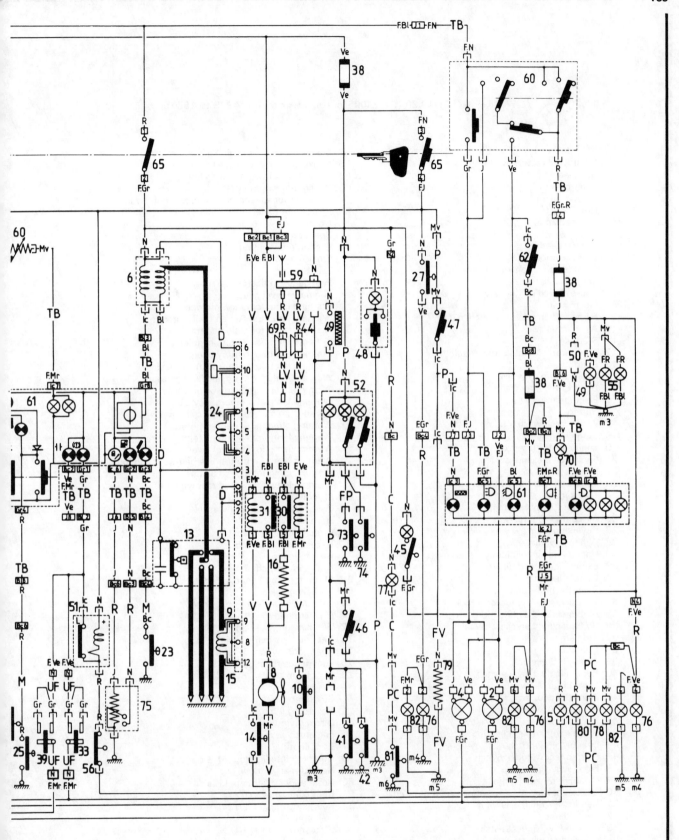

Fig. 10.20 Wiring diagram for CX 2400 (carburettor model), 1978 to 1980 (continued)

Key to Fig. 10.20 (CX 2400 – carburettor model, 1978 to 1980)

1 RH sidelamp:
   Front RH direction indicator
2 RH headlamp:
   Main beam
   Dipped beam
3 Horn
4 LH headlamp:
   Main beam
   Dipped beam
5 LH sidelamp:
   Front LH direction indicator
6 Ignition coil
7 Socket for coil HT sensor
8 Electric fan
9 HT socket on reference spark plug
10 Air thermal switch
11 Starter
12 Alternator with integrated regulator
13 Distributor
14 Water thermal switch
15 Horn with compressor
16 Electric fan resistor
17 Battery
18 Windscreen washer pump
19 Diagnostic socket
20 Engine oil level sensor
21 Engine oil pressure switch
22 Idle cut-off
23 Engine oil thermal switch
24 TDC sensor
25 Coolant thermal switch
26 Air compressor relay
27 Reversing lamp switch
28 Window winder relay
29 Heater and air conditioning relay
30 Electric fan speed relay
31 Electric fan relay
33 Front RH brake unit
34 Windscreen wiper motor
35 Air blower and air flap motor
36 Hydraulic fluid pressure switch
37 Stoplamp switch
38 Fuse box
39 Front LH brake unit
40 Hydraulic fluid level switch
41 Front LH door switch
42 Front RH door switch
43 RH window winder motor
44 RH loudspeaker
45 Glove compartment lighting
46 Interior lamp switch
47 Heated rear window switch
48 Front swivelling lamp
49 Cigar lighter and lighting
50 Socket for map reading lamps (sun roof fitted)
51 Handbrake 'on' flasher unit
52 Centre lamp
53 RH window winder switch
54 LH window winder switch
55 Air conditioning control lighting
56 Handbrake switch

57 Electronic unit for engine oil gauge
58 Choke control with warning lamp
59 Radio control with warning lamp
60 RH lighting control unit:
   Rheostat for speedometer and tachometer lighting
61 Instrument panel:
   Lighting
   Speedometer
   Tachometer lighting
   Clock
   Tachometer
   Fuel gauge indicator
   Engine oil level gauge
   Warning lamp for rear foglamps
   Warning lamp for side and tail lamps
   Warning lamp for main beams
   Warning lamp for direction indicators
   Warning lamp for battery charge
   Warning lamp for hazard warning device
   Warning lamp for hydraulic fluid pressure
   Warning lamp for engine oil pressure
   Warning lamps for emergency 'stop'
   Test-button for 'stop' warning lamps
   Warning lamp for water temperature
   Warning lamp for engine oil temperature
   Warning lamp for low fuel level
   Warning lamp for front brake pad wear and handbrake wear
   Warning lamp for dipped beams
   Warning lamp for heated rear window
62 LH control unit:
   Windscreen wiper and washer
   Horns
   Direction indicators
   Hazard warning lamps
   Rear foglamps
65 Anti-theft switch
68 Motor for front window-winder, LH side
69 LH loudspeaker
70 Ignition key switch
71 Flasher unit
72 Windscreen wiper timer unit
73 Rear door switch, LH side
74 Rear door switch, RH side
75 Fuel gauge rheostat
76 Rear lamp cluster, RH side:
   Tail lamp
   Stoplamp
   Reversing lamp
   Direction indicator
   Foglamp
77 Boot lighting
78 Number plate lighting, RH side
79 Heated rear window
80 Number plate lighting, LH side
81 Boot lighting switch
82 Rear lamp cluster, LH side:
   Tail lamp
   Stoplamp
   Reversing lamp
   Direction indicator
   Foglamp

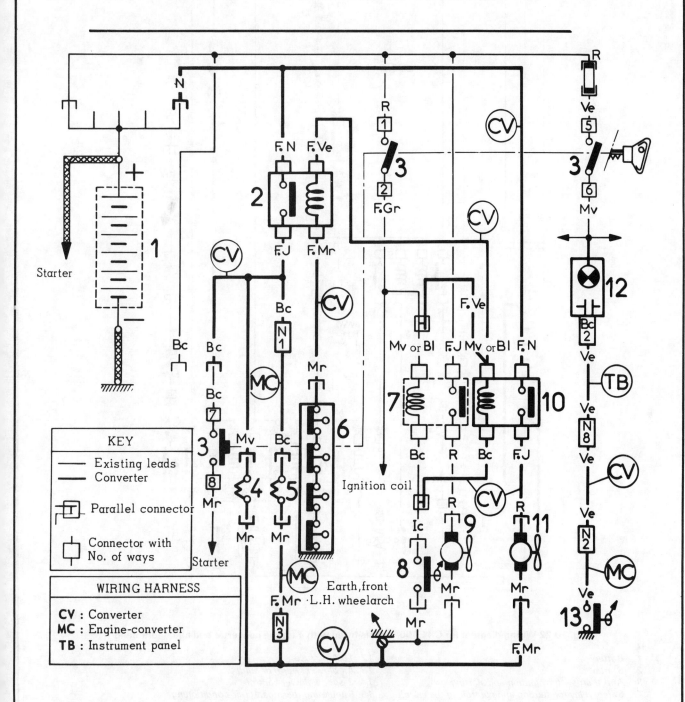

Fig. 10.21 Wiring diagram for models fitted with a torque converter (January 1976 on)

1   Battery
2   Relay
3   Ignition and starting contact
4   Electro-valve controlling fast idle
5   Electro-valve controlling clutch
6   Gearbox switch housing
7   Control relay for electric fan
8   Thermal switch controlling the electric fans
9   Electric fan
10 Relay controlling supplementary electric fan
11 Supplementary electric fan
12 Warning lamp for converter oil temperature
13 Converter oil thermal switch

KEY

— Existing leads
— Converter

Parallel connector

Connector with No. of ways

WIRING HARNESS

CV : Converter
MC : Engine-converter
TB : Instrument panel

Starter

Ignition coil

Earth, front L.H. wheelarch

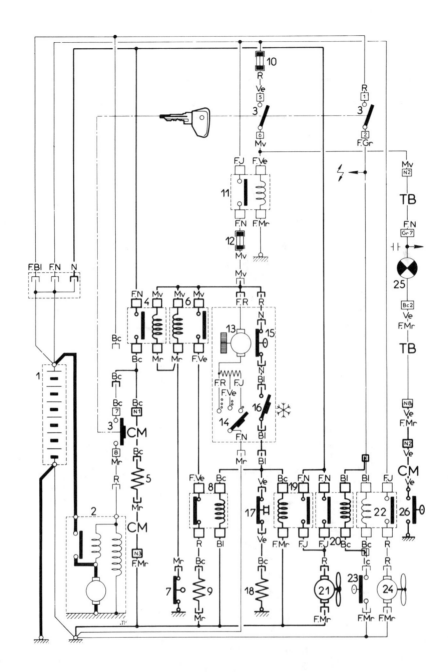

Fig. 10.22 Wiring diagram for CX 2400 models fitted with a torque converter and air conditioning

1 Battery
2 Starter
3 Anti-theft switch, ignition and starting
4 Safety relay for starting and controlling the clutch
   electro-valve (converter)
5 Clutch electro-valve (converter)
6 Control relay for idling speeds (converter):
   Relay energized = normal idling speed
   Relay not energized = fast idling speed
7 Switch housing on gearbox (converter)
8 Fast idle control relay (air-conditioning):
   Relay energized = contact open = fast idle
9 Electro-valve for fast idle:
   Energized = normal idle
   Not energized = fast idle
10 16 Amp fuse
11 General control relay

12 16 Amp fuse
13 Air blower (warm or cold)
14 3-speed blower control
15 Regulating thermostat (air-conditioning)
16 Air-conditioning switch
17 Pressure switch on de-watering tank (air-conditioning)
18 Compressor clutch (air-conditioning)
19 Control relay for LH supplementary electric fan (21) (air-
   conditioning)
20 Control relay for electric fan (21) (cooling of radiator water)
21 Supplementary electric fan for condenser (air conditioning) and
   water radiator (cooling)
22 Control relay for RH electric fan (24) (cooling)
23 Thermal switch on water radiator (cooling control)
24 RH electric fan for gearbox oil cooler and coolant radiator
25 Converter oil temperature warning lamp (converter)
26 Thermal switch for converter oil (converter)

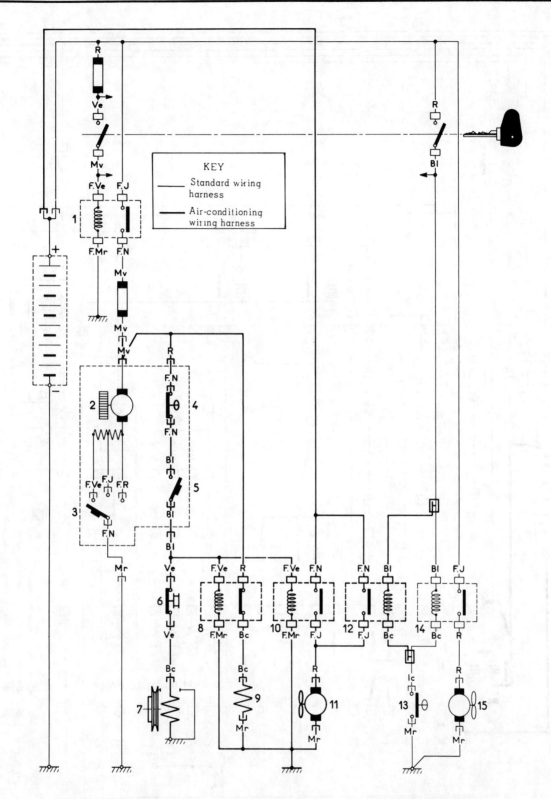

Fig. 10.23 Wiring diagram for models manufactured from July 1976 with air conditioning

1 Heater relay (Standard)	7 Compressor clutch	12 Relay for LH supplementary electric fan (cooling)
2 Air blower (Standard)	8 Control relay for fast-idle electro-valve	13 Control thermostat for electric fans (Standard)
3 Speed control for blower (Standard)	9 Fast idle electro-valve	14 Relay for RH electric fan (Standard)
4 Regulating thermostat	10 Relay for LH supplementary electric fan (air-conditioning)	15 Electric cooling fan (Standard)
5 Air-conditioning switch	11 Supplementary LH electric fan (cooling)	
6 Pressure switch (on de-watering tank)		

KEY
Standard wiring harness
Air-conditioning wiring harness

174

Fig. 10.24 Wiring diagram for models with fuel injection manufactured from May 1977 on

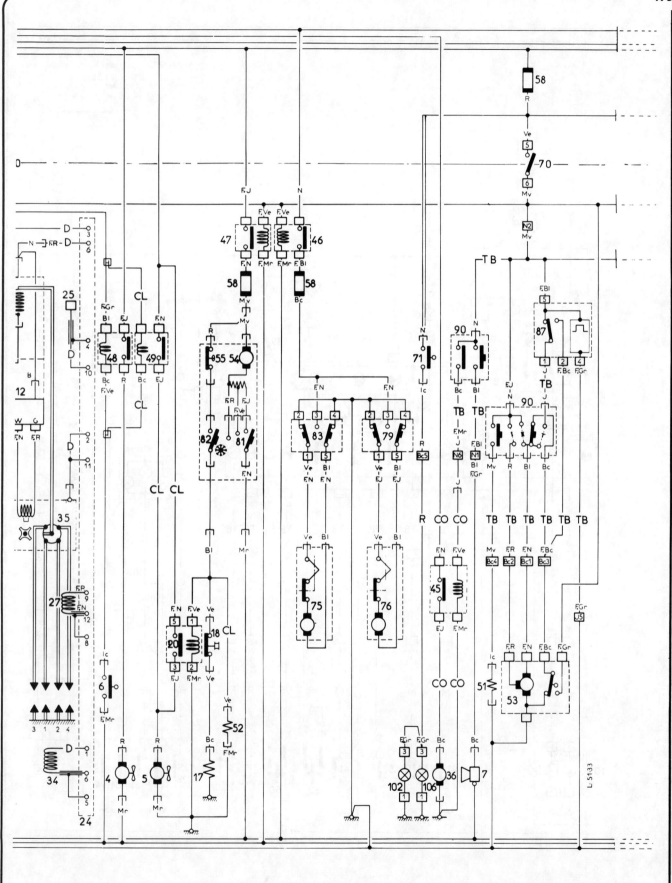

Fig. 10.24 Wiring diagram for models with fuel injection manufactured from May 1977 on continued

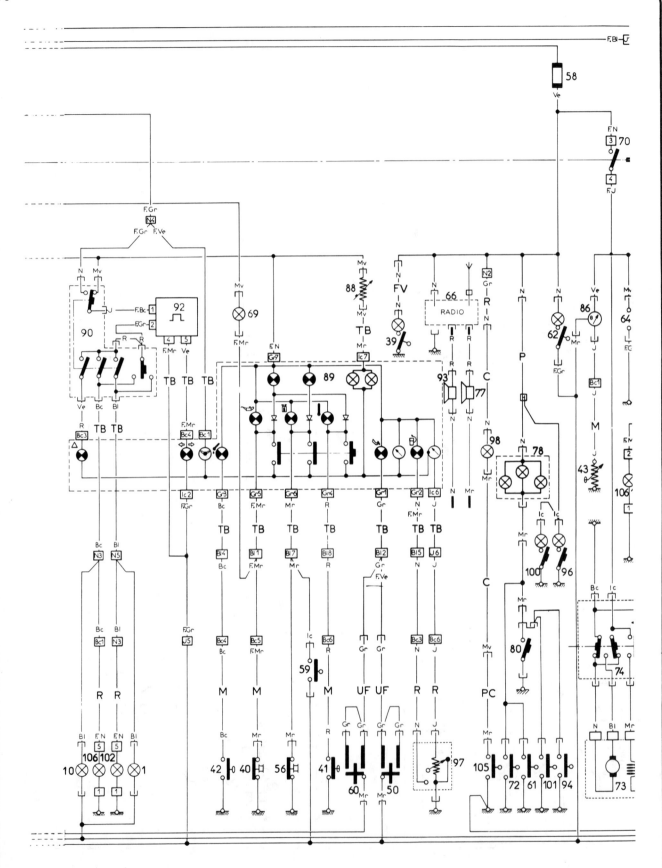

Fig. 10.24 Wiring diagram for models with fuel injection manufactured from May 1977 on continued

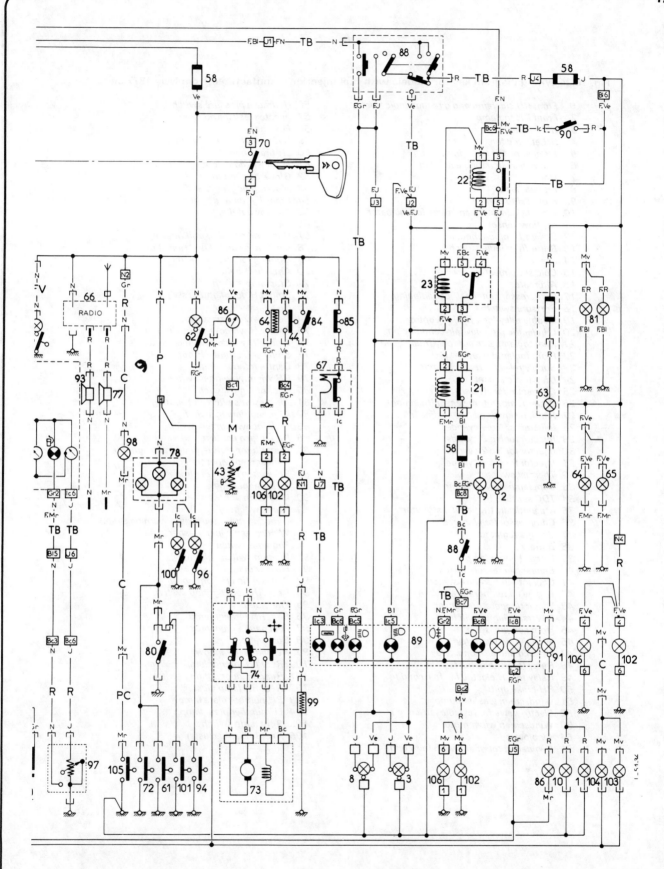

Fig. 10.24 Wiring diagram for models with fuel injection manufactured from May 1977 on continued

Fig. 10.24 Wiring diagram key for models with fuel injection manufactured from May 1977 on

1   Front RH sidelamp and direction indicator
2   Front RH foglamp
3   RH headlamp
4   RH electric fan
5   LH electric fan (air-conditioning)
6   Thermal switch for electric fan
7   Horn
8   LH headlamp
9   Front LH foglamp
10 Front LH sidelamp and direction indicator
11 Air-flow sensor
12 Coil and ignition module
13 Butterfly spindle switch
14 Starter
15 Cold start injector
16 Alternator
17 Compressor clutch (air-conditioning)
18 Pressure switch
19 Double relay for injection control
20 LH electric fan relay (air-conditioning)
21 Rear foglamp cut-out relay (main beam)
22 Front foglamp relay
23 Supply relay for rear foglamps
24 Diagnostic socket
25 Connector for HT sensor
26 Water temperature sensor (Injection)
27 Ignition sensor on No 4 cylinder
28 Injector for No 4 cylinder
29 Injector for No 3 cylinder
30 Injector for No 2 cylinder
31 Injector for No 1 cylinder
32 Thermal switch
33 Supplementary air control
34 TDC sensor
35 Magnetically triggered distributor
36 Compressor for air horns
37 Voltage regulator
38 Battery
39 Under-bonnet lamp
40 Engine oil pressure switch
41 Coolant temperature switch
42 Engine oil temperature switch
43 Water temperature sensor
44 Reversing lamp switch
45 Horn compressor relay
46 Window-winder relay
47 Heating and air-cond. relay
48 Relay for RH electric fan
49 Relay for LH electric fan (air-cond.)
50 RH brake unit
51 Windscreen washer pump
52 Electro-valve for fast idle (air-cond.)
53 Windscreen wiper motor
54 Air blower
55 Regulating thermal switch (air-cond.)

56 Hydraulic pressure switch
57 Injector resistor housing
58 Fuse box
59 Hydraulic fluid level switch
60 LH brake unit
61 Front RH door lighting switch
62 Glove-box lighting
63 Map-reading lamp and fuse
64 Cigar-lighter and lighting
65 Ashtray lighting
66 Radio
67 Handbrake flasher unit housing
68 Electronic control unit (injection)
69 Lighting for pneumatic oil-gauge
70 Anti-theft switch
71 Stoplamp switch
72 Front LH door lighting switch
73 Rear view mirror
74 Rear view mirror switch
75 Front LH window-winder motor
76 Front RH window-winder motor
77 Speaker (in front RH door)
78 Centre interior lamp
79 RH window-winder switch
80 Interior lamp switch
81 Air-blower switch and lighting
82 Air-conditioning switch
83 LH window-winder switch
85 Handbrake contact
86 Water temperature gauge and lighting
87 Windscreen wiper timer
88 RH switch unit for lighting
89 Instrument panel
90 LH switch unit:
     Horn switch
     Direction indicator/hazard warning switch
     Windscreen wiper/washer switch
     Foglamp switch
91 Ignition switch lighting
92 Flasher unit
93 Speaker (in LH front door)
94 Rear RH door lighting switch
95 Fuel pump
96 Rear RH interior lamp
97 Fuel gauge rheostat
98 Boot lamp
99 Heated rear window
100 Rear LH interior lamp
101 Rear LH door lighting switch
102 Rear RH lamp cluster
103 RH number plate lamp
104 LH number plate lamp
105 Boot lamp switch
106 Rear LH lamp cluster

Chapter 11 Suspension and steering

For modifications, and information applicable to later models, see Supplement at end of manual

Contents

Specifications

Front suspension

Type	Independent, with upper and lower arms and steering knuckle, hydropneumatic suspension cylinders supplied with fluid from main hydraulic system via front height corrector, anti-roll bar, bump and rebound stops
Suspension height (normal position)	165 ± 8.0 mm (6.49 ± 0.31 in)

Anti-roll bar:
Diameter	23.0 mm, (0.91 in) except GTI, 24.0 mm (0.94 in)
Bearing preload	30 kg f (66 lbf)

Rear suspension

Type	Independent, with trailing arms, hydropneumatic suspension cylinders supplied with fluid from main hydraulic system via rear height corrector, anti-roll bar, bump and rebound stops

Suspension height (normal position):
Saloons	215.0 ± 8.0 mm (8.46 ± 0.31 in)
Estates	228.0 ± 8.0 mm (8.98 ± 0.31 in)
Anti-roll bar diameter	17.5 mm (0.69 in)

Steering

Type	Rack-and-pinion with optional power steering, steering column with universal joint and coupling

Turning circle (between walls):
Saloon	11.8 m (38.7 ft)
Estate	12.7 m (41.7 ft)

Steering wheel diameter:
Manual	410 mm (16.14 in)
Power	380 mm (15.00 in)

Front wheel alignment

Camber	$0° \pm {13' \atop 29'}$
Castor	1° 40' to –1°
Toe-in	1.0 to 4.00 mm (0.04 to 0.16 in)

Steering angle:
Inner wheel	43° 30' + 1°
Outer wheel	32° 50' + 1°

Rear wheel alignment

Camber	0° – 24'
Toe-in (not adjustable)	0.04 to 0.16 in (1.0 to 4.0 mm)

Wheels and tyres

Roadwheels . . . . Pressed steel 5½J x 14 or light alloy option

Tyres:

	Manual steering	Power steering
Saloon – front	185SR14	185HR14
Saloon – rear	175SR14	175HR14
Saloon – rear (alternative)	185SR14	185HR14
Estate – front	185SR14	185HR14
Estate – rear	185SR14	185HR14
Estate – front (alternative)	185HR14	185R14
Estate – rear (alternative)	185HR14	185R14

Tyre pressures in bar (lbf/in^2)

	Manual steering	Power steering
Saloon – front	2 (29)	1.9 (28)
Saloon – rear	2.1 (30)	2.1 (30)
Estate – front	2 (29)	1.9 (28)
Estate – rear	2.2 (32)	2.1 (30)

Torque wrench settings

	lbf ft	kgf m
Track-rod locknuts	26 to 29	3.6 to 4.0
Track-rod clamp bolts	6.5	0.9
Steering gear to crossmember	18.0 to 20.5	2.5 to 2.8
Anti-roll bar link (upper):		
Bush	21.5	3.0
Locking nut	32.5 to 36.0	4.5 to 5.0
Anti-roll bar link (lower)	32.5 to 36.0	4.5 to 5.0
Anti-roll bar bearing	19.5	2.7
Anti-roll bar preload clamp	9.5	1.3
Height corrector control rod clamp	11.0	1.5
Anti-roll bar to trailing arm	43.5	6.0
Steering column flange	9.5 to 10.0	1.3 to 1.4
Steering column coupling	22.5 to 24.5	3.1 to 3.4
Steering column	13.5 to 15.0	1.9 to 2.1
Steering rack balljoint	36 to 40	5.0 to 5.5
Steering crossmember to subframe	18.0 to 20.5	2.5 to 2.8
Track-rod end	65.0 to 72.5	9.0 to 10.0
Steering wheel retaining nut	45.5 to 58.0	6.0 to 8.0
Front upper balljoint	50.5	7.0
Front suspension upper arm pivot	87 to 94	12.0 to 13.0
Front lower balljoint	36.0	5.0
Front suspension lower arm pivot	87 to 94	12.0 to 13.0
Flexible brake hose retaining nut	15.5 to 17.5	2.1 to 2.4
Height corrector collar	10.75	1.5
Steering wheel retaining nut	43.5 to 58.0	6.0 to 8.0
Rear hub bearing nut:		
Saloon	253 to 326	35 to 45
Estate	398 to 470	55 to 65
Wheel bolts	50.5 to 65.0	7.0 to 9.0
Rear anti-roll bar clamp bolt:		
5.0 mm (0.197 in) thick	58.0	8.0
6.0 mm (0.236 in) thick	72.5	10.0
Suspension pneumatic sphere	21.5	3.0

1 General description

The front suspension is of independent hydropneumatic type, incorporating upper and lower arms supporting the steering knuckle. The suspension cylinders are supplied with hydraulic fluid from the main hydraulic system via the front height corrector which is actuated by the front anti-roll body. Bump and rebound straps are fitted to the upper suspension arms (photo). The anti-roll bar is attached to the upper suspension arms with two links.

The rear suspension is also of independent hydropneumatic type, incorporating trailing arms. The suspension cylinders are supplied with hydraulic fluid from the main hydraulic system via the rear height corrector which is actuated by the rear anti-roll bar. The trailing arms are fitted with bump and rebound stops, and the anti-roll bar is attached to the trailing arms.

The ground height clearance may be adjusted with a lever mounted inside the car, the lever being connected by operating rods to the front and rear height correctors (photo). Automatic damping is incorporated in the suspension cylinders.

The steering is of rack-and-pinion type, mounted on a crossmember attached to the front subframe. The steering column incorporates a universal joint and a coupling. Power steering is fitted to some models and this system incorporates a self-centering action which varies according to the speed of the car.

2 Maintenance and inspection

1   At the intervals specified in Routine Maintenance, check and adjust the front wheel alignment, inspect the condition of the flexible bellows, balljoint dust excluders and suspension hydraulic lines, and renew them as necessary.
2   At the same time, check the tightness of all nuts and bolts on the suspension and steering components in accordance with the torque wrench figures in the Specifications.
3   The suspension spheres should be checked by your dealer at the specified intervals and re-charged with gas to bring them up to the correct pressure.

3 Front suspension upper arm – removal, servicing and refitting

1   Jack-up the front of the car and support it on axle stands. Chock the rear wheels.
2   Remove the roadwheel. Move the ground clearance lever fully to the rear in the minimum height position.
3   Loosen the hydraulic system pressure regulator bleed screw 1 to 1½ turns.

1.1 The front suspension bump and rebound stops in the front subframe

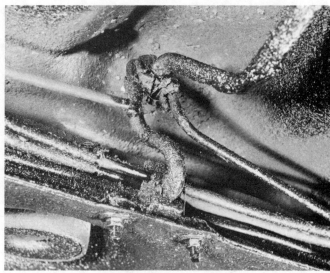

1.3 Ground clearance lever operating rod joint

3.4A Removing the nut ...

3.4B ... and anti-roll bar link from the upper suspension arm

3.4C Removing the front suspension cylinder pushrod split-pin

3.4D Removing the front suspension cylinder pushrod

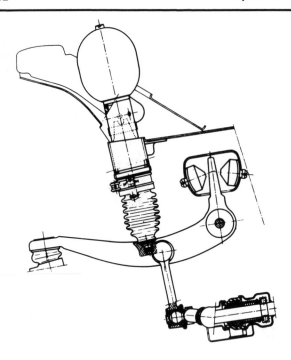

Fig. 11.1 Sectional view of front suspension upper arm, cylinder and anti-roll bar (Sec 1)

4   Unscrew the nut securing the anti-roll bar link to the suspension arm. The link must now be separated from the arm (photos). To do this use a wedge type fork and drive it between the link balljoint and the arm. If the link is very tight, an extractor may be required. Bend the legs and remove the pin securing the cylinder pushrod to the suspension arm, then remove the pushrod to allow room for the extractor to be fitted (photos).

5   Unscrew the steering knuckle upper balljoint nut, and separate the joint with a suitable separator whilst supporting the steering knuckle.

6   Support the steering knuckle with an axle stand, taking care not to strain the flexible brake hose.

7   Unscrew the nut and drive the pivot bolt through the suspension arm and subframe.

8   Remove the upper suspension arm from the subframe, making a special note of any shims located between the front of the arm and the subframe.

9   Mount the arm in a soft-jawed vice and use a soft metal punch to drive out the spacer and thrust washers.

10   Remove the taper roller bearings and identify them side for side.

11   Drive out the bearing outer races with the punch and identify these also side for side.

12   Clean all components with paraffin and dry with a lint-free cloth. Examine the bearings for wear and damage and the races for pitting. Renew them as necessary.

13   Using a tube of suitable diameter, drive the bearing races into the arm.

14   If new components are being fitted, the correct thickness of the thrust washers must be determined to obtain a bearing preload of 50 kgf (110 lbf). If possible, obtain the Citroen tool No 6311-T from your dealer to check the dimensions, otherwise proceed as follows.

15   Fit the tapered bearings on their races and use a suitable size bolt to determine the distance between the outer surfaces of the bearing inner races.

16   Measure the length of the spacer with vernier calipers.

17   The difference between the dimensions obtained in paragraph 15 and 16 represent the overall thickness of the thrust washers. The rear thrust washer must always be 9.34 mm (0.37 in) thick, therefore the front thrust washer thickness will be the difference between the rear washer thickness and the overall thickness.

18   Make sure that the thrust washer seals are serviceable; if not, renew them.

19   Coat the bearings with a multi-purpose grease, then fit them into the suspension arm followed by the thrust washers (in their correct

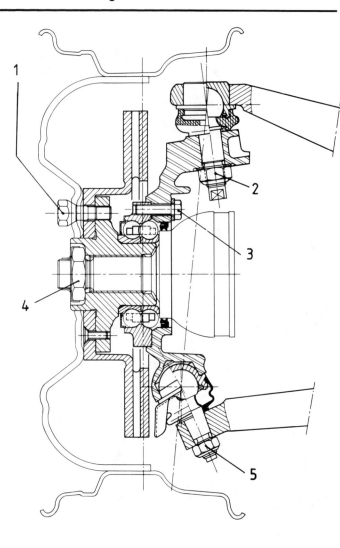

Fig. 11.2 Cross-section of the steering knuckle (Sec 1)

1	Wheel bolt	4	Driveshaft nut
2	Upper balljoint nut	5	Lower balljoint nut
3	Hub retaining bolt		

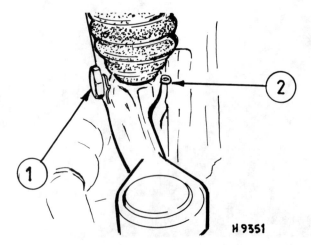

Fig. 11.3 Location of anti-roll bar link nut (1) and cylinder pushrod retaining pin (2) (Sec 3)

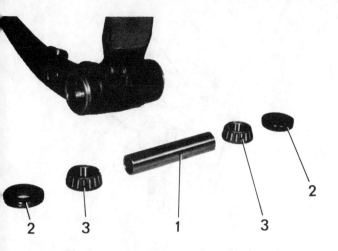

Fig. 11.4 Front suspension upper arm components (Sec 3)

1 Spacer
2 Thrustwashers
3 Taper roller bearings

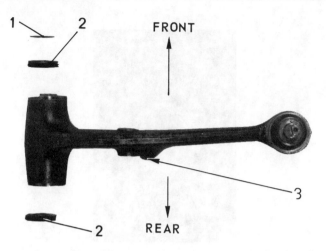

Fig. 11.5 Front suspension upper arm fitting diagram (Sec 3)

1 Shim
2 Thrustwashers
3 Boss

Fig. 11.6 Separating the lower balljoint (Sec 4)

1 Separator tool

Fig. 11.7 Track-rod end retaining nut (1) (Sec 5)

positions), and the spacer.

0 If the upper balljoint requires renewal it may be prised from the arm using a hydraulic press. Press the new balljoint into the arm in the same manner, but take care not to distort the arm. Never fit a used balljoint, as it will have insufficient grip.

1 Refitting is a reversal of removal, but do not forget to fit any previously renewed shims between the front of the arm and the subframe. Tighten all nuts to the specified torque, and tighten the pressure regulator bleed screw. Note that the boss on the arm nut face towards the rear of the car (see Fig. 11.5).

Front suspension lower arm – removal, servicing and refitting

Jack-up the front of the car and support it on axle stands. Chock the rear wheels.

Remove the roadwheel. Move the ground clearance lever fully to the rear in the minimum height position.

Loosen the hydraulic system regulator bleed screw 1 to 1½ turns.

Disconnect the brake disc pad wear warning lamp wires from the boom.

Unscrew the lower balljoint nut (photo) and separate the joint with suitable separator.

Prise the plastic cover from the end of the pivot bolt, then unscrew the nut.

Draw the pivot bolt through the suspension arm and subframe,

then withdraw the arm. Make a special note of the location of the shims at the front and rear of the arm as these determine the steering castor angle.

8 Mount the arm in a soft-jawed vice.

9 To facilitate the removal of the plastic encased bushes it will be necessary to obtain an expanding dowel or a tap of suitable diameter. Pull the bushes from each side of the arm whilst turning them slowly.

10 To remove the outer rubber bushes, obtain Citroen tool No 6314-T and extract both bushes from the arm.

11 Thoroughly clean the interior of the arm.

12 To fit the new rubber bushes, first coat the exterior contact arm with a rubber solution, then press the bush into the arm with a suitable press, at the same time making sure that the location lug is in line with the rib on the suspension arm.

13 Smear silicon grease on the exterior of the plastic bush, then drive it into the rubber bush with a wooden or hide mallet.

14 Make sure that the two bushes are touching at the centre of the arm by compressing them in a vice. Temporarily insert the pivot bolt through the bushes to check that they are aligned with each other. If they are not, obtain Citroen tool No 6312-T and insert the expander over the bush joint. The expander can be driven out when the pivot bolt is fitted.

15 The remaining refitting procedure is a reversal of removal, but make sure that the shims are fitted in the correct position. Tighten all nuts to the specified torque and tighten the pressure regulator bleed screw.

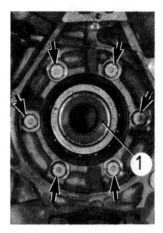

Fig. 11.8 Front hub (1) retaining bolt location – arrowed (Sec 5)

H9352

Fig. 11.9 Steering knuckle lower balljoint (Sec 5)

1   Bolts   2   Circlip   3   Guard plate

5   Front steering knuckle – removal, servicing and refitting

1   Remove the wheel embellisher, and extract the split-pin from the driveshaft nut.
2   Have an assistant depress the footbrake (with the engine running), then loosen the nut; an extension bar will be necessary as the nut is very tight.
3   Jack-up the front of the car and support it on axle stands. Chock the rear wheels.
4   Remove the roadwheel and release the handbrake.
5   Move the ground clearance lever fully to the rear in the minimum height position.
6   Loosen the hydraulic system pressure regulator bleed screw 1 to 1½ turns.
7   Remove the brake disc as described in Chapter 9.
8   Unscrew the handbrake cable adjustment unit and locknut and detach the cable from the steering knuckle; note the number of shims at the end of the cable.
9   Disconnect the brake caliper supply hose from the rigid hydraulic line and the support bracket.
10 Unscrew the steering knuckle lower balljoint nut and detach it from the lower suspension arm with a suitable separator.
11 Unscrew the upper balljoint nut and detach it from the steering knuckle with a suitable separator.
12 Unscrew the track-rod end nut and detach the track-rod end from the steering knuckle with a suitable separator.
13 Unscrew and remove the driveshaft nut and withdraw the steering knuckle from the car.
14 Unscrew the retaining bolts and remove the disc cooling deflector (photo).
15 Unscrew the union bolt and support bolts and detach the brake pipes from the steering knuckle.
16 Press the handbrake mechanism as described in Chapter 9.
17 Unscrew the bolts from the rear of the knuckle and withdraw the hub complete with bearing.
18 Drive the hub oil seal from the steering knuckle with a soft metal punch.
19 Unscrew the lower balljoint retaining bolts and remove the guard plate.
20 Extract the circlip and remove the dust cover,
21 To remove the lower balljoint, obtain the Citroen extractor No 6305-T and slide hammer 1671-T, and clamp the tool over the balljoint. Extract the balljoint from the steering knuckle. It is possible to remove the balljoint from its hub recess if the hub or disc is well supported while the suspension arm is temporarily reconnected to the balljoint taper pin and the arm then driven downwards using one or two heavy blows.
22 Clean all components with paraffin and dry with a lint-free cloth. Examine the bearing for wear by trying to move the outer race laterally; if excessive play is evident, or if the bearing sounds rough when spun in the hand, it must be renewed. To do this, use a suitable

puller to remove the outer race and ball bearings, then use the same puller to remove the remaining inner race from the hub. Press the new bearing onto the hub with a tube located on the inner races; do no attempt to dismantle the new bearing.
23 Examine the lower balljoint for wear and renew it if necessary. Obtain a new hub oil seal.
24 Refitting is a reversal of removal, but the following additional points should be noted.
   (a) Use long bolts and spacers to press the lower balljoint into the steering knuckle
   (b) After assembling the guard plate, peen the plate over the balljoint retaining bolts to lock them
   (c) Fit the hub oil seal squarely into the steering knuckle
   (d) Tighten all nuts and bolts to the specified torque. Lock the driveshaft nut with a new split-pin
   (e) Refit the brake hose as described in Chapter 9
   (f) Adjust the handbrake as described in Chapter 9
   (g) Check the wheel alignment

6   Front anti-roll bar – removal and refitting

1   Jack-up the front of the car and support it on axle stands. Chock the rear wheels then remove the front wheels.
2   Move the ground clearance lever fully to the rear in the minimum height position.
3   Loosen the hydraulic system pressure regulator bleed screw 1 to 1½ turns.
4   Remove the spare wheel from the engine compartment.
5   Mark the anti-roll bar and height corrector clamp in relation to each other, then unscrew the clamp bolt and remove the clamp.
6   Detach the exhaust pipe guard from beneath the exhaust pipe (where fitted).
7   Remove the rubber shields from the wheel arches.
8   Unscrew the nuts securing the anti-roll bar links to the upper suspension arms.
9   Separate the links from the arms with an impact wedge. If they are very tight, it will be necessary to remove the pin and disconnect the suspension cylinder pushrods from the arms in order to use an extractor.
10 Release the rubber covers from the anti-roll bar bearings, then mark the positions of the spring clamps.
11 Loosen the clamp bolts to release the spring pressure.
12 Unscrew and remove the two brake valve retaining bolts, then remove the plastic covers from the sides of the subframe.
13 Unscrew the anti-roll bar retaining bolts, and withdraw the bar from the car.
14 If necessary, remove the components shown in Fig. 11.13 from the anti-roll bar. Note that the split bearing shells incorporate a location notch.
15 Examine all components for wear and damage, and renew them if such is evident.

Fig. 11.10 Front wheel bearing (1) and hub (2) (Sec 5)

Fig. 11.11 Height connector clamp (1) on the anti-roll bar, and
exhaust pipe guard (2) (Sec 6)

Fig. 11.12 Front anti-roll bar spring clamp (1) and retaining bolts
(2) (Sec 6)

16 Assemble the components on the anti-roll bar and lubricate them with a multi-purpose grease.
17 Jack-up the suspension on both sides until the upper arms are in their normal central running positions. Citroen tool No 6301-T may be used for this operation, but if not available, make sure that the centre of each driveshaft nut is an equal distance from the ground, which must be level.
18 Refit the anti-roll bar and insert the links in the upper suspension arms. Fit the nuts and hand tighten them.
19 Insert and hand tighten the bearing retaining bolts.
20 Compress the springs and tighten the clamp bolts with the clamp in the previously noted position. Tighten the bearing bolts to the specified torque. If a new anti-roll bar has been fitted, proceed as follows to obtain the correct bearing preload. First obtain Citroen tools No 6401-T.
21 Compress the springs with the tools to hold the split bearing shells in place. Check that both bearings touch the subframe; if one does not touch, fit shims in the gap as necessary.
22 With the bearing bolts tightened, compress the springs until coil-bound, then loosen the two nuts on the tools half a turn. Make sure that the anti-roll bar is located centrally in the subframe by measuring the protrusion on each side; a tolerance of 2.0 mm (0.079 in) is allowed.
23 Tighten the clamp bolts and remove the tools.
24 The remaining refitting procedure is a reversal of removal, but tighten all nuts and bolts to the specified torque. Adjust the front height corrector if necessary as described in Section 12. Tighten the pressure regulator bleed screw.

7 Rear hub bearing – removal

1 Jack-up the rear of the car and support it on axle stands. Apply the handbrake and remove the rear roadwheel.
2 Move the ground clearance lever fully to the rear in the minimum height position.
3 Loosen the hydraulic system pressure regulator bleed screw 1 to 1½ turns.
4 Remove the brake disc as described in Chapter 9 (photo).
5 Using an Allen key inserted through the holes in the hub, unscrew and remove the flange retaining bolts together with the lockwashers (photo).
6 Withdraw the hub and flange from the trailing arm, and prise out the plastic cover (photo).
7 The hub must now be held stationary while the nut is unscrewed. To do this, bolt a length of steel plate to the hub using two wheel bolts, and grip the plate in a vice.
8 Unscrew and remove the hub nut. The nut is very tight and unless you have suitable removal tools, leave the renewal of the bearing to your dealer.
9 Using a puller, separate the bearing outer race and balls from the hub together with one inner race.
10 Remove the remaining inner race from the hub using a puller which must be clamped to the race.
11 Wash the hub, bearing, and arm recess with paraffin and wipe dry with a lint-free cloth. Check the hub locknut for damage, also the threads of the hub. Renew the components as necessary. Once removed, the hub bearing must never be reassembled; always renew it.
12 Refitting is a reversal of removal, but the following additional points must be noted:

(a) Drive the new bearing into position with a tube located on the inner races
(b) Lubricate the bearing and hub threads with multi-purpose grease before tightening the hub nut to the specified torque. Lock the nut by peening the metal in two places (photo)
(c) Tighten the hub retaining bolts to the specified torque
(d) Refit the brake disc as described in Chapter 9

8 Rear suspension arm – removal, servicing and refitting

1 Jack-up the rear of the car and support it on axle stands. Apply the handbrake and remove the rear roadwheel.
2 Move the ground clearance lever fully to the rear in the minimum height position.

4.5 Removing the front suspension lower balljoint nut

5.14 Front brake disc cooling deflector location

7.4 Removing the rear brake disc

7.5 Removing the rear hub flange bolts

7.6 Removing the rear hub

7.12 Rear hub nut must be locked by peening over

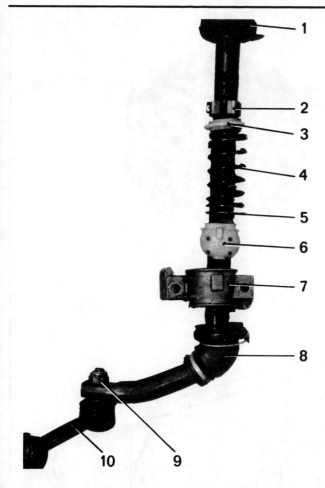

Fig. 11.13 Front anti-roll bar components (Sec 6)

1 Seal	6 Split bearing shell
2 Clamp	7 Bearing
3 Washer	8 Cover
4 Spring	9 Nut
5 Shim	10 Link

Fig. 11.14 Adjusting the front anti-roll bar bearing preload using tool 6401-T (Sec 6)

1 Clamp
2 Spring

3   Loosen the hydraulic system pressure regulator bleed screw 1 to 1½ turns.

4   If removing the left-hand rear suspension arm, disconnect the exhaust system and lower it from the underframe.

5   Remove the rear anti-roll bar as described in Section 9.

6   Unscrew the rear brake line union nuts from the caliper and rear brake circuit, release the retaining clamp, and withdraw the brake line coil.

7   Release the spring pin securing the suspension cylinder pushrod to the suspension arm.

8   Unscrew the nut and drive out the pivot bolt using a soft metal punch. Note the location of the bearing washers from each side of the arm if they fall out when the arm is being removed.

9   Remove the bump stops from inside the rear subframe (photo).

10 Mount the suspension arm in a soft-jawed vice and remove the thrust washer from each side together with the seals. Mask each washer in relation to the side it is removed from.

11 Withdraw the taper roller bearings and identify them side for side. At the same time remove the spacer sleeve.

12 Using a soft metal punch, drive the bearing outer races from the arm keeping them identified side for side.

13 Clean all components with paraffin and wipe dry with a lint-free cloth. Examine the bearings for wear and damage and the races for pitting. Check the bump stops for wear. Examine the thrust washer seals for deterioration and wear. Renew the components as necessary.

14 Using a tube of suitable diameter drive the bearing races into the arm.

15 If new components are being fitted, the correct thickness of the thrust washers must now be determined in order to obtain a bearing preload of 50 kgf (110 lbf). If possible, obtain the Citroen tool No 6311-T from a tool hire agent to check the dimensions, otherwise proceed as follows.

16 Fit the tapered bearings in their races and use a suitable size bolt to determine the distance between the outer surfaces of the bearing inner races.

17 Measure the length of the spacer sleeve with vernier calipers.

18 The difference between the dimensions obtained in paragraphs 16 and 17 represents the overall thickness of the thrust wahsers. The inner thrust washer must always be 9.34 mm (0.37 in) thick, therefore the outer thrust washer will be the difference between the inner washer thickness and the overall thickness.

19 Make sure that the thrust washer seals are serviceable; if not, renew them.

20 Coat the bearings with a multi-purpose grease, then fit them into the suspension arm, followed by the thrust washers (in their correct positions) and the spacer sleeve.

21 Refitting is a reversal of removal, but the following additional points should be noted:

    (a) Refit the bump stops using a soapy water solution

    (b) Refit the anti-roll bar as described in Section 9

    (c) Bleed the brake hydraulic system as described in Chapter 9

    (d) Grease the pivot bolt threads before refitting the nut

    (e) Tighten all nuts and bolts to the specified torque

    (f) Tighten the pressure regulator bleed screw

9   Rear anti-roll bar – removal and refitting

1   Jack-up the rear of the car and support it on axle stands. Apply the handbrake.

2   Move the ground clearance lever fully to the rear in the minimum height position, then unscrew the pressure regulator bleed screw 1 to 1½ turns.

3   Remove the rear roadwheels.

4   Mark the anti-roll bar and height corrector clamp in relation to each other, then unscrew and remove the clamp bolt (photo).

5   Unscrew and remove the four retaining bolts, at the same time noting the location of the bearing blocks and spacers (photo).

6   Withdraw the anti-roll bar from the right-hand side of the car after removing it from the clamp on the height corrector control shaft.

7   To refit the anti-roll bar, first locate it in the clamp on the height corrector control shaft.

8   Support each suspension arm with the extension plates half way between the bump stops. If available, use Citroen tool No 6302-T to position the arms.

9   Temporarily fit the retaining bolts and bearing blocks to the anti-

188

Fig. 11.15 Location of three of the rear hub retaining bolts -
arrowed (Sec 7)

Fig. 11.16 Rear wheel hub and bearing (Sec 7)

1   Nut
2   Bearing
3   Hub

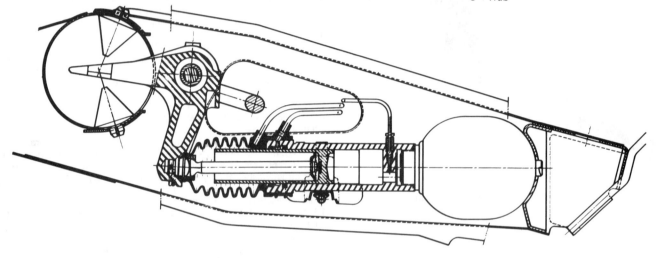

Fig. 11.17 Sectional view of a rear suspension cylinder on saloon models (Sec 8)

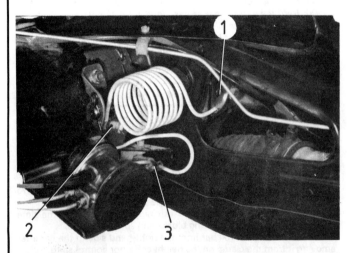

Fig. 11.18 Location of rear brake line clamps (1 and 2), and union
nut (3) (Sec 8)

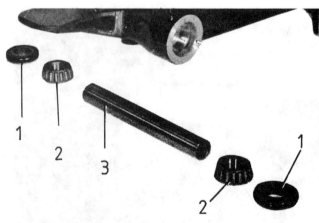

Fig. 11.19 Rear suspension arm components (Sec 8)

1   Thrustwashers
2   Taper roller bearings
3   Spacer sleeve

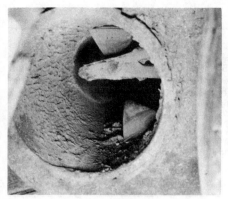

8.9 Rear suspension bump stop

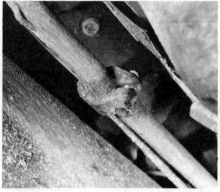

9.4 Rear suspension height corrector to anti-roll bar clamp

9.5 Rear anti-roll bar retaining bolt locations

10.4A Unscrewing a front suspension cylinder sphere

10.4B Holding the front suspension cylinder stationary

10.6A Removing the front suspension cylinder upper union nut

10.6B The front suspension cylinder bellows and hydraulic pipe connections

10.7A Removing the retaining clip from the front suspension cylinder

10.7B Removing the front suspension cylinder

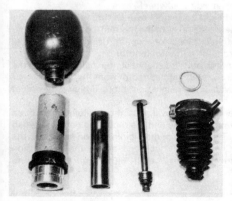

10.7C Component parts of the front suspension cylinder

11.6A Front height corrector

11.6B Rear height corrector

Fig. 11.20 Rear suspension arm positioning tool 6302-T (Sec 9)

Fig. 11.21 Location of front suspension cylinder hydraulic pipes
(1 and 2) (Sec 10)

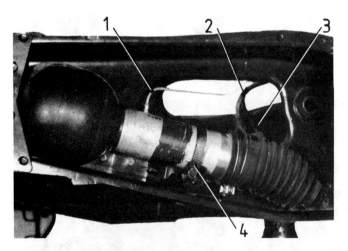

Fig. 11.22 Location of rear suspension cylinder (Sec 10)

  1   Overflow pipe
  2   Hydraulic pipe
  3   Hydraulic pipe
  4   Clip

roll bar so that there is an equal clearance from the arms on each side. Measure the clearances and obtain shims as necessary; they are available up to 4.0 mm (0.157 in) thick for the rear bolts and up to 3.0 mm (0.0118 in) thick for the front bolts. The shims must be within 0.3 mm (0.012 in) thickness on both sides.
10 With the ground clearance lever in the 'normal' position, tighten the retaining bolts and height corrector clamp to the specified torque after inserting the shims.
11 Fit the rear roadwheels, tighten the pressure regulator bleed screws and lower the car to the ground.
12 Check and adjust the rear suspension height as described in Section 12.

10 Suspension cylinders – removal and refitting

1   Jack-up the front or rear of the car and support it on axle stands.
2   Move the ground clearance lever fully to the rear in the minimum height position. Unscrew the pressure regulator bleed screw 1 to $1\frac{1}{2}$ turns.
3   Remove the roadwheel.

Front cylinder
4   Using a strap wrench or oil filter removing tool, unscrew the pneumatic sphere from the top of the cylinder whilst holding the cylinder stationary (photos).
5   Extract the pin securing the cylinder pushrod to the upper suspension arm.
6   Identify each hydraulic pipe using masking tape, then unscrew the union nut and remove the pipes (photos).
7   Detach the pushrod from the suspension arm, and lower the cylinder from the subframe after removing the clip (photos).

Rear cylinder
8   Release the spring pin securing the cylinder pushrod to the suspension arm and remove the pushrod.
9   Identify each hydraulic pipe using masking tape, then unscrew the union nut and remove the pipes.
10 Unscrew and remove the retaining worm drive clip.
11 Withdraw the suspension cylinder from the rear subframe, and if necessary unscrew the pneumatic sphere using a strap wrench.

All cylinders
12 Refitting of both front and rear suspension cylinders is a reversal of removal, but if the pneumatic unit has been removed always fit a new O-ring seal, and tighten the sphere to the specified torque. Make sure that the rear penumatic sphere is correctly located in the subframe. Tighten the hydraulic union screws to the specified torque (see Chapter 8).

11 Suspension height correctors – removal and refitting

1   Jack-up the front or rear of the car and support it on axle stands.
2   Move the ground clearance lever fully to the rear in the minimum height position. Unscrew the pressure regulator bleed screw 1 to $1\frac{1}{2}$ turns.
3   Remove the right-hand side roadwheel.
4   Remove the plastic height corrector cover (where fitted).
5   Move the ground clearance lever to the 'normal' position.
6   Identify all the hydraulic pipes for location using masking tape, then disconnect them from the corrector (photo).
7   Unscrew the mounting bolts, disconnect the balljoint from the control lever, and withdraw the height corrector from the car.
8   It is not possible to repair the height correctors; if faulty, they must be renewed.
9   Refitting is a reversal of removal, but the balljoint should be lubricated with multi-purpose grease and the mounting bolts tightened to the specified torque. Tighten the hydraulic pipe union screws to the specified torque (see Chapter 8). Check and adjust the suspension height as described in Section 12 after tightening the pressure regulator bleed screw.

12 Suspension height – adjustment

1   Check that the tyre pressures are correct (see the Specifications).

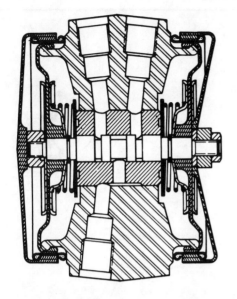

Fig. 11.23 Sectional view of a height corrector (Sec 11)

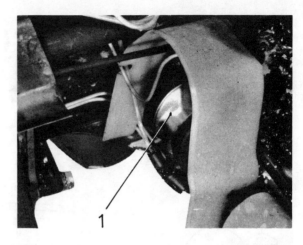

Fig. 11.24 Location of front height corrector (1) (Sec 11)

Fig. 11.25 Front height corrector control lever (1) (Sec 11)

Fig. 11.26 Rear height corrector control lever (1) (Sec 11)

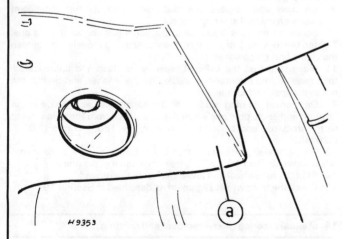

Fig. 11.27 Front suspension height measuring point (a) (Sec 12)

Fig. 11.28 Rear suspension height measuring point (b) (Sec 12)

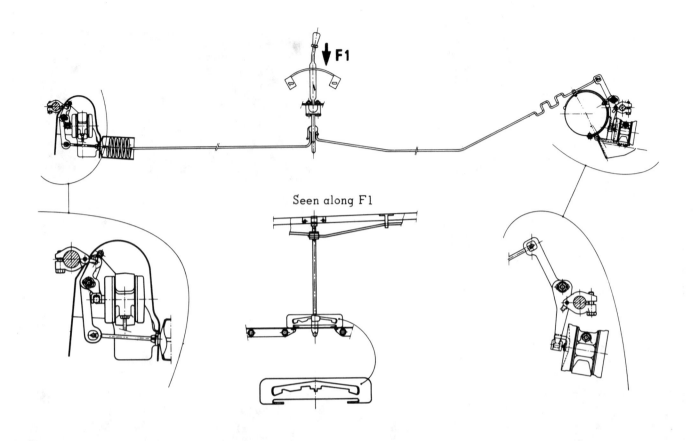

Fig. 11.29 Diagram showing height control mechanism (Sec 12)

2   With the ground clearance lever in the 'normal' position and the car on level ground, start the engine and allow it to idle.

3   Refer to Figs. 11.27 and 11.28, then check that the front and rear suspension heights are as given in the Specifications. If not, remove the relevant cover from the height corrector and check that the manual height control rod is not touching the height corrector lever.

4   Loosen the control rod clamp on the anti-roll bar, and adjust its position until the correct height is achieved. Tighten the clamp bolt to the specified torque.

5   Loosen the nut which holds the two sections of the operating lever together, and adjust the movable section so that the manual control rod is central. Tighten the nut.

6   Make sure that the height corrector balljoints are not seized in their forks.

7   With the engine still idling and the ground clearance lever still in the 'normal' position, check the front and rear suspension heights as follows. Lift the car by hand as far as possible, then release it and let it stabilise. Note the suspension height. Press the car down as far as possible, then release it and let it stabilise. Note the suspension height again. The average of the two measurements should be within the specified limits.

8   Refit the covers as necessary to the height correctors.

13 Track-rod and balljoints – testing and renewal

1   At the intervals specified in Routine Maintenance, examine the track-rod ends for wear and deterioration. The balljoints incorporate nylon seats and require no lubrication.

2   First check the rubber dust covers for splitting.

3   Check the balljoint for wear by gripping the track-rod and attempting to move it up and down.

4   If excessive movement is evident in the balljoint, or if the dust cover is split, the track-rod end must be renewed. Jack-up the front of

the car and remove the roadwheel.

5   Unscrew and remove the track-rod end nut and plain washer.

6   Remove the rubber cover from the side of the subframe, then loosen the track-rod locknut approximately $\frac{1}{4}$ of a turn on manual steering models; loosen the outer clamp bolt on power steering models. Note the track-rod thread protrusion.

7   On manual steering models note the angle and location of the handbrake cable guide, then remove it from the track-rod.

8   Using a suitable balljoint separator, disconnect the track-rod from the steering knuckle.

9   Unscrew and remove the track-rod; hold the inner balljoint stationary on manual steering models.

10 Screw on the new track-rod to the same position as the old one. Tighten the locknut $\frac{1}{4}$ of a turn on manual steering models, and tighten the clamp bolt on power steering models.

11 Make sure that the balljoint taper pin is clean and unlubricated, then insert it into the steering knuckle, fit the washer, and tighten the nut to the specified torque.

12 On manual steering models, fit the handbrake cable guide in the location and angle previously noted; the distance from the guide clamp to the track-rod end balljoint centre must be 180 ± 5 mm (7.09 ± 0.20 in).

13 On all models, make sure that the handbrake cable guide clamp tilts backwards from 15° to 20°. Insert the cable in the guide.

14 Refit the roadwheel and lower the car to the ground.

15 Check the front wheel alignment as described in Section 19.

14 Manual steering gear – removal and refitting

1   Jack-up the front of the car and support in on axle stands. Chock the rear wheels.

2   Move the ground clearance lever fully to the rear. Loosen the pressure regulator bleed screw 1 to $1\frac{1}{2}$ turns.

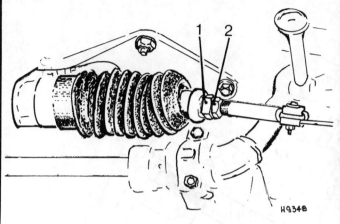

Fig. 11.30 Manual steering inner balljoint (1) and track-rod locknut (2) (Sec 13)

Fig. 11.31 Power steering track-rod clamps (1) and adjusting sleeve (2) (Sec 13)

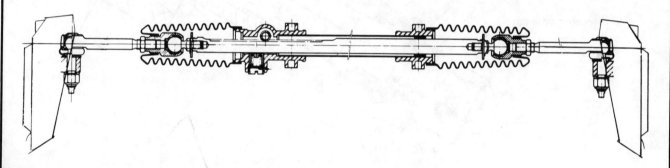

Fig. 11.32 Sectional view of manual steering gear (Sec 15)

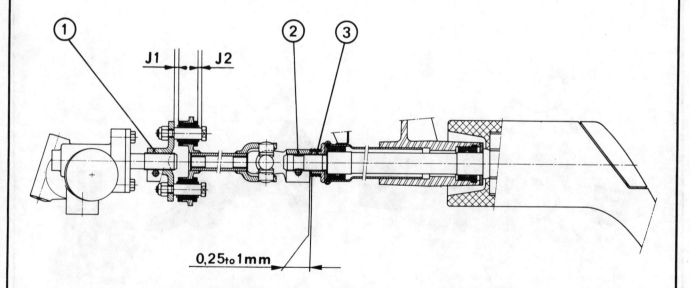

J1   J2

0,25 to 1mm

Fig. 11.33 Sectional view of steering column fitted before September 1976 (J1 must equal J2)

1   Flange   2   Steering column   3   Spacer

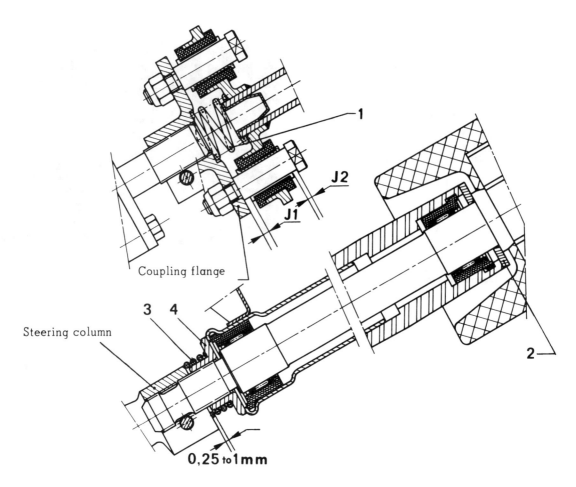

Fig. 11.34 Sectional view of steering column fitted from September 1976 on (J1 must equal J2)

1 Spring   2 Spacer   3 Spring   4 Spacer

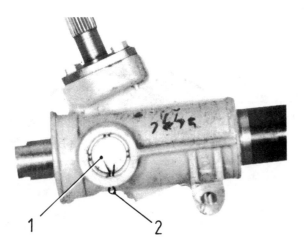

Fig. 11.35 Manual steering damper nut (1) and pin (2) (Sec 15)

Fig. 11.36 Manual steering retaining plate (1) and pinion (2) (Sec 15)

3   Remove the front roadwheels.
4   Remove the rubber covers from the sides of the subframe.
5   Detach the handbrake cable guides from the track-rods.
6   Unscrew and remove the track-rod end nuts and, using a suitable separator, disconnect the track-rods from the steering knuckles.
7   Unbolt the steering column from the shaft coupling, leaving the flange attached to the steering gear pinion.
8   Unbolt the steering gear from the subframe crossmember and withdraw it from the car. **Do not** attempt to remove the crossmember, as this would alter the steering geometry.
9   Refitting is a reversal of removal, but the following additional points should be noted:

(a) *A clearance of 2.0 to 3.0 mm (0.079 to 0.118 in) must exist between the flexible coupling and the pinion flange (see Fig. 11.33). If not, reposition the flange*
(b) *Tighten all nuts and bolts to the specified torque*
(c) *Fit the handbrake cable guides as described in Section 13*
(d) *Check the front wheel alignment as described in Section 19*

15   Manual steering gear – overhaul

1   Clean the exterior of the steering gear then mount it in a soft-jawed vice.
2   Remove the rubber bellows from the housing.
3   Hold the rod stationary and unscrew the balljoints from each side after bending back the lock tabs.
4   Extract the split-pin and unscrew the damper nut using two crossed screwdrivers in the slots. Remove the spring and damper pad.
5   Unscrew the two bolts, remove the retaining plate, and withdraw the pinion. Remove the rack from the housing.
6   Using a suitable soft metal punch, drive out the pinion bush from inside the housing after removing the needle bearing.
7   Extract the rubber guide ring from the end of the housing, and if necessary, pull out the retaining bush.
8   Clean all components with paraffin and wipe dry with a lint-free cloth.
9   Examine the components for wear, and renew as necessary. Check the pinion teeth for wear and the bearings for pitting. If the bearings feel rough when spun in the hand, renew them. Renew the seal in the pinion retaining plate whenever the steering gear is overhauled.
10   Commence reassembly by driving the pinion bush into the housing to a depth of 1.7 mm (0.067 in) from the outer face of the housing. Retain it in position by centre punching the housing at three points.
11   Refit the retaining bush and rubber guide ring to a depth of 11.0 mm (0.43 in) from the end of the housing.
12   Coat the needle bearing with multi-purpose grease and insert it into the pinion bush.
13   Coat the rack with multi-purpose grease and insert it into the housing.
14   Lubricate the pinion and ball bearing with multi-purpose grease, and insert it into the housing.
15   Locate the retaining plate over the pinion with the closed end of the seal outermost, and tighten the bolts to the specified torque.

16   Coat the damper pad with multi-purpose grease, then fit it into the housing, followed by the spring and nut. Tighten the nut fully, then back off $\frac{1}{8}$th to $\frac{1}{6}$th of a turn. Move the rack from side to side and check that there are no high spots; if there are, loosen the nut slightly until the movement is smooth. Lock the nut with the split-pin.
17   Hold the rack stationary and tighten the track-rod balljoints into each end to the specified torque. Bend over the lock tabs.
18   Refit the rubber bellows.

16   Power steering gear – removal and refitting

1   Jack-up the front of the car and support it on axle stands. Chock the rear wheels.
2   Prise the plug from the centre of the steering wheel, unscrew the nut, and remove the steering wheel (photo).
3   Start the engine and allow the steering to centralise, then insert a 6.5 mm (0.26 in) diameter rod through the steering gear pinion. If the hole is not aligned, adjust the eccentric on the flexible coupling.
4   Switch off the engine and remove the ignition key to lock the steering. Using Citroen tool No 6454-T and a 5 or 6 mm diameter ball inserted in the steering wheel shaft, lock the control unit in the straight-ahead position.
5   Remove the front roadwheels and loosen the hydraulic system pressure regulator bleed screw 1 to $1\frac{1}{2}$ turns. Depress the brake pedal several times to release the pressure.
6   Remove the rubber covers from each side of the subframe.
7   Detach the handbrake cable guides from the track-rods.
8   Unscrew and remove the track-rod end nuts and, using a suitable separator, disconnect the track-rods from the steering knuckles.
9   Unbolt the steering column from the flexible coupling (photo). Loosen the pinion flange clamp nut and turn the coupling eccentric to its central position.
10   Detach the exhaust pipe shield and hydraulic pipe shield.
11   Remove the hydraulic pipe retaining collar from the steering gear, note the location of the feed and return pipes, then unscrew the union nuts and remove the return pipe.
12   Unbolt the steering gear from the subframe crossmember; **do not** attempt to remove the crossmember, as this would alter the steering geometry.
13   Select third gear and disconnect the pinion flange, then withdraw the steering gear from the car.
14   Refitting is a reversal of removal, but the following additional points should be noted:

(a) *Do not remove the locking pin until the steering gear is refitted*
(b) *The coupling eccentric must be positioned at the top, and the coupling centre plate must be in a central position*
(c) *Make sure that the gear linkage does not touch the hydraulic pipe*
(d) *Tighten all nuts and bolts to the specified torque*
(e) *Fit the handbrake cable guides as described in Section 13*
(f) *Check the front wheel alignment as described in Section 19*
(g) *Road test the car to check that the steering returns to the straight-ahead position. If necessary, loosen the coupling bolts and adjust the eccentric to correct*

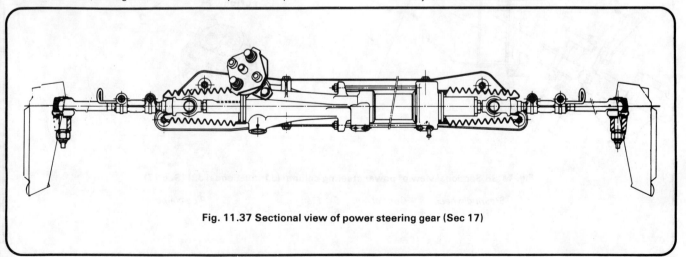

Fig. 11.37 Sectional view of power steering gear (Sec 17)

17 Power steering gear – overhaul

1   Clean the exterior of the steering gear, then mount it in a soft-jawed vice.
2   Remove the rubber bellows from the housing.
3   Loosen the locknuts and unscrew the track-rods from each side of the steering rack.
4   Check that the rack protrusion on each side is equal, then lock the pinion with a 6.5 mm (0.26 in) diameter rod.
5   Mark the position of the pinion retaining plate, then unscrew the two bolts.
6   Extract the split-pin and unscrew the damper nut using two crossed screwdrivers in the slots; remove the spring and damper pad.
7   Remove the retaining plate and pinion.
8   Unscrew the rack housing rod nuts and separate the housing from the rack.
9   Pull the rack and piston from the cylinder.
10 Mount the rack in a soft-jawed vice and unscrew the sleeve nut. Withdraw the rack, piston tube, seal and piston rod, and if necessary unscrew the extension rod from the rack.
11 Remove the seals from the piston rod, rack housing and cylinder as shown in Figs. 11.44, 11.45, 11.46 and 11.47.
12 Using a suitable soft metal punch, drive out the pinion bush from inside the housing after removing the needle bearing.
13 Clean all components with paraffin and wipe thoroughly dry with a piece of lint-free cloth.

14 Examine the components for wear and renew as necessary. Check the rack-and-pinion teeth for wear, and the bearings for pitting. Spin the bearings by hand; if they feel rough, renew them. Obtain a complete set of seals.
15 During the reassembly procedure, all seals must be coated with LHM fluid and the rack-and-pinion lubricated with multi-purpose grease.
16 Commence reassembly by driving the pinion bush into the housing to a depth of 2.0 mm (0.079 in) from the outer face of the housing. Peen the metal in three places to retain it.
17 Refit the seals to the cylinder, rack housing and piston rod in the reverse order of removal.
18 Assemble the piston rod, seal, piston tube and rack, then tighten the sleeve nut to 6.5 kgf m (46.0 lbf ft).
19 Insert the rack into the housing.
20 Slide the cylinder onto the piston, using a length of shim to guide the seal into position.
21 Locate the piston tube housing in the rack housing with the hydraulic pipe outlets facing the same direction, then tighten the rod nuts.
22 Locate the pinion in the retaining plate and insert the locking pin.
23 Check that the rack protrusion is equal on both sides, then insert the pinion so that the previously made marks are aligned. Insert and tighten the retaining bolts to 1.4 kgf m (10.0 lbf ft).
24 Refit the damper pad, spring, and nut. Tighten the nut fully, then back off $\frac{1}{8}$th of a turn. Move the rack from side to side and check that there are no high spots; if evident, loosen the nut slightly. Lock the nut with the split-pin and insert the rubber plug.

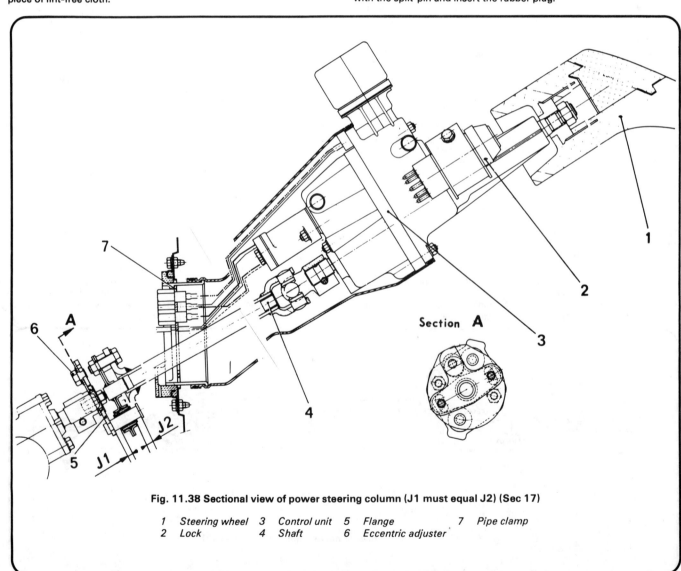

Fig. 11.38 Sectional view of power steering column (J1 must equal J2) (Sec 17)

1	Steering wheel	3	Control unit	5	Flange	7 Pipe clamp
2	Lock	4	Shaft	6	Eccentric adjuster	

Fig. 11.39 Steering coupling on power steering models (Sec 17)

1   Bolts   3   Clamp nut
2   Eccentric   J1 = J2

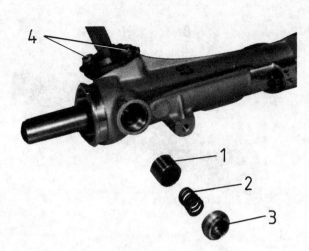

Fig. 11.40 Power steering damper pad (1), spring (2), nut (3), and retaining plate bolts (4) (Sec 17)

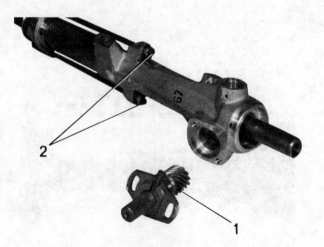

Fig. 11.41 Power steering gear pinion (1) and rack housing rod nuts (2) (Sec 17)

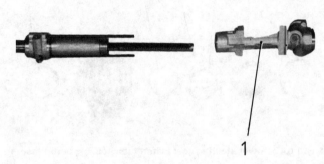

Fig. 11.42 Power steering gear rack housing (1) (Sec 17)

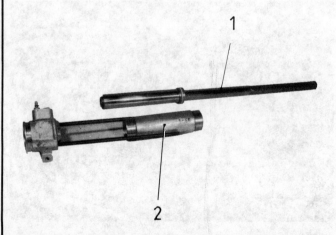

Fig. 11.43 Power steering gear rack (1) and cylinder (2) (Sec 17)

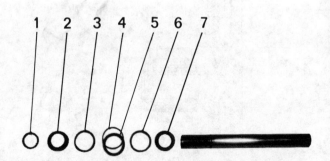

Fig. 11.44 Power steering gear piston rod components (Sec 17)

1   Ring seal   4   Seal   6   Washer
2   Piston   5   Sliding seal   7   Washer
3   Washer

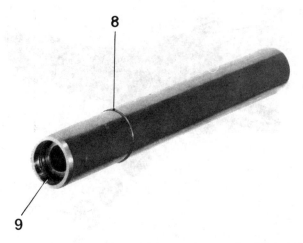

Fig. 11.45 Power steering gear piston tube stop rings (8 and 9)
(Sec 17)

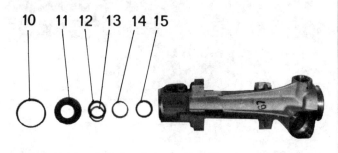

Fig. 11.46 Power steering gear rack housing components (Sec 17)

10	Ring seal	12	Seal	14	Washer
11	Bush	13	Sliding seal	15	Ring seal

Fig. 11.47 Power steering gear piston tube housing components
(Sec 17)

1	Ring seal	3	Seal	5	Washer
2	Bush	4	Sliding seal	6	Ring seal

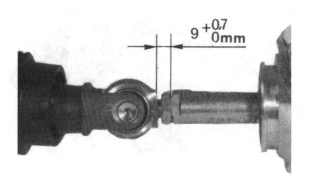

Fig. 11.48 Power steering gear track-rod adjustment dimension
(Sec 17)

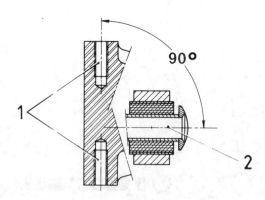

Fig. 11.49 Power steering track-rod positioning diagram (Sec 17)

1	Steering gear retaining bolt	2	Track-rod swivel eye
	holes		

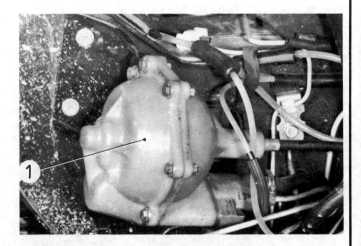

Fig. 11.50 Steering governor (1) location on power steering
models (Sec 18)

16.2 View of the steering wheel retaining nut

16.9 Steering column flexible coupling

18.1 Power steering control unit pipes

18.2 Power steering governor location

20.4 Upper steering column showing steering wheel splines

25 Screw the track-rods into the rack until the distance from the eye flat to the rack is 9.0 to 9.7 mm (0.35 to 0.38 in) with the eyes at 90° to the retaining bolt holes (see Fig. 11.49). Tighten the locknuts to 5.5 kgf m (40 lbf ft) whilst holding the rack stationary.
26 Refit the rubber bellows.

18 Power steering control unit and governor – description

1 The control unit is located beneath the steering wheel and comprises a slide valve operated by rockers when the steering wheel is turned. Fluid under high pressure from the main hydraulic system is fed from the control unit to the piston in the steering gear where it provides assistance to the steering movement (photo).
2 The steering governor is located on the front subframe and is driven by cable from the differential unit (photo). Internal centrifugal weights determine the pressure exerted on an eccentric cam inside the control unit. The cam is turned by the action of the steering wheel, and as the road speed of the car increases, the self-centering effect of the steering is also increased, thus giving greater control at higher speeds.
3 It is not possible to repair either the control unit or the steering governor, and if these components are faulty, renewal is the only course of action.

19 Wheel alignment – checking and adjusting

1   Accurate wheel alignment is essential for good steering and slow tyre wear. Before checking it, make sure that the suspension heights are correct and that the tyres are correctly inflated.
2   Place the car on level ground with the wheels in the straight-ahead position.
3   With the ground clearance lever in the 'normal' position and the engine idling, measure the toe-in of the front wheels using a wheel alignment gauge. The amount of toe-in must be as given in the Specifications.
4   If adjustment is necessary, proceed as follows.

Manual steering models
5   Hold the track-rod inner balljoint stationary and loosen the locknut on each side.
6   Turn the balljoints by equal amounts until the alignment is correct, then tighten the locknut. Note that a complete turn of the balljoint alters the alignment by 4.0 mm (0.16 in).

Power steering models
7   Loosen the clamp bolts on both sides of the steering rack.
8   Turn the sleeves by equal amounts until the alignment is correct, then tighten the clamp bolts, making sure that the clamps as positioned as described in Section 13.

All models
9   Castor and camber angles can only be checked with special equip-ment and this work is best entrusted to a Citroen garage.

20 Steering wheel – removal and refitting

1   Set the front roadwheels in the straight-ahead position.
2   Prise out the medallion from the centre of the steering wheel.
3   Unscrew and remove the steering wheel retaining nut using a socket and extension.
4   Pull the steering wheel off its splines and remove it from the car (photo).
5   Refitting is a reversal of removal, but make sure that the steering wheel spoke is vertical with the roadwheels in the straight-ahead posi-tion before tightening the retaining nut to the specified torque.

21 Roadwheels and tyres – general

1   Clean the insides of the roadwheels whenever they are removed. If necessary, remove any rust and repaint them.
2   Remove any flints or stones which may have become embedded in the tyres. Examine the tyres for damage and splits. Where the depth of tread is less than the legal minimum, renew them.
3   The wheels should be rebalanced half way through the life of the tyres to compensate for loss of rubber.
4   Check and adjust the tyre pressures regularly and make sure that the dust caps are correctly fitted. Remember to check the spare tyre also.

22 Fault diagnosis – suspension and steering

Symptom	Reason/s
Excessive free movement in steering wheel	Worn steering gear Worn track-rod end balljoints Worn flexible coupling
Wander	Incorrect wheel alignment Worn steering knuckle balljoints Uneven tyre pressures Faulty suspension cylinder Worn or seized suspension arm bearings
Heavy or stiff steering	Incorrect wheel alignment Tyre pressures incorrect Seized balljoint Faulty steering gear Faulty control unit or governor (power steering)
Wheel wobble and vibration	Roadwheels out of balance Incorrect wheel alignment Worn wheel bearings
Low suspension height	Fault in hydraulic system Incorrect adjustment of height correctors Seized height corrector balljoints Faulty suspension cylinder Damaged hydraulic pipe
Excessive tyre wear	Incorrect wheel alignment Incorrect tyre pressures

Chapter 12 Bodywork and fittings

For modifications, and information applicable to later models, see Supplement at end of manual

Contents

1 General description

The bodyshell is of all-steel welded construction and is attached to the underframe by rubber mountings. The underframe comprises the front subframe, the sidemembers and the rear subframe. The front subframe supports the front suspension components and the engine/gearbox unit; the rear subframe supports the rear suspension components.

Although the bodyshell can be removed from the underframe, special jigs are required to check the alignment of the subframes, therefore this work is definitely not possible for the home mechanic. The bodyshell mountings must never be loosened, otherwise distortion of the underframe may occur.

2 Maintenance – bodywork and underframe

1 The general condition of a car's bodywork is the one thing that significantly affects its value. Maintenance is easy but needs to be regular and particular. Neglect, particularly after minor damage, can lead quickly to further deterioration and costly repair bills. It is important also to keep watch on those parts of the car not immediately visible, for instance the underside, inside all the wheel arches and the lower part of the engine compartment.

2 The basic maintenance routine for the bodywork is washing – preferably with a lot of water, from a hose. This will remove all the loose solids which may have stuck to the car. It is important to flush these off in such a way as to prevent grit from scratching the finish.

The wheel arches and underbody need washing in the same way to remove any accumulated mud which will retain moisture and tend to encourage rust. Paradoxically enough, the best time to clean the underbody and wheel arches is in wet weather when the mud is thoroughly wet and soft. In very wet weather the underbody is usually cleaned of large accumulations automatically and this is a good time for inspection.

3 Periodically it is a good idea to have the whole of the underside of the car steam cleaned, engine compartment included, so that a thorough inspection can be carried out to see what minor repairs and renovations are necessary. Steam cleaning is available at many garages and is necessary for removal of accumulation of oily grime which sometimes is allowed to cake thick in certain areas near the engine and gearbox. If steam facilities are not available, there are one or two excellent grease solvents available which can be brush applied. The dirt can then be simply hosed off.

4 After washing paintwork, wipe off with a chamois leather to give

an unspotted clear finish. A coat of clear protective wax polish will give added protection against chemical pollutants in the air. If the paintwork sheen has dulled or oxidised, use a cleaner/polish combination to restore the brilliance of the shine. This requires a little effort, but is usually caused because regular washing has been neglected. Always check that the door and ventilator opening drain holes and pipes are completely clear so that water can drain out. Bright work should be treated the same way as paintwork. Windscreens and windows can be kept clear of the smeary film which often appears if a little ammonia is added to the water. If they are scratched, a good rub with a proprietary metal polish will often clear them. Never use any form of wax or other body or chromium polish on glass.

3 Maintenance – upholstery and carpets

1 Mats and carpets should be brushed or vacuum cleaned regularly to keep them free of grit. If they are badly stained remove them from the car for scrubbing or sponging and make quite sure they are dry before replacement. Seats and interior trim panels can be kept clean by a wipe over with a damp cloth. If they do become stained (which can be more apparent on light coloured upholstery) use a little liquid detergent and a soft nail brush to scour the grime out of the grain of the material. Do not forget to keep the head lining clean in the same way as the upholstery. When using liquid cleaners inside the car do not over-wet the surfaces being cleaned. Excessive damp could get into the seams and padded interior causing stains, offensive odours or even rot. If the inside of the car gets wet accidentally it is worthwhile taking some trouble to dry it out properly, particularly where carpets are involved. **Do not** leave oil or electrical heaters inside the car for this purpose.

4 Minor body damage – repair

The photo sequence on pages 206 and 207 illustrates the operations detailed below

Repair of minor scratches in the car's bodywork

If the scratch is very superficial, and does not penetrate to the metal of the bodywork, repair is very simple. Lightly rub the area of the scratch with a paintwork renovator or a very fine cutting paste, to remove loose paint from the scratch and to clear the surrounding bodywork of wax polish. Rinse the area with clean water.

Apply touch-up paint to the scratch using a thin paint brush. Con-

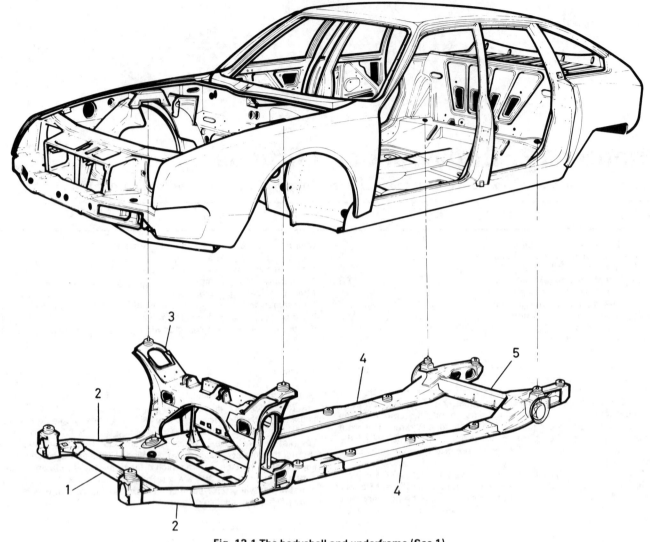

Fig. 12.1 The bodyshell and underframe (Sec 1)

1   Front crossmember   3   Front subframe   5   Rear subframe
2   Front extensions   4   Sidemembers

tinue to apply thin layers of paint until the surface of the paint in the scratch is level with the surrounding paintwork. Allow the new paint at least two weeks to harden; then blend it into the surrounding paintwork by rubbing the paintwork in the scratch area with a paintwork renovator, or a very fine cutting paste. Finally apply wax polish.

Where the scratch has penetrated right through to the metal of the bodywork, causing the metal to rust, a different repair technique is required. Remove any loose rust from the bottom of the scratch with a penknife, then apply rust inhibiting paint to prevent the formation of rust in the future. Using a rubber or nylon applicator fill the scratch with bodystopper paste. If required, this paste can be mixed with cellulose thinners to provide a very thin paste which is ideal for filling narrow scratches. Before the stopper-paste in the scratch hardens, wrap a piece of smooth cotton rag around the top of a finger. Dip the finger in cellulose thinners and then quickly sweep it across the surface of the stopper-paste in the scratch; this will ensure that the surface of the stopper-paste is slightly hollowed. The scratch can now be painted over as described earlier in this Section.

Repair of dents in the car's bodywork

When deep denting of the car's bodywork has taken place,the first task is to pull the dent out, until the affected bodywork almost attains its original shape. There is little point in trying to restore the original shape completely, as the metal in the damaged area will have

stretched on impact and cannot be reshaped fully to its original contour. It is better to bring the level of the dent up to a point which is about $\frac{1}{8}$ inch (3 mm) below the level of the surrounding bodywork. In cases where the dent is very shallow anyway, it is not worth trying to pull it out at all.

If the underside of the dent is accessible, it can be hammered out gently from behind, using a mallet with a wooden or plastic head. Whilst doing this, hold a suitable block of wood firmly against the impact from the hammer blows and thus prevent a large area of bodywork from being 'belled-out'.

Should the dent be in a section of the bodywork which has a double skin or some other factor making it inaccessible from behind, a different technique is called for. Drill several small holes through the metal inside the dent area – particularly in the deeper sections. Then screw long self-tapping screws into the holes just sufficiently for them to gain a good purchase in the metal. Now the dent can be pulled out by pulling on the protruding heads of the screws with a pair of pliers.

The next stage of the repair is the removal of the paint from the damaged area, and from an inch or so of the surrounding 'sound' bodywork. This is accomplished most easily by using a wire brush or abrasive pad on a power drill, although it can be done just as effectively by hand using sheets of abrasive paper. To complete the preparations for filling, score the surface of the bare metal with a screwdriver or the tang of a file, or alternatively, drill small holes in the affected area. This will provide a really good 'key' for the filler paste.

To complete the repair see the Section on filling and respraying.

Repair of rust holes or gashes in the car's bodywork

Remove all paint from the affected area and from an inch or so of the surrounding sound bodywork, using an abrasive pad or a wire brush on a power drill. If these are not available a few sheets of abrasive paper will do the job just as effectively. With the paint removed you will be able to gauge the severity of the corrosion and therefore decide whether to renew the whole panel (if this is possible) or to repair the affected area. Replacement body panels are not as expensive as most people think and it is often quicker and more satisfactory to fit a new panel than to attempt to repair large areas of corrosion.

Remove all fittings from the affected area except those which will act as a guide to the original shape of the damaged bodywork (eg headlamp shells etc). Then, using tin snips or a hacksaw blade, remove all loose metal and any other metal badly affected by corrosion. Hammer the edges of the hole inwards in order to create a slight depression for the filler paste.

Wire brush the affected area to remove the powdery rust from the surface of the remaining metal. Paint the affected area with rust inhibiting paint; if the back of the rusted area is accessible treat this also.

Before filling can take place it will be necessary to block the hole in some way. This can be achieved by the use of zinc gauze or aluminium tape.

Zinc gauze is probably the best material to use for a large hole. Cut a piece to the approximate size and shape of the hole to be filled, then position it in the hole so that its edges are below the level of the surrounding bodywork. It can be retained in position by several blobs of filler paste around its periphery.

Aluminium tape should be used for small or very narrow holes. Pull a piece off the roll and trim it to the approximate size and shape required, then pull off the backing paper (if used) and stick the tape over the hole; it can be overlapped if the thickness of one piece is insufficient. Burnish down the edges of the tape with the handle of a screwdriver or similar, to ensure that the tape is securely attached to the metal underneath.

Bodywork repairs – filling and respraying

Before using this Section, see the Sections on dent, deep scratch, rust hole and gash repairs.

Many types of bodyfiller are available, but generally speaking those proprietary kits which contain a tin of filler paste and a tube of resin hardener are best for this type of repair. A wide, flexible plastic or nylon applicator will be found invaluable for imparting a smooth and well contoured finish to the surface of the filler.

Mix up a little filler on a clean piece of card or board – use the hardener sparingly (follow the maker's instructions on the packet) otherwise the filler will set very rapidly.

Using the applicator, apply the filler paste to the prepared area; draw the applicator across the surface of the filler to achieve the correct contour and to level the filler surface. As soon as contour that approximates the correct one is achieved, stop working the paste – if you carry on too long the paste will become sticky and begin to pick-up on the applicator. Continue to add thin layers of filler paste at twenty-minute intervals until the level of the filler is just proud of the surrounding bodywork.

Once the filler has hardened, excess can be removed using a metal plane or file. From then on, progressively finer grades of abrasive paper should be used, starting with a 40 grade production paper and finishing with 400 grade wet or dry paper. Always wrap the abrasive paper around a flat rubber, cork, or wooden block – otherwise the surface of the filler will not be completely flat. During the smoothing of the filler surface the wet-or-dry paper should be periodically rinsed in water. This will ensure that a very smooth finish is imparted to the filler at the final stage.

At this stage the dent should be surrounded by a ring of bare metal, which in turn should be encircled by the finely feathered edge of the good paintwork. Rinse the repair area with clean water, until all of the dust produced by the rubbing-down operation is gone.

Spray the whole repair area with a light coat of grey primer – this will show up any imperfections in the surface of the filler. Repair these imperfections with fresh filler paste or bodystopper, and once more smooth the surface with abrasive paper. If bodystopper, is used, it can be mixed with cellulose thinners to form a really thin paste which is ideal for filling small holes. Repeat this spray and repair procedure until you are satisfied that the surface of the filler, and the feathered edge of the paintwork are perfect. Clean the repair area with clean water and

allow to dry fully.

The repair area is now ready for spraying. Paint spraying must be carried out in a warm, dry, windless and dust free atmosphere. This condition can be created artificially if you have access to a large indoor working area, but if you are forced to work in the open, you will have to pick your day very carefully. If you are working indoors, dousing the floor in the work area with water will lay the dust which would otherwise be in the atmosphere. If the repair area is confined to one body panel, mask off the surrounding panels; this will help to minimise the effects of a slight mis-match in paint colours. Bodywork fittings (eg chrome strips, door handles etc), will also need to be masked off. Use genuine masking tape and several thickness of newspaper for the masking operation.

Before commencing to spray, agitate the aerosol can thoroughly, then spray a test area (an old tin, or similar) until the technique is mastered. Cover the repair area with a thick coat of primer; the thickness should be built up using several thin layers of paint rather than one thick one. Using 400 grade wet or dry paper, rub down the surface of the primer until it is really smooth. While doing this the work area should be throughly doused with water, and the wet or dry paper periodically rinsed in water. Allow to dry before spraying on more paint.

Spray on the top coat, again building up the thickness by using several thin layers of paint. Start spraying in the centre of the repair area and then, using a circular motion, work outwards until the whole repair area and about 2 inches of the surrounding original paintwork is covered. Remove all masking material 10 to 15 minutes after spraying on the final coat of paint.

Allow the new paint at least 2 weeks to harden fully; then, using a paintwork renovator or a very fine cutting paste, blend the edges of the new paint into the existing paintwork. Finally, apply wax polish.

5   Major body damage – repair

Where serious damage has occurred or large areas need renewal due to neglect, it means certainly that completely new sections or panels will need welding in and this is best left to professionals. If the damage is due to impact it will also be necessary to completely check the alignment of the bodyshell structure. Due to the principle of construction the strength and shape of the whole car can be affected by damage to a part. In such instances the services of a Citroën agent with specialist checking jigs are essential. If a body is left misaligned it is first of all dangerous as the car will not handle properly and secondly uneven stresses will be imposed on the steering, engine and transmission, causing abnormal wear or complete failure. Tyre wear may also be excessive.

6   Maintenance – hinges and locks

1   Oil the hinges of the bonnet, doors and boot or tailgate with a drop or two of light oil periodically. A good time is after the car has been washed.
2   Oil the bonnet release catch mechanism and striker pin periodically.
3   Do not over lubricate door latches and strikers. Normally a little oil on the lock spindle is sufficient.

7   Door rattles – tracing and rectification

1   Check that the door is not loose at the hinges and that the latch is holding it firmly in position. Check also that the door lines up with the aperture in the body.
2   If the door is out of alignment, adjust it as described in Section 9.
3   If the latch is holding the door in the correct position but the latch still rattles, the lock mechanism is worn out and requires renewal.
4   Other rattles from the door could be caused by wear in the window operating mechanism or electric motors, interior lock mechanism, or loose glass channels.

8   Bonnet – removal, refitting and adjustment

1   Support the bonnet in its open position, and place some cardboard

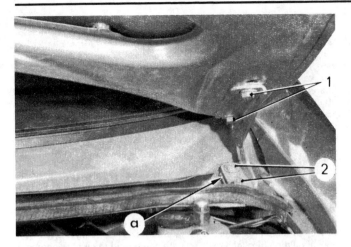

Fig. 12.2 Bonnet hinge location (Sec 8)

1   Upper retaining bolts   2   Lower retaining bolts
                              a   Shim location

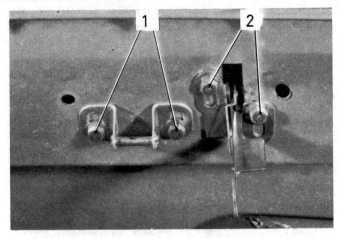

Fig. 12.3 Bonnet striking plate and safety catch (Sec 8)

1   Retaining bolts   2   Retaining bolts

Fig. 12.4 Bonnet lock shield (Sec 8)

1   Retaining bolt   3   Retaining bolts
2   Shield

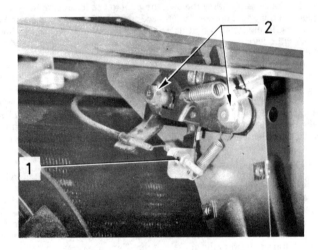

Fig. 12.5 Bonnet lock location (Sec 8)

1   Cable adjusting nut   2   Retaining bolts

or rags beneath the corners by the hinges.

2   Mark the location of the hinges with a pencil, then loosen the four retaining bolts (photo).

3   With the help of an assistant, unscrew the four retaining bolts, noting that an earth strap is located on the rear ones. Lift the bonnet from the car after unscrewing the support strap nut.

4   Refitting is a reversal of removal, but adjustments are necessary for the bonnet location and lock operation.

5   The rear of the bonnet must be flush with the front wings or a maximum of 2·0 mm (0·08 in) below them. If adjustment is necessary, unbolt the hinges from the bulkhead and locate shims beneath the hinges.

6   The distance between the bonnet and the front wings must be between 5·0 and 8·5 mm (0·20 and 0·33 in) with a maximum difference between sides of 2·5 mm (0·10 in). The front contour of the bonnet and wings must be within 3·0 mm (0·12 in) of each other. If adjustment is necessary, loosen the retaining bolts in the bonnet and reposition the bonnet.

7   Check that the striking plate at the front of the bonnet is central to the lock. If not, loosen the two bolts and reposition it.

8   Check that the safety catch engages under the weight of the bonnet only. If not, loosen the two bolts and reposition it.

9   With the bonnet locked, the height of the bonnet at the front should equal that given in paragraph 5. If adjustment is necessary, remove the shield and loosen the lock retaining bolts. Reposition the lock and tighten the bolts. Adjust the cable to eliminate any slackness. The bonnet should lock with ease when released from a height of 250

mm (10 in).

9   Front and rear doors – adjustment

1   The clearance at the front and rear of the doors must be between 3·0 and 9·0 mm (0·12 and 0·35 in). If necessary, add or remove shims from the hinges. On the upper hinge, remove the inner bolt and loosen the two outer bolts; on the lower hinge, remove the check strap and loosen the outer bolts.

2   The clearance at the top of the doors must be between 5·0 and 9·0 mm (0·20 and 0·35 in). In addition the maximum recess of the front edge of the door in relation to the front wing or front door must be 2·0 mm (0·08 in). If adjustment is necessary, loosen the hinge bolts and reposition the door.

3   The striker plate must be located so that the catch engages with it centrally. The plate also determines the amount by which the door seal is compressed, and the position of the rear edge of the door in relation to the rear door or rear wing. If necessary, loosen the crosshead screw and reposition the plate; shims may be added behind the plate to align it with the catch.

10 Boot lid – removal, refitting and adjustment

1   Disconnect the battery negative terminal.

2   Open the boot lid and disconnect the wiring from the number plate

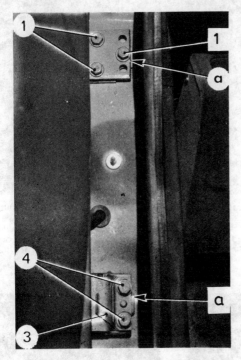

Fig. 12.6 Door hinge locations (Sec 9)

1 Bolts
3 Check strap
4 Bolts
a Shim locations

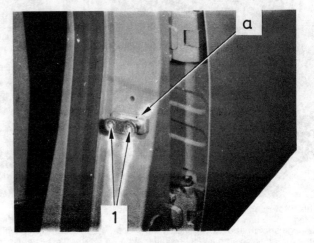

Fig. 12.7 Door striker plate location (Sec 9)

1 Crosshead screws
a Shim location

Fig. 12.8 Boot lid hinge location (Sec 10)

1 Bolts

lamps. Remove the rear window trim strips.

3   Extract the pin, remove the washer, and detach the gas-filled strut from the boot lid.

4   Mark the hinge locations with a pencil, then unbolt them from the body and withdraw the boot lid from the car.

5   Refitting is a reversal of removal, but, if necessary, adjust the boot lid as follows.

6   The clearance between the boot lid and the rear wings must be between 5·0 and 8·5 mm (0·20 and 0·33 in) with a maximum difference between sides of 2·0 mm (0·08 in). The contour of the bootlid and wings must be within 3·0 mm (0·12 in) of each other. If adjustment is necessary, loosen the hinge nuts on the boot lid and reposition it.

7   The clearance between the boot lid and the rear bumper must be 10·0 mm (0·4 in). This will give a clearance between the boot lid and rear window of 2·5 to 10·5 mm (0·1 to 0·4 in). If adjustment is necessary, remove the upper and side trim strips from the rear window if they are still in position, loosen the hinge bolts, and reposition the boot lid.

8   Check that the boot lid compresses the sealing rubber when shut. If not, loosen the lock mounting bolts and/or the striker plate, and reposition them as necessary (photo).

11 Door lock – removal and refitting

1   Using a screwdriver, prise the plastic cover from the window winder handle (where fitted) and remove the spring clip. Withdraw the handle (photos).

2   Prise out the two plastic plugs and remove the special screws (photos).

3   Prise out the ashtray (where fitted).

4   Pull off the locking knob (photo).

5   Prise out the spring clip and withdraw the door inner handle (photo).

6   Using a wide blade screwdriver, prise the trim panel away and lift it at the same time. Remove the plastic sheeting, and the spring from the window winder spindle (where fitted) (photos).

8.2 Bonnet hinge location. Note earthing strap

This photographic sequence shows the steps taken to repair the dent and paintwork damage shown above. In general, the procedure for repairing a hole will be similar; where there are substantial differences, the procedure is clearly described and shown in a separate photograph.

First remove any trim around the dent, then hammer out the dent where access is possible. This will minimise filling. Here, after the large dent has been hammered out, the damaged area is being made slightly concave.

Next, remove all paint from the damaged area by rubbing with coarse abrasive paper or using a power drill fitted with a wire brush or abrasive pad. 'Feather' the edge of the boundary with good paintwork using a finer grade of abrasive paper.

Where there are holes or other damage, the sheet metal should be cut away before proceeding further. The damaged area and any signs of rust should be treated with Turtle Wax HI-Tech Rust Eater, which will also inhibit further rust formation.

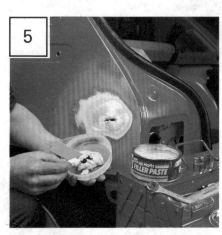

For a large dent or hole mix Holts Body Plus Resin and Hardener according to the manufacturer's instructions and apply around the edge of the repair. Press Glass Fibre Matting over the repair area and leave for 20-30 minutes to harden. Then ...

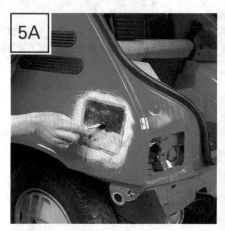

... brush more Holts Body Plus Resin and Hardener onto the matting and leave to harden. Repeat the sequence with two or three layers of matting, checking that the final layer is lower than the surrounding area. Apply Holts Body Plus Filler Paste as shown in Step 5B.

For a medium dent, mix Holts Body Plus Filler Paste and Hardener according to the manufacturer's instructions and apply it with a flexible applicator. Apply thin layers of filler at 20-minute intervals, until the filler surface is slightly proud of the surrounding bodywork.

For small dents and scratches use Holts No Mix Filler Paste straight from the tube. Apply it according to the instructions in thin layers, using the spatula provided. It will harden in minutes if applied outdoors and may then be used as its own knifing putty.

Use a plane or file for initial shaping. Then, using progressively finer grades of wet-and-dry paper, wrapped round a sanding block, and copious amounts of clean water, rub down the filler until glass smooth. 'Feather' the edges of adjoining paintwork.

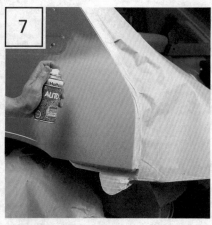

Protect adjoining areas before spraying the whole repair area and at least one inch of the surrounding sound paintwork with Holts Dupli-Color primer.

Fill any imperfections in the filler surface with a small amount of Holts Body Plus Knifing Putty. Using plenty of clean water, rub down the surface with a fine grade wet-and-dry paper – 400 grade is recommended – until it is really smooth.

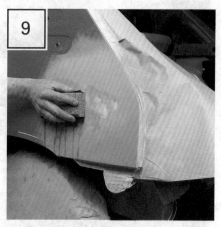

Carefully fill any remaining imperfections with knifing putty before applying the last coat of primer. Then rub down the surface with Holts Body Plus Rubbing Compound to ensure a really smooth surface.

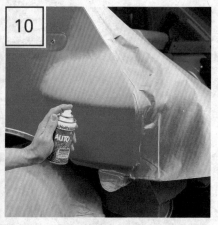

Protect surrounding areas from overspray before applying the topcoat in several thin layers. Agitate Holts Dupli-Color aerosol thoroughly. Start at the repair centre, spraying outwards with a side-to-side motion.

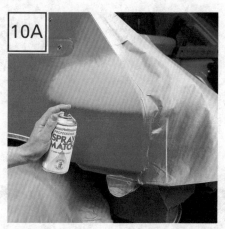

If the exact colour is not available off the shelf, local Holts Professional Spraymatch Centres will custom fill an aerosol to match perfectly.

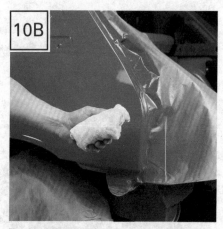

To identify whether a lacquer finish is required, rub a painted unrepaired part of the body with wax and a clean cloth.

If *no* traces of paint appear on the cloth, spray Holts Dupli-Color clear lacquer over the repaired area to achieve the correct gloss level.

The paint will take about two weeks to harden fully. After this time it can be 'cut' with a mild cutting compound such as Turtle Wax Minute Cut prior to polishing with a final coating of Turtle Wax Extra.

When carrying out bodywork repairs, remember that the quality of the finished job is proportional to the time and effort expended.

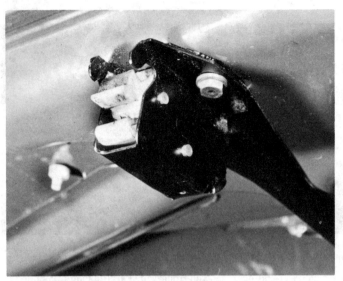

10.8 Boot lid lock

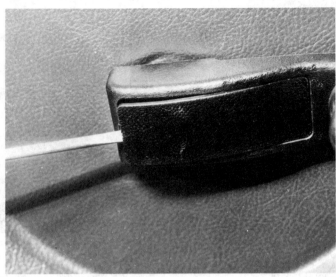

11.1A Removing the cover from the window regulator handle

11.1B Window regulator handle spring clip location

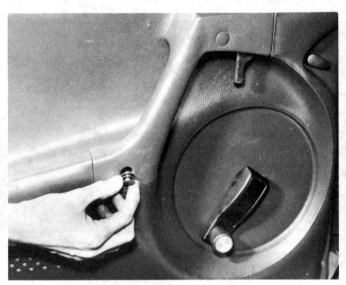

11.2A Removing the trim panel plugs ...

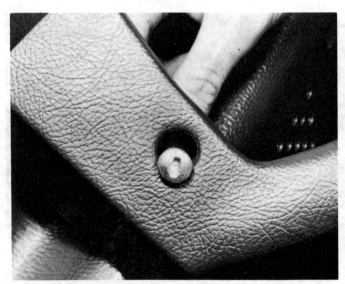

11.2B ... and special screws

11.4 Removing the door locking knob

11.5 Removing the door inner handle

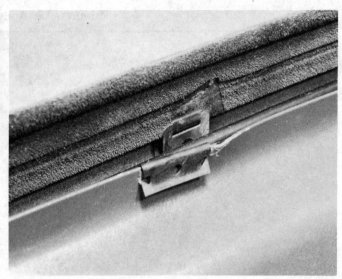
11.6A Door trim panel clip

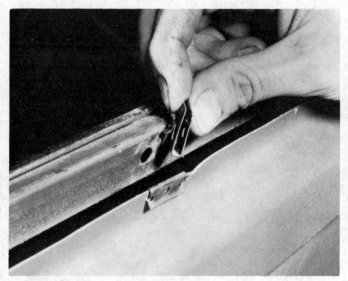
11.6B Removing a door trim panel clip

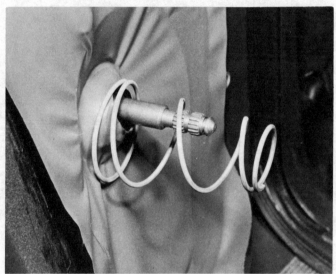
11.6C Window regulator spindle and spring

11.7A Door exterior handle retaining nut and door lock

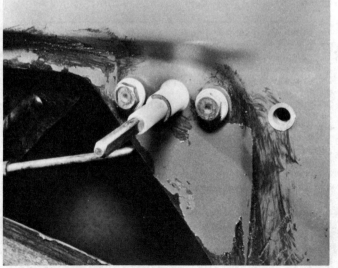
11.7B Door lock control

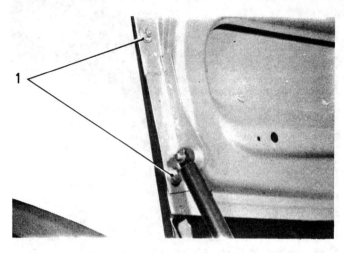

Fig. 12.9 Boot lid hinge nut (1) locations (Sec 10)

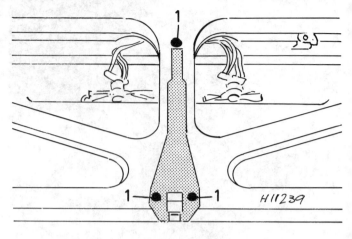

Fig. 12.10 Boot lid lock location (Sec 10)

1   Bolts

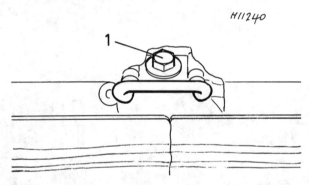

Fig. 12.11 Boot lid striker plate location (Sec 10)

1   Bolt

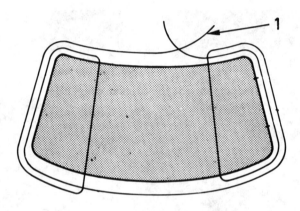

Fig. 12.12 Cord location diagram for refitting the windscreen
(Sec 14)

1   Cord

7   Release the window channel and disconnect the control rods from
the lock (photos).
8   Unscrew the crosshead screws and withdraw the lock from the
door.
9   Refitting is a reversal of removal.

12 Window regulator and glass – removal and refitting

1   Remove the trim panel as described in in Section 11, paragraphs 1
to 6 inclusive.
2   Unscrew the regulator retaining nuts and push the regulator into
the door cavity.
3   Support the glass and release the rollers from the runner channel
(photo).
4   Withdraw the regulator from the door (photos).
5   To remove the window glass, first remove the front guide channel
and channel rubbers (photo).
6   Lower the window and remove the inner and outer weatherstrips.
7   Tilt the glass and remove it from the door (photo).
8   Refitting is a reversal of removal.

13 Bumpers – removal and refitting

1   To remove the front bumper, first unscrew the securing nuts from
the middle section (photo).
2   Remove the bolts at the top of the middle section, and also the
bolts on each side of the bumper.
3   Withdraw the bumper after disconnecting the lighting wires.

4   To remove the rear bumper, unscrew the bolts in the luggage compartment and remove the underpanel and nuts.
5   Unbolt the quarter sections and remove the bumper.
6   Refitting is a reversal of removal.

14 Windscreen glass – removal and refitting

1   If the windscreen has shattered, cover the facia panel with a large
sheet of polythene to catch the pieces of glass. If available, adhesive
sheeting will facilitate the removal of the shattered windscreen.
2   Where the screen is to be removed intact, release the rubber surround from the bodywork with a blunt screwdriver. Take care not to
damage the paintwork.
3   Remove the windscreen wiper arm, the interior mirror, and the
windscreen pillar trimmings.
4   Have an assistant support the outside of the windscreen. Sit inside
the car and carefully push the upper part of the windscreen with the
feet, at the same time easing the rubber surround from the body
aperture. When the surround is released from the upper flange and
side pillars, withdraw the windscreen from the car.
5   Remove the rubber surround from the windscreen.
6   Check the body aperture flange for damage and file away any high
spots. Offer the windscreen up to the opening in order to check the
flange. After removing the old sealing compound, stick the roof trim
back in position.
7   Smear the groove of the rubber surround with soapy water, then
fit the surround to the windscreen glass, with the point at the centre
bottom of the glass.
8   Obtain a length of strong cord and locate it in the rubber surround

12.3 Window glass runner and roller

12.4A Removing the window regulator

12.4B Inner view of the window regulator

12.4C Outer view of the window regulator

12.4D Location of the electric window motor

12.4E Electric window motor mounting nut locations

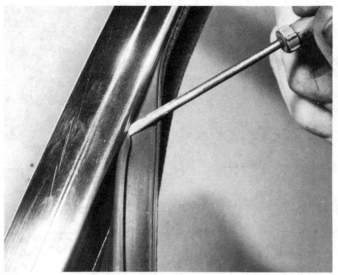

12.5 Removing the window front guide

12.7 Removing a window glass

13.1 Front bumper securing nut

16.4 Heater intake duct and interior lower
panel retaining nut

16.5A Heater motor location on the bulkhead

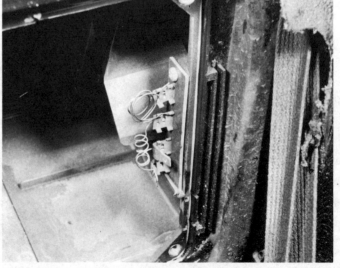

16.5B Heater motor supply wire terminal

16.9 Heater control knobs with cover removed

16.11 Air distribution duct location

16.13 Glovebox retaining nut and plug

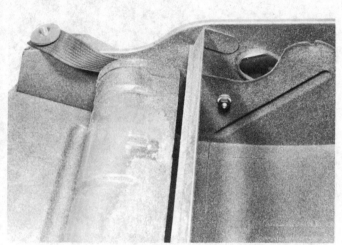

16.14A Glovebox pivot and check strap

16.14B Glovebox lamp location

16.14C Bonnet release handle, with glovebox removed

16.18 Heater control valve and inlet/outlet hoses

16.19 Heater temperature control cable location

16.20 Air distribution control cable and clamp

16.21 Air distribution control arm location

16.23 Heater valve control gear and mating marks (arrowed)

16.24 Control valve and inlet/outlet assembly

16.25 Removing the flap control arm using an Allen key

16.26 Heater side cover location

16.27 Removing the heater supply terminals

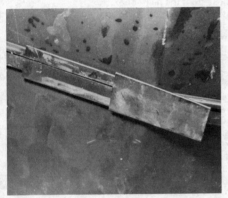

16.29A Tapered side case clip

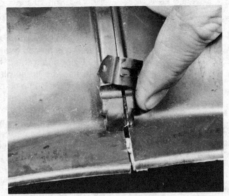

16.29B Removing a side case clip

16.30A Air control flap locations in the side case

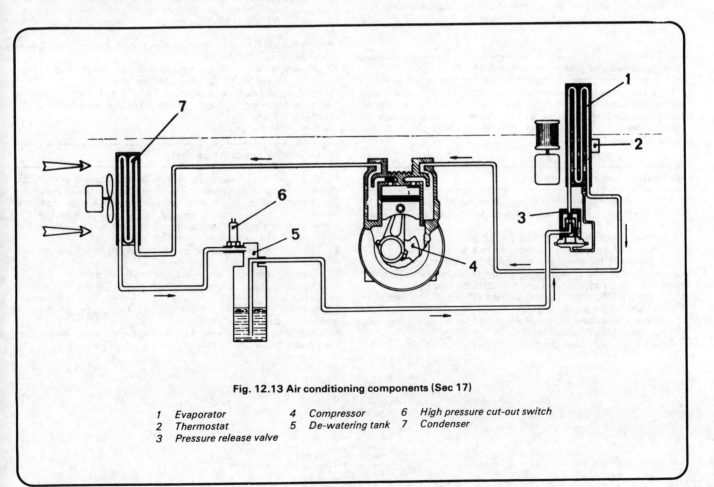

Fig. 12.13 Air conditioning components (Sec 17)

1 Evaporator	4 Compressor	6 High pressure cut-out switch
2 Thermostat	5 De-watering tank	7 Condenser
3 Pressure release valve		

16.30B Removing the heater matrix

as shown in Fig. 12.12. Note that the cord is double along the sides to make sure that the surround seats correctly on the side pillars.
9   Locate the windscreen on the aperture and have the assistant press gently from the outside.
10 From inside the car, pull each loop in turn until the surround is located on the side pillars, then pull the cord right round the glass so that the windscreen is fully seated. Tap the glass with the palm of the hand to make sure that it is seated.
11 Refit the windscreen pillar trimmings and the wiper arm. Stick the interior mirror in the centre of the windscreen, 15·0 mm (0·60 in) from its top edge.

15 Rear screen and quarter glass – renewal

1   The rear screen and quarter glass are bonded to the body flange with special adhesive which is supplied in strips. Although the procedure is straight forward, a special 27 volt transformer is required in order to heat the bonding strip, and therefore the work is outside the scope of the home mechanic.

16 Heater – removal and refitting

1   Drain the cooling system as described in Chapter 2.
2   Disconnect the battery negative terminal and remove the spare wheel.
3   Unbolt the expansion bottle from the bulkhead.
4   Unbolt the heater intake duct from the bulkhead (photo).
5   Unscrew the four bolts and withdraw the heater motor assembly from the bulkhead far enough to disconnect the supply wires from the terminal block. Remove the heater motor assembly (photos).
6   Working inside the car, remove the ashtray, unscrew the gear lever knob and extract the gear lever gaiter.
7   Prise the cover from the top of the console, unscrew the retaining screws, and remove the upper bracket.
8   Prise out the air distribution outlets and remove the transfer ducts.

9   Unscrew the retaining screws and lift the console cover far enough to disconnect the wiring. Make a careful note of the location of each wire. Disconnect the radio and map light in-line fuses (photo).
10 Remove the console cover, making sure that the switches remain in their correct locations.
11 Unscrew the two screws and remove the rear seat supply tunnel from the heater box (photo).
12 Unclip and remove the hydraulic system LHM fluid reservoir.
13 Unscrew the nuts retaining the glovebox and steering column lower panel to the bulkhead. Working inside the car, unscrew the crosshead screws and remove the moulding strips (photo).
14 Remove the glovebox and disconnect the switch wires. Remove the lower panel. The glovebox may be dismantled if necessary by removing the switch, check straps, and retaining bolts (photos).
15 Disconnect the air hoses from the top of the heater box.
16 Uncrew and remove the heater box mounting bolts, located on the bulkhead, from inside the car.
17 Disconnect the air hose from the heater box.
18 Disconnect the water inlet and outlet hoses from the heater box and identify each hose for location (photo). A little water will be spilt during this operation, and it is recommended that a piece of polythene sheeting is placed over the carpets to protect them.
19 Disconnect the cable from the control arm (photo).
20 Prise the small plastic cover from the side of the heater box, then unscrew the cable clamp at the front of the heater box (photo).
21 Prise off the retaining washers and disconnect the spring, then remove the plastic arm and disconnect the cable. Note that the plastic arm is located on the two air flaps (photo).
22 Remove the cable and recover the anti-rattle clip and foam.
23 Unscrew the screw and remove the plastic gear from the shaft; note the mating marks (photo).
24 Remove the inlet/outlet assembly (photo).
25 Using an Allen key, release the flap control arm (photo).
26 Remove the side cover and rubber gasket (photo).
27 Withdraw the heater box far enough to remove the wiring loom plastic cover, then pull the four spade terminals from the block and release the loom (photo). Note the location of the loom retaining clips.
28 Remove the heater box from the car and place it on its side on the bench.
29 Prise off the side case retaining clips and separate the two halves of the heater box (photos).
30 Lift out the two air control flaps and ease the matrix from its location. Take care not to damage the matrix fins (photos).
31 Refitting is a reversal of removal, but refill and bleed the cooling system as described in Chapter 2, and check the operation of all the switches and heater controls.

17 Air condition system – general

1   Where the car is equipped with an air conditioning system, the maintenance operations must be limited to the items below. *No part of the system must be disconnected due to the danger from the refrigerant which would be released.* A Citroën garage or refrigeration engineer must be employed if the system has to be evacuated or recharged. (Refer to Chapter 1, Section 5).
2   Regularly check the condition of the system hoses and connections.
3   Clean the condenser fins regularly with a small brush.
4   Regularly check and adjust the tension of the compressor drivebelt.
5   Keep the air conditioner drain tube clear to allow the internal condensation to disperse.
6   During the winter period, operate the system for a few minutes every one or two weeks to keep the compressor in good order.

Chapter 13 Supplement:
Revisions and information on later models

Contents

1 Introduction

This Supplement covers the main changes and modifications which have been made to the Citroën CX range during the later years of production.

Minor changes have been numerous and apply to trim and to the re-design of small mechanical components. As they do not affect overhaul procedures, they are ignored.

Major items covered in this Supplement include the fully automatic transmission, 2500 cc engine, turbocharger, anti-lock braking system, central door locking, electrically-operated windows and revised wiring circuits.

In order to use the Supplement to best advantage, it is suggested that it is consulted before the main Chapters of the Manual. This will ensure that any relevant information can be collated and absorbed into Chapters 1 to 12.

Maintenance intervals – later models

The major service interval for later models is 12 000 miles (20 000 km), with a minor service due at 6000 miles (10 000 km). The detailed maintenance schedule for 1985 model year vehicles is given below as an example.

Vehicles operating under adverse conditions (eg full-time trailer or taxi work, extremes of climate or dusty conditions) should have the major service interval reduced to 10 000 miles (16 000 km).

Vehicles covering a low mileage (less than 6000 miles/ 10 000 km per annum) should have the following tasks performed regardless of mileage:

(a) *Change the engine oil at least once a year*
(b) *Change the gearbox oil every two years*
(c) *Change the hydraulic fluid every two years*

Although not specified by the makers, it is prudent to renew the coolant every two years or so to maintain its anti-corrosive properties.

Maintenance schedule – 1985 model year
Every 6 000 miles (10 000 km)
    Change engine oil
    Renew engine oil filter (Turbo only)
    Inspect spark plugs, re-gap or renew (Turbo only)
    Check gearbox oil level
    Check coolant level
    Check hydraulic fluid level
    Top up screen washer reservoir(s)
    Check battery electrolyte (except maintenance-free type)
    Check tyre pressures and condition
    Check steering rack and driveshaft gaiters
    Check operation of lights, signals etc
    Inspect pipes and hoses for leaks or damage

Every 12 000 miles (20 000 km) – additional work
    Renew engine oil filter
    Inspect spark plugs, re-gap or renew
    Check clutch adjustment (when applicable)
    Check condition and tension of auxiliary drivebelts
    Check operation of handbrake, adjust if necessary
    Lubricate clutch linkage
    Check valve clearances (at first 12 000 miles/20 000 km only)

Every 18 000 miles (30 000 km) – additional work
    Renew air cleaner element
    Clean LHM suction and return filters
    Lubricate door hinges and check straps

Every 24 000 miles (40 000 km) – additional work
    Change manual gearbox oil
    Inspect rear brake pads

Every 30 000 miles (48 000 km) – additional work
    Change automatic transmission fluid

Every 36 000 miles (60 000 km) – additional work
    Change hydraulic fluid

2 Specifications

These Specifications are revisions of, or supplementary to, the Specifications given at the beginning of the preceding Chapters.

Engine – 2500 cc (except Turbo)
General

Type	M25/659 – electronic fuel injection
Capacity	2500 cc (152.5 cu in)
Bore	93.0 mm (3.66 in)
Stroke	92.0 mm (3.62 in)
Compression ratio	8.75 : 1
Maximum power	138 bhp (101 kW) at 5000 rev/min
Maximum torque	148 lbf ft (20.6 kgf m) at 4000 rev/min

Valves

Valve seat contact angle	90°

Valve timing*

Inlet valve opens	3° 30′ BTDC
Inlet valve closes	45° 0′ ABDC
Exhaust valve opens	38° 30′ BBDC
Exhaust valve closes	1° 0′ ATDC

With valve clearance of 1.0 mm (0.039 in) – for checking valve timing only

Crankshaft
Main bearing journal diameter:

Class A	$67.04 \begin{smallmatrix} +0.010 \\ -0.005 \end{smallmatrix}$ mm		$(2.6394 \begin{smallmatrix} +0.0004 \\ -0.0002 \end{smallmatrix}$ in)	
Class B	$66.79 \begin{smallmatrix} +0.010 \\ -0.005 \end{smallmatrix}$ mm		$(2.6295 \begin{smallmatrix} +0.0004 \\ -0.0002 \end{smallmatrix}$ in)	

Lubrication system

Oil capacity (from May 1986)	5.5 litres (9.7 pints) drain and refill, including filter change

Torque wrench settings

	lbf ft	kgf m
Camshaft pulley nut	72	10.0
Exhaust downpipe nuts	15	2.0
Transmission mouting plate nut	120	16.6
Transmission mounting plate bolts	71	9.8
Suspension swivel nuts	42	5.8
Anti-roll bar link nut	35	4.9
Driveshaft nut	246	34.0
Drivebelt tensioner nut	28	3.8
Camshaft extension bearing bolt	20	2.7
Engine stabiliser bolts	71	9.8
Oil cooler pipe unions	28	3.9
Engine bearer spindle	71	9.8
Cylinder head bolts	See text (Section 3)	See text (Section 3)

Engine – 2500 cc (Turbo)
General
As above, except for the following:

Compression ratio	7.75 : 1
Maximum power	168 bhp (122 kW) at 5000 rev/min
Maximum torque	217 lbf ft (30.0 kgf m) at 3250 rev/min

Cooling system (Turbo)
Fan thermoswitch

Low speed cuts in	88 ± 3°C (190 ± 5°F)
Low speed cuts out	83 ± 3°C (181 ± 5°F)
High speed cuts in	92 ± 3°C (198 ± 5°F)
High speed cuts out	87 ± 3°C (189 ± 5°F)

Fuel system
Carburettor – Solex 34 CICF – 161

Application	CX 2400 March 1978 on	
	Primary	**Secondary**
Venturi bore	24.0 mm	27.0 mm
Main jet	130.0	122.5
Air correction jet	190.0	150.0
Emulsion tube	No. 21479	No. 21643
Mixture jet	No. 20461050	No. 20461000
Emulsion well	5.2	5.2
Idle jet	65.0	60.0
Idle vent	Variable	90.0
Bypass:		
(first-lowest)	0.100 mm	0.100 mm
(second)	0.110 mm	–
Anti-spill hole	0.160 mm	–
Accelerator pump cam	No. 20498082	–
Injector	60.0	–
Accelerator pump output	1.40 to 1.90 cc	
Enrichment device	–	160.0
Retarding hole	–	100.0
Cold start device:		
Opening (device)	16° 10' to 16° 80'	
Opening (strangler flap)	3.98 to 4.02 mm	
Strangler flap cam	No. 20720054	
Anti-flooding spring	No. 58714012	
Diaphragm return spring	No. 56155032	
Vacuum advance take off	1.20	
Needle valve	1.80	
Float chamber fuel level	18.0 to 22.0 mm	

Carburettor – Weber 34 DATC

Application	CX 2400 1981 on	
Identification:		
1/100 – W105-50	Manual choke (air conditioner)	
1/200 – W106-50	Automatic choke, coolant and electrically heated (without air conditioner)	
	Primary	**Secondary**
Venturi bore	24.0 mm	27.0 mm
Main jet	0.115	0.125
Air correction jet	0.230	0.160
Emulsion tube	F51	F25
Mixture jet	4.0	4.0
Idle jet	0.052	0.050
Air jet	0.130	0.070

Under-bonnet view of a Citroën CX Turbo

1 Coolant expansion tank	9 Front suspension spheres	16 Throttle cable	23 Spark plug bung
2 Fast idle valve (air conditioning)	10 Air conditioning receiver/dryer	17 Drivebelt guard	24 Oil filler cap
3 Fast idle adjustment screw	11 Hydraulic pump	18 Ignition coils	25 Idle speed adjustment screw
4 Fuel pressure regulator	12 Air conditioning compressor	19 Cold start injector	26 Fuel injector rail
5 Air intake tower	13 Horns	20 Air pressure lines (turbo boost control)	27 Fuel supply line
6 Wheelbrace	14 Battery	21 Throttle valve switch	28 Fuel return line
7 Jack	15 Radiator top hose	22 Breather	29 Manifold pressure line
8 LHM reservoir			

	Primary	Secondary
Progression holes:		
First (lowest)	0.100 mm	0.100 mm
Second	0.130 mm	1.100 mm
Third	0.100 mm	–
Accelerator pump cam	No. 150	–
Injector	0.050	–
Pump – ejected per stroke	0.6 to 1.0 cc	–
Cold start fuel jet	0.060	–
Econostat fuel jet	–	110.0
Econostat air jet	–	100
Enrichment jet	–	200
Cold start butterfly opening under strangler flap	1.3 mm diameter rod	
Strangler flap opening (with 400 mm Hg vacuum applied)	4.5 mm diameter rod	
Resistor	80W	
Resistance	1.0 Ohms	
Fuel inlet valve	No. 200	
Float setting	6.75 to 7.25 mm	
Advance vacuum port	0.110	

Idle adjustment (Weber 34 DATC carburettor)

Manual transmission:
- Without air conditioning ... 800 to 850 rev/min
- With air conditioning (switched off) ... 800 to 850 rev/min
- With air conditioning (switched on) ... 850 to 950 rev/min adjusted by means of primary valve plate screw

Automatic transmission:
- Without air conditioning (lever in A) ... 700 to 750 rev/min
- With air conditioning (switched off) ... 700 to 750 rev/min
- With air conditioning (switched on) ... 700 to 750 rev/min adjusted by means of primary valve plate screw

CO content ... 1.0 to 2.5%

Fuel injection system (CX 25)

Idle speed – except Turbo:
- Manual transmission without air conditioner ... 750 to 800 rev/min
- Automatic transmission (in P) without air conditioner ... 750 to 800 rev/min
- Manual transmission with air conditioner ... 800 to 850 rev/min
- Automatic transmission (in P) with air conditioner off ... 800 to 850 rev/min
- Fast idle (manual transmission, air conditioning on) ... 1000 to 1050 rev/min

Idle speed – Turbo:
- Nominal idle ... 800 to 850 rev/min
- Fast idle (air conditioning on) ... 1000 to 1050 rev/min

CO content at idle (all fuel injected models) ... 0.8 to 1.5%

Ignition system

Distributor (1978/79)
- Type ... SEV-Marchal
- Number ... 41701602
- Rotational direction ... Anti-clockwise
- Static setting (flywheel) ... 10°
- Dynamic setting ... 25° at 2500 rev/min

Spark plugs (CX 25)

Type:
- Except Turbo ... Champion L82YC or Eyquem 755 SX
- Turbo ... Champion L82C or Eyquem 755 X

Electrode gap (all models) ... 0.8 mm (0.032 in)

Ignition coils (CX 25)

- Primary resistance ... 2.5 Ohms
- Secondary resistance ... 3000 to 4000 Ohms

Torque wrench setting

	lbf ft	kgf m
Knock sensor (Turbo only)	17	2.3

Manual transmission

Gear ratios (1980 on) – 5-speed

	Except Turbo	Turbo
1st	3.16 : 1	3.17 : 1
2nd	1.83 : 1	1.83 : 1
3rd	1.25 : 1	1.21 : 1
4th	0.93 : 1	0.88 : 1
5th	0.73 : 1	0.67 : 1
Reverse	3.75 : 1	3.15 : 1

Final drive ratio (1980 on)
- Except Turbo ... Between 4.06 : 1 and 4.53 : 1, depending on model and year
- Turbo ... 4.21 : 1

Automatic transmission

Type .... Fully automatic ZF with Fitchel and Sachs torque converter

Speed ratios

	2400 cc	2500 cc
1st	1.814 : 1	2.479 : 1
2nd	1.082 : 1	1.479 : 1
3rd	0.730 : 1	1.000 : 1
Reverse	1.526 : 1	2.085 : 1
Final drive	4.769 : 1	4.769 : 1

Lubricant type .... Dexron (R)II D20 – 356

Fluid capacity
From dry .... 10.4 pint (6.5 litre)
Drain and refill .... 4.4 pint (2.5 litre) approx

Torque wrench settings

	lbf ft	kgf m
Engine/torque converter housing bolts	13	1.7
Driveplate/torque converter bolts	64	8.7
Driveplate/crankshaft bolts	64	8.7
Camshaft housing screw	20	2.7

Electrical system

Fuses (pre-1986 vehicles with automatic transmission)

Colour	Rating (A)	Circuits protected
Mauve	16	Heater blower
		Air inlet flap motor
		Air conditioner
		Stoplamps
		Warning lamps
		Clock
Red	16	Anti-theft switch
		Heater relay
		Window winder relay
		Horns
		Windscreen wiper motor and timer unit
		Windscreen washer pump
		Direction indicators
		Instrument lighting rheostat
		Oil pressure gauge relay
		Instrument panel warning lamps
Green	16	Alternator regulator
		Handbrake warning switch
		Coolant temperature switch
		Automatic transmission speed selector lever indicator
		Reversing lamps
		Heated rear window
		Radio
		Central door locks
		Interior lamps
		Luggage boot lamp
		Glove compartment lamp
White	16	Electric window winders
Yellow	10	Heater illumination
		Selector position on instrument panel (automatic transmission)
		Ashtray illumination
		Cigar lighter illumination
		Map reading lamp socket
		Ignition key illumination
		Engine compartment illumination
		Side and tail lamps
		Rear number plate lamp
		Instrument illumination
Blue	10	Rear foglamps

Fuses (1986 model year) – typical

No	Colour	Rating (A)	Circuits protected
1	Red	10	Reversing lamps
2	White	25	Heater/air conditioner, instruments, direction indicators, warning lamps
3	White	25	Window winder relays, height control relay, heated rear window relay, wiper delay, stop-lamps, sunroof motor, ABS (when applicable)
4	Green	30	Engine cooling fans

No	Colour	Rating (A)	Circuits protected
5	Red	10	Hazard warning
6	Green	30	Rear window motors
7	Green	30	Interior lights, height control motor, computer, radio, central locking
8	White	25	Horn relay, heated rear window, heated mirrors
9	Green	30	Front window motors
10	Brown	5	Rear foglamps
11	Brown	5	Number plate lamps
12	Brown	5	Tail lamps
13	Brown	5	Sidelamps, under-bonnet light, ashtray/cigarette lighter/key/digital unit/keyboard lighting, interior light delay, foglamp relays
14	–	–	Spare

Bulbs (later models)

Function	Wattage
Headlamp (main/dip)	60/55
Auxiliary headlamp (main only)	55
Sidelamps	5
Direction indicators	21
Direction indicator repeaters	4
Stop/tail lamps	21/5
Reversing lamps	21 or 25
Rear foglamps	21
Number plate lamps	5
Interior lamps	7 or 21
Rear reading lamps	7
Boot and under-bonnet lamps	5
Glove compartment lamp	2
Speedometer and tachometer illumination	4
Minor instrument illumination	2 (wedge base)
Indicator and warning lamps	1.2 (wedge base)

Suspension and steering

Tyre sizes – CX 25 (1984 on)

Standard (except GTi Saloon, Turbo, and some TRI Estates)	195/70 R14 MXV
Option (standard on GTi Saloon and some TRI Estates)	190/65 HR390 TRX
Turbo – standard	210/55 VR390 TRX
Turbo – alternative	210/55 R390 TRX M + S, 200/60 R390 TRX M + S

Tyre pressures – CX 25 (1984 on)

Recommended tyre pressures vary widely from year to year. For confirmation consult a Citroën dealer or tyre specialist

	Front	Rear
1984/85 – Saloon (except Turbo):		
195/70 tyres	2.4 bar (35 lbf/in²)	2.0 bar (29 lbf/in²)
190/65 tyres	2.2 bar (32 lbf/in²)	1.4 bar (20 lbf/in²)
1984/85 – Estate:		
195/70 tyres	2.5 bar (36 lbf/in²)	2.3 bar (33 lbf/in²)
190/65 tyres	2.4 bar (35 lbf/in²)	1.9 bar (28 lbf/in²)
1984/85 – Turbo:		
210/55 tyres	2.3 bar (33 lbf/in²)	1.5 bar (22 lbf/in²)
200/60 tyres	2.5 bar (36 lbf/in²)	1.7 bar (25 lbf/in²)
1986 – Saloon (except Turbo):		
All tyre sizes	2.4 bar (35 lbf/in²)	2.0 bar (29 lbf/in²)
1986 – Estate:		
195/70 tyres	2.5 bar (36 lbf/in²)	2.3 bar (33 lbf/in²)
190/65 tyres	2.6 bar (38 lbf/in²)	2.3 bar (33 lbf/in²)
1986 – Turbo	As for 1984/85 models	As for 1984/85 models
Compact spare tyre (see text)	2.8 bar (41 lbf/in²) front or rear, all models	

Rear wheel alignment (Turbo)

Toe-out (not adjustable)	0 to 3.8 mm (0 to 0.15 in)

Dimensions and weights

CX 2400 – Safari, Familiale

Overall length	4953.0 mm (195.0 in)
Overall width	1733.6 mm (68.25 in)
Height	1460.5 mm (57.5 in)
Ground clearance	152.4 mm (6.0 in)
Wheelbase	3098.8 mm (122.0 in)
Front track	1473.2 mm (58.0 in)
Rear track	1384.3 mm (54.75 in)
Kerb weight	1405 kg (3097 lb)
Maximum trailer weight	1300 kg (2866 lb)

CX 25 (except Turbo) – 1984

Overall length:	
Except Prestige	4597.4 mm (181.0 in)
Prestige	4902.2 mm (193.0 in)
Overall width	1727.2 mm (68.0 in)
Height	1371.6 mm (54.0 in)
Ground clearance	152.4 mm (6.0 in)
Wheelbase:	
Except Prestige	2844.8 mm (112.0 in)
Prestige	3098.8 mm (122.0 in)
Front track	1473.2 mm (58.0 in)
Rear track	1358.9 mm (53.5 in)
Kerb weight:	
Pallas (auto)	1297 kg (2856 lb)
GTi	1373 kg (3024 lb)
Prestige (auto)	1373 kg (3024 lb)
Maximum trailer weight	1300 kg (2866 lb)

CX 25 (except Turbo) – 1985

Overall length:	
Saloon (except Prestige)	4660 mm (183.46 in)
Prestige	4910 mm (193.31 in)
Estate	4950 mm (194.88 in)

No other information is available for 1985 vehicles

CX 25 – 1986 (and all Turbo)

Overall length:	
Saloon (except Prestige and Turbo)	4653 mm (183.19 in)
Turbo (except Prestige)	4650 mm (183.07 in)
Prestige (including Turbo)	4900 mm (192.91 in)
Estate	4920 mm (193.70 in)
Overall width	1770 mm (69.69 in)
Height:	
Saloon (except Prestige)	1360 mm (53.54 in)
Prestige	1375 mm (54.13 in)
Estate	1475 mm (58.07 in)
Ground clearance	160 mm (6.30 in)
Wheelbase:	
Saloon (except Prestige)	2845 mm (112.01 in)
Prestige and Estate	3095 mm (121.85 in)
Front track	1522 mm (59.92 in)
Rear track	1368 mm (53.86 in)
Kerb weight:	
Saloon (except Prestige and Turbo)	1370 kg (3021 lb)
Turbo (except Prestige)	1385 kg (3054 lb)
Prestige (except Turbo)	1450 kg (3197 lb)
Prestige Turbo	1480 kg (3263 lb)
Estate – Familiale	1420 kg (3131 lb)
Estate – Safari	1435 kg (3164 lb)
Maximum trailer weight	1300 kg (2867 lb) (or 1500 kg (3308 lb) subject to local legislation and gross train weight)

---

3 Engine

2500 cc engine – description

1 In July 1983, the 2347 cc engine was modified and its capacity increased to 2500 cc. Although the overhaul operations remain largely as described in Chapter 1, the revised specifications should be noted in Section 2 of this Supplement. The following essential differences apply to the new engine.

Cylinder head bolts

2 Initial tightening is carried out as follows after overhaul, but no subsequent re-tightening should be done between overhauls.

Stage 1: Tighten in specified sequence to 28 lbf ft (38 Nm)
Stage 2: Turn each bolt in specified sequence through 100° to tighten
Stage 3: Turn each bolt in specified sequence through 100° to tighten
Stage 4: Start engine and warm up until electric cooling fan cuts in, switch off and allow to cool (minimum of three hours) then turn each bolt in specified sequence through 45° to tighten

3 **It is imperative that all cylinder head bolts are renewed whenever the cylinder head is removed.**

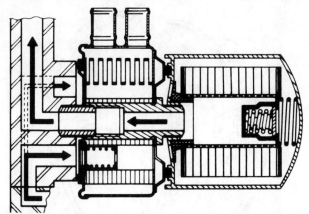

Fig. 13.1 Sectional view of oil cooler and filter (Sec 3)

Engine oil cooler
4   This consists of an oil cooler heat exchanger located at the oil filter mounting base with connections to the engine cooling system (photo).

Sump cover
5   From May 1986 a different sump cover is fitted; having a baffle fitted to the internal ribs. This baffle allows an increased engine oil capacity. Eventually only the new cover will be supplied as a spare – fit the baffle before using the cover (all models).

Crankshaft
6   From January 1987 a different crankshaft is fitted; having a larger crankpin journal blending radius. This means that matching big-end bearing shells are not as wide on later models. It is possible to use the new bearing shells with an old crankshaft, but a new crankshaft can only be used with new, narrower, shells.

General
7   The introduction of the new engine brings about the following changes which are described in greater detail in other Sections of this Supplement.

Modified fuel injection system
New clutch actuation eliminating free movement
Revised gear ratios

Flywheel spigot bearing
8   On later models, the flywheel spigot bearing is of interference fit type in its recess. The circlip used on earlier models is no longer fitted.

Piston rings (CX 2400)
9   As from October 1981, the profile of the second (scraper) piston ring on CX 2400 engines has been altered by removal of the step.

Engine/transmission mountings (November 1978 on)
10 As from November 1978, the engine/transmission is mounted on three flexible mountings instead of the four employed on some models.
11 From January 1984 the engine mounting torque bar has been modified as shown (Fig. 13.3). The new components can be fitted to earlier 2500 cc engine.

Driveplate-to-crankshaft bolts (automatic transmission models)
12 On later automatic transmission models, the driveplate-to-crankshaft bolts have washers under their heads and in consequence longer bolts are used.

Camshaft pulley nut (later models)
13 From January 1984 the camshaft pulley nut is flanged instead of plain. The flange goes nearest the pulley.
14 The flanged nut may be fitted in place of the plain one if wished. The tightening torque is unchanged. Oil the threads and the contact face of the nut before fitting; do not use thread locking compound.

Starter ring gear renewal (later models)
15 On models fitted with the AEI ignition system (Section 6), the position of the starter ring gear teeth is used to provide information

3.4 Oil cooler seen from below (oil filter removed). Central nut is arrowed

controlling ignition timing.
16 Before removing the starter ring gear on pre-1987 models (ignition system with two sensors), mark the position of one tooth relative to the flywheel. Fit the new ring gear, ensuring that one of the teeth is exactly aligned with the flywheel mark.
17 On 1987 models (single ignition sensor), one particular ring gear tooth is 0.3 mm lower than the rest. If a new ring gear can be obtained,

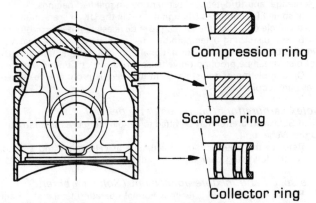

Fig. 13.2 Piston ring profiles – later CX 2400 models (Sec 3)

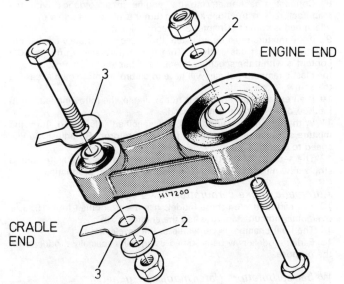

Fig. 13.3 Modified engine mounting torque bar (1) (Sec 3)
2   Washers   3   Shims

this tooth must be identified on the old and new gears, and the new gear must be fitted with the tooth in exactly the same position.
18 1984 and later automatic transmission models have a torque converter on which the starter ring can be renewed. The procedure is similar to that for manual transmission (Chapter 1, Section 24, and the above paragraphs).

4 Cooling system

Coolant level sensor (1986 on) – description
1 later models are fitted with a coolant level sensor. The sensor is a bayonet fit in the side of the coolant expansion tank (photo).
2 Unlike ordinary mechanical level sensors, this type of sensor relies on the difference in conductivity between air and water. The two electrodes on the detector are connected to an electronic unit mounted next to the under-bonnet air intake. The electronic unit is connected to the instrument panel warning light.

Coolant temperature warning light function
3 Note that on some models the coolant temperature warning light illuminates when the coolant is below normal operating temperature as well as when overheating is occurring. This feature is intended to remind the driver to exercise restraint until the engine has warmed up.

5 Fuel and exhaust systems

Fuel system adjustments (all models) – caution
1 To comply with EEC anti-pollution regulations, some carburettor or fuel injection adjusting screws are covered by 'tamperproof' caps, plugs or similar devices. The purpose of tamperproofing is to discourage, and to detect, adjustment by unqualified persons.
2 In some EEC countries (though not yet in the UK) it is an offence to use a vehicle on which the tamperproof devices are missing or broken.
3 Before disturbing a tamperproof device, satisfy yourself that you will not be breaching local or national anti-pollution regulations. Do not disturb tamperproofing on vehicles which are still under warranty.
4 On completion of adjustments, fit new tamperproof devices where these are required by law.

Solex carburettors (later models) – general
5 A Solex carburettor may be fitted to certain models as an alternative to the Weber unit.
6 Refer to the Specifications for details of calibration and settings and to the following paragraphs for adjustment procedures.

Idle speed and mixture adjustment (Solex carburettors)
7 Run the engine until it reaches normal operating temperature and the radiator cooling fan cuts in.
8 Connect a tachometer to the engine in accordance with the manufacturer's instructions and then turn the idle speed screw until the idle speed is correct (Chapter 3, Specifications).
9 If the mixture must be adjusted, this is most accurately carried out using an exhaust gas analyser. Turn the mixture screw until the CO content is within the specified tolerance (Chapter 3). On most models, the plastic tamperproof cap will have to be broken off to gain access to the screw.
10 If an exhaust gas analyser is not available, the following lean drop method of adjustment may be used.
11 With the engine running at the specified idle speed, turn the mixture screw in until the speed just starts to drop. Re-adjust the idle speed to specification.
12 The settings of the throttle stop screw and the accelerator pump stop screw must never be altered as they are set in production.

Automatic choke carburettor (CX 2400)
13 The carburettor on these models has been modified from 1983 to overcome difficult starting when the engine is hot.
14 The float chamber is ventilated to the air cleaner.
15 Earlier models may be modified using parts specially produced for the purpose.

Weber carburettors (later models) – general
16 Later vehicles have different series carburettors.
17 Refer to the specifications for details of calibration and settings.

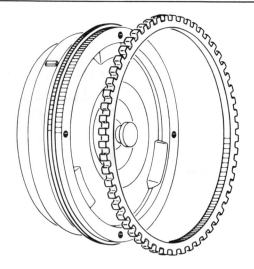

Fig. 13.4 Starter ring gear and torque converter (Sec 3)

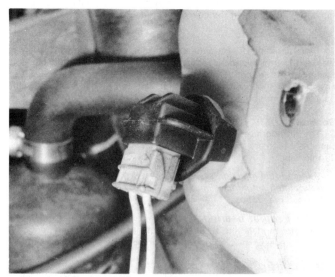

4.1 Coolant level sensor

Weber carburettor (Type 34 DATC) – adjustments
Idle speed and mixture
18 Before carrying out any adjustment, make sure that the valve clearances and ignition timing are correctly set and that the engine is at working temperature, with the radiator cooling fans having just cut out.
19 Connect a reliable tachometer to the engine and set the idle speed to the specified level by turning the primary valve plate stop screw. *On no account alter the secondary choke valve plate stop screw. This is set during production.*
20 If an exhaust gas analyser is available, the tamperproof cap should be broken off the mixture adjustment screw, and the screw turned until the CO level is as specified.
21 Re-set the primary valve plate stop screw to bring the idle speed to the specified level.
22 If an exhaust gas analyser is not available, turn the mixture screw in until the idle speed just starts to fall, then adjust the idle speed to bring it back to the specified level.

Automatic choke
23 When the engine is cold, set the choke by depressing the accelerator pedal fully and then releasing it.

Fig. 13.5 Adjustment points – Solex 34 CICF carburettor (Sec 5)

1   Throttle stop screw (sealed)   2   Idle speed adjustment screw   3   Mixture adjustment screw

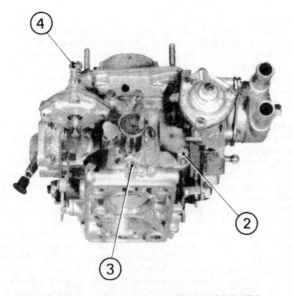

Fig. 13.6 Adjustment points – Weber 34 DATC carburettor (Sec 5)

Fig. 13.7 Secondary choke valve plate stop screw (1) – Weber 34 DATC. Do not adjust this screw (Sec 5)

2   Primary valve stop plate   4   Fast idle adjustment screw
    (idle speed) screw   (with air conditioning)
3   Mixture adjustment screw

Fig. 13.8 Choke valve plate gap (a) – Weber 34 DATC
(Sec 5)

Fig. 13.9 Automatic choke details – Weber 34 DATC
(Sec 5)

1	Housing cover screws	3	Housing cover
2	Coolant connections	4	Centre bolt

Fig. 13.10 Carburettor float chamber vent filter (Sec 5)

24 Refer to Fig. 13.8. With the choke in the cold start position, the gap (a) between the edge of the choke valve plate and the venturi wall should conform to the following table. If it does not, release the housing cover screws and turn the choke housing as necessary to adjust the gap.

Ambient temperature	Choke valve plate gap (a)
27°C (81°F)	1.5 mm (0.059 in)
30°C (86°F)	4.0 mm (0.158 in)
36°C (98°F)	6.5 mm (0.256 in)
39°C (102°F)	9.5 mm (0.374 in)
43°C (109°F)	12.7 mm (0.500 in)
48°C (118°F)	16.5 mm (0.650 in)
Over 48°C (118°F) fully open	17.5 mm (0.690 in)

Carburettor float chamber vent filter – CX 2400

25 On vehicles produced from January 1979, a small supplementary air filter is fitted to the air intake duct on carburettor models.
26 Clean the filter in fuel or solvent at the same time as the main air filter is cleaned or renewed.

Fuel injection (CX 2400) – over-enrichment

27 It is possible on models built since 1981 that when the engine is warm it will misfire or emit black smoke from the exhaust pipe. This is due to a fault in the signal to the electronic control unit and can be rectified in the following way.
28 Verify that the over-enrichment (black smoke etc) ceases if the heater blower relay is temporarily disconnected.
29 Obtain the appropriate relay (No 95 493 312) and electrical connectors from a Citroën dealer. Make up a wiring harness as shown in Fig. 13.11.
30 Disconnect the battery negative lead.
31 Disconnect the wiring plug from the heater relay.
32 From the heater relay brown wire, pull off the clip and fit it into the newly acquired relay wiring plug (socket 1).
33 Pull the clip from the yellow wire and fit it into the newly acquired relay wiring plug (socket 3).
34 Fit the clip of the grey wire on the new wiring harness into socket 1 of the heater relay wiring plug.
35 Fit the clip of the red wire on the new wiring harness into socket 3 of the heater relay plug.
36 Reconnect the wiring plug to the heater relay.
37 Mount the new relay adjacent to the horn compressor relay and connect the new relay wiring plug.
38 Reconnect the battery.

Fuel pump wiring (CX 2400)

39 On CX 2400 models with fuel injection, it is imperative that the two small wiring connecting plugs are correctly connected in the starter motor to fuel pump circuit, otherwise the fuel pump will not operate.
40 The plugs are located near the battery. If disconnected during overhaul operations, make sure that they are identified so that they can be correctly reconnected. As the plugs are both of the same colour, confusion can easily arise.

Electronic fuel injection (CX 25) – description

41 The fuel injection system used on these models differs from that used on 2400 models in the following respects.
42 Except on some Turbo models, the cold start injector is eliminated, enrichment being arranged by the system computer in accordance with the coolant temperature sensor. A further result of this arrangement is that the cold start time delay switch is no longer fitted.
43 The fuel injectors are fed directly from the battery (+) terminal without the use of resistors (except on Turbo models).
44 Below an engine speed of 250 rev/min, or when the ignition is switched off, a new relay cuts off the feed to the injection mechanism and the fuel pump. As with 2400 models, actuation of the starter motor energises the fuel injection system.
45 The fuel filter is now located next to the fuel pump (photo).

Fuel injection hoses and clamps
46 The mounting of the fuel injection system hoses is shown in Figs. 13.13 and 13.14.
47 When a hose is renewed, the hose clamps must be renewed also. Two diameters of hose are in use. Make sure that the correct size hose clamps are fitted.

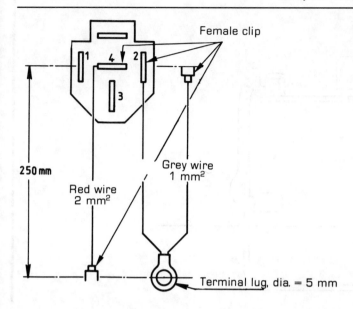

Fig. 13.11 Fuel injection wiring modifications (Sec 5)

5.45 Unclipping the fuel filter. Arrow shows direction of flow

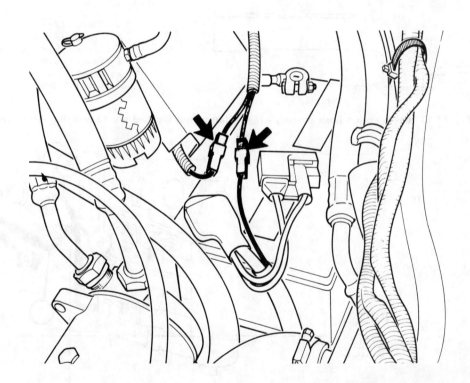

Fig. 13.12 Fuel pump wiring connectors (arrowed) (Sec 5)

Exhaust coupling (CX 2400)

48 On vehicles with a spring-loaded exhaust flange connecting joint, a machined flange has been fitted on later models, instead of the original pressed-steel type, in order to overcome resonance at engine speeds between 2500 and 3000 rev/min.

49 The modification may be carried out on earlier models by obtaining the new type of flange from your dealer.

50 Apply anti-seize grease to the exhaust swivel joint surfaces, tighten the coupling nuts to compress the coil springs until their coils just touch and then unscrew them through one and a half turns. Tighten the locknuts.

Cruise control system – description

51 This system is an option on 1982 and later models equipped with fuel injection.

52 The main components consist of an electrically-operated vacuum pump, a vacuum capsule and two valves.

53 The control circuit incorporates a speed sensor, an electronic control unit and an engine overspeed unit.

54 Various switches are fitted, including a main three-position switch, a brake pedal switch and a 'clutch depressed' switch which operates when changing gear.

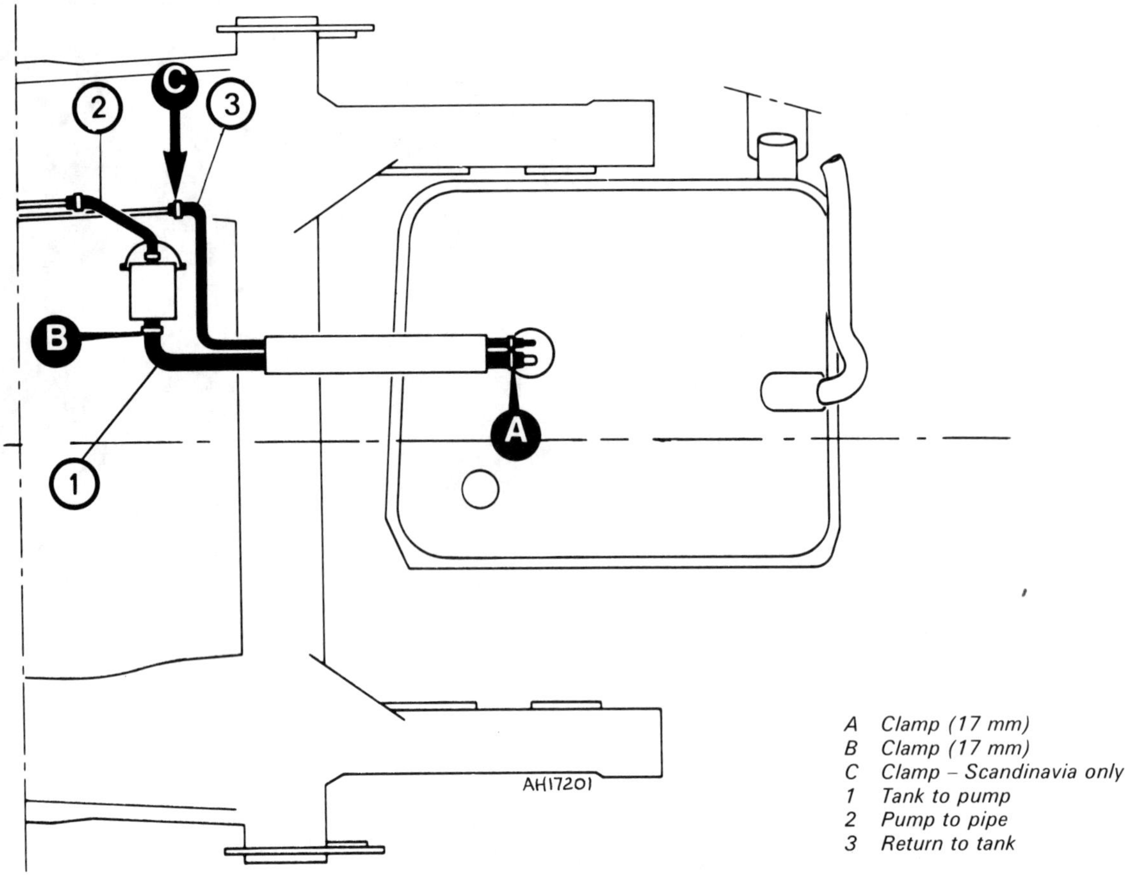

230

A Clamp (17 mm)
B Clamp (17 mm)
C Clamp – Scandinavia only
1 Tank to pump
2 Pump to pipe
3 Return to tank

AHI7201

Fig. 13.13 Fuel injection hose routing – rear. Clamps not marked are 13 mm diameter (Sec 5)

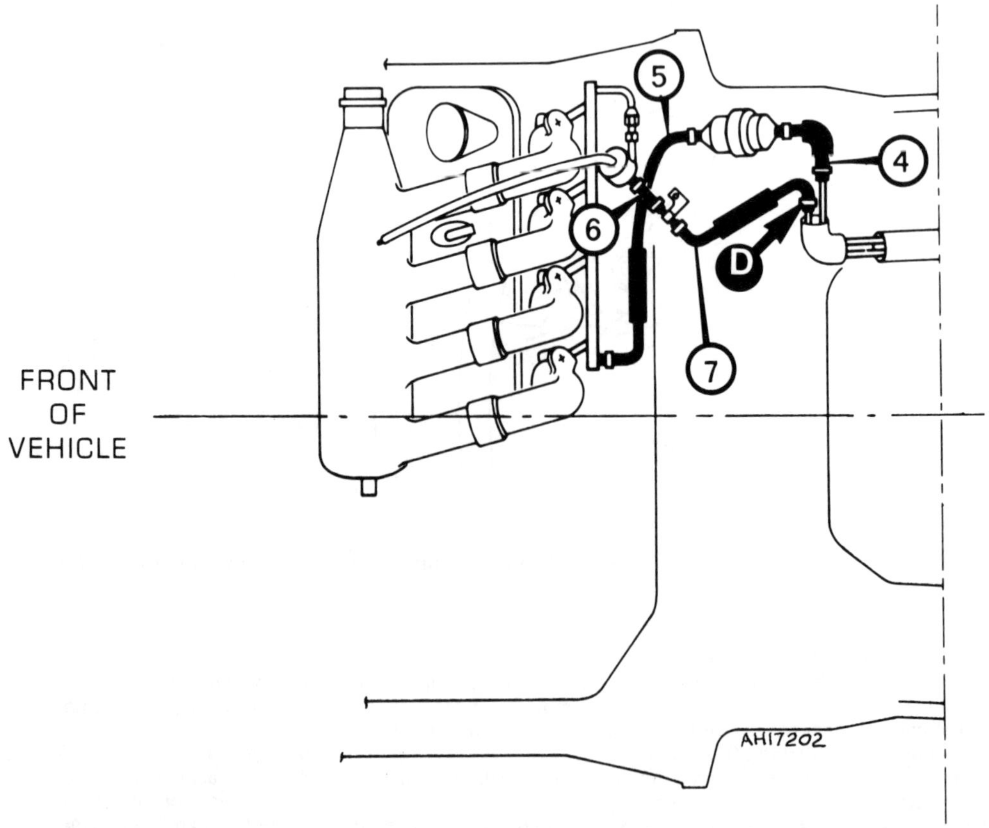

FRONT
OF
VEHICLE

D Clamp – Scandinavia only
4 Pipe to filter
5 Filter to rail
6 Regulator to connector
7 Connector to return pipe

AHI7202

Fig. 13.14 Fuel injection hose routing – front (Sec 5)

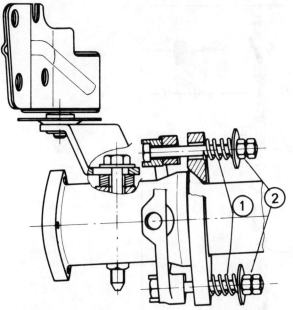

Fig. 13.15 Modified exhaust coupling (Sec 5)

1   Springs   2   Nuts

Cruise control system – adjustments
55 Any malfunction of the system may be due to incorrect adjustment. If this is the case check the following and adjust as described.

Accelerator guide pulley
56 Release the locknut at the bracket.
57 Insert a washer, 4.0 mm thick, between the threaded cable end fitting and the plastic stop.
58 Insert a washer, 5.0 mm thick, between the air flap stop and the operating eccentric on the inlet manifold.
59 Adjust the cable to just remove all slack. Remove the temporary washers.

Guide pulley pedal cable
60 Fully depress the accelerator pedal and check that full throttle can be obtained and the cable coil spring is compressed by between 0.5 and 2.0 mm. If not, release the nut and locknut on the cable end fitting and adjust as necessary.

Pneumatic capsule
61 Adjust the end fitting on the pullrod so that there is the slightest (1.0 mm) slackness in the cable when the pulley is in the released position.

Clutch switch
62 The switch should be positioned in its retainer so that the cruise control electrical circuit is open when the clutch pedal is depressed between 15.0 and 30.0 mm, and remains open during further depression of the pedal.

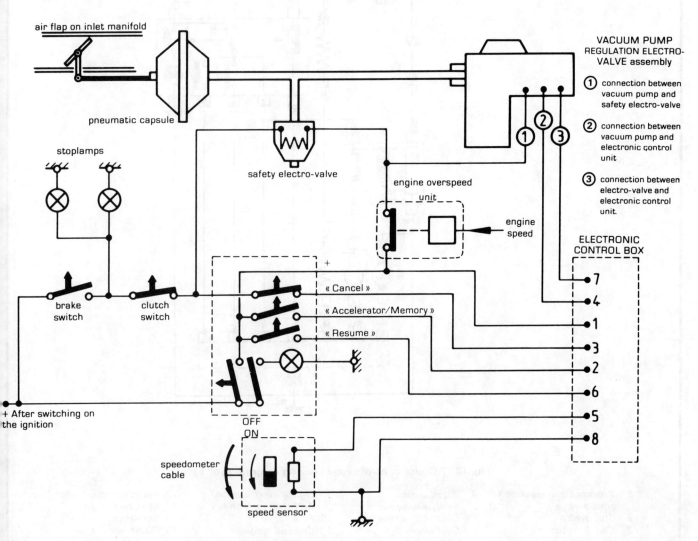

Fig. 13.16 Cruise control system schematic (Sec 5)

232

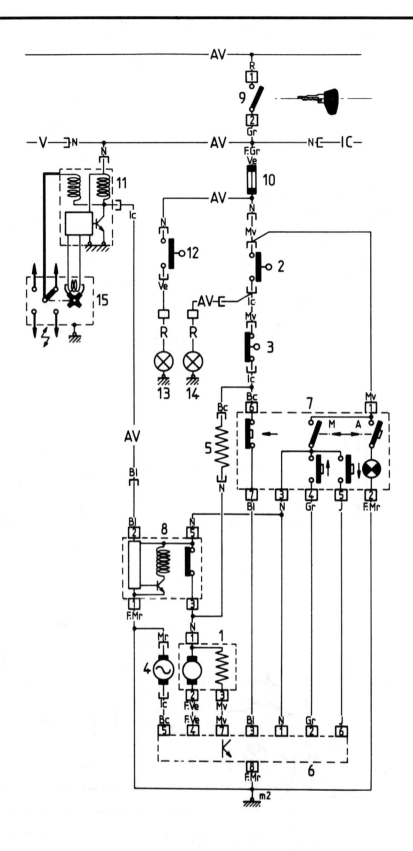

Fig. 13.17 Cruise control system wiring diagram (Sec 5)

1	Vacuum pump regulation electro-valve	4 Speed sensor	8 Engine overspeed unit	12 Reversing lamp switch

1 Vacuum pump regulation electro-valve
2 Stop switch
3 Clutch switch
4 Speed sensor
5 Safety electro-valve
6 Electronic control unit
7 Control switch
8 Engine overspeed unit
9 Anti-theft ignition key
10 Fuse
11 Coil and module
12 Reversing lamp switch
13 Reversing lamps
14 Stoplamps
15 Distributor

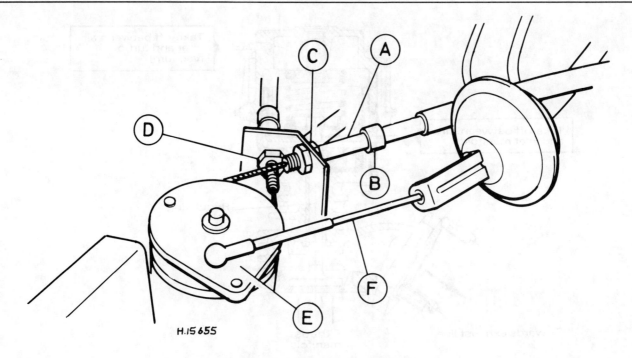

Fig. 13.18 Cruise control linkage (Sec 5)

A Cable threaded end fitting   C Bracket   E Pulley
B Plastic end piece   D Locknut   F Pullrod

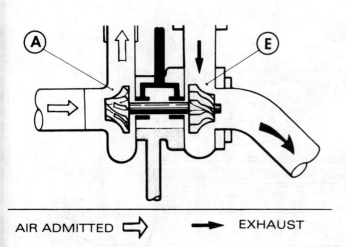

AIR ADMITTED ⇨ ➡ EXHAUST

Fig. 13.19 Schematic view of turbocharger (Sec 5)

A Inlet   E Exhaust

Stop-lamp switch
63 The adjustment must be set as described in Chapter 9, Section 15.

Turbocharger – description
64 The turbocharger increases the efficiency of the engine, and hence raises its power output, by pressurising the inlet manifold. The amount by which manifold pressure exceeds atmospheric pressure is called boost pressure.
65 The parts of the turbocharger are a turbine wheel, driven by the exhaust gases, and a compressor wheel, positioned between the air cleaner and the inlet manifold. The two wheels run on a common shaft. Each wheel is surrounded by a housing which contains and ducts the gases. The turbocharger shaft bearings are pressure lubricated from the engine's lubrication system.

66 Boost pressure is limited by a blow-off valve (also known as a wastegate). When the boost pressure reaches a certain value, the blow-off valve opens and allows exhaust gas to bypass the turbine wheel. If the blow-off valve fails and boost pressure becomes excessive, a pressure sensor in the inlet manifold cuts off the fuel injection.
67 On 1987 model year vehicles, an intercooler (heat exchanger) is placed between the turbocharger and the inlet manifold. The intercooler further increases engine efficiency by cooling the compressed air.

Turbocharger – precautions
68 The turbochager operates at very high speeds and temperatures (up to 150 000 rev/min and 1000°C/1832°F). Efficient lubrication is therefore vital. Observe the following points:

   (a) *Only use good quality engine oil of the correct viscosity*
   (b) *Observe the prescribed oil change intervals. Renew the oil filter at every oil change*
   (c) *After a run, allow the engine to idle for half a minute or so before switching off. If the engine is stopped while the turbo is still spinning at high speed, the turbo bearings may be destroyed*
   (d) *To avoid personal injury, do not allow the turbocharger to operate when partially dismantled, particularly if the inlet or exhaust ports are exposed. Before working on or near the turbocharger allow it to cool sufficiently to avoid burns*

Turbocharger – removal and refitting
69 Start by applying a releasing agent to the exhaust flange nuts which will have to be undone later.
70 Disconnect the oil feed union from the turbocharger. This is secured by two Allen screws. Be prepared for some oil spillage. Recover the gasket.
71 Disconnect the air pressure line(s) on the right-hand side of the turbocharger. (1987 models have one line, earlier models have two with different unions). Recover the banjo union washers (photo).
72 Unbolt the spring clip which secures the air pressure lines. This bolt also secures one end of the air outlet pipe-to-turbo strap. Undo the nut at the other end of the strap and remove the strap (photo).

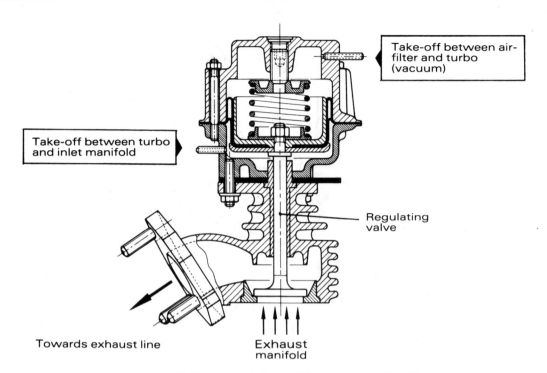

Take-off between air-filter and turbo (vacuum)

Take-off between turbo and inlet manifold

Regulating valve

Towards exhaust line

Exhaust manifold

Fig. 13.20 Sectional view of blow-off valve (Sec 5)

5

H17203

Fig. 13.21 Intercooler (5) fitted to 1987 model year vehicles (Sec 5)

5.71 Air pressure lines connected to turbocharger. Rigid pipe is oil feed

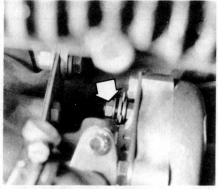

5.72 Nut (arrowed) securing outlet pipe-to-turbo strap

5.74 Turbo air inlet hose and clip

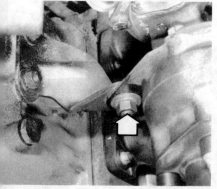

5.75 Turbo-to-bracket bolt (arrowed)

5.77 Turbo oil drain pipe

5.79 Separating the turbocharger from the exhaust flange

5.82 Refitting the air outlet union to the turbocharger

5.84 Exhaust flange connection with blow-off valve pipe

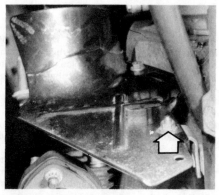

5.85 One of the heat shield securing nuts (arrowed)

5.86 Air pressure line banjo union (arrowed)

5.87 Air pressure line secured by a hose clip

5.89A Removing the blow-off valve

73 Remove the two turbo-to-exhaust manifold flange nuts which are accessible from above and recover the spacers. Raise and support the front of the vehicle, then remove the other two nuts and spacers.

74 Disconnect the air inlet hose from the turbo by undoing its clip (photo).

75 Remove the single nut and bolt which secures the turbo to the bracket (photo). Recover the washers.

76 Remove the four nuts which secure the exhaust flange to the side of the turbo. Recover three of the spacers; the fourth cannot be removed from the stud yet.

77 Remove the rubber pipe which connects the turbo oil drain to the sump (photo). Be prepared for some oil spillage.

secured by a hose clip (photo). (On 1987 models this pressure line is replaced by a short vent hose).

88 Remove the four nuts and washers which secure the valve to the exhaust manifold.

89 Work the valve off the manifold studs and remove it. The radiator top hose obstructs removal, but with care there is no need to remove the hose. Recover the gasket and sealing ring (photos).

90 Do not drop the blow-off valve, it is fragile. Do not attempt to dismantle the valve unless it is to be scrapped: the top cover nuts are sealed to detect tampering. No spares are available.

91 Refit by reversing the removal operations. Use a new gasket and sealing ring (photo).

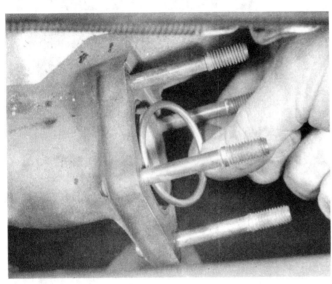

5.89B Manifold sealing ring

5.91 Inserting a new gasket between the flanges

78 The turbocharger is now held in place only by the exhaust flange studs. To provide enough free movement of the exhaust system, remove the three nuts and bolts which clamp the exhaust flange to the bottom of the blow-off valve pipe. Recover the flange gasket.

79 Work the exhaust flange off the side of the turbo – if necessary, slacken the exhaust unions towards the rear of the vehicle to provide enough movement. Recover the gasket and the remaining spacer (photo).

80 Draw the turbocharger downwards, freeing it from the exhaust manifold and the air output tube. Remove the turbo from under the vehicle. Do not drop it, it is fragile.

81 Overhaul of the turbocharger is not a practical proposition for the home mechanic. Spares are not available in any case.

82 Refit by reversing the removal operations, noting the following points:

(a) Use new seals, gaskets, fixing hardware etc as necessary
(b) Loosely fit the air outlet pipe-to-turbo strap to the turbo before refitting, but be careful not to trap or bend it; it is very awkward to fit later. (This does not apply to intercooler models)
(c) Apply a little liquid soap to the air outlet union O-rings (photo) (not intercooler models)
(d) Remember to fit the single exhaust flange nut spacer (paragraph 79) before the flange is fully home

83 If much oil was spilt during removal, check the engine oil level after refitting and top up as necessary. Check for oil feed and drain leaks when the engine is next run.

Blow-off valve (wastegate) – removal and refitting

84 Raise and support the front of the vehicle. Remove the three nuts and bolts which secure the exhaust flange to the bottom of the blow-off valve pipe (photo).

85 Remove the valve heat shield, which is secured by two nuts and bolts (photo).

86 Disconnect the air pressure line banjo union from the valve (photo). Recover the washers.

87 Lower the vehicle. Disconnect the other air pressure line, which is

Anti-pulsation valve (later Turbo models) – description

92 Fitted to 1987 Turbo models, the anti-pulsation valve allows a small quantity of inducted air to bypass the turbocharger. Its function is to stop the airflow sensor flap chattering after rapid throttle closure.

93 The anti-pulsation valve is located in the air trunking which leads from the airflow sensor to the idle speed adjustment screw. The valve resembles a crankcase breather valve in appearance.

---

6   Ignition system

Distributor (SEV-Marchal electronic) – description

1   For a limited period during 1979, a distributor of this type was fitted to Prestige, GTi and Pallas C-matic vehicles.

2   Refer to the Specifications at the beginning of this Supplement for details of this unit.

Distributor (SEV-Marchal electronic) – overhaul

3   Remove the distributor as described in Chapter 4.

4   Remove the distributor cap, rotor and protective shield.

5   Drive out the pin and take off the pinion gear.

6   Extract the circlip and remove the thrust washers.

7   Extract the fixing screw and remove the wiring harness, distributor shaft, sensor and vacuum capsule.

8   Do not lose the balance weight washers. Remove the magnet.

9   Reassembly is a reversal of dismantling, but fit the magnet so that the yellow mark is visible and towards the drive pinion.

All electronic ignition (AEI) system – description

10   The AEI system is fitted to all CX 25 vehicles. The components of the system are an ignition computer, either one or two synchronization sensors, a vacuum sensor, two ignition coils, the spark plugs and associated wiring. There is no distributor.

11   Initial ignition timing is determined by the synchronization sensor which are mounted close to the flywheel. One sensor responds to the passage of a 'slug' fixed to the flywheel at the static or idle firing point

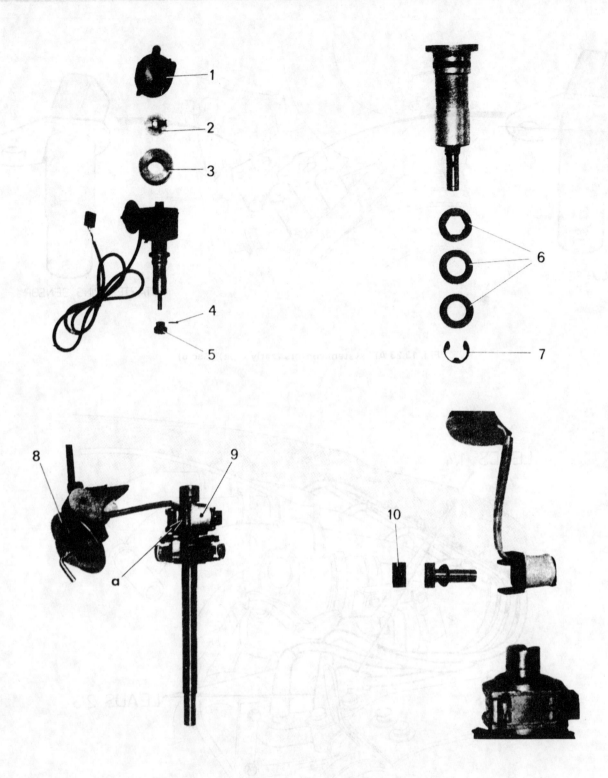

Fig. 13.22 Components of the SEV-Marchal electronic distributor (Sec 6)

1 Distributor cap	4 Pin	7 Circlip	10 Magnet
2 Rotor	5 Drive pinion	8 Vacuum capsule	a Yellow alignment mark
3 Shield	6 Washers	9 Sensor	

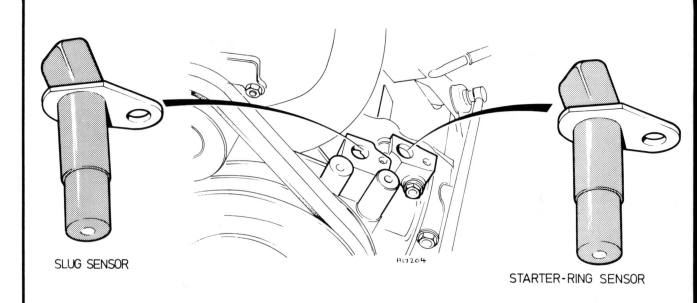

SLUG SENSOR

H17204

STARTER-RING SENSOR

Fig. 13.23 AEI system sensors (early type) (Sec 6)

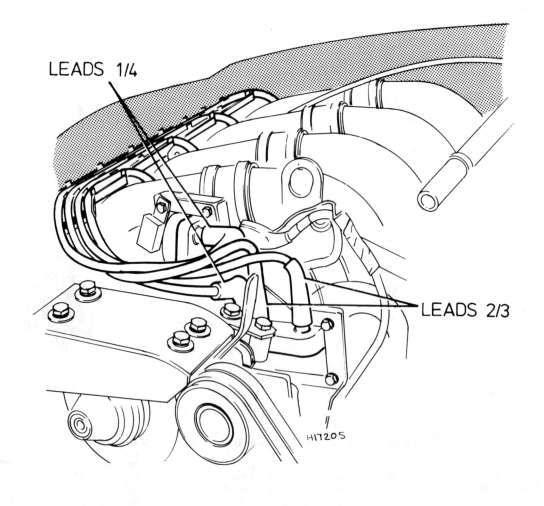

LEADS 1/4

LEADS 2/3

H17205

Fig. 13.24 AEI system ignition coils (Sec 6)

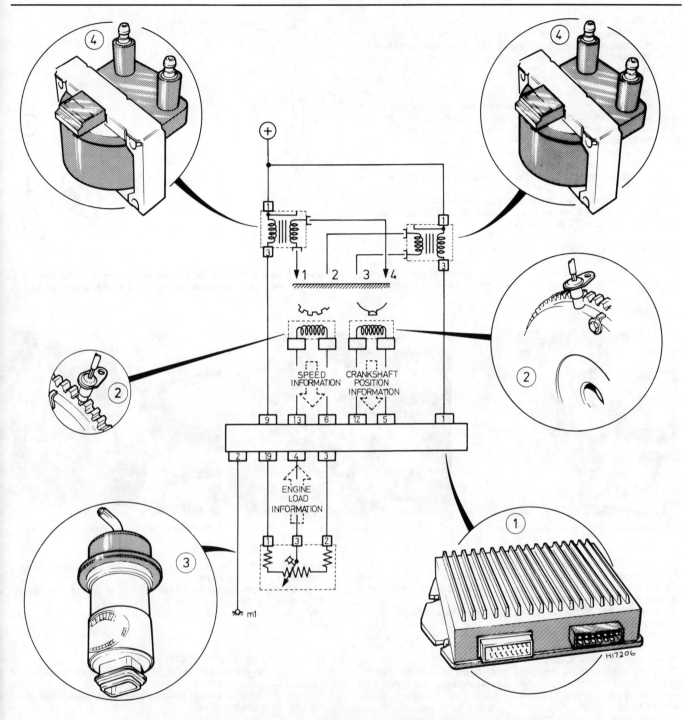

Fig. 13.25 AEI system schematic (Sec 6)

1   Computer (under dash or on   2   Flywheel sensors   3   Vacuum sensor   4   Ignition coils
*   inner wing)*

for cylinders 1 and 4. The second sensor detects engine speed by the speed of the starter ring gear teeth passing it; this information is used by the computer to determine speed-related ('centrifugal') advance. (On 1987 model year vehicles there is only one dual function sensor, which picks up from a datum tooth on the starter ring).

12 The vacuum sensor enables the computer to read inlet manifold vacuum and make an appropriate correction to the ignition timing.

13 On Turbo models, a crankcase-mounted knock sensor detects the onset of pre-ignition (pinking) and causes the ignition timing to be retarded until the pre-ignition stops. A warning light alerts the driver to any malfunction in this system. The knock sensor is on the right-hand end of the engine, in front of the timing cover.

14 Each ignition coil has two HT terminals, one spark plug being connected to each terminal. The coil secondary windings are not earthed. When the computer triggers the appropriate coil to provide a spark at No 1 cylinder, a spark occurs at No 4 as well. Since No 4 is then on the exhaust stroke, this spark is 'wasted'; after one rotation of the crankshaft, No 4 fires and the spark at No 1 is 'wasted'. This is a similar system to that used for many years on the two-cylinder Citroën engines.

15 There is no sensor which directly indicates the firing point for cylinders 2 and 3, but the computer triggers that coil halfway between the firing points for Nos 1 and 4.

AEI system – maintenance

16 Maintenance of the system is limited to inspection and renewal of the spark plugs at the specified intervals, and inspection and cleaning of the HT leads and coil towers. No direct adjustment of the ignition timing is possible.

AEI system – fault finding

17 If misfiring occurs, check the condition and electrode gap of the spark plugs before suspecting other faults. Turbocharged models are particularly sensitive to the type and condition of the plugs.
18 If the knock sensor malfunction warning light comes on, check that the knock sensor is properly seated on the crankcase. The insertion of a flat washer between the sensor and the crankcase may improve matters. After fitting the washer, tighten the sensor to the specified torque.
19 Apart from simple continuity checks, further fault finding requires special test equipment, or a supply of known good units for testing by substitution. Consult a Citroën dealer.

Spark plugs (all models) – removal and refitting

20 Disconnect the HT leads from the spark plugs or extension rods by pulling the sealing bungs out of the spark plug wells (photo). Do not pull on the HT leads themselves. Label the HT leads with their cylinder

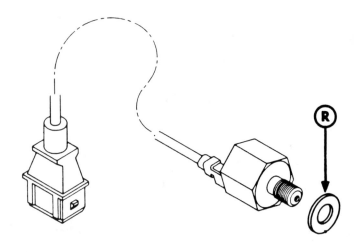

Fig. 13.26 Knock sensor, showing flat washer (R) which must be fitted between sensor and crankcase (Sec 6)

6.20 Disconnecting a spark plug HT lead

6.23 Unscrewing a spark plug

6.24 Removing a spark plug from its well

numbers if there is any possibility of confusion.
21 On models with separate extension rods and insulator tubes, pull out the tubes and unscrew the rods. (On later models the extensions are integral with the HT leads).
22 Blow out any dirt from around the spark plugs, using a bicycle pump or an air line.
23 Unscrew the spark plugs. A long box spanner, or a plug socket and extension bar, will be needed for this (photo).
24 Remove the spark plugs from their wells (photo).
25 When refitting, use a piece of rubber or plastic tube to start the spark plugs in their threads. It should be possible to screw the plugs nearly all the way home by hand (ie without using a tommy bar or ratchet handle on the plug socket). Do not force the plug if it is cross-threaded, or damage to the cylinder head may result.
26 Tighten the plugs to the specified torque (see Chapter 4, Specificatons). In the absence of a torque wrench, tighten by no more than 90° (a quarter-turn) beyond the point where the plug washer contacts the cylinder head.
27 On models with separate extension rods and insulators, refit them (Chapter 4, Section 9, paragraph 12).
28 Reconnect the HT leads and push the sealing bungs home.

7 Clutch

Clutch cable – setting (CX 25)

1 Working within the vehicle, locate a shim (0.22 in – 5.5 mm) thick at (J) shown in Fig. 13.27.
2 Prop the pedal fully upwards using a rod.
3 Working within the engine compartment, release the locknut at the

release lever and turn the adjuster nut until the clutch release bearing is felt to contact the diaphragm.
4 Tighten the locknut without altering the position of the adjuster nut. Remove the shim and the rod.
5 When correctly adjusted, the pedal stroke should not be less than 5.3 in (135.0 mm).

Hydraulic clutch actuation (Prestige)

6 Some Prestige models have hydraulic instead of cable actuation of the clutch.
7 The clutch hydraulic system operates using LHM green fluid as for the rest of the hydraulic system.

Clutch pedal (hydraulic clutch) – adjustment

8 Refer to Fig. 13.29. Release the locknuts on the stop screw and turn the screw to obtain a clearance (J) of between 0.1 and 0.5 mm.
9 Make sure that the pushrod is in contact with the master cylinder piston and then loosen the stop screw by half a turn. Re-tighten the locknuts. The pedal will now have the correct free movement.

Clutch slave cylinder (hydraulic clutch) – adjustment

10 Working at the slave cylinder, disconnect the return spring.
11 Tighten the adjuster screw until the thrust bearing is just felt to make contact with the clutch diaphragm spring fingers.
12 Unscrew the adjuster screw by one and a quarter turns and reconnect the return spring.
13 This will give a free movement at the bearing of between 1.0 and 1.5 mm.

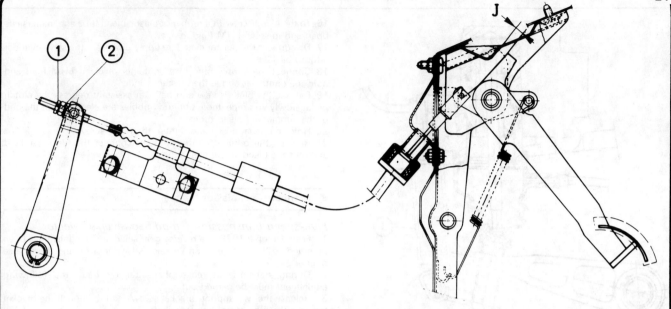

Fig. 13.27 Clutch cable setting – CX 25 (Sec 7)

1   *Locknut*   2   *Adjuster nut*   J   *Shim gap (see text)*

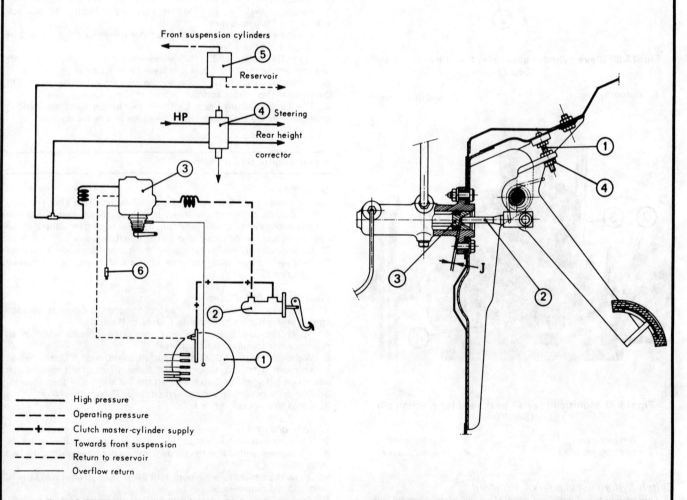

Fig. 13.28 Hydraulic clutch schematic (Sec 7)

1	*Fluid reservoir*	4	*Safety valve*
2	*Master cylinder*	5	*Front height corrector*
3	*Slave cylinder*	6	*Bleed screw*

Fig. 13.29 Pedal adjustment – hydraulic clutch (Sec 7)

1	*Stop screw*	4	*Locknut*
2	*Pushrod*		*J = 0.1 to 0.5 mm*
3	*Master cylinder piston*		*(0.004 to 0.020 in)*

High pressure
Operating pressure
Clutch master-cylinder supply
Towards front suspension
Return to reservoir
Overflow return

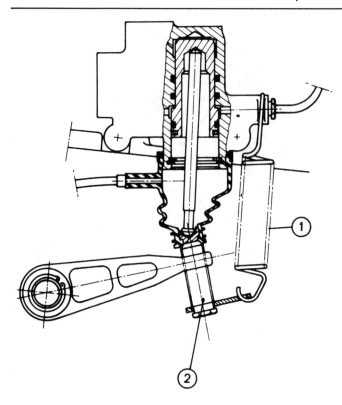

Fig. 13.30 Slave cylinder adjustment – hydraulic clutch (Sec 7)

1   Return spring   2   Adjuster screw

Fig. 13.31 Modified reverse gear selector mechanism (Sec 8)

1   Reverse gear   3   Selector shaft
2   Locking spindle   4   Support bracket

Clutch hydraulic cylinders – overhaul
14 Overhaul of the clutch master and slave cylinders is carried out in a similar way to that described for the brake assemblies in Chapter 9.

Clutch hydraulic system – bleeding
15 Remove the rubber dust cap from the bleed screw which is located above the gearbox.

16 To the bleed screw fit a rubber or plastic bleed tube and immerse its open end in some LHM fluid in a jar.
17 Disconnect the master cylinder supply pipe from the slave cylinder return hose.
18 Connect the supply pipe to a container of clean LHM fluid and hold the container above the master cylinder.
19 Release the bleed screw and have an assistant depress the clutch pedal slowly and repeatedly until no bubbles are ejected from the end of the submerged bleed tube.
20 Hold the pedal down and tighten the bleed screw.
21 Remake the original connections, disconnect the bleed jar fluid and refit the bleed screw dust cap.

8   Manual transmission

Five-speed transmission – modified reverse selector
1   From October 1979, the reverse gear selector mechanism has been modified so that 1st gear can be selected without driving the reverse pinion.
2   During transmission reassembly after overhaul, the following adjustment must be carried out.
3   Release the two support bracket screws and then push the bracket towards the 5th/reverse selector shaft.
4   Retain the shaft in this position and tighten the screws.

Bearing modifications (later models)
5   From October 1985, the primary shaft bearing at the clutch end has an integrated seal. The bearing/seal assembly is fitted with its black side facing 1st gear pinion.
6   This new bearing can be fitted to older transmissions (4-speed or 5-speed) during overhaul.
7   From December 1985, the primary shaft and secondary shaft bearings at the 5th gear cover end have been increased in size. There are consequential modifications to the bearing retaining plate, 5th driven gear and spacer and the secondary shaft nut.
8   The larger bearings can be fitted to old pattern transmissions provided that the other parts mentioned are also renewed.

9   Automatic transmission

Description
1   The three-speed fully automatic transmission fitted after February 1981 consists of a three-element torque converter and a gearbox which contains an epicyclic geartrain, a hydraulic unit for control of the speed changes, an oil pump and a centrifugal regulator.
2   During starting and acceleration, the torque converter multiplies the engine torque and replaces the clutch used with manual transmissions.

Fluid level – checking
3   Have the engine cold, preferably first thing in the morning. Start the engine and run it for one minute with N or P selected.
4   Apply the handbrake fully and move the selector lever to all positions several times, finishing in P.
5   Withdraw the dipstick from the transmission, wipe it clean, reinsert it, withdraw it for the second time. Read off the fluid level which should be between the two marks on the flat section of the dipstick.
6   Top up if necessary with specified fluid. Do not overfill. Pour the fluid into the dipstick guide hole.

Fluid – changing
7   The transmission fluid should be renewed at the specified intervals.
8   It is recommended that the fluid is drained hot by removing the two drain plugs.
9   Allow the transmission to cool, refit the plugs and pour two litres of fluid into the transmission.
10 Start the engine and check the fluid level as previously described.

Adjustments
Idling speed
11 It is important that the engine idling speed is correctly set, otherwise the transmission fluid pressure will be low.

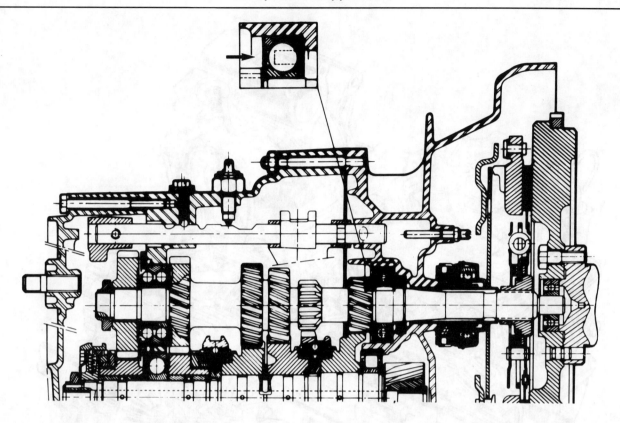

Fig. 13.32 Transmission with modified primary shaft bearing. Black side (arrowed, inset) must face 1st gear pinion (Sec 8)

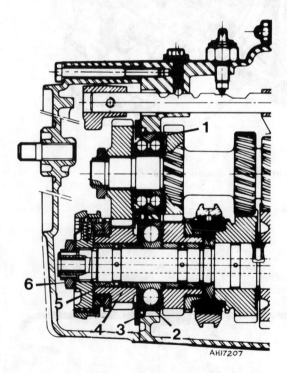

Fig. 13.33 Transmission modifications – 5th gear cover end (Sec 8)

1   Primary shaft bearing
2   Secondary shaft bearing
3   Bearing retaining plate
4   5th driven gear
5   5th gear spacer
6   Secondary shaft nut

Kickdown cable

12 The engine idle speed must be correctly set.

13 Disconnect the air intake duct at the manifold and then have an assistant fully depress the accelerator pedal. Check that the throttle valve plate is fully open.

14 Release the accelerator pedal. There should be no slack in the kickdown cable and it should be seen to move immediately the valve plate begins to rotate.

15 There should be a clearance between the stop, which is crimped to the kickdown cable, and the threaded end fitting of the cable conduit of between 0.039 and 0.079 in (1.0 and 2.0 mm). Where necessary adjust the cable by releasing the locknuts and turning them.

16 When correctly adjusted, the distance between the crimped stop and the end of the threaded end fitting should be 1.6 in (41.0 mm) with the accelerator pedal depressed to the cam hard spot.

Speed selector lever

17 Working inside the vehicle, extract the two screws which are located beneath the selector lever anti-draught brush and pull the cover plate up the lever.

18 Disconnect the link rod ball coupling.

19 Move the selector lever to P, release the fixing bolts and slide the lever mounting plate until there is sufficient clearance for the hand to pass between the knob of the lever and the centre console. Tighten the bolts.

20 Move the hand control lever to N and set the control arms in the neutral mode.

21 Release the locknut and alter the length of the link rod to allow the ball socket of the coupling to slip onto the ball-pin. Re-tighten the locknut.

22 With the selector lever still in N, unscrew the switch securing nut and pass a suitable rod into the switch holes to align it. Re-tighten the nut and remove the rod.

23 Check the selection of all speed ratios and the illumination of the selector lamps.

24 Refit the lever cover plate.

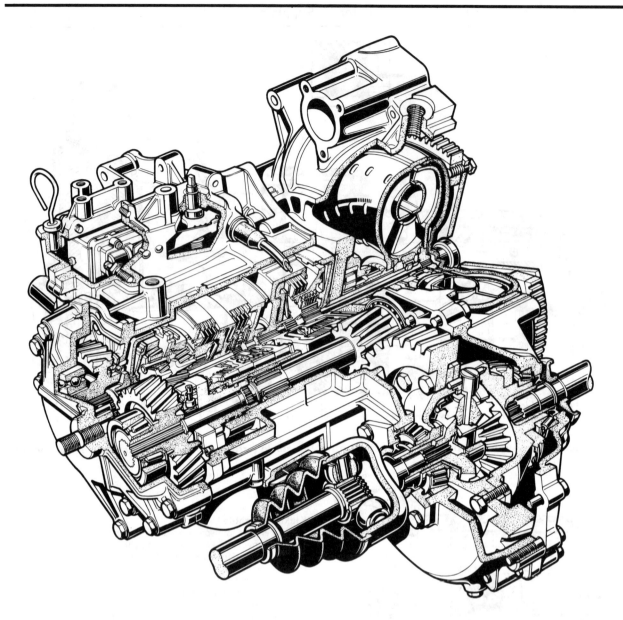

Fig. 13.34 Cutaway view of the automatic transmission (Sec 9)

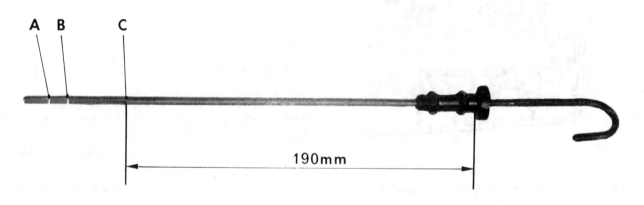

190mm

Fig. 13.35 Automatic transmission dipstick (Sec 9)

A Min cold   B Max cold   C Max hot (not marked on dipstick)

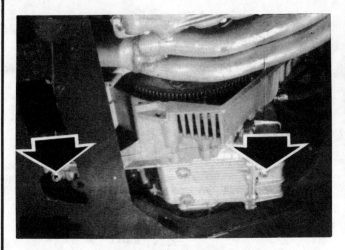

Fig. 13.36 Two drain plugs (arrowed) on automatic transmission (Sec 9)

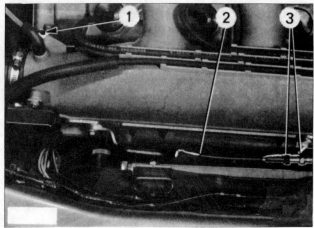

Fig. 13.37 Kickdown cable adjustment (Sec 9)

1   Valve plate screw   3   Locknuts
2   Cable inner

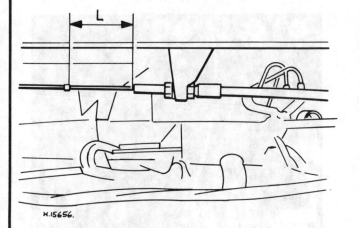

Fig. 13.38 Kickdown cable stop-to-end fitting distance – pedal depressed to hard spot (Sec 9)

L = 41 mm (1.6 in)

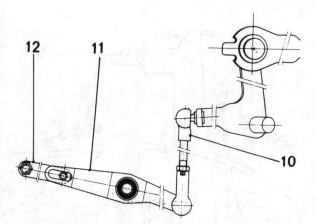

Fig. 13.39 Speed selector linkage (Sec 9)

10 Link rod   12 Control arm
11 Control arm

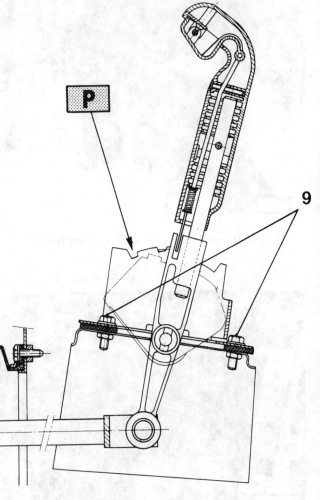

Fig. 13.40 Speed selector lever (Sec 9)

P   Park notch   9   Fixing bolts

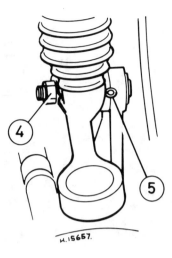

Fig. 13.41 Anti-roll bar at upper link rod (Sec 9)

4 Nut   5 Split pin

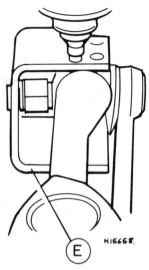

Fig. 13.42 Disconnecting a suspension balljoint (Sec 9)

E Extractor

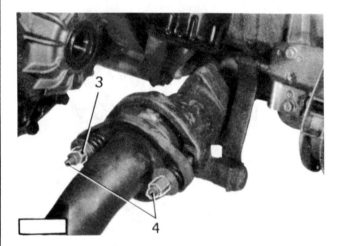

Fig. 13.43 Disconnect the exhaust coupling (Sec 9)

3 Nut   4 Studs

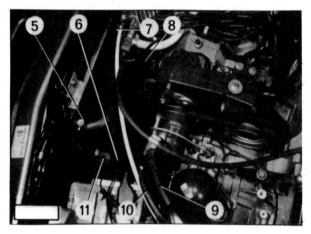

Fig. 13.44 Disconnection points – left-hand side (Sec 9)

5 Coolant hose   9   Fluid supply hose
6 Coolant hose   10 Fluid return hose
7 Air temperature sensor 11 Temperature sensor
8 Coolant hose

Fig. 13.45 Disconnection points – left-hand side (cont'd)
(Sec 9)

12 Wiring harness plug   13 Brake accumulator

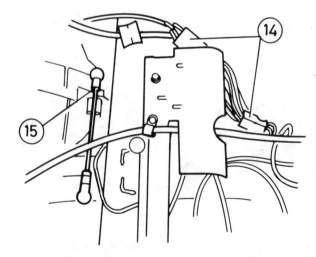

Fig. 13.46 Disconnect the wiring plugs (14) and the speed
selector control rod (15) (Sec 9)

Automatic transmission – removal (with engine)

25 The transmission and the engine are removed together and separated after removal.

26 Depending upon the type of roadwheel trim it may be possible to extract the split pins and release the driveshaft/hub nuts before raising the front of the vehicle. The nuts are very tight and the handbrake should be fully applied before attempting to unscrew them.

27 Raise the front of the vehicle and support securely on axle stands.

28 Disconnect the battery.

29 With the help of an assistant, remove the bonnet (refer to Chapter 12).

30 Remove the spare wheel and the two front roadwheels.

31 Allow time for the pressure to drop in the hydraulic system and in the front brake accumulator.

32 Drain the cooling system (Chapter 2).

33 If the driveshaft nuts have not already been released (paragraph 26) extract the split pins and remove the nut retainers and the thrust washers. Unscrew the nuts using a socket and a long bar as a lever. To prevent the hub from rotating, bolt a length of flat steel or angle iron to two of the roadwheel bolt holes.

34 Disconnect the anti-roll bar at the upper link rods.

35 Remove the nuts and the split pins and push the suspension cylinders backwards.

36 Disconnect the balljoints using the special extractor (OVT-306320-T) or similar.

37 Remove the nuts from the lower balljoints and using a conventional balljoint extractor disconnect the balljoints.

38 Release the disc pad wear sensor leads.

39 Remove the left-hand driveshaft as described in Chapter 7.

40 Remove the right-hand driveshaft also as described in Chapter 7.

41 Disconnect the exhaust pipe at the manifold flange.

42 Remove the radiator grille.

43 Remove the left-hand headlamp.

44 Remove the battery and its mounting tray.

45 Disconnect the fluid supply hose from the hydraulic pressure pump (Fig. 13.44).

46 Disconnect the fluid return hose from the pressure regulator.

47 Disconnect the three hydraulic pipes from the brake accumulator.

48 Disconnect the wiring harness plug (Fig. 13.45).

49 Disconnect the lead from the coolant temperature sensor and the air temperature sensor from the radiator.

50 Disconnect the wiring plugs (Fig. 13.46).

51 Disconnect the speedometer drive cables from the transmission.

52 Disconnect the ball-joint speed selector control rod.

53 Disconnect the coolant hoses (5,6,8 and 16) (see Figs. 13.44 and 13.47).

54 Disconnect the fuel pipes (21 and 22).

55 Disconnect the breather hoses (17, 18, 19 and 20) and withdraw the air duct.

56 Disconnect the HT cable from the ignition coil.

57 Disconnect the wiring plugs (24, 25, 26 and 27) (Fig. 13.48).

58 Remove the air cleaner resonator.

59 Refer to Fig. 13.49 and extract the bumper screws, then remove the lower valance screws. Remove the valance.

60 Remove the brake accumulator.

61 Disconnect the fluid cooler pipe unions and allow the oil to drain (Fig. 13.50).

62 Remove the fixing screws and withdraw the fluid cooler.

63 Unscrew the bolt from the horn bracket and disconnect the wiring harness plug from the radiator cooling fan (Fig. 13.51).

64 Unbolt and remove the radiator/fans downwards.

65 Attach a chain or lifting sling to the engine so that it is hooked under the exhaust manifold and also connected to the engine block with a bolt (Fig. 13.52).

66 Raise the hoist to just take the weight of the engine.

67 Remove the spindle (Fig. 13.53).

68 Remove the engine/transmission mounting bolts and disconnect the engine stabiliser bar.

69 Raise the engine/transmission until the accelerator cable can be released from the air inlet box.

70 Hoist the power unit up and out of the engine compartment.

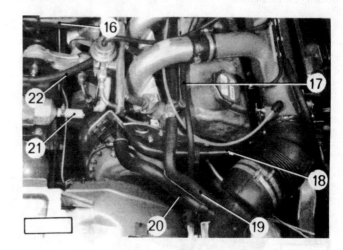

Fig. 13.47 Disconnection points – right-hand side (Sec 9)

16 Coolant hose	*20 Breather hose*
17 Breather hose	*21 Fuel inlet pipe*
18 Breather hose	*22 Fuel return hose*
19 Breather hose	

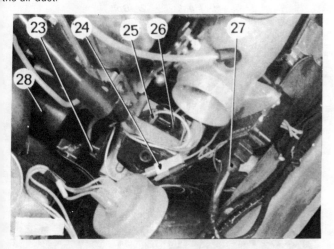

Fig. 13.48 Disconnection points – right-hand side (cont'd) (Sec 9)

23 Coil lead	*26 Wiring connector*
24 Wiring connector	*27 Switch connector*
25 Wiring connector	*28 Air cleaner resonator*

Fig. 13.49 Lower valance screw (29) and bumper screws (30) (Sec 9)

Automatic transmission – separation from engine

71 With the engine/transmission removed, clean away external dirt using paraffin and a brush or a water soluble solvent.

72 Remove the hydraulic pressure pump and the pressure regulator. To do this, first slacken the drivebelt tensioner screw (Fig. 13.54). Unbolt the tensioner support screw and then free the pump/regulator pipe flanges. Remove the pressure regulator support bolts, also the pump bolt. Remove the pump and regulator.

73 Remove the pulley which drives the pump drivebelt.

74 Release the drivebelt tensioner and take off the drivebelts.

75 Unscrew the crankshaft pulley nut and using a puller, draw off the pulley. Retain any adjustment shims.

76 Unscrew the bolts and remove the camshaft extension bearing housing.

77 Release the kickdown cable from the air inlet box.

78 Remove the alternator (Chapter 10).

79 With the cover plate removed from the base of the torque converter housing, unscrew the four driveplate to torque converter bolts. The torque converter will have to be rotated using a screwdriver inserted in the starter ring gear teeth in order to bring each bolt into view. Lock the torque converter when unscrewing the bolts, once again using a screwdriver in the ring gear teeth.

80 Unscrew and remove the bolts which secure the torque converter housing to the engine.

Fig. 13.50 Fluid cooler pipe unions (31), cooler fixing screws (32) and brake accumulator (13) (Sec 9)

Fig. 13.51 Horn bracket bolt (1) (Sec 9)

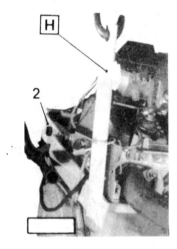

Fig. 13.52 Engine hoisting point (Sec 9)

H   Hook   2   Bolt

Fig. 13.53 Engine bearer spindle (3) (Sec 9)

Fig. 13.54 Hydraulic pump drivebelt tensioner screw (8), support screw (9) and pulley (10) (Sec 9)

81 Support the weight of the transmission and withdraw it from the engine. It is important that the torque converter is retained in its fully engaged position in its housing. To ensure this, bolt a short length of metal to a torque converter housing flange hole as a retainer.

Automatic transmission – reconnection to engine

82 Set the engine so that No 1 piston (flywheel end) is at TDC. The centring dowel on the driveplate will now be located as shown in the lower part of the driveplate (Fig. 13.56).
83 Turn the torque converter on the transmission until the PM mark on the converter is in alignment with the (a) mark on the housing.
84 Apply grease to the torque converter centre spigot.
85 Offer the torque converter to the engine and tighten the housing bolts to the specified torque.
86 Use new bolts for connecting the driveplate to the torque converter. Tighten to the specified torque wrench setting after having applied thread locking fluid to the threads.
87 Fit the camshaft pulley, replacing any shims removed at dismantling. Tighten the retaining nut to the specified torque.
88 Fit the alternator and drivebelt.
89 Fit the hydraulic pump and pressure regulator, returning any shims to their original positions.
90 Adjust the kickdown cable as described earlier.

Automatic transmission – refitting (with engine)

91 Hoist the engine/transmission into the engine compartment. As it is lowered into position, locate the accelerator cable.
92 Fit the engine bearer spindle and connect the engine/transmission mountings and the engine stabiliser bar.
93 Tighten all nuts and bolts to the specified torque.
94 Re-fit the radiator/electric cooling fan, reconnect the wiring and fit the horn.

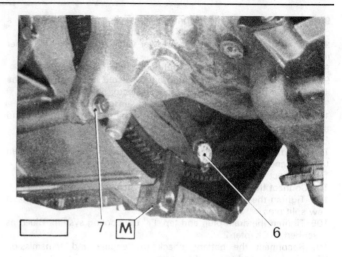

Fig. 13.55 Torque converter retainer tool (M) (Sec 9)

6 Converter-to-driveplate bolt   7 Converter
                                           housing-to-engine bolt

Fig. 13.56 Driveplate position, No 1 piston at TDC (Sec 9)

10 Driveplate   11 Dowel

Fig. 13.57 Torque converter position for mating with driveplate (Sec 9)

a Alignment marks   12 Centre spigot
M Retainer tool

95 Fit the oil cooler and reconnect the pipes, making sure that a copper washer is located at each side of the banjo union.
96 Fit the brake accumulator, the lower valance and the air cleaner resonator.
97 Reconnect the coolant, fuel and hydraulic pipes and hoses.
98 Reconnect the hydraulic pump and pressure regulator pipes, the speedometer drive cable and the speed selector link rod.
99 Reconnect all the electrical plugs and sensor leads.
100 Refit the radiator grille, the headlamp, battery mounting tray and the battery.
101 Reconnect the air duct and the exhaust pipe.
102 Refit the right-hand driveshaft as described in Chapter 7 and then the left-hand one.
103 Connect the lower swivel balljoints.
104 Connect the anti-roll link rods to the suspension upper arms.
105 Tighten the driveshaft nuts, position the nut retainers and insert new split pins.
106 Tighten the drain plug and tap. Fill the cooling system. Bleed as described in Chapter 2.
107 Reconnect the battery, check the engine and transmission lubricant levels and top up if necessary.
108 Fit the roadwheels and the bonnet.

Fault diagnosis – automatic transmission
109 Any faults which cannot be attributed to incorrect fluid level, or cured by the adjustments described in this Section, should be referred to a Citroën dealer or transmission specialist.

10 Driveshafts

Driveshaft renewal (all models)
1   Several different lengths and patterns of driveshaft have been fitted to the CX range. Make sure that a new driveshaft is the correct one for the vehicle in question.

2   Apart from rubber bellows and circlips, no spares for the driveshafts are available. Reconditioned driveshafts may be available as well as new ones – consult a Citroën dealer for details.

11 Braking system

Compensator/brake control valve (1982 on) – description
1   From July 1982, GTi vehicles are fitted with a combined brake control valve and brake pressure limiter. The same type of combined unit is fitted to Safari models from March 1985.
2   The combined unit (called a compensator/brake control valve) is shown in Fig. 13.58, which may be compared with Figs. 9.10 and 9.14 in Chapter 9.
3   No specific dismantling instructions exist, but repair kits for the valve are available.
4   The fitting of the new valve has caused changes to be made to the hydraulic pipe runs and (when applicable) the clutch cable.
5   The new valve cannot be fitted to earlier models.

Compensator/brake control valve – bleeding procedure
6   Bleed the front and rear brake hydraulic circuits as described in Chapter 9, Section 11.
7   Bleed the compensator/brake control valve at the bleed nipple on the valve with the engine running, the pressure regulator bleed screw tightened and the brake pedal applied.
8   Tighten the bleed nipple when LHM free of air bubbles emerges from it.
9   Top up the hydraulic fluid level (Chapter 8, Section 4).

Handbrake cable – renewal (all models)
10 Chock the rear wheels, slacken the front wheel bolts and release the handbrake. Raise and support the front of the vehicle and remove the front wheels.
11 Remove the cover plates to expose the cable locknuts at the calipers.

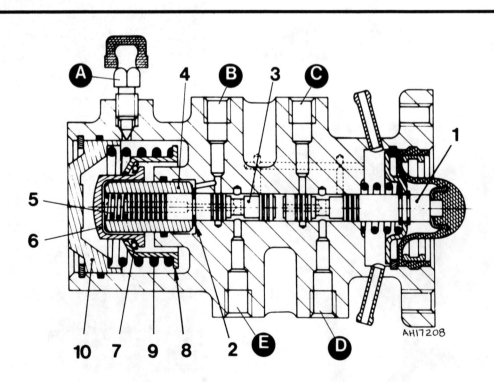

Fig. 13.58 Sectional view of compensator/brake control valve (Sec 11)

A Bleed nipple	E To rear brakes	4 Shuttle	8 Spring cap
B From rear suspension	1 Slide valve (front circuit)	5 Slide valve spring	9 Compensator spring
C High pressure inlet	2 Circlip	6 Cup	10 Cover
D To front brakes	3 Slide valve (rear circuit)	7 Intermediate bearing	

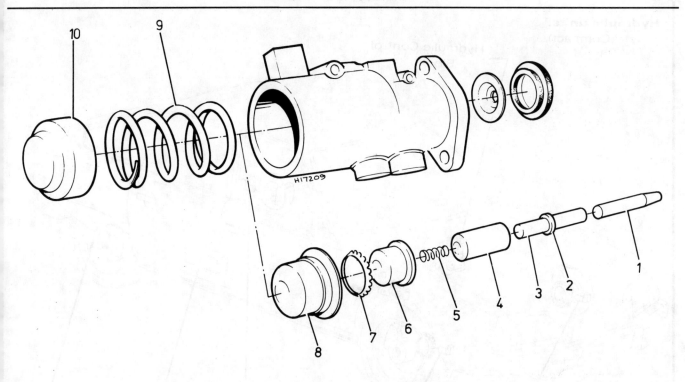

Fig. 13.59 Compensator/brake control valve components (Sec 11)

For key see Fig. 13.58

12 Unscrew the nuts and withdraw the cables from the caliper arm trunnions.

13 Remove the left-hand side panel from the centre console and hinge the panel downwards on the left-hand side of the heater casing.

14 Disconnect the cables from the equaliser now exposed at the dashboard.

15 Pull the cables out of the dashboard.

16 Refitting is a reversal of removal, grease all pivots and smear the threaded end fittings of the cables with high melting point grease.

17 Adjust the handbrake as described in Section 12, Chapter 9.

Brake disc securing screws (1982 on)

18 As from February 1982, the brake disc is secured to the hub by a single screw instead of two used previously.

Rear disc pad anti-rattle springs (1978 on)

19 As from December 1978 on CX Saloon and Prestige models, the anti-rattle springs fitted to the rear disc pads are inverted so that the ears of the spring are located at the top of the caliper aperture instead of the bottom as was the case on earlier models.

Anti-lock braking system (ABS) – description

20 An anti-lock braking system (ABS) has been available on some CX models since March 1985.

21 The ABS monitors the rotational speed of each roadwheel during braking. If any wheel begins to slow at a faster rate than the others, showing that it is on the point of locking, the ABS reduces the hydraulic pressure to that wheel's brake caliper. (In fact both rear calipers receive the same hydraulic pressure, even if only one rear wheel is locking). As the wheel grips again, its rotational speed matches the others and hydraulic pressure to the caliper is restored. This cycle can be repeated several times per second.

22 The main components of the ABS are the four wheel sensors, the electronic control unit (ECU) and the hydraulic control block. The hydraulic control block contains three electrically-operated valves – one for each front brake caliper and one for the rear brake circuit.

23 The electronic control unit incorporates a self-test facility. In normal operation, the ABS warning light on the instrument panel will light when the ignition is switched on and go out when the engine is started. If the light stays on, or comes on during driving, this shows

Fig. 13.60 Rear disc pad anti-rattle springs – later models (Sec 11)

that the ECU has detected a fault and that the ABS is not working. Normal braking is unaffected.

24 There are also two relays, located under the spare wheel, associated with the ABS. One relay protects the ECU from voltage surges, and is known as the overload relay; the other feeds the valves in the control block and is known as the electro-valve relay.

25 No repairs are possible to ABS components. Even the valves in the control block cannot be renewed separately.

26 The ABS cannot overturn the laws of physics: stopping distances will inevitably be greater on loose or slippery surfaces. However, it does give even inexperienced drivers a good chance of retaining control of the vehicle under panic braking conditions.

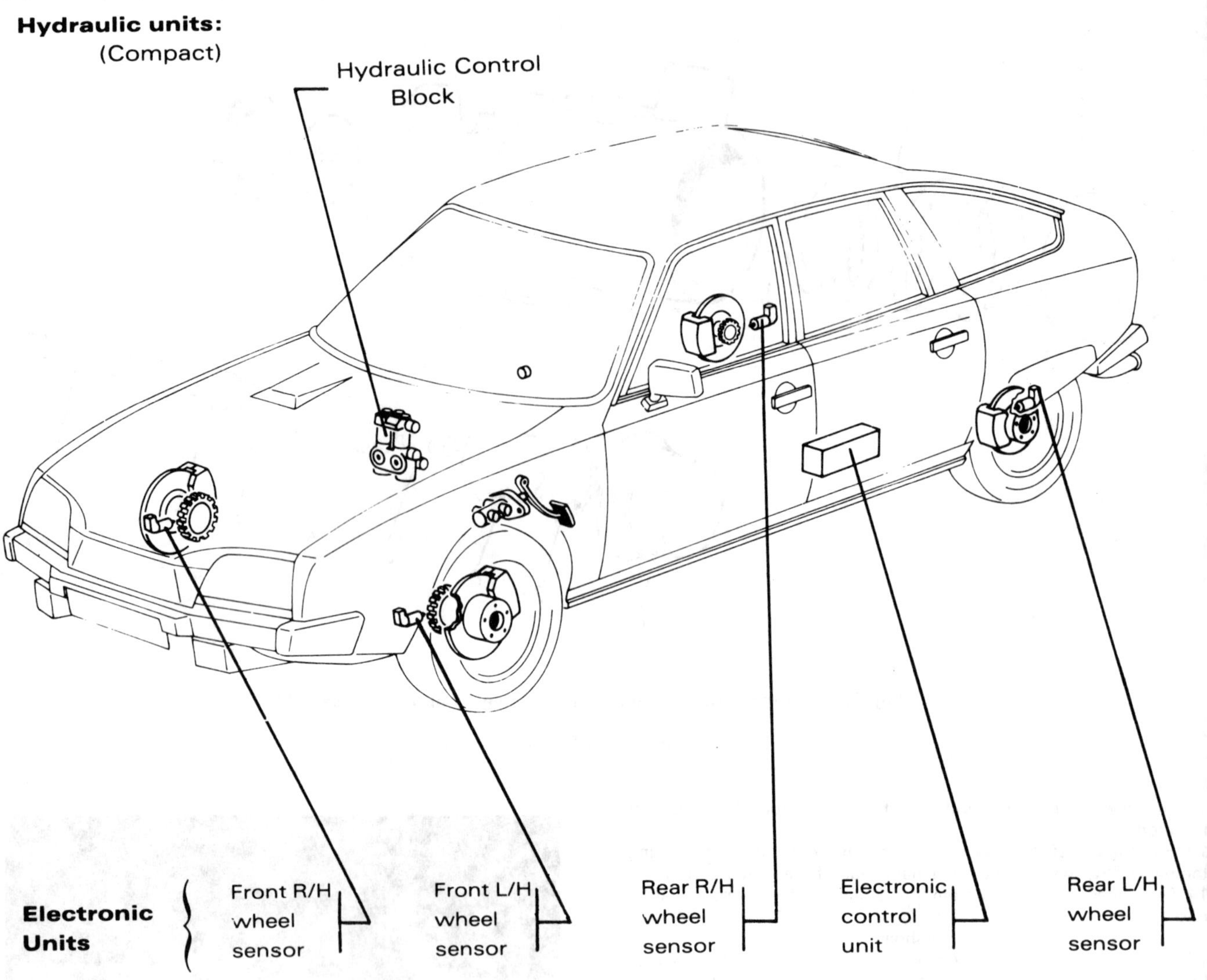

Hydraulic units:
(Compact)

Hydraulic Control
Block

Electronic Units {

Front R/H wheel sensor

Front L/H wheel sensor

Rear R/H wheel sensor

Electronic control unit

Rear L/H wheel sensor

Fig. 13.61 ABS system components. LHD shown, RHD similar (Sec 11)

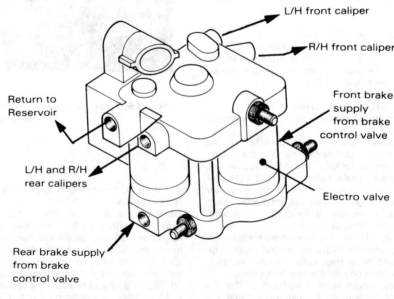

L/H front caliper

R/H front caliper

Return to Reservoir

Front brake supply from brake control valve

L/H and R/H rear calipers

Electro valve

Rear brake supply from brake control valve

Fig. 13.62 ABS hydraulic control block (Sec 11)

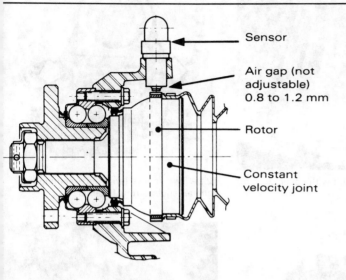

Sensor

Air gap (not adjustable) 0.8 to 1.2 mm

Rotor

Constant velocity joint

Fig. 13.63 Sectional view of front hub, showing ABS wheel sensor (Sec 11)

ABS components – removal and refitting
Wheel sensor
27 Slacken the wheel nuts, raise the vehicle and remove the roadwheel.
28 Disconnect the sensor wiring plug and free the wiring from any clips or ties.
29 Remove the sensor securing screw and withdraw the sensor from its bore (photos).

30 Clean the sensor and/or bore as necessary.
31 Refit by reversing the removal operations.

Hydraulic control block
32 Depressurise the brake hydraulic system (Chapter 9, Section 7 and elsewhere).
33 Remove the spare wheel. Remove the spare wheel undertray, which is secured by two bolts (photo).
34 Disconnect the control block multi-plug. This is housed in a special protective case, which is held shut by two 'Torx' screws (photos).
35 Identify and disconnect the hydraulic unions from the control block. Be prepared for some spillage of hydraulic fluid.
36 Unbolt the control block and remove it.
37 Refit by reversing the removal operations. Use new seals on the hydraulic unions.
38 Bleed the complete braking system on completion.

Electronic control unit (ECU)
39 Remove the rear seat cushion.
40 Unbolt the ECU and its cover plate from the brackets (photos).
41 Disconnect the multi-plug and remove the ECU.
42 Refit by reversing the removal operations.

12 Electrical system

Battery maintenance
1 Later models are fitted with a 'maintenance-free' battery; earlier models may be fitted with such a battery as a replacement for the original type.
2 Maintenance is limited to keeping the battery and terminals clean and dry. Topping-up of the electrolyte is not required, and there may not be any provision even for inspecting the electrolyte level.
3 Observe the battery manufacturer's instructions concerning long-term checks of the electrolyte and precautions with regard to charging.

11.29A Undoing an ABS wheel sensor screw

11.29B Removing the wheel sensor from its bore

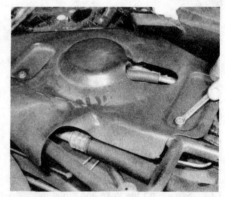

11.33 Unbolting the spare wheel under-tray

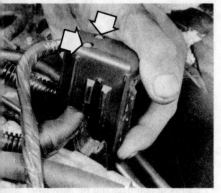

11.34A Unclipping the ABS control block multi-plug case. Two 'Torx' screws arrowed

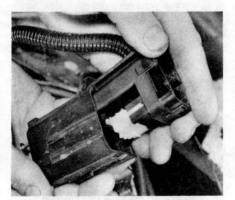

11.34B Separating the two halves of the multi-plug case

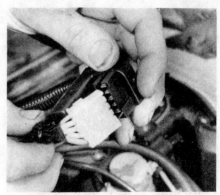

11.34C Disconnecting the multi-plug

11.40A Unbolting the ABS control unit cover

11.40B ABS control unit with cover removed

12.8A Two screws (arrowed) securing the voltage regulator/brush carrier

12.8B Removing the voltage regulator/brush carrier

12.9 Brush soldering points (arrowed)

12.15 Removing a starter motor through-bolt

12.17 Separating the yoke and armature from the drive end housing

12.19 Removing the commutator end cover

12.21A Removing the pinion shaft cover

12.21B Removing the U-clip and washer

12.22 Removing the drive end housing through-bolt

12.23 Reduction gear and thrust washer

12.25 Removing the solenoid from the drive end housing

12.26A Removing the rubber plug and spring ...

12.26B ... followed by the operating lever

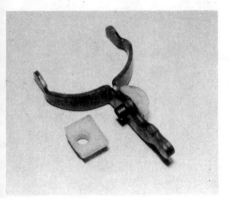
12.26C Operating lever and pivot halves

12.27A Driving down the pinion collar

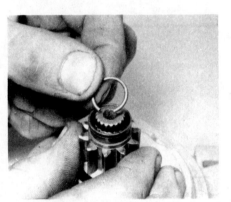
12.27B Remove the spring ring and collar ...

Alternator – Paris-Rhone

4   The voltage regulator used in conjunction with Paris-Rhone alternators is of remotely mounted type located on the front left inner wing valance.
5   The diode rectifier bridge is also remotely mounted on the upper rail just to the rear of the right-hand headlamp.

Alternator with integral regulator – brush renewal

6   Some later models are fitted with an alternator which has an integral voltage regulator. The voltage regulator is mounted on the rear of the alternator housing and also carries the brushes.
7   To remove the brushgear on such an alternator, first unclip the rear cover.
8   Remove the two screws which secure the voltage regulator/brush carrier. Disconnect the field lead and remove the regulator (photos).
9   The brushes can be removed independently of the regulator if they are worn, but the old brushes will have to be unsoldered and the new brushes soldered into place (photo). This work should be done by someone who has experience of soldering small electronic components.
10   Reconnect and secure the voltage regulator/brush carrier and refit the cover.

Starter motor (Mitsubishi) – description

11   A starter motor made by Mitsubishi is fitted to some models from mid-1979. It differs from the other makes of starter motor described in Chapter 10 by having reduction gearing between the armature and the drive pinion.
12   The principle of operation of this type of starter motor is unchanged. The effect of the reduction gearing is to reduce the rotational speed of the drive pinion and to increase its torque.
13   In operation this starter motor makes a noise unlike that made by direct drive motors. Provided that it is performing satisfactorily, do not attempt to overhaul the motor in an attempt to correct this noise.

Starter motor (Mitsubishi) – dismantling and reassembly

14   Clean the motor externally. Scribe or paint alignment marks between the commutator end cover and the yoke, and between the yoke and the drive end housing.
15   Remove the two through-bolts from the commutator end cover (photo).
16   Disconnect the motor lead from the solenoid terminal.
17   Carefully pull the yoke and armature off the drive end housing (photo).
18   Remove the two cross-head screws from the commutator end cover. These screws are very tight.
19   Remove the commutator end cover to expose the brushplate (photo). Unhook the brush springs and withdraw the positive (field) brushes, then pull the brushplate off the commutator.
20   The armature may now be removed from the yoke.
21   To dismantle the drive end housing, remove the pinion shaft cover, which is retained by two screws. Recover the U-clip and washer from the pinion shaft (photos).
22   Remove the through-bolt which holds the two halves of the housing together (photo). Separate the housing halves.
23   Remove the thrust washer and the reduction gear from the pinion shaft (photo).
24   Remove the two screws which secure the solenoid to the drive end housing. These screws are tight.
25   Pull the solenoid out of the drive end housing, unhooking it from the operating lever (photo). Do not lose the large washer.
26   Remove the rubber plug, spring and operating lever. The operating lever pivot is in two halves (photos).
27   Remove the pinion by driving the collar down the shaft with a socket or tube, then removing the spring ring, collar and pinion. Recover the spring (photos).
28   The pinion shaft can now be removed from the housing (photo).
29   Examine all components and renew as necessary. Check the availability and price of spare parts, and the price of a new or reconditioned motor, before proceeding. The armature ball-bearings

are available separately, but the pinion shaft bearing is not. Brushes are only available complete with brushplate.

30 Commence reassembly by inserting the pinion shaft into the drive end housing. Fit the spring, pinion and collar. Insert the spring ring and cover the pinion and collar upwards so that the ring enters the groove in the collar.

31 The remainder of reassembly is a reversal of the dismantling procedure, noting the following points:

(a) Apply a little grease to the reduction gear teeth and to the inside of the pinion shaft cover. Take care not to get grease on the commutator or brushes

(b) Prepare the brushplate by raising the negative (earth) brushes and holding them with their springs as shown (photo). Fit the brushplate, raise the springs onto the tops of the brushes, then insert the positive brushes and apply their springs

(c) If difficulty is experienced in inserting the long through-bolts, slacken the drive end housing through-bolt temporarily to allow the housings to take up their correct alignment

Front foglamp (1986 on) – removal and refitting

32 Remove the closing panel (if fitted) below the foglamp. This is secured by three screws.

33 Remove the two screws and nuts which secure the foglamp. Do not disturb the aiming screw (photo).

34 Withdraw the foglamp and disconnect its wiring. The bulb may now be renewed (photos).

35 Refit by reversing the removal operations. Check the aiming of the light if a new unit is being fitted.

Auxiliary headlight bulbs – renewal

36 Some models have auxiliary headlight bulbs which are lit during main beam operation.

37 Remove the auxiliary bulb cover screw and release the cover (photo).

38 Disconnect the bulb wire, release the spring clip and withdraw the bulb (photo).

39 Do not touch the new bulb with the fingers (see Chapter 10, Section 18).

12.27C ... and the pinion and spring

12.28 Removing the pinion shaft from the housing

12.31 Negative brushes retained by springs bearing on their sides (arrowed)

12.33 Removing a foglamp retaining nut (bumper removed for clarity)

12.34A Remove the rubber cover ...

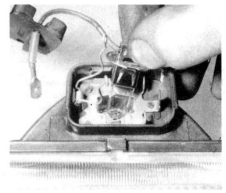
12.34B ... and unclip the front foglamp bulb

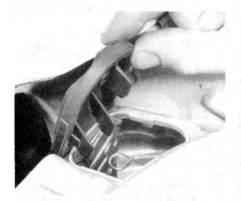
12.37 Removing the auxiliary headlight bulb cover

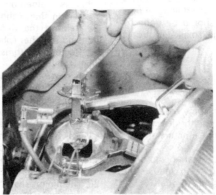
12.38 Removing an auxiliary headlight bulb

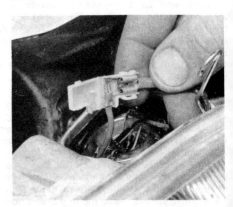
12.40 Wiring connector insulating cover (open to show connector)

40 Fit the new bulb by reversing the removal operations. Make sure that the wiring connector is protected by its insulating cover (photo).

Central door locking system – description

41 This is fitted to certain later models to control the side doors, luggage boot and fuel filler flap. (On estate models the tailgate and fuel filler flap are not included in the system).
42 The electrical door locking units are located within the door cavities, while the one for the fuel filler flap is mounted on a plate fitted between the filler neck collar and the flap (photo).
43 A control unit and warning lamp timer are positioned behind the glovebox.
44 In the event of failure in the fuel filler flap lock, the flap may be released by inserting a long screwdriver through the cut-out provided in the rear wheel arch lining to release the lock pin.

Remote locking system – description

45 Fitted to some 1986 and later models, the remote locking system allows the operator to lock and unlock all the doors using a pocket transmitter. The transmitter sends a coded infra-red signal to a receiver mounted in the interior light surround. If the code received is correct,

the receiver triggers the central locking system control unit to lock or unlock the doors.
46 The transmitter is powered by three small batteries, which can be renewed after unclipping the key ring end of the casing. Observe correct polarity when fitting batteries.
47 A signal lamp mounted on the driver's door trim lights for a few seconds when the doors have been locked using the transmitter. When the doors are unlocked by the same means, the vehicle interior light is switched on.
48 The key can still be used to open the driver's door, and so operate the central locking system, in the usual way.

Bulb failure warning system – description

49 Fitted to 1986 and later models, the bulb failure warning system monitors the current drawn by the tail lights, stop-lights and (1986 models only) rear foglights. If a bulb fails, the current drawn is reduced and a warning light on the instrument panel comes on.
50 Monitoring is carried out by the bulb failure warning controller, located in the left-hand rear wheel arch (Saloon) or under the rear seat (Estate). Warning of bulb failure is only given when the particular rear light circuit is in use, although in the case of the stop-lights, the

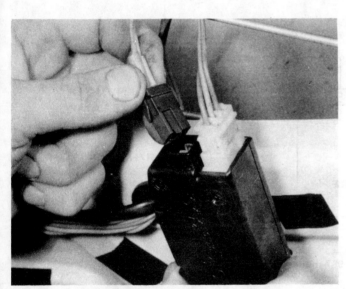

12.42 Disconnecting a front door locking unit

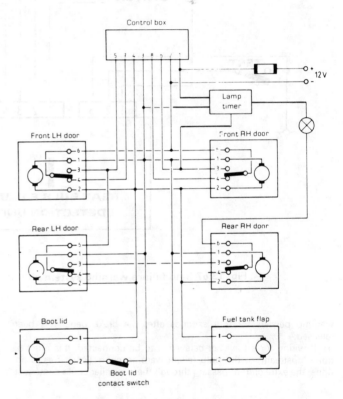

Fig. 13.64 Central door locking system circuit (Sec 12)

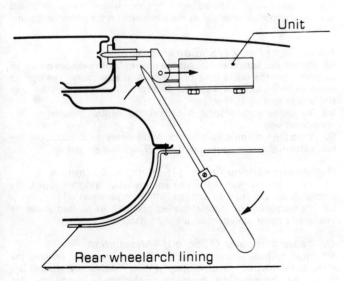

Fig. 13.65 Releasing the fuel filler flap (Sec 12)

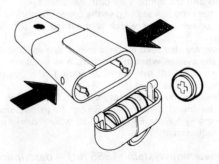

Fig. 13.66 Remote locking system transmitter. Squeeze sides (arrowed) to release battery carrier (Sec 12)

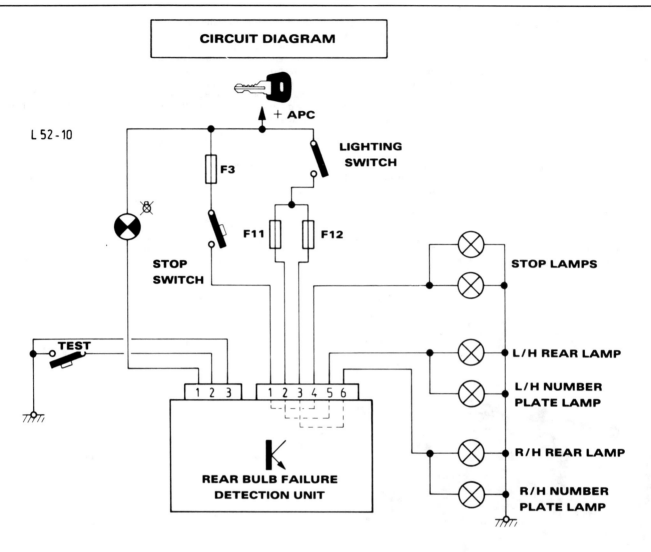

Fig. 13.67 Bulb failure warning system circuit. 1987 model year shown – 1986 similar (Sec 12)

warning persists for four seconds after the brake pedal has been released.

51 If wiring for a trailer or caravan is to be connected, this must be done 'upstream' of the bulb failure warning controller. If this is not done, the extra current passing through the controller could damage it.

'Dim-dip' headlights – general

52 To comply with current legislation, 1987 model year vehicles have 'dim-dip' headlights. These headlights are lit at reduced intensity when the sidelights and the ignition are both switched on.

53 The voltage drop needed to give the correct brightness is achieved by using a power resistor which is mounted on the bonnet front crossmember.

54 Two relays are also used in the 'dim-dip' system. One relay is used to activate the system when the ignition and sidelights are on. The other relay switches off the 'dim-dip' lighting when dipped or main beam headlights are selected.

55 No futher information was available at the time of writing. No circuit will be found in the main wiring diagrams since these are prepared primarily for the French market, where 'dim-dip' lighting is not a legal requirement.

Door ajar warning system (1986 on) – description

56 The door ajar warning system operates by means of a microswitch in each door lock. Similar switches are fitted to the boot or tailgate lock and to the bonnet front crossmember (photo).

57 When the doors and bonnet are fully shut, the switch contacts are open. When a door or the bonnet is not shut, the contacts are closed and the appropriate segment of the silhouette on the instrument panel is illuminated.

Interior light delay (1986 on) – description

58 The interior light delay causes the interior light to remain on for 15 seconds after the doors have been closed. It also causes the light to come on for 15 seconds when the doors are unlocked using the key or the remote locking transmitter.

59 The delay unit is located behind the centre console on the right-hand side.

60 When the ignition is switched on or the doors are locked, the delay unit extinguishes the light even if the 15 seconds are not up.

'Lights on' warning buzzer (1986 on) – description

61 The 'lights on' warning buzzer sounds when a door is open, the sidelights are switched on and the ignition is switched off.

62 The buzzer and its associated electronic unit are located under the instrument panel top cover on the right-hand side (photo).

On-board computer (1986 on) – description

63 Fitted to fuel injection models only, the computer enables the driver to receive information relating its time, distance covered and fuel consumed. Normal clock functions (including an alarm) are also available. Setting up and use of the computer are described in the vehicle operator's handbook.

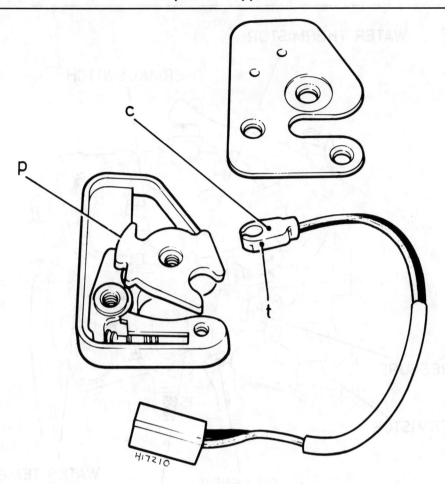

Fig. 13.68 Door ajar microswitch (c). With door shut, switch lug (t) engages in notch (p) (Sec 12)

64 The components of the computer are as follows:

   (a) A keyboard/calculator unit, located in the centre console
   (b) A fuel calculator, linked to the fuel injection system, located below the console next to the gearshift lever
   (c) A distance sensor, located on the speedometer cable in the engine compartment (photo)

65 Output from the computer is displayed on one of the panels in the digital display unit. The illumination of the display is automatically dimmed when the lights are switched on.

On-board computer (1986 on) – fault diagnosis
66 If a fault develops in the computer, detailed testing should be left to a Citroën dealer or other competent specialist. As a rule of thumb, however, the following points apply.
67 When the fault is time-related, the keyboard is faulty.
68 When the fault is distance-related, the distance sensor is faulty.
69 When the fault relates to fuel consumption, the fuel calculator is faulty, or the computer has not been programmed correctly by the driver. (Remember that the amount of fuel put into the tank must be entered into the computer at each refuelling).

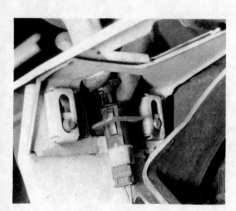

12.56 'Bonnet ajar' warning switch

12.62 Warning buzzer inside the instrument panel

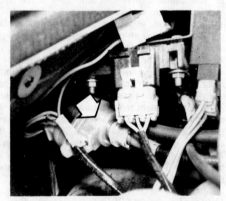

12.64 Distance sensor (arrowed) connected in speedometer cable

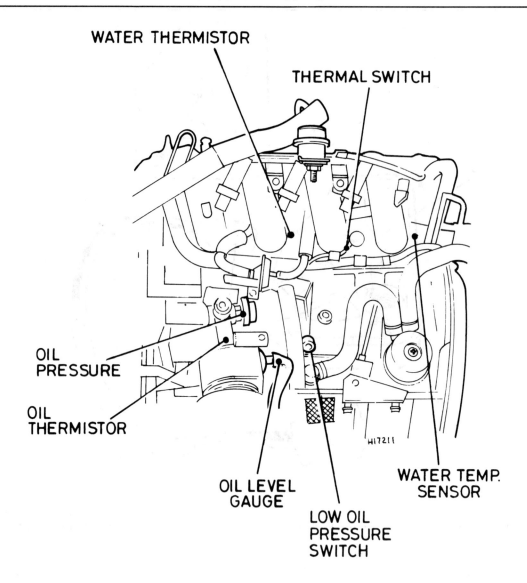

Fig. 13.69 Engine oil temperature, pressures and level sensors (Sec 12)

70 If there is no display from the computer, check fuse No 2. (This fuse also protects other circuits – see Specifications).

71 If the computer only displays the last function used, check fuse No 7. Again, this fuse protects other circuits.

Digital display unit (1986 on) – description

72 The digital display unit is located in the centre of the dashboard and contains up to four liquid crystal displays. Three displays supply information on engine oil temperature, coolant temperature and ambient (outside) air temperature. The remaining display carries clock or computer output.

73 As well as the LCDs themselves, the digital display unit contains integrated circuits which translate the information from the temperature sensors or computer into a signal appropriate for the LCDs. If any part of the unit malfunctions, it must be renewed complete.

74 Oil and coolant temperature functions are linked to the instrument panel warning lights. When the critical temperatures are exceeded (114°C/237°F for coolant, 145°C/293°F for oil) the warning lights will come on and the temperature displays will flash.

75 The oil and coolant temperature sensors are located on the side of the engine. The ambient air temperature sensor is located in the front bumper on the left-hand side (photo).

Oil level gauge (1986 on) – description

76 Instead of the pneumatic oil level gauge described in Chapter 1,

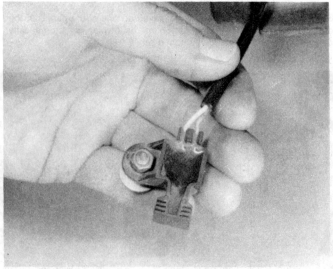

12.75 Ambient air temperature sensor

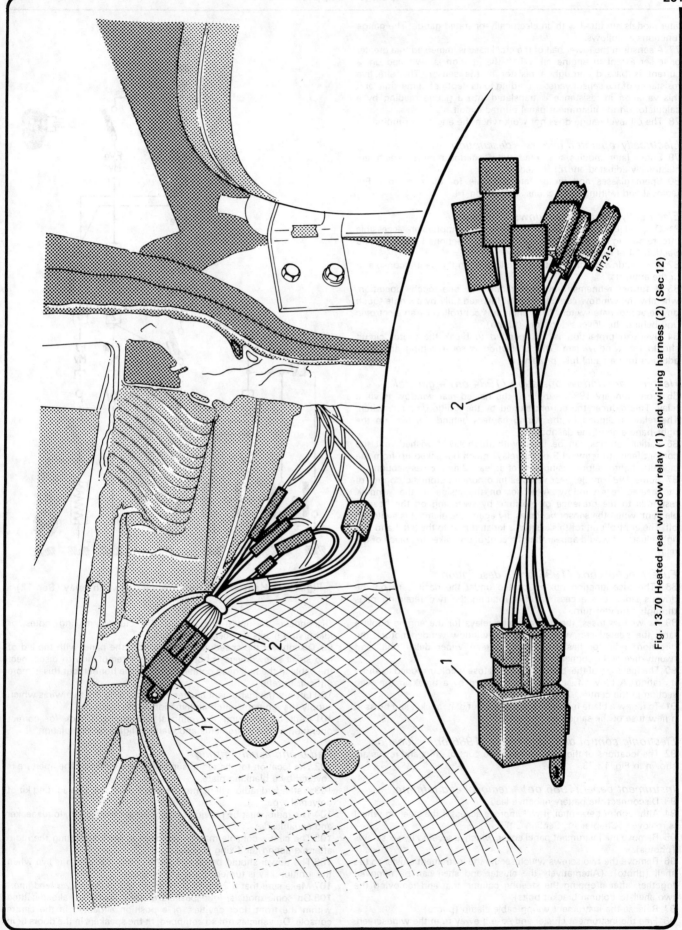

Fig. 13.70 Heated rear window relay (1) and wiring harness (2) (Sec 12)

later models are fitted with an electrically-operated gauge. The gauge functions as follows.

77 A sensor in the lower half of the crankcase is immersed to a greater or lesser extent in engine oil. When the ignition is switched on, a current is passed through a resistor in the sensor. The effective resistance of the sensor varies according to its depth of immersion, and this variation in resistance is translated into a gauge reading by a calculator on the instrument panel printed circuit.

78 The oil level gauge does not work when the engine is running.

Electrically-operated mirrors – description
79 Some later models are fitted with exterior mirrors which are electrically adjusted and/or heated.

80 Spare glasses and motors are available for these mirrors. For removal and refitting instructions see Section 14.

Electrically-operated windows – general
81 On models so equipped, the window winder motors are accessible after removing the door trim. See Chapter 12, Sections 11 and 12, and Section 14 of this Chapter.

82 The window control switches are located in the centre console or in the armrests.

83 A further refinement on later models is 'one-touch' operation, whereby the window can be raised or lowered fully by a single touch on the appropriate switch. This function is controlled by an electronic unit behind the driver's door trim (photo).

84 Overload protection is incorporated to break the motor circuit should the window jam. This protection is self-resetting and is in addition to the usual fuse protection.

Heated rear window operation (1984 on) – general
85 From January 1984, supply to the heated rear window is via a relay. This reduces the current carried by the ignition/starter switch. The relay is clipped to the wiring harness behind the trim on the right-hand side of the dashboard.

86 Earlier vehicles can be fitted with this relay if wished, but the contact feed (to terminal 3 of the relay) much be picked up from the cigarette lighter supply using wire of at least 2 mm² cross-section.

87 Some 1987 model year vehicles incorporate automatic control of the heated rear window. A sensor on the inside of the window responds to the presence of moisture by switching on the heating element; when the sensor becomes dry again, the element is switched off. The control unit for this system is located next to the left-hand rear light cluster. It would appear that the control unit takes the place of the relay.

Fuse/junction box (1986 on) – description
88 The fuse/junction box is located under the dashboard on the driver's side. It is accessible after rotating the two retaining pegs through a quarter-turn.

89 As well as fuses, the box contains relays for the engine cooling fans; the heated rear window and the window winder motors; the direction indicator flasher; the windscreen wiper delay unit, and twenty-five multi-connectors.

90 The fuses are of the 'blade' type. Each fuse is colour-coded to show its rating. A blown fuse can be recognised by a break in the wire section in the centre.

91 To renew a blade fuse, pull the old one out of its socket and press in a new fuse of the same rating (photo).

Electronic control units and relays (1986 on) – location
92 The locations of the various electronic control units and relays are shown in Fig. 13.73.

Instrument panel (1986 on) – removal and refitting
93 Disconnect the battery negative lead.

94 Although not essential, it will improve access if the steering wheel is removed (Chapter 11, Section 20).

95 Remove the instrument panel cover, which is secured by six screws (photos).

96 Remove the two screws which secure the instrument cluster to the shell (photo). (Alternatively the cluster and shell can be removed together, after dropping the steering column trim and removing the two shell-to-column bracket bolts).

97 Release the instrument wiring cable clamp (photo).

98 Free the instrument cluster and ease it away from the windscreen.

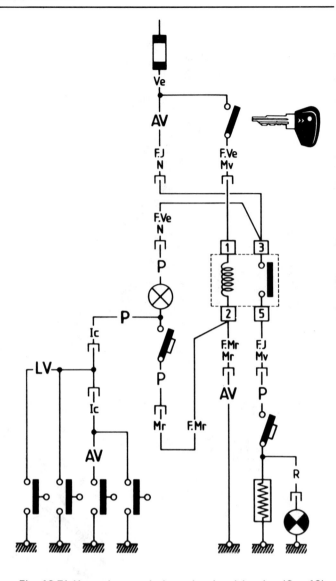

Fig. 13.71 Heated rear window circuit with relay (Sec 12)

Disconnect the multi-plugs from the cluster, making notes or identifying marks if necessary (photo).

99 Disconnect the speedometer cable from the panel with the aid of two small screwdrivers (photo). There is a temptation to disconnect the cable at the bulkhead connector under the bonnet, but this is more difficult to refit.

100 Lift out the instrument cluster, disconnecting the two wires which supply the ignition switch illumination light (photo).

101 Refit by reversing the removal operations. Check for correct operation of the instruments and warning lights on completion.

Radio and aerial – fitting
102 The location for the radio is in the centre console. The aperture is covered by a blanking plate.

103 A standard radio will fit into the space provided. Use a fitting kit of universal type.

104 The radio must be provided with a power feed, earth, loudspeaker and aerial leads.

105 The centre console may be removed to facilitate fitting the radio after extracting the fixing screws.

106 The power should be taken from a connector which is live when the ignition key is turned to the (1) position.

107 Make sure that a 2A fuse is incorporated in the power feed line.

108 On some models, loudspeakers or their leads, are already fitted within the front door cavities, or a position allocated in the centre console. On vehicles not so equipped, fit the speakers in the doors or in

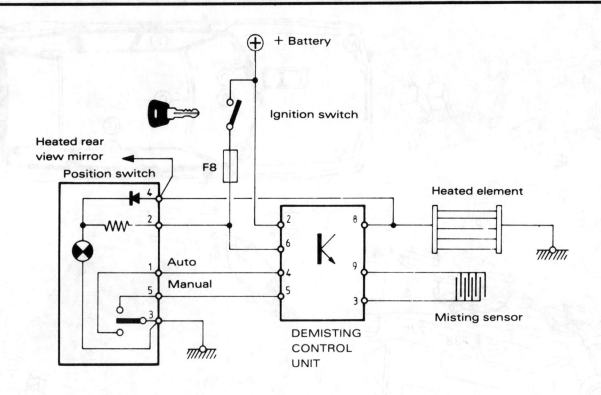

Fig. 13.72 Heated rear window circuit with automatic control (Sec 12)

12.83 'One-touch' window control unit

12.91 Removing a blade type fuse. Some relays and connectors are visible above

12.95A Instrument panel cover screws: two from the top of the meter hood ...

12.95B ... one (arrowed) at each end ...

12.95C ... and one on each side from below

12.96 Removing an instrument cluster-to-shell screw

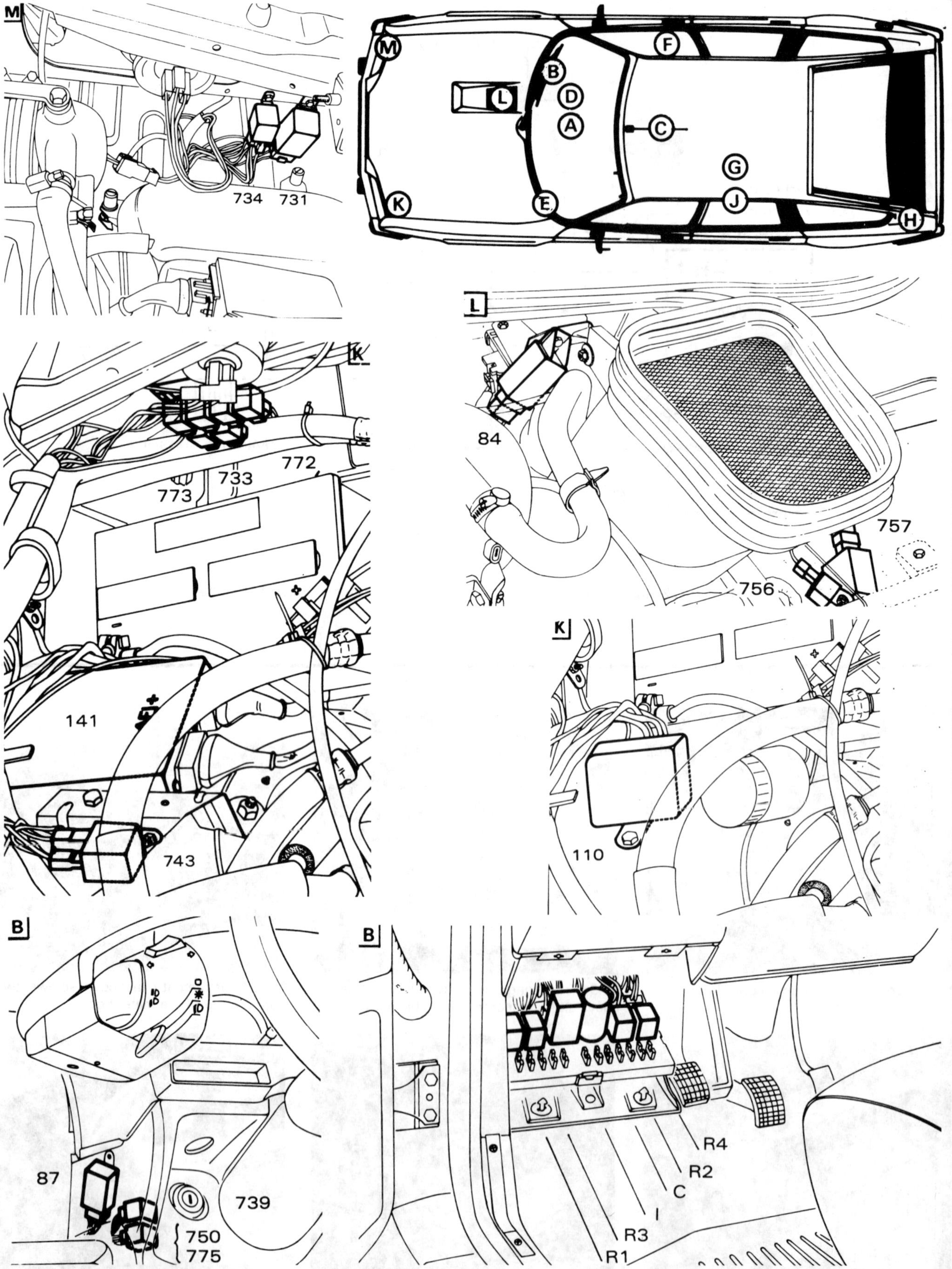
M
734
731
M
B
D
L
A
C
F
G
K
E
J
H
L
84
757
756
K
773
733
772
141
743
K
110
B
87
739
750
775
B
R4
R2
C
I
R3
R1

Fig. 13.73 Electronic control unit and relay location. Not all items are fitted to all models (Sec 12). Key on page 266

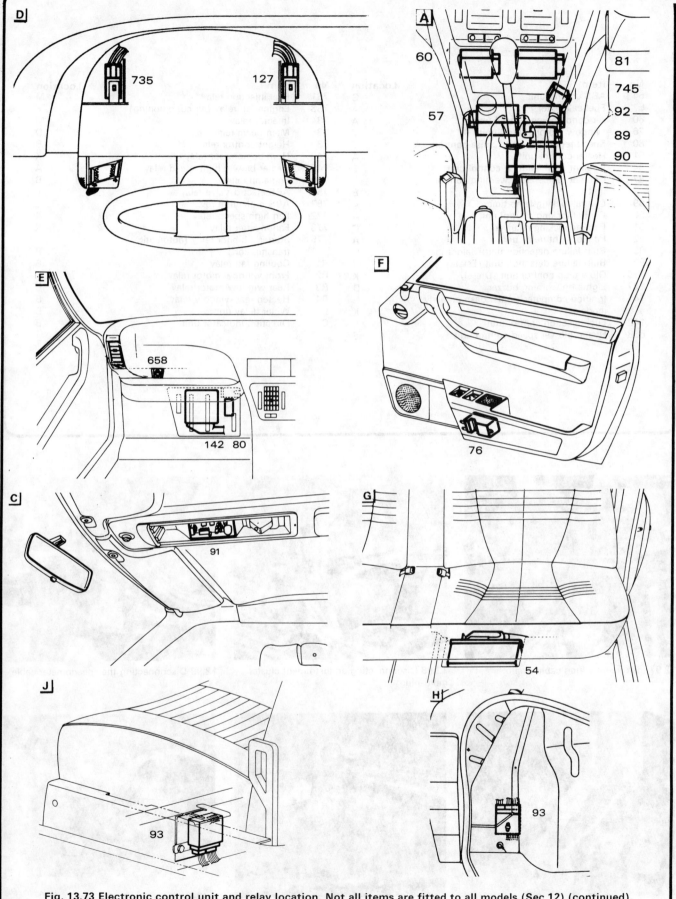

Fig. 13.73 Electronic control unit and relay location. Not all items are fitted to all models (Sec 12) (continued).
Key on page 266

No	Item	Location	No	Item	Location
54	ABS control unit	G	731	Fuel injection relay	M
57	Fuel calculator	A	733	Engine fan relay (air conditioning)	K
60	Air conditioning control unit	A	734	Injector relay	M
76	Window motor control unit	F	735	Main beam relay	D
80	Speed regulating unit (cruise control)	E	739	Height control relay	B
81	Heater control unit	A	743	Horn compressor relay	K
84	Coolant level warning control unit	L	745	Heater blower high speed relay	A
87	Coolant temperature warning control unit	B	750	Foglamp relay	B
89	Central locking lamp timer	A	756	ABS electro-valve relay	L
90	Central locking control unit	A	757	ABS protection relay	L
91	Remote locking receiver	C	772	Fan high speed relay	K
92	Interior light delay unit	A	773	Fan inverter relay	K
93	Bulb failure detection unit (Saloon)	H	775	Starter inhibitor relay (automatic transmission)	B
93	Bulb failure detection unit (Estate)	J	R1	Cooling fan relay	B
110	Glow plug control unit (Diesel)	K	R2	Front window motor relay	B
127	Lights on warning buzzer	D	R3	Rear window motor relay	B
141	Ignition computer (under dash on early models)	K	R4	Heated rear window relay	B
142	Fuel injection control unit	E	I	Wiper delay unit	B
658	Heater blower speed control unit	E	C	Direction indicator unit	B

12.97 Instrument wiring cable clamp

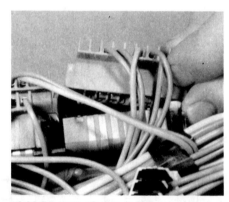

12.98 Disconnecting an instrument cluster multi-plug

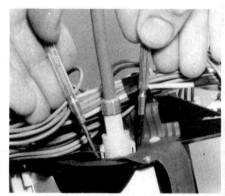

12.99 Disconnecting the speedometer cable

12.100 Ignition switch illumination connectors

13.12 Height control motor – crankarm spindle nut arrowed

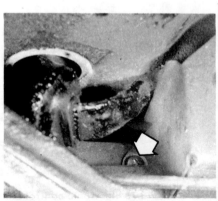

13.13 Fourth screw (arrowed) securing the motor shroud

the luggage compartment side panels, or use pod type speakers, according to individual choice.
109 The recommended location for the aerial is on the roof. The fitting operations are as follows.
110 Remove the right-hand and centre sun visor supports.
111 Pull the door seal away from the upper part of the windscreen pillar.
112 Remove the speaker grille (if fitted), gear change lever and ashtray from the centre console.
113 Carefully cut the headlining between the centre sun visor mounting holes so that a 10.5 mm hole can be drilled in the roof panel at the centre line of the roof and 100.00 mm rearwards from the screen rubber surround.
114 Feed the aerial cable under the headlining and down inside the windscreen pillar to emerge behind the glove compartment. An extension cable may be necessary to route the cable to the centre console and connect it to the radio.
115 The radio must now be 'trimmed' to the aerial in accordance with the manufacturer's instructions.
116 As the vehicle is fully suppressed against radio interference it is unlikely that this problem will arise with reception, but should interference be evident, first check the coil suppressor, the state of the ignition HT leads and possibly the need for a suppressor on the alternator.

Wiring diagrams (later models) – general
117 Wiring diagrams for later models will be found at the end of this Chapter.

118 Space limitations prevent the inclusion of all possible wiring diagrams, but those selected are representative and will normally apply to all vehicles of the year in question, making due allowance for difference in trim level.

13 Suspension and steering

Front track – modification
1 As from July 1980 the front track of all models is increased by 40.0 mm. This results in modification of many of the suspension components including fitting of longer driveshafts.

Rear anti-roll bar knock (all models)
2 Knocking or tapping from the rear suspension over rough surfaces may be caused by the rear anti-roll bar bearing blocks being dry. Proceed as follows.
3 Raise and support the rear of the vehicle so that the rear wheels are off the ground.
4 Unbolt and remove the two bearing blocks. Recover the shims, noting their positions.
5 Clean up the anti-roll bar bearing areas with abrasive paper.
6 Lubricate the bearing blocks and their bolts with multi-purpose grease.
7 Refit the shims and bearing blocks. Tighten the bolts to the specified torque (Chapter 11, Specifications), then lower the vehicle.

Height control system (1986 on) – description
8 From 1986, operation of the height control is by means of an electric motor connected to the control rods. Instead of the manual control lever previously used, a four-position latching switch conveys the driver's commands to the motor.

Height control motor (1986 on) – removal and refitting
9 Raise and support the vehicle.
10 Unclip the rear height control rod from the motor shroud.
11 Remove the two nuts which secure the motor.
12 Mark the position of the crankarm on the motor spindle. Remove the spindle nut and pull off the arm (photo).
13 Remove the four 'Torx' screws which secure the motor shroud. Three of these screws are around the spindle, the other is towards the front (photo).

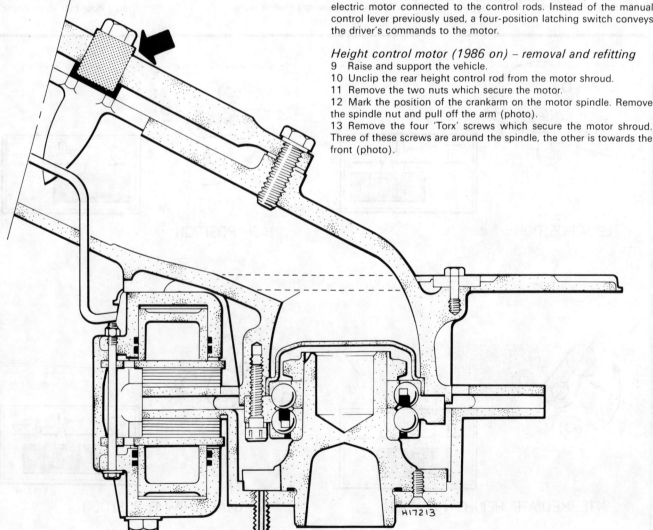

Fig. 13.74 Rear anti-roll bar bearing block (arrowed) (Sec 13)

14 Inside the vehicle, prise the height control switch out of the centre console (photo). Disconnect the motor wiring from the switch and from the live connector adjacent.

15 Below the vehicle again, free the rubber grommet from the floorpan and withdraw the motor, shroud and wiring (photo). (If a new motor is to be fitted, it might be better to cut the wires close to the old motor, then tie the new wires to the old and use the old wires to draw the new ones into position.)

16 Refit by reversing the removal operations. If a new motor is being fitted, connect the switch and apply power to bring the motor to the 'normal' position, then determine the crankarm position by referring to Fig. 13.75.

Height control (all models) – adjustment

17 With the engine idling and normal height selected, remove the covers from the height correctors. Check the clearances between the control rods and the height corrector lever – see Figs. 13.76 and 13.77. Note that the desired clearances are different for manually-operated and electrically-operated systems.

18 If adjustment to the clearances is necessary, stop the engine, slacken the nuts on the height corrector levers and move them as necessary. Tighten the nuts.

19 The suspension heights may now be adjusted if necessary as described in Chapter 11, Section 12.

13.14 Removing the height control switch

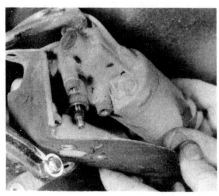
13.15 Removing the height control motor

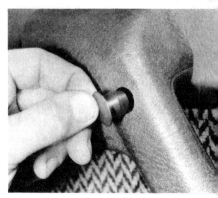
14.5A Removing a door pull screw cover

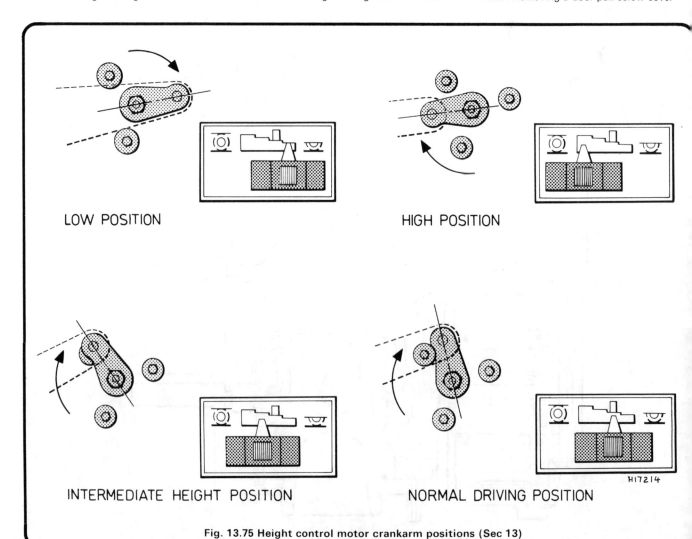

LOW POSITION

HIGH POSITION

INTERMEDIATE HEIGHT POSITION

NORMAL DRIVING POSITION

H17214

Fig. 13.75 Height control motor crankarm positions (Sec 13)

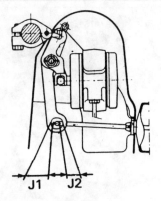

Fig. 13.76 Height control adjustment – front (Sec 13)

Manual control – $J_1 = J_2$
Electric control – $J_1 = 3.5$ mm, $J_2 = 4.5$ mm

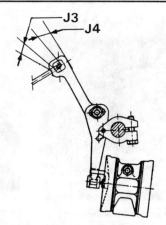

Fig. 13.77 Height control adjustment – rear (Sec 13)

Manual control – $J_3 = J_4$
Electric control – $J_3 = 3.5$ mm, $J_4 = 4.5$ mm

Compact spare wheel – description and use

20 On some later models a compact spare wheel may be supplied. This wheel carries a tyre of narrower section than standard – typically 185/70. It is inflated to a higher pressure than the standard tyres and is subject to a speed restriction of 80 mph (130 km/h).
21 The use of tyres of different sizes and/or tread patterns on the same axle is certainly undesirable and in some countries illegal. Observe any applicable regulations when using the compact spare, and drive with caution, especially when cornering or braking. Have the punctured tyre repaired or renewed at the first opportunity.

Front and rear suspension arms

22 From January 1987 the means for setting the bearing preload for the suspension arms has changed, although the procedure remains the same (Chapter 11, Sections 3 and 8).
23 On later models both thrust washers are of the same thickness (9.34 mm/0.37 in) – any adjustment being made by the addition of extra shims between the thrust washer and the bearing.
24 Shims are fitted inside the **front** thrust washer for the front suspension arm, and inside the **outer** thrust washer for the rear suspension.

14 Bodywork and fittings

Rear wing lower panel removal – all models

1 The screw which is accessible after opening a rear door and retains the rear wing lower panel, should be kept well greased to prevent corrosion of the threads.
2 Should the screw seize owing to rust, and the plastic knob shear off, the screw can usually be removed downwards, with the coil spring, if it is first gripped and pulled upwards to release the wing panel. Use self-locking pliers to grip the screw in this case.

Door trim panel (later models) – removal and refitting

3 On some models with loudspeakers mounted in the doors, the speaker leads must be disconnected as the trim panel is withdrawn. The same applies to window and mirror control switches, when fitted.
4 On 1986 and later models, the door trim is in three sections: a centre panel, an upper trim strip and a lower trim strip.
5 Commence removal with the centre panel. Unclip the armrest, remove the three Allen screws and remove the door pull/armrest support. Unclip the centre panel and remove it. If manually adjusted mirrors are fitted, release the adjuster control from the panel (photos).
6 Remove the lower trim strip by unclipping the speaker grille(s) and removing the seven securing screws. Disconnect the control switches and loudspeakers and withdraw the trim strip (photos).
7 To remove the upper trim strip, first remove the window interior seal, the door lock knob and the door interior handle (photos). Unclip the trim strip and remove it, when applicable disconnecting the central locking warning light.
8 Refit by reversing the removal operations.

Front bumper (1986 on) – removal and refitting

9 Remove the front foglamps (when fitted) as described in Section 12. (Alternatively, disconnect the foglamps and remove them with the bumper.)
10 Release the direction indicator/sidelight assemblies from the bumper by inserting a small screwdriver at their inboard ends. Disconnect the wiring and remove them.
11 Remove the six screws which hold the bumper to the front crossmember. Two of these screws also secure the grille; the other four are accessible from below (photos).
12 Prise out the two pegs which secure the bumper side sections (photo).
13 Free the bumper side sections from the 'keyhole' fastenings on the front wings. Remove the bumper.
14 Refit by reversing the removal operations. If a new bumper is being fitted, holes will have to be drilled in it to accept the bright trim strip.

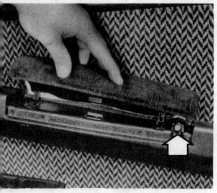

14.5B Unclip the armrest to expose another screw (arrowed)

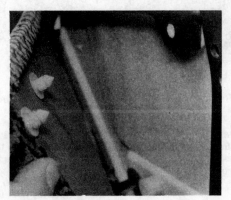

14.5C Unclipping the door trim centre panel

14.6A Removing a speaker grille

14.6B Removing a switch from the door lower trim strip

14.7A Removing the window interior seal

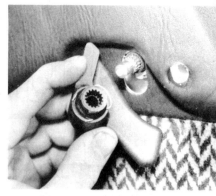

14.7B Removing the door interior handle

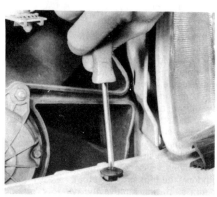

14.11A Removing a bumper-to-front crossmember screw. This one secures the grille (already removed) also

14.11B Removing another bumper securing screw from in front of a foglamp

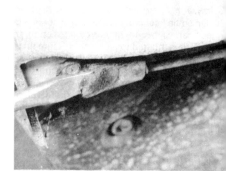

14.12 Prising out a bumper side section peg

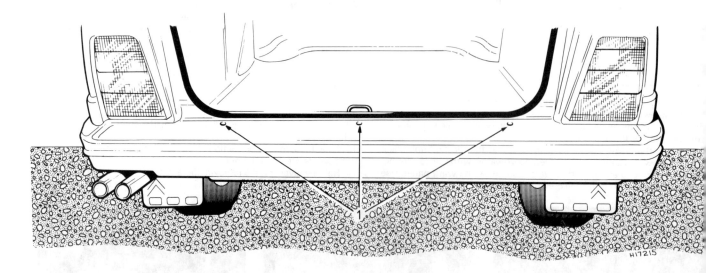

Fig. 13.78 Rear bumper screws (1) accessible from above (Sec 14)

Rear bumper (1986 on) – removal and refitting
15 Open the tailgate. Remove the three screws from the upper side of the bumper.
16 Remove the four screws from the underside of the bumper.
17 Free the bumper side sections from the 'keyhole' fastenings. Remove the bumper.
18 The position of the bumper support strip can be adjusted if necessary after slackening its securing screws. Adjust the strip so that

the tailgate just clears the bumper comfortably.
19 Refit by reversing the removal operations. If a new bumper is being fitted, holes will have to be drilled in it to accept the bright trim strip.

Door mirror (1986 on) – removal and refitting
20 Remove the door trim panel. Disconnect the mirror wiring harness or release the control cables, as appropriate.
21 The Allen screw which secures the mirror to its base must now be

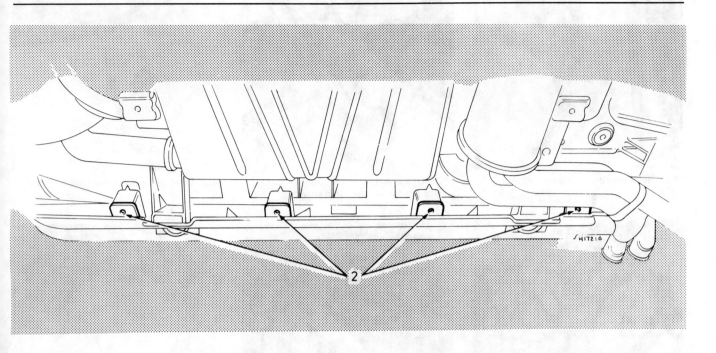

Fig. 13.79 Rear bumper screws (2) accessible from below (Sec 14)

removed. Twist the plastic collar and pull it away from the door to expose the screw (photo). Beware of using levers to move the collar, as it is easy to damage the paintwork; better to drill a hole in the collar as shown (Fig. 13.80).

22 With the mirror freed from its base, the base can be unscrewed from the door using a peg spanner or a couple of screwdrivers (photo).

23 Withdraw the mirror, base and wiring or control cables from the door.

24 Refit by reversing the removal operations. If a hole was drilled in the plastic collar, turn the collar after tightening the screw so that the hole points downwards.

Door mirror glass (1986 on) – removal and refitting

25 There is no need to remove the mirror from the door for this operation.

26 Tilt the mirror to expose the lowest part of the glass. Release the mirror support plate by inserting a small screwdriver and pushing the lug towards the door. Remove the glass and support plate, disconnecting the demister wires when applicable (photos).

27 Commence refitting by positioning the lug on the support plate to engage with the fingers in the mirror body. Reconnect the demister wires, when applicable, and offer the glass and support plate to the body.

28 Rotate the lug to lock the support plate in position.

Door mirror motor (1986 on) – removal and refitting

29 Remove the mirror glass as just described.

30 Remove the three 'Torx' screws which secure the motor to the mirror body. Withdraw the motor and disconnect its leads (photos).

31 Refit by reversing the removal operations.

Dashboard (1986 on) – removal and refitting

32 Disconnect the battery negative lead.

33 Open the glovebox and remove the two nuts and two screws which secure it to the dashboard. Disconnect the glovebox light and remove the glovebox (photo).

34 Remove the two screws which secure each of the centre console side panels. Free the panels from the top edge of the console and remove them.

35 Remove the steering wheel (Chapter 11, Section 20).

36 Open the fuse/junction box. Remove the bolt and the nut which hold it to the dashboard and side panels. Move the box out of the way without disconnecting it.

37 Remove the securing screws and lower the trim from around the steering column.

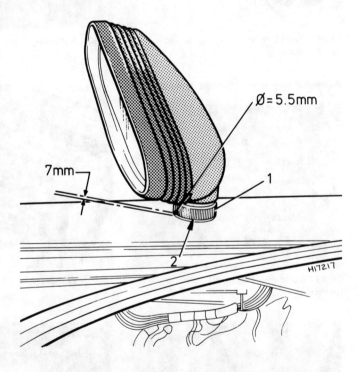

Fig. 13.80 Door mirror removal. If collar (1) will not move, drill a hole at (2) – dimensions in mm (Sec 14)

38 Remove the instrument panel and shell as described in Section 12. Also unbolt the relay bracket from around the steering column.

39 Prise free the heater control panel without disconnecting it. Remove the six securing screws and withdraw the front part of the centre console (photos).

40 Remove the digital display unit by undoing the two screws and disconnecting its multi-plug (photo).

41 Remove the computer keyboard (when fitted) by prising it out and disconnect its multi-plug (photo).

42 Unclip the side air vents from the dashboard (photo).

14.21 Removing a door mirror securing screw

14.22 Unscrewing the mirror base – be careful not to damage the paintwork

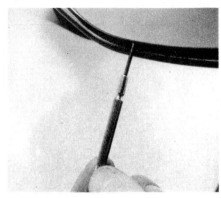

14.26A Releasing the mirror support plate lug

14.26B Removing the mirror glass and support plate

14.30A Removing a mirror motor screw

14.30B Disconnecting the mirror motor

14.33 Two screws (arrowed) securing the glovebox

14.39A Withdrawing the heater control panel

14.39B One of the centre console securing screws

14.40 Disconnecting the digital display unit

14.41 Disconnecting the computer keyboard

14.42 Unclipping a dashboard air vent

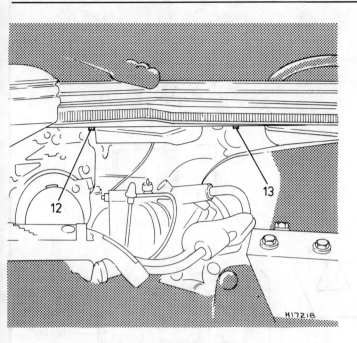

Fig. 13.81 Two nuts (12 and 13) which secure the dashboard to the bulkhead (Sec 14)

43 Open the bonnet and remove the two nuts which secure the middle of the dashboard to the bulkhead.
44 Carefully pull the dashboard off its locating lugs. Remove the centre storage pockets.
45 Refit by reversing the removal operations.

Locks and doors (all models) – compatibility
46 If new doors are fitted and old locks transferred to them, spacer washers may be needed between the lock and the door panel. Consult a Citroen dealer.
47 In the case of the Saloon boot lid, new lids are suitable for manual locking only. The lock opening must be enlarged as shown in Fig. 13.82 if it is to accept a central locking solenoid.

Heater (1978 on) – description
48 From May 1978 a new type of heater, made by Behr, was fitted. The main difference between this heater and the one previously fitted is the means of temperature regulation. Instead of varying the flow of coolant through the heater matrix, the proportion of hot air to cold air is varied by means of flaps. Coolant flows through the matrix all the time, even when hot air is not required.
49 No specific removal, overhaul or refitting procedures for this heater exist. If problems are experienced, first check the security of attachment of the control cables.

Heater (1984 on) – temperature regulation
50 On some 1984 and later vehicles, temperature regulation within the passenger compartment is automatic. A temperature sensor in the roof compares the air temperature with that selected on the heater control panel. An electronic control unit compares the two temperatures and operates a motor which moves the cold/hot air mix flap (photos). This device is completely independent of the air conditioning system (if fitted).
51 On vehicles without air conditioning, the regulation system is only effective if the temperature selected is higher than the outside air temperature. If the contrary occurs, the control unit will cause the heater to admit fresh air only.
52 If problems are experienced with the heater output remaining constant regardless of the position of the temperature control, check that the flap control spindle has not become disengaged from the control motor. The control motor and flap spindle are accessible after removing the glovebox; a spring clip can be fitted to the spindle to stop it becoming disengaged again. Make sure that the motor and flap are both in the same position ('full hot' or 'full cold') before engaging the spindle.

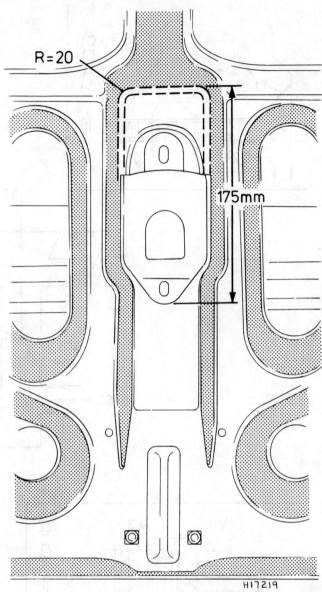

Fig. 13.82 Boot lid modification to accept central locking solenoid – dimensions in mm (Sec 14)

53 Later models (1985 on) have been modified so that the spindle is captive.
54 If it is ever necessary to remove the temperature control motor, do not allow the motor and geartrain to be separated, otherwise the calibration may be lost.
55 New temperature control motors are supplied in the 'full cold' position.

Heater/air conditioning unit (1986 on) – removal and refitting
56 Have the air conditioning system discharged by a Citroën dealer or other specialist.
Warning: *Refrigerant can cause injury, blindness or death if carelessly handled.*
57 Disconnect the battery negative lead.
58 Remove the dashboard as described earlier in this Section.
59 Disconnect the air conditioning control panel and remove it.

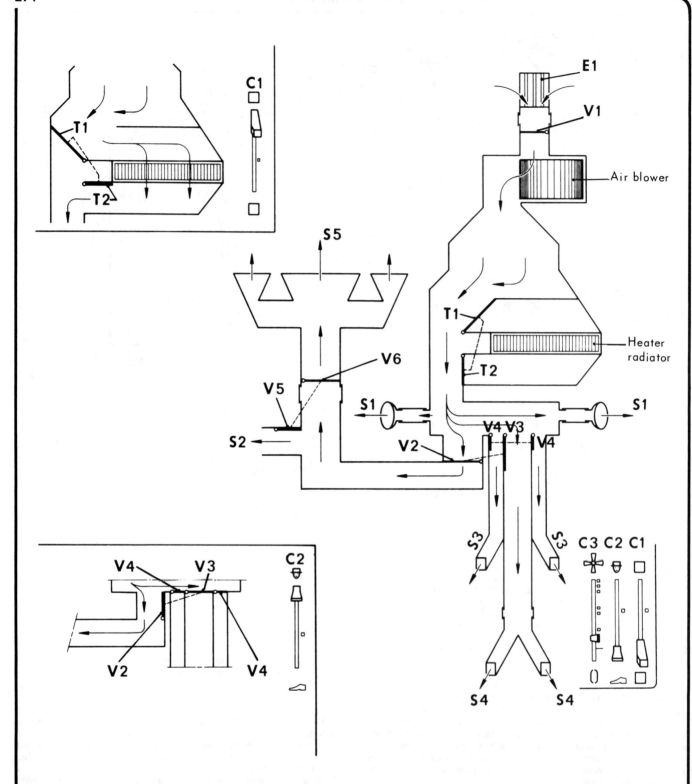

Fig. 13.83 Airflow diagrams for the Behr heater (Sec 14)

C1 Temperature control
C2 Distribution control
C3 Air intake/blower speed control
E1 Exterior air intake
S1 Side vents
S2 Centre vent

S3 Lower front outlets
S4 Lower rear outlets
S5 Windscreen vents
T1 Incoming air flap
T2 Hot air flap
V1 Intake cut-off flap

V2 S2/55 cut-off flap
V3 S4 cut-off flap
V4 S3 cut-off flap
V5 S2cut-off flap
V6 S5 cut-off flap

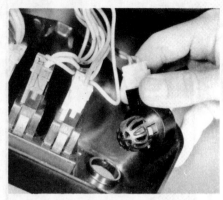

14.50A Cabin air temperature sensor being withdrawn from roof console

14.50B Temperature control motor (in passenger footwell)

14.50C Temperature regulation electronic control unit (arrowed) under centre console

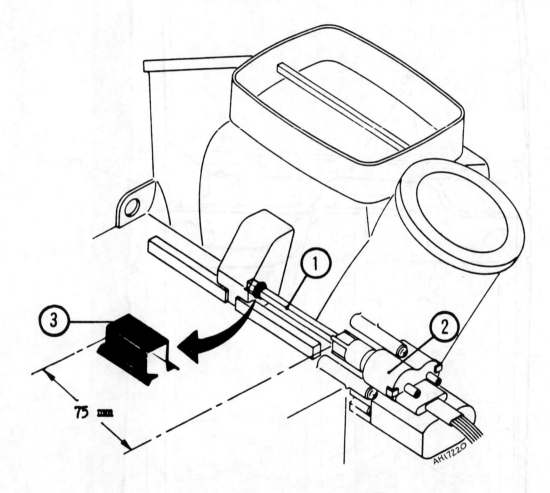

Fig. 13.84 Temperature control motor (2) and flap spindle (1) (Sec 14)

3 Spring clip

60 Remove the rear compartment air duct.

61 Working under the bonnet, unbolt the coolant expansion tank and move it aside. Remove the air ducting from behind the expansion tank and unbolt the air intake tower.

62 Disconnect the yellow connector from the air conditioning compressor clutch. Also disconnect the twin connector, under the expansion tank, which supplies the air intake flap motor.

63 Disconnect the two refrigerant hoses at the bulkhead. Be careful not to lose or damage the seals.

64 Clamp the two coolant pipes at the bulkhead to minimise subsequent spillage; alternatively drain the cooling system.

65 Back inside the vehicle, disconnect the wiring from the heater/air conditioning unit.

66 Disconnect the two coolant pipes from the unit; be prepared for some spillage.

67 Remove the four screws which secure the unit to the bulkhead.

68 Remove the unit, preferably with the help of an assistant. It will be necessary to displace the air intake tower from its mounting studs, and to release the heater ducts from the top of the unit.

69 Recover the defroster drain gaiter.

70 Refit by reversing the removal operations; have the air conditioning system recharged on completion.

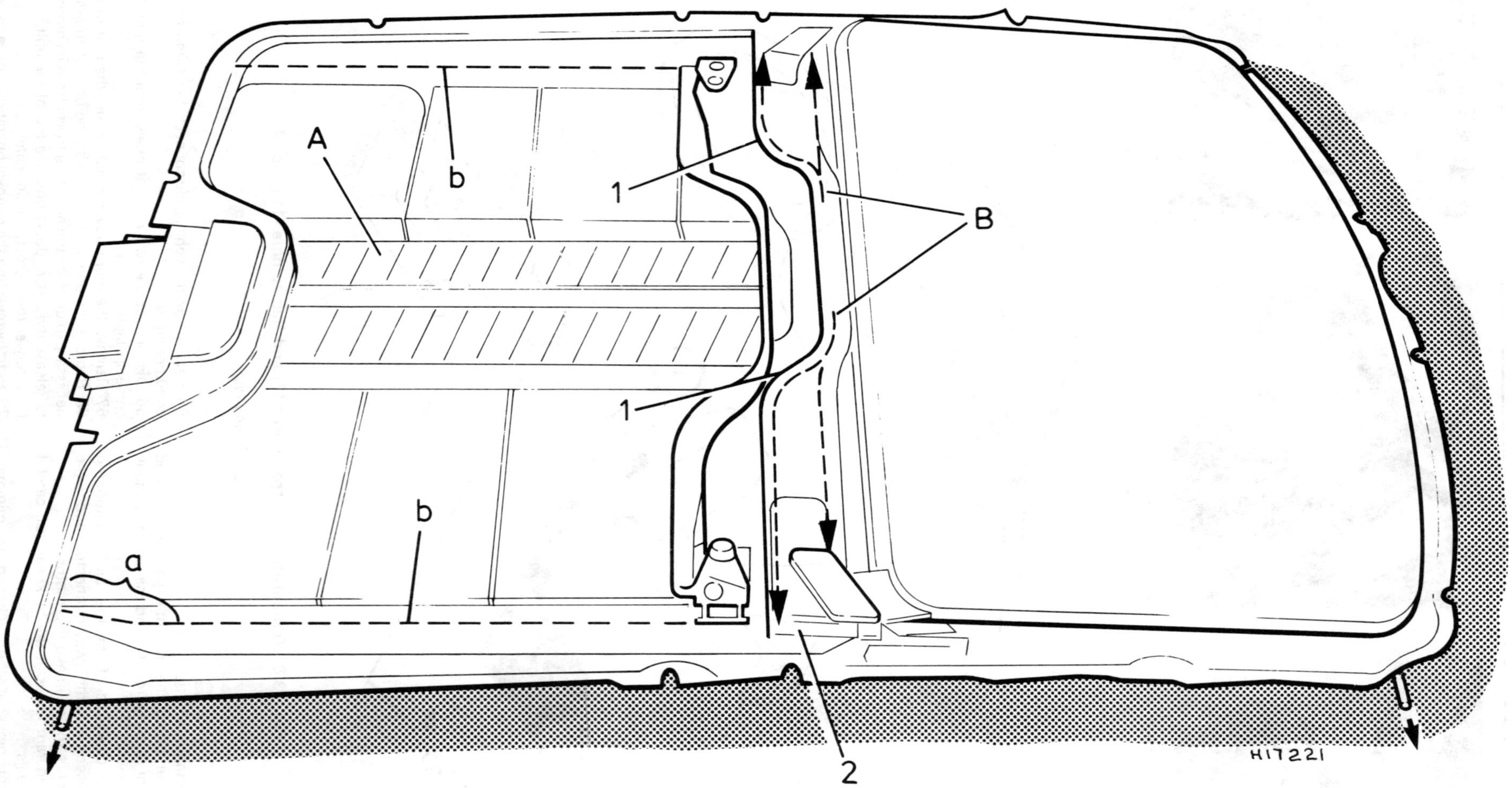

Fig. 13.85 Rectifying sunroof water leaks (Sec 14)

A Water collects here
B Desired drainage route

a Apply sealant
b Runner rails

1 Corner edges
2 Flange

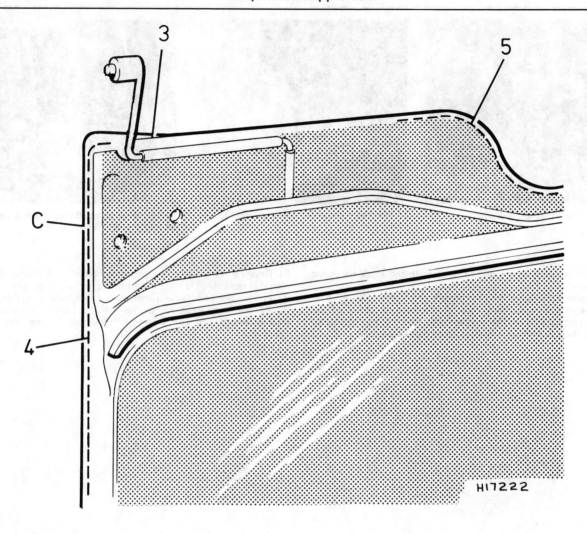

Fig. 13.86 Apply sealant to the junction of plates 3 and 4 (Sec 14)

C   Gusset   5   Plate

Water leaks from sunroof

71 If a problem is experienced with water leaking into the centre part of the sunroof lining, check first that all four drain pipes are clear.

72 If the drain pipes are clear, make sure that the runner rails are tightly in contact with the roof lining, and apply a thick bead of sealant to area 'a' (Fig. 13.85) to prevent water flowing towards the middle of the sunroof.

73 If there is still a problem, refer to Fig. 13.86. Check that the gusset 'C' allows water to flow out into the rain channels. Apply a bead of sealant at the junction of plates 3 and 4, and bend up the edge of plate 5 slightly to stop the water overflowing.

Rear seat – removal and refitting

74 This procedure applies to later Saloon models. Allowance should be made for differences in other models.

75 Remove the cushion by lifting it at the front and giving a firm tug to release it from its clips.

76 To remove the squab, slacken the two bolts which secure the 'keyhole' fittings and disengage the fittings (photo). Thump the squab to free the top clips, and remove it.

77 Refit by reversing the removal operations.

Seat belts – general

78 Periodically inspect the belts for fraying or other damage. If

14.76 Rear seat squab 'keyhole' fitting

14.82A Rear seat belt under-cushion anchorage

14.82B Rear seat belt anchorage next to door opening

14.82C Rear seat belt inertia reel mounting on parcel shelf (Saloon)

evident, renew the belt.

79 Clean the belt if necessary using a damp cloth and a little detergent – nothing else.

80 Never alter the original belt anchorage and if the belts are ever removed, always take a careful note of the fitted sequence of the mounting components. If the washers and spacers are incorrectly positioned, the belt will not swivel as it has been designed to do.

Rear seat belts – fitting

81 Obtain a set of belts and mounting components designed for the model in question. Do not attempt to improvise components.

82 Follow the belt maker's instructions concerning anchor points. Anchor points are located under the rear seat cushion, rearward of the door openings and (on Saloon models) on the rear parcel shelf (photos).

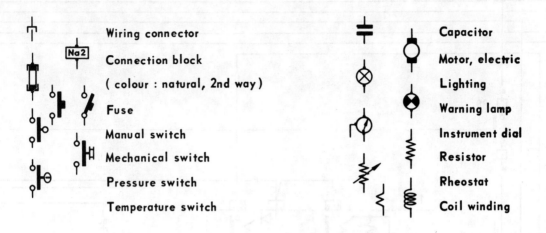

Key to symbols of the circuit diagrams

The symbols key includes:

- Wiring connector
- Connection block (colour : natural, 2nd way) — Na2
- Fuse
- Manual switch
- Mechanical switch
- Pressure switch
- Temperature switch
- Capacitor
- Motor, electric
- Lighting
- Warning lamp
- Instrument dial
- Resistor
- Rheostat
- Coil winding

Wiring diagram colour code

B or Bc	White	Ic	Neutral	Na	Natural
Bl	Blue	M or Mr	Brown	Or	Orange
G	Grey	Mr	Mauve	R	Red
J	Yellow	N	Black	V or Ve	Green

Harness code – Figs 13.87 to 13.89

AR	Rear wiring	LG	Door window winder	RG	Rear LH side
AV	Main front wiring	M	Engine	RT	Rear view exterior mirror
C	Luggage boot	PC	Luggage boot	T	Roof
CO	Horn with compressor	PAR	Interior lamps	TB	Dashboard
D	Diagnostic plug	PD	Right-hand rear door	TO	Sunroof
FV	Flying lead	PG	Left-hand rear door	UF	Front pad wear
H	Tailgate	PR	Rear doors	V	Electric fan
IC	Fuel injection (engine)	RD	Rear RH side		
IM	Fuel injection (body)				
K	Console				

Harness code – Fig. 13.90

A	Horn	G	Left-hand front	PC	Driver's door
AB	Front foglamps	H	Interior	PD	Right-hand rear door
B	Junction box	IC	Fuel injection (chassis)	PG	Left-hand rear door
BA	Digital display unit	IM	Fuel injection (engine)	PP	Passenger front door
C	Boot locking	J	Fuel gauge	Q	Heater blower
CA	Alternator	K	Heating	R	Rear
CD	Turbo boost	L	Bulb failure monitoring	T	Instrument panel
CN	Battery negative	LV	Window winder extension	U	Front brake pad wear
CP	Battery positive	M	Engine	V	Engine cooling fans
D	Right-hand front	MB	Junction box earth	W	Bulb failure monitoring
E	Number plate lighting	ML	Heated rear window earth	X	Fuel filler flap locking
EC	Under-bonnet lighting	MP	Fuel pump earth	Y	ABS
F	Rear light interconnection	O	Computer	Z	Ignition
FP	Fuel pump	P	Interior lighting		

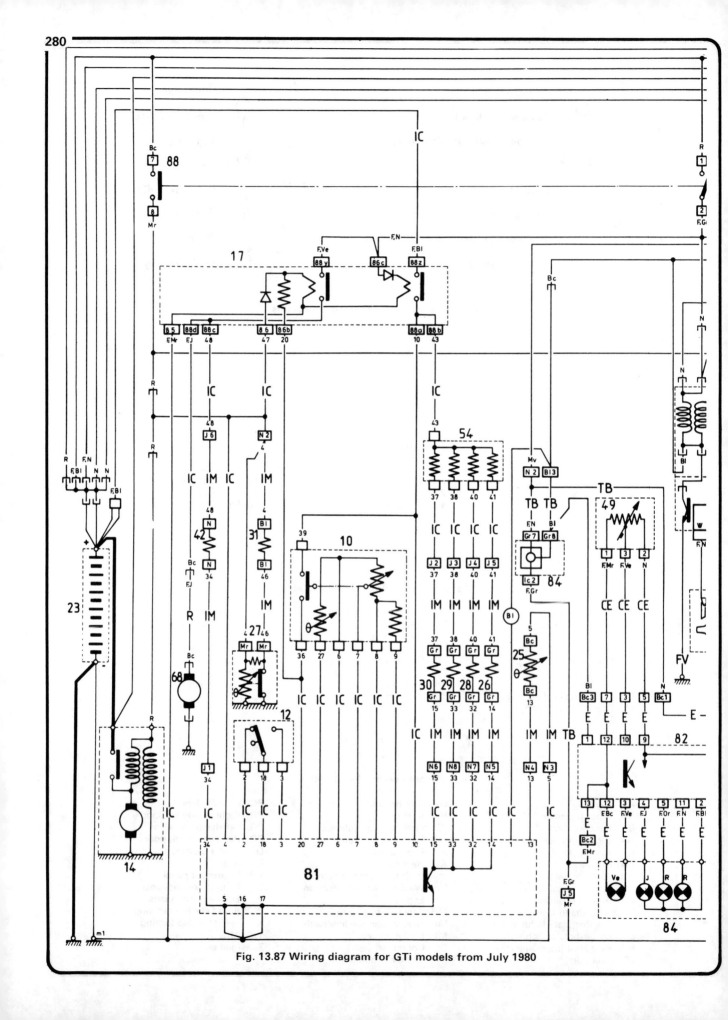

Fig. 13.87 Wiring diagram for GTi models from July 1980

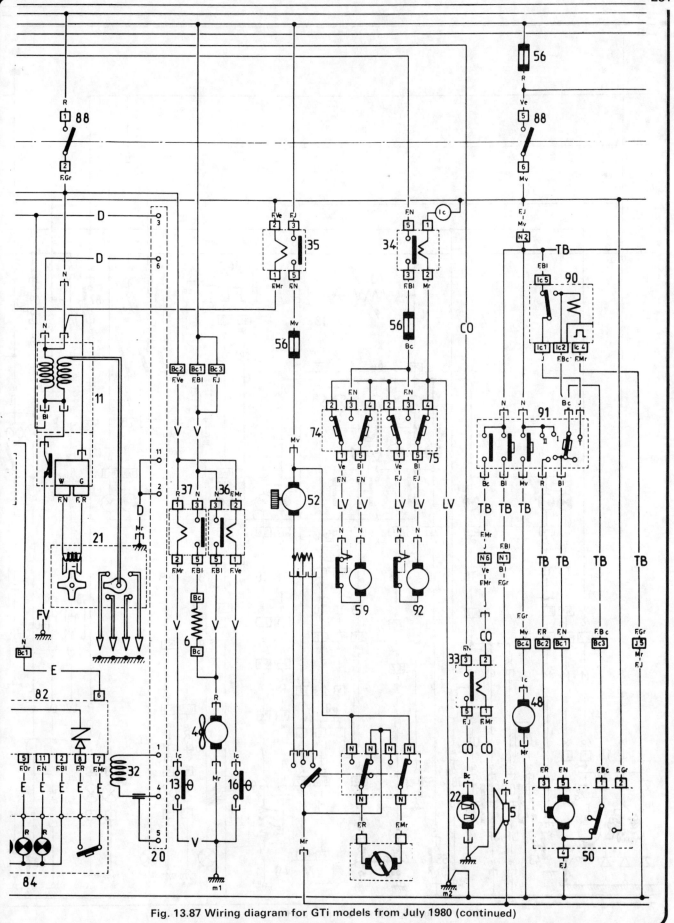

Fig. 13.87 Wiring diagram for GTi models from July 1980 (continued)

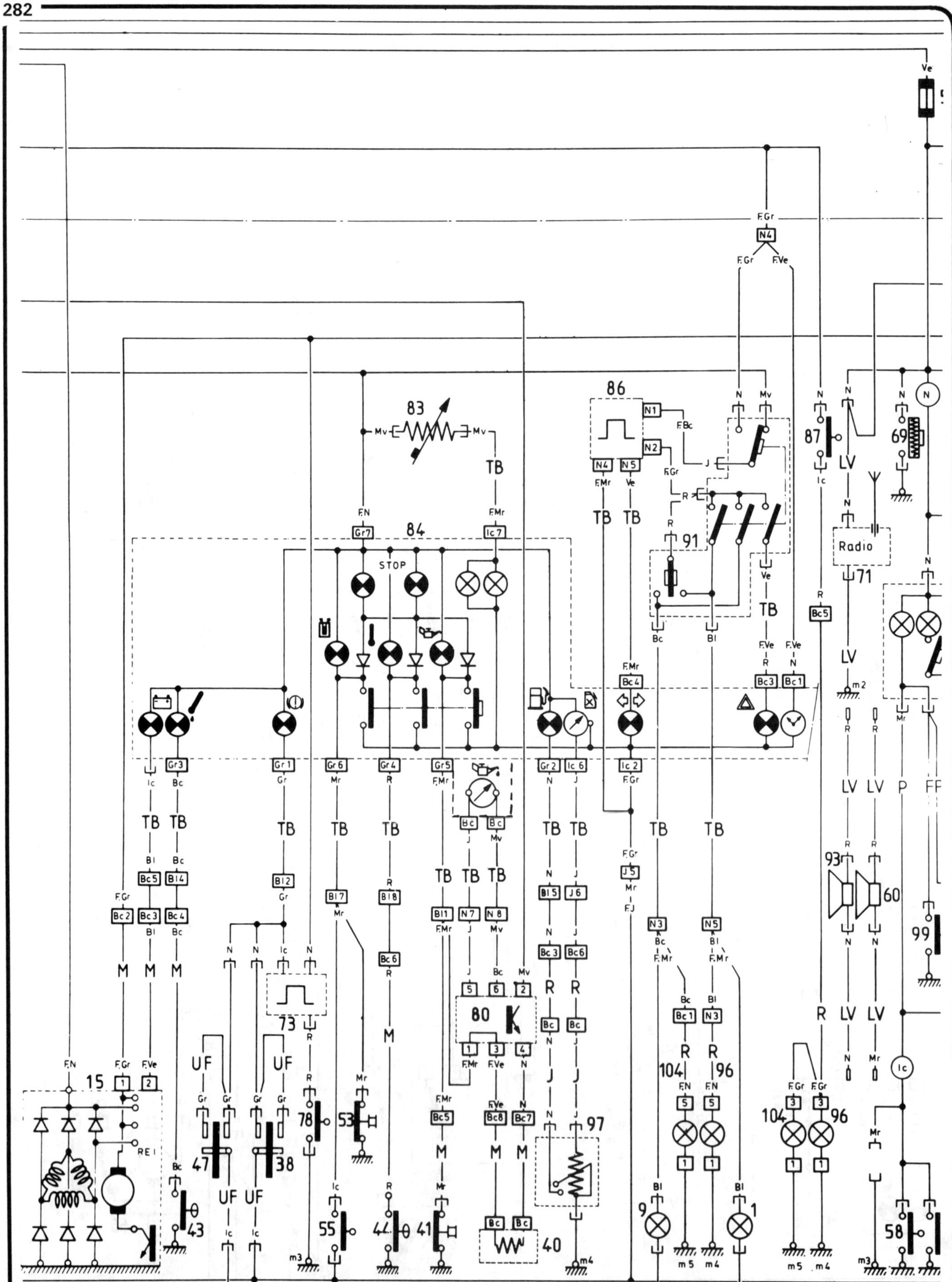

Fig. 13.87 Wiring diagram for GTi models from July 1980 (continued)

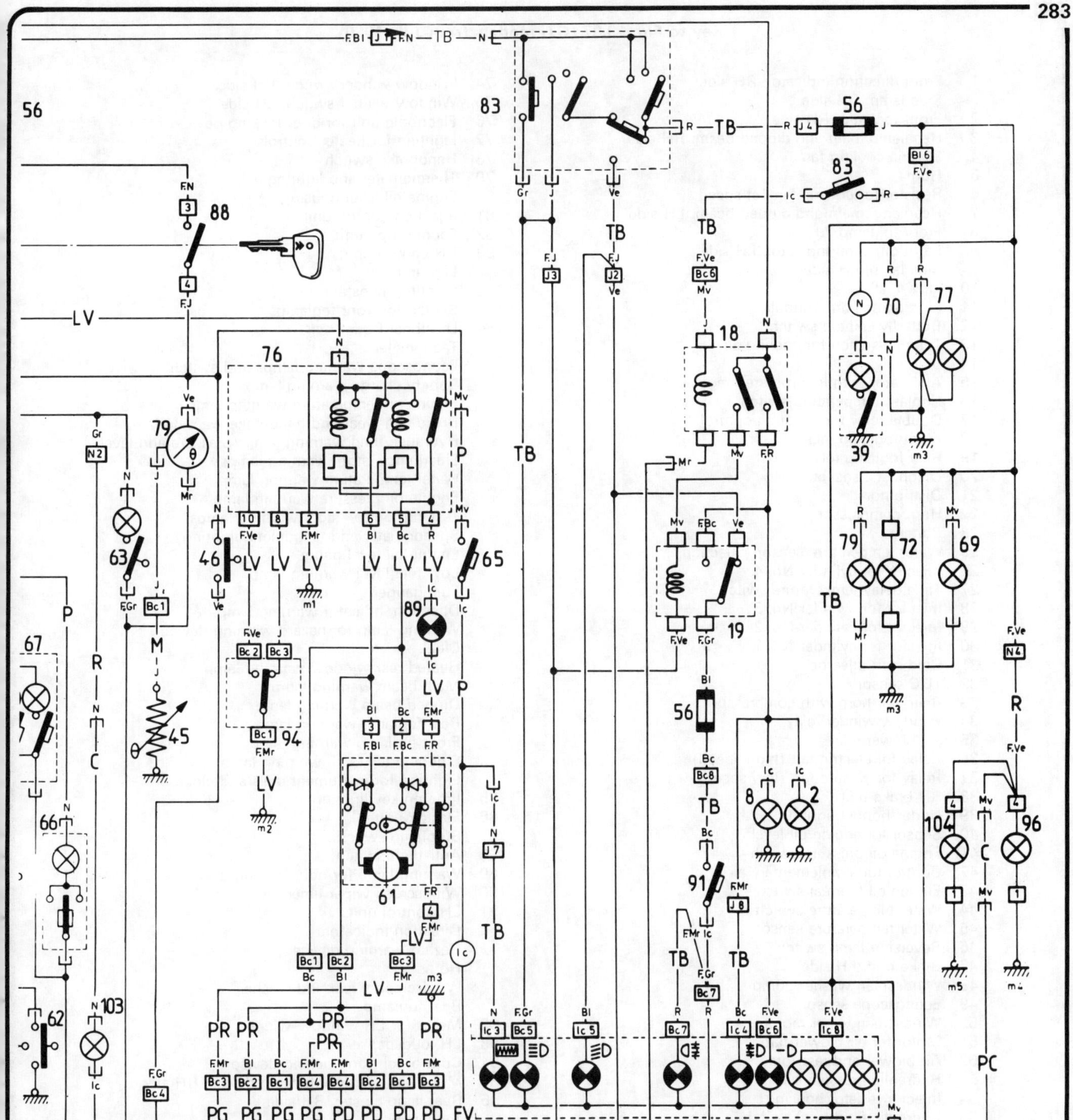

Fig. 13.87 Wiring diagram for GTi models from July 1980 (continued)

Key to Fig. 13.87 (GTi models from July 1980)

1 Front direction indicator, RH side:
   Side lamp: RH side
2 Front foglamp, RH side
3 Headlamp main and dipped beam: RH side
4 Electric cooling fan
5 Horn
6 Resistor for electric fan 1st speed
7 Headlamp main and dipped beam, LH side
8 Front foglamp, LH side
9 Front direction indicator, LH side:
   Side lamp, LH side
10 Flow meter
11 Ignition coil and module
12 Butterfly spindle switch
13 Thermal switch for cooling air
14 Starter
15 Alternator with incorporated regulator
16 Coolant temperature switch
17 Double relay for injection control
18 Front foglamp relay
19 Rear foglamp relay
20 Diagnostic socket
21 Distributor
22 Horn compressor
23 Battery
25 Water temperature sensor (injection)
26 Injector for cylinder No. 4
27 Time delay temperature switch
28 Injector for cylinder No. 3
29 Injector for cylinder No. 2
30 Injector for cylinder No. 1
31 Cold start injector
32 TDC sensor
33 Relay for horn with compressor
34 Window winder relay
35 Air blower relay
36 Relay for electric fan (high speed)
37 Relay for electric fan (low speed)
38 RH brake unit
39 Under-bonnet lighting
40 Sensor for engine oil level
41 Engine oil pressure switch
42 Control for supplementary air
43 Engine oil thermal switch
44 Water temperature switch
45 Water temperature sensor
46 Reversing lamp switch
47 Brake unit, LH side
48 Windscreen washer pump
49 Econoscope sensor
50 Windscreen wiper motor
51 Motor for air blower flap
52 Air blower and resistors
53 Hydraulic pressure switch
54 Injector resistor housing
55 Hydraulic fluid level switch
56 Fuse box
57 Front door switch, RH side
58 Front door switch, LH side
59 Window winder motor, RH side
60 Loudspeaker, RH side
61 Motor for front door locking device, RH side
62 Rear door switch, RH side
63 Lighting for glove compartment
64 Interior lamp switch
65 Heated rear window switch
66 Front seat swivelling lamps
67 Centre lamp
68 Fuel pump
69 Cigar lighter and lighting
70 Map reading lamp socket
71 Radio terminals (+ and loudspeaker)
72 Ashtray lighting
73 Handbrake 'on' flasher

74 Window winder switch, RH side
75 Window winder switch, LH side
76 Electronic unit for door locking device
77 Lighting for heater controls
78 Handbrake switch
79 Thermometer and lighting
80 Engine oil level housing
81 Injection control unit
82 Econoscope unit
83 RH control unit:
   Lighting
   Lighting rheostat
   Switch for front foglamps
84 Dashboard:
   Tachometer
   Econoscope warning lamps and switch
   Battery charge warning lamp
   Engine oil temperature warning lamp
   Brake pad wear and handbrake warning lamp
   Hydraulic fluid warning lamp (pressure and level)
   Emergency 'stop' warning lamps
   Water temperature warning lamp
   Engine oil pressure warning lamp
   Test-button for 'stop' warning lamps
   Speedometer and tachometer lighting
   Engine oil level gauge
   Low fuel level warning lamp
   Fuel gauge
   Direction indicator warning lamp
   Warning lamp for hazard warning device
   Clock
   Heated rear window warning lamp
   Main beam warning lamp
   Dipped beam warning lamp
   Rear foglamp warning lamp
   Front foglamp warning lamp
   Side and tail lamp warning lamp
   Lighting for instrument dials and clock
85 Ignition key lighting
86 Flasher unit
87 Stoplamp switch
88 Anti-theft switch
89 Warning lamp for door locking device
90 Windscreen wiper timer unit
91 LH control unit:
   Direction indicators
   Hazard warning device
   Horns
   Windscreen wiper and washer
   Rear foglamp
92 Motor for LH window-winder
93 LH loudspeaker
94 Control for door locking device
95 Motor for rear door locking device, RH side
96 Rear lamp cluster, RH side:
   Tail lamp
   Stoplamp
   Direction indicator
   Reversing lamp
   Foglamp
97 Fuel gauge rheostat
98 Heated rear window
99 Rear door switch, LH side
100 Number plate lighting, RH side
101 Number plate lighting, LH side
102 Boot lighting switch
103 Boot lighting
104 Rear lamp cluster, LH side:
   Tail lamp
   Stoplamp
   Direction indicator
   Reversing lamp
   Foglamp
105 Motor for rear door locking device, LH side

Key to Fig. 13.88 (Carburettor models from July 1980)

1 Sidelamp, RH side:
   Front direction indicator, RH side
2 RH headlamp:
   Main beam
   Dipped beam
3 Electric cooling fan
4 15°C air temperature switch (choke)
5 Horn
6 LH headlamp:
   Main beam
   Dipped beam
7 Sidelamp, LH side:
   Front direction indicator, LH side
8 55°C air temperature switch (cooling)
9 Ignition coil
10 Water temperature switch (cooling)
11 Resistor (electric fan low speed)
12 Choke relay (oil pressure)
13 Choke relay (air temperature)
14 Starter
15 TDC sensor
16 Alternator with integrated regulator
17 Air horn compressor
18 Battery and supply connector
19 Diagnostic socket
20 Ignition sparking plugs
21 Distributor
22 Engine oil level sensor
23 Engine oil pressure switch
24 Choke water temperature switch (60°C)
25 Automatic choke resistor
26 Idle cut-off
27 Engine oil temperature switch
28 Coolant temperature switch
29 Water temperature sensor (optional)
30 Relay for horn with compressor
31 Window winder relay
32 Heater relay
33 Electric fan relay (normal speed)
34 Electric fan relay (low speed)
35 Front brake unit, RH side
36 Windscreen washer pump
37 Econoscope vacuum sensor
38 Windscreen wiper motor
39 Air blower and flap motor
40 Hydraulic fluid pressure switch
41 Reversing lamp switch
42 Hydraulic fluid level switch
43 Front brake unit, LH side
44 Fuse box
45 Front door switch, RH side
46 Front door window winder, RH side
47 Front door loudspeaker, RH side
48 Motor for front door locking device, RH side
49 Glove compartment lighting
50 Centre lamp switch
51 Heated rear window switch
52 Front seat swivelling lamps
53 Centre lamp
54 Ashtray lighting
55 Cigar lighter and lighting
56 Front window winder switch, RH side
57 Map reading lamp socket (sunroof fitted)
58 Front window winder switch, LH side
59 Handbrake 'on' flasher unit
60 Electronic unit for door locking device
61 Heater control lighting

62 Handbrake switch
63 Radio terminals
64 Oil level electronic unit
65 Econoscope electronic unit
66 Lighting switch and rheostat
67 Dashboard:
   Instrument dial lighting
   Speedometer and tachometer lighting
   Engine oil level gauge
   Fuel gauge indicator
   Tachometer
   Clock
   Rear foglamp warning lamp
   Side and tail lamp warning lamp
   Main beam warning lamp
   Dipped beam warning lamp
   Battery charge warning lamp
   Hazard warning device warning lamp
   Hydraulic fluid warning lamp (pressure and level)
   Emergency 'stop' warning lamps
   Test-button for 'stop' warning lamps
   Engine oil pressure warning lamp
   Coolant temperature warning lamp
   Engine oil temperature warning lamp
   Low fluid level warning lamp
   Front brake pad wear, handbrake wear warning lamp
   Dipped beam warning lamp
   Heated rear window warning lamp
   Econoscope warning lamps and switch
68 Ignition key lighting
69 Stoplamp switch (braking)
70 Ignition starting switch
71 Direction indicator flasher unit
72 Windscreen wiper timer unit
73 LH control unit:
   Direction indicators
   Hazard warning lamps
   Horns
   Windscreen wiper and washer
   Rear foglamp switch
74 Front door switch, LH side
75 Motor for front window winder, LH side
76 Door locking device warning lamp
77 Front door loudspeaker, LH side
78 Control unit for door locking device
79 Rear door switch, RH side
80 Motor for rear door locking device, RH side
81 Fuel gauge rheostat
82 Heated rear window
83 Rear door switch, LH side
84 Motor for rear door, locking device, LH side
85 Rear lamp cluster, RH side:
   Foglamp
   Direction indicator
   Reversing lamp
   Tail lamp
   Stoplamp
86 Number plate lighting, RH side
87 Number plate lighting, LH side
88 Boot lighting switch
89 Boot lighting
90 Rear lamp cluster, LH side:
   Foglamp
   Direction indicator
   Reversing lamp
   Tail lamp
   Stoplamp

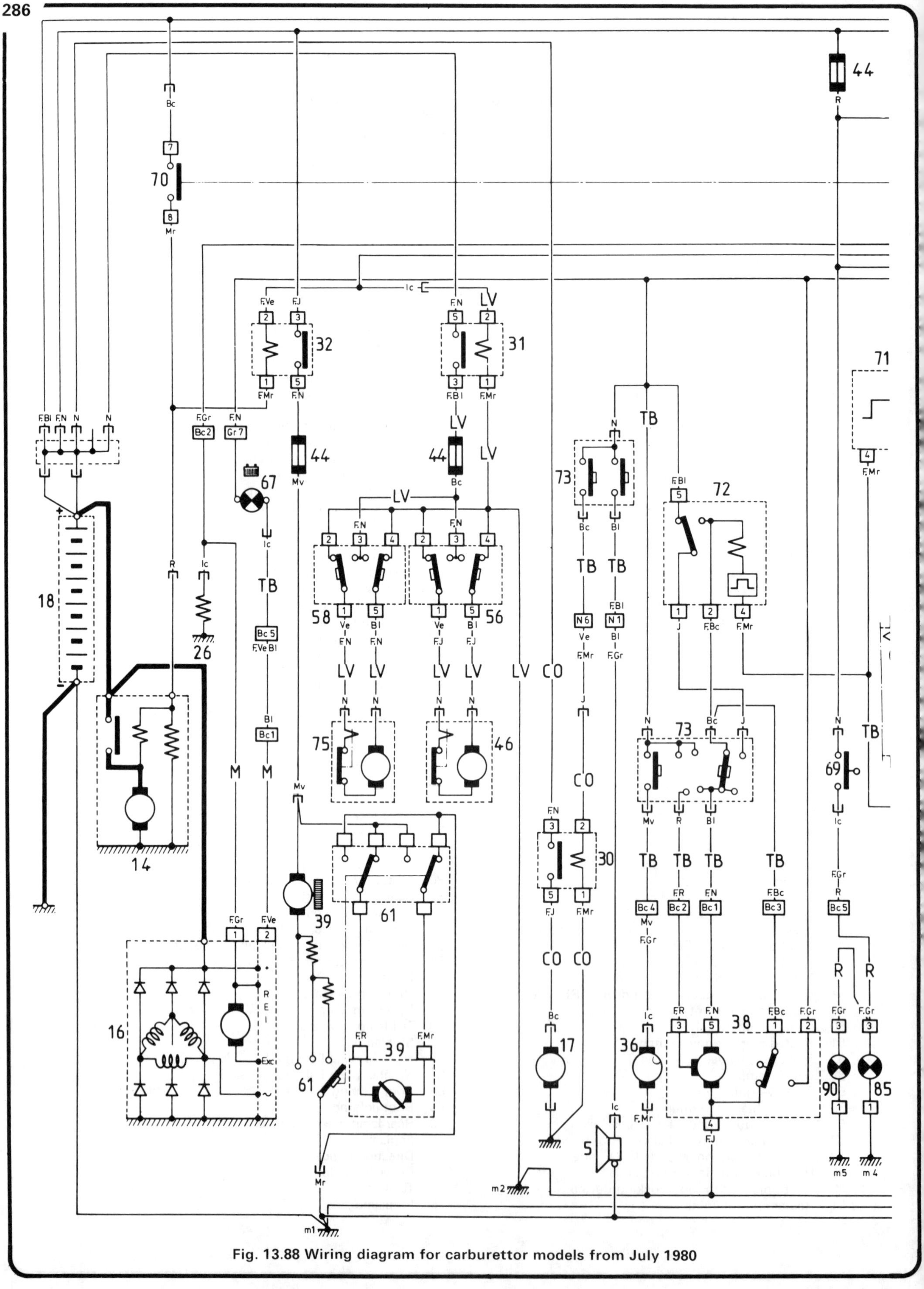

Fig. 13.88 Wiring diagram for carburettor models from July 1980

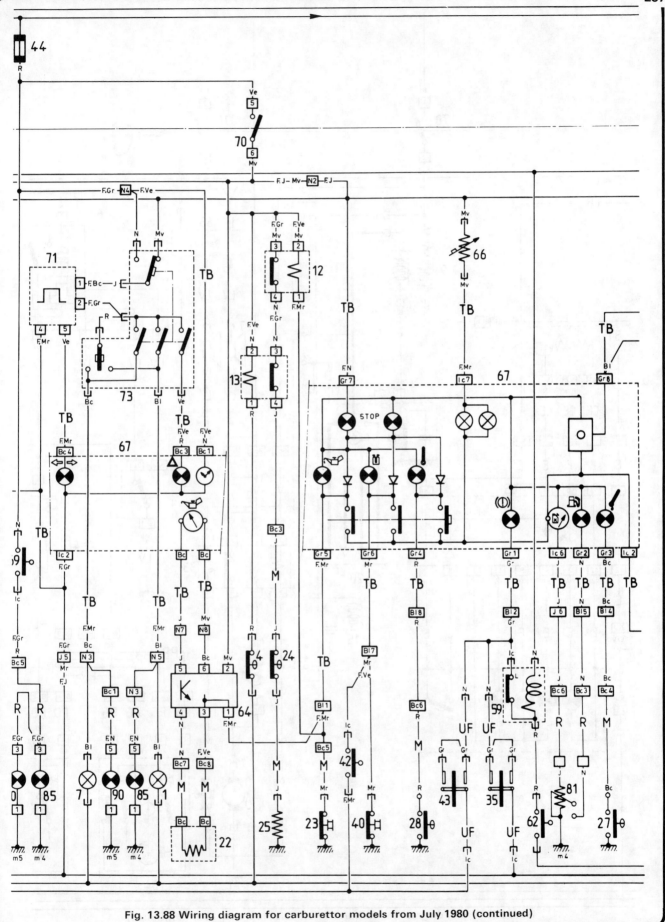

Fig. 13.88 Wiring diagram for carburettor models from July 1980 (continued)

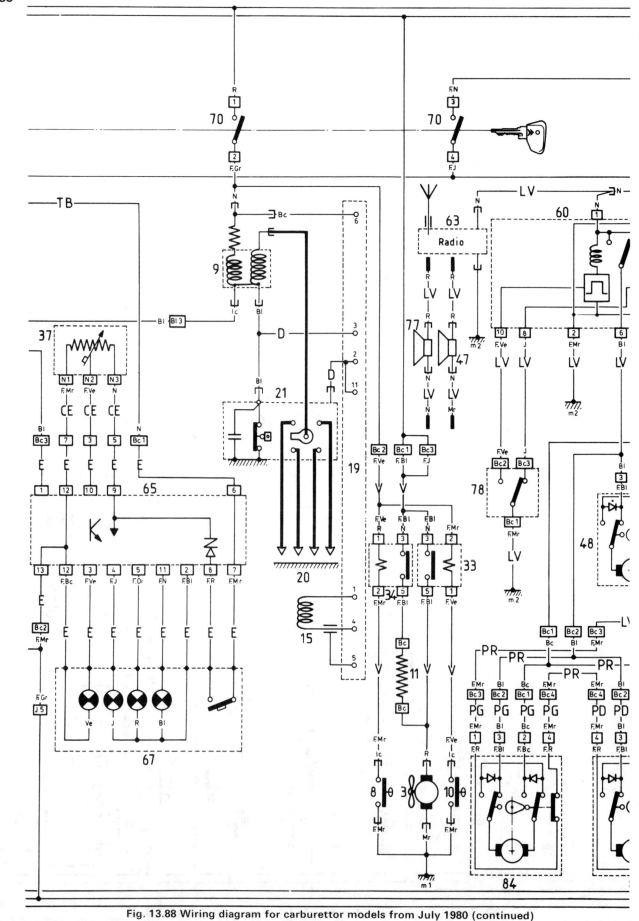

Fig. 13.88 Wiring diagram for carburettor models from July 1980 (continued)

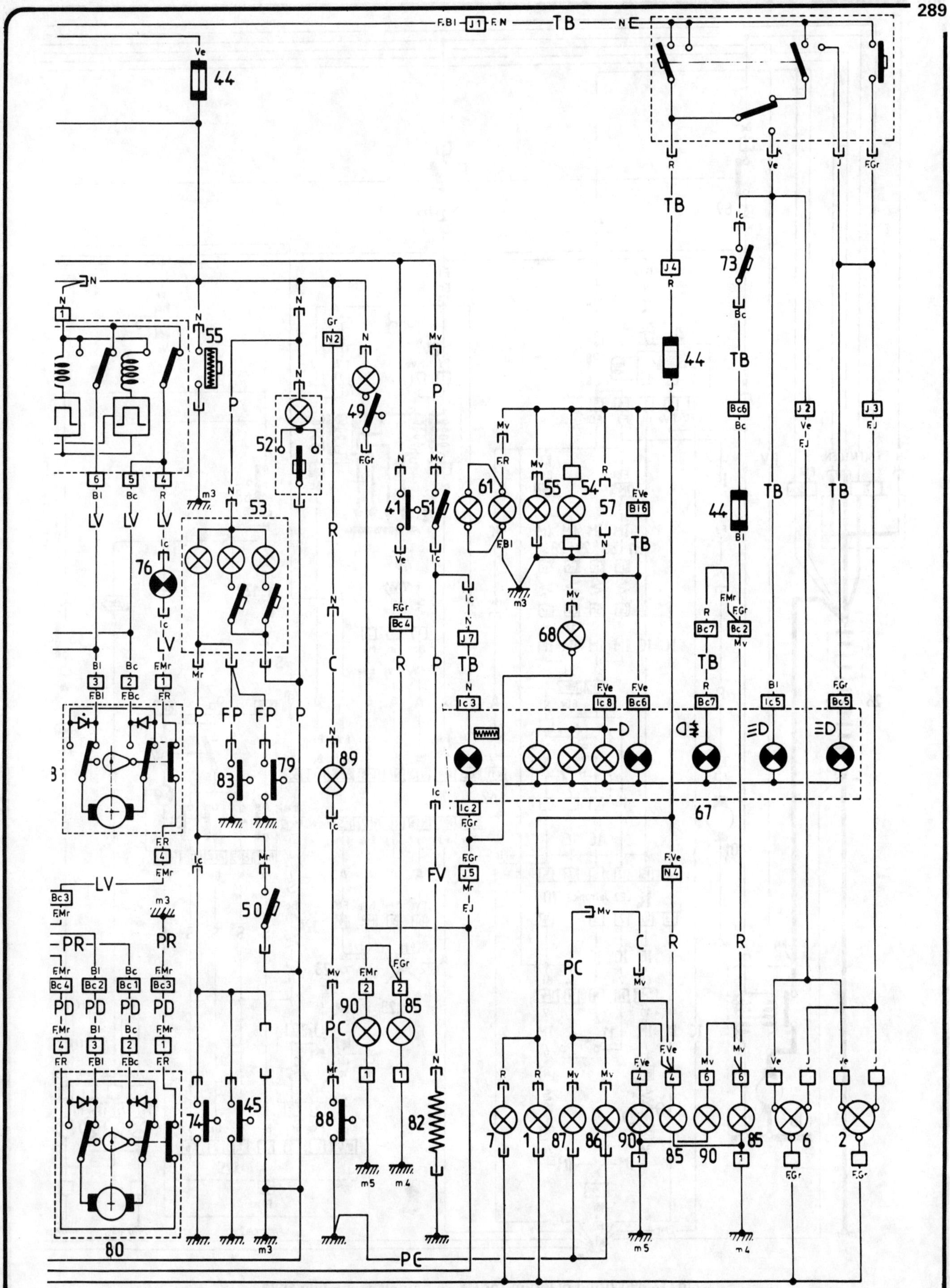

Fig. 13.88 Wiring diagram for carburettor models from July 1980 (continued)

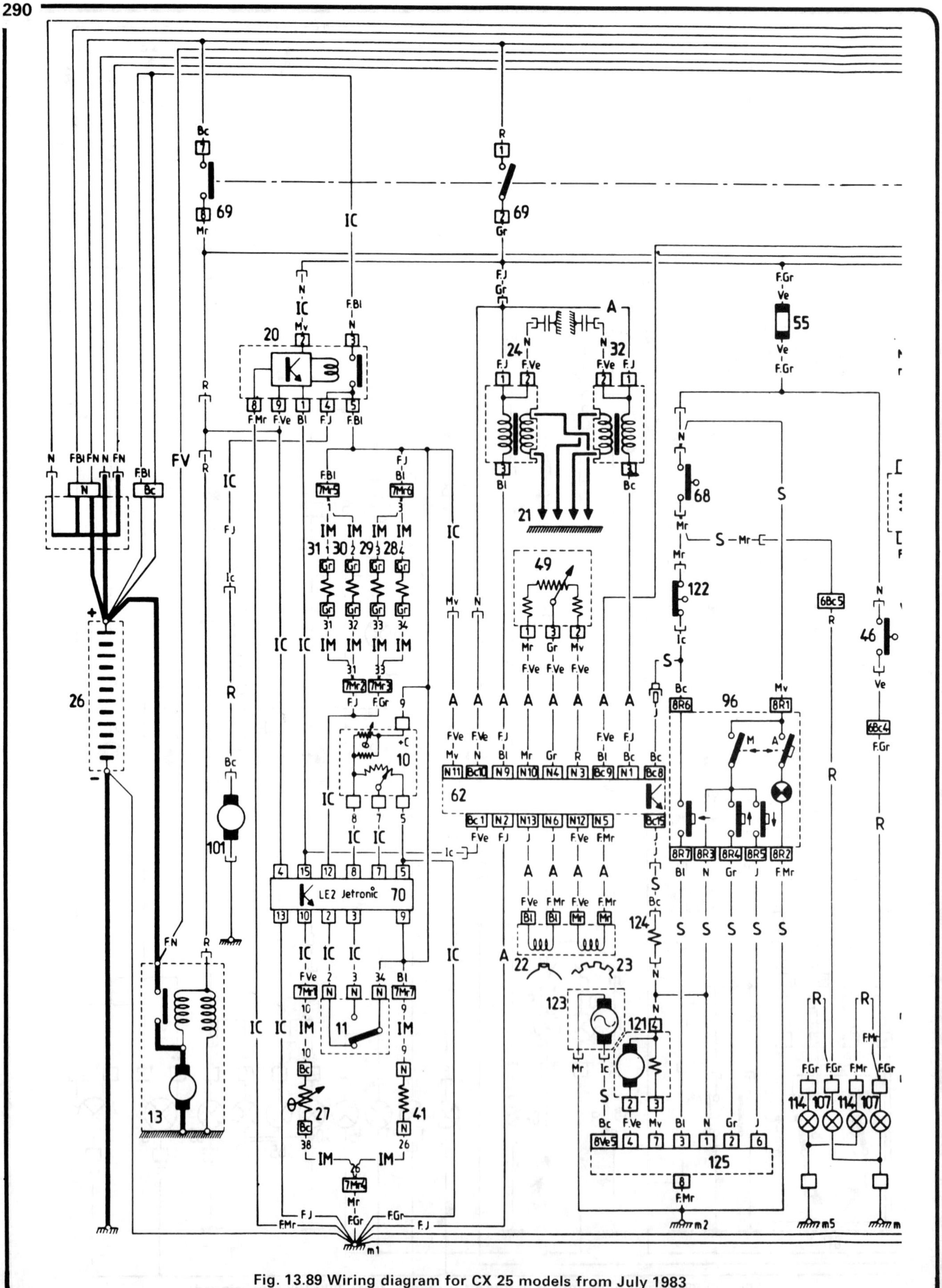

Fig. 13.89 Wiring diagram for CX 25 models from July 1983

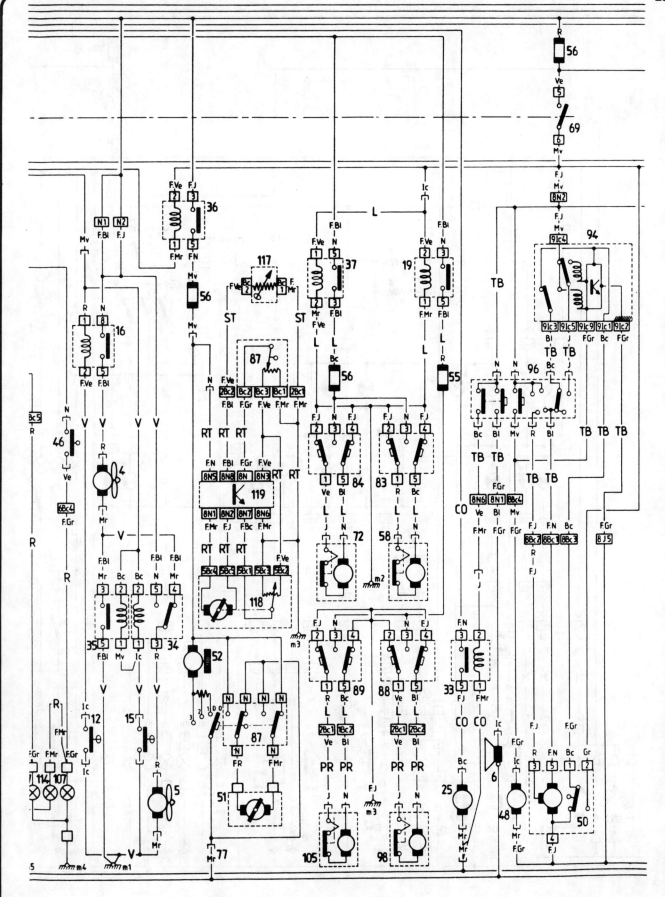

Fig. 13.89 Wiring diagram for CX 25 models from July 1983 (continued)

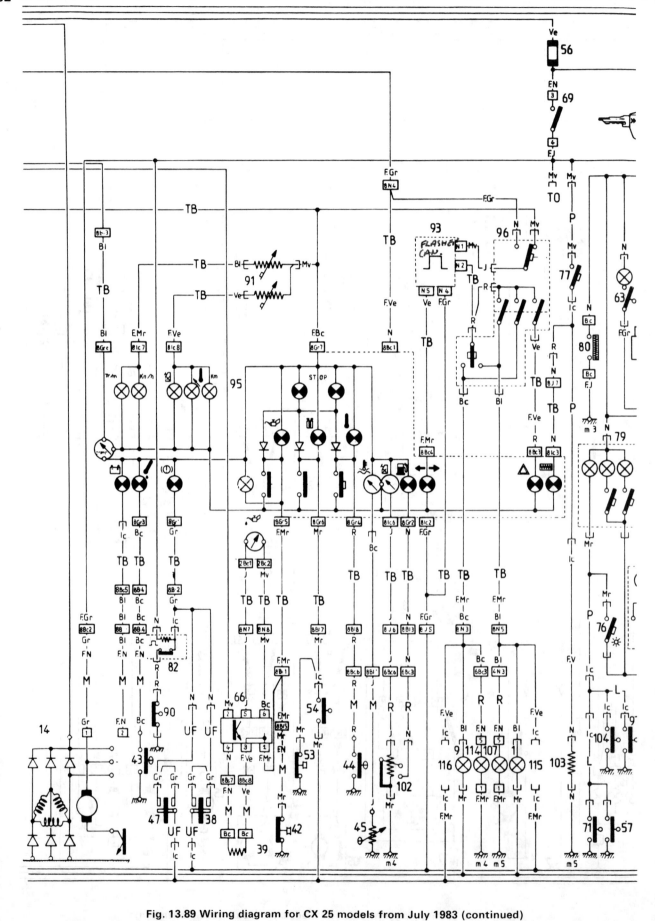

Fig. 13.89 Wiring diagram for CX 25 models from July 1983 (continued)

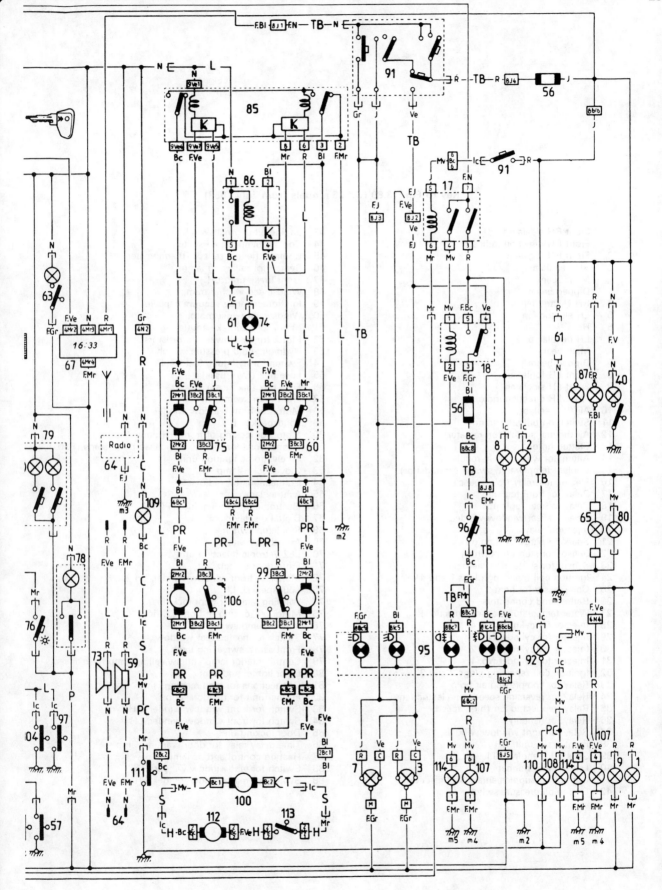

Fig. 13.89 Wiring diagram for CX 25 models from July 1983 (continued)

Key to Fig. 13.89 (CX 25 models from July 1983)

1 Front RH sidelamp:
   Front RH direction indicator
2 Front RH foglamp
3 RH headlamp:
   Main beam
   Dipped beam
4 RH electric fan
5 LH electric fan
6 Horn
7 LH headlamp:
   Main beam
   Dipped beam
8 Front LH foglamp
9 Front LH sidelamp
   Front LH direction indicator
10 Air flow sensor
11 Switch on butterfly spindle
12 Air thermal switch (on radiator)
13 Starter motor
14 Alternator with built-in regulator
15 Coolant temperature switch (on radiator)
16 Electric fan relay (low speed)
17 Relay for front foglamp
18 Relay for rear foglamps
19 Relay for rear window winders
20 Injection relay
21 Sparking plugs for ignition
22 Sensor for stud on flywheel
23 Sensor for starter ring teeth
24 Ignition coil (sparking plugs 1 and 4)
25 Compressor for horn
26 Battery and connectors
27 Water temperature sensor (injection)
28 Injector for cylinder No. 4
29 Injector for cylinder No. 3
30 Injector for cylinder No. 2
31 Injector for cylinder No. 1
32 Ignition coil (sparking plugs 2 and 3)
33 Relay for compressed air horn
34 Relay for reversing speeds on electric fans
35 Relay for electric fan (high speed)
36 Relay for heating
37 Relay for front window winders
38 Front brake unit, RH
39 Sensor for engine oil level
40 Lamp under bonnet
41 Control for supplementary air (injection)
42 Engine oil pressure switch

43 Engine oil thermal switch
44 Coolant temperature switch
45 Coolant thermal sensor (thermometer)
46 Switch for reversing lamps
47 Front brake unit, LH
48 Windscreen washer pump
49 Ignition advance vacuum capsule
50 Windscreen wiper motor
51 Motor for air intake shutter
52 Motor for air blower and resistors
53 Hydraulic fluid pressure switch
54 Switch for hydraulic fuel level
55 Fuse box (two fuses)
56 Fuse box (six fuses)
57 Front door switch, RH
58 Motor for front window winder
59 Loudspeaker, RH
60 Motor for locking of front RH door
61 Connections for locking device warning lamps (RHD)
62 All electronic ignition unit
63 Glove locker lamp
64 Connections for radio set
65 Ashtray lamp
66 Electronic unit for engine oil level
67 Digital display clock
68 Stoplamp switch
69 Anti-theft switch
70 LE2 Jetronic injection unit
71 Front door switch, LH
72 Motor for front window winder, LH
73 Loudspeaker, LH
74 Warning lamp for door locking
75 Motor for locking of front LH door
76 Interior lamp switch
77 Switch for heated rear window
78 Front seats, swivelling lamp
79 Central interior lamp and swivelling lamp for rear seats
80 Cigar lighter and lamp
81 Connections for map reading lamp
82 Flasher unit for handbrake 'on'
83 Switch for front window winder, RH
84 Switch for front window winder, LH
85 Door locking unit
86 Time delay relay for door warning lamp
87 Heating control and its lamp
88 Switch for rear window winder, RH
89 Switch for rear window winder, LH

Key to Fig. 13.89 (CX 25 models from July 1983) (continued)

90 Handbrake 'on' warning switch
91 RH control unit:
    Lighting
    Instrument panel lighting rheostats
    Switch for front foglamps
92 Ignition keyhole lamps
93 Flasher unit for direction indicators
94 Windscreen wiper timer
95 Dashboard:
    Warning lamps for:
        Rear foglamps
        Front sidelamps
        Headlamp main beam
        Direction indicator
        Battery charge
        Hazard warning device
        Hydraulic fluid pressure and level
        Emergency 'stop'
    Test button for 'stop' warning lamp
    Warning lamps for:
        Engine oil pressure
        Coolant temperature
        Engine oil temperature
        Low fuel level in tank
        Brake pad wear and handbrake 'on'
        Headlamp dipped beam
        Front foglamps
        Heated rear window
    Water thermometer
    Tachometer
    Fuel gauge indicator
    Engine oil level indicator
    Lighting for speedometer and tachometer
    Lighting for indicators
96 LH control unit:
    Direction indicators
    Horn
    Rear foglamps
    Windscreen wipe/wash
    Hazard warning lamp
97 Rear door switch, RH
98 Motor for rear window winder, RH
99 Motor for locking of rear RH door
100 Motor for locking of fuel tank flap
101 Fuel pump
102 Fuel gauge rheostat
103 Heated rear window
104 Rear door switch, LH

105 Motor for rear window winder, LH
106 Motor for locking of rear LH door
107 Rear lamp cluster, RH:
    Reversing lamp
    Stoplamp
    Tail lamp
    Direction indicator lamp
    Foglamp
108 Number plate lamp, RH
109 Boot lamp
110 Number plate lamp, LH
111 Switch for boot lamp
112 Motor for locking of boot
113 Motor switch for locking of boot
114 Rear lamp cluster, LH:
    Reversing lamp
    Stoplamp
    Tail lamp
    Direction indicator lamp
    Foglamp
Export:
115 Direction indicator side repeater, RH
116 Direction indicator side repeater, LH
Option: Temperature regulation
117 Sensor for temperature in passenger compartment
118 Motor unit for heating shutter
119 Electronic unit
(87) Potentiometer on control
Option: Sunroof
120 Switch
126 Relay
127 Motor
Options: Cruise control device
(96) Switch unit, LH
121 Vacuum pump and regulator
122 Switch for declutching
123 Tachymetric sensor
124 Electrovalve for venting (security)
125 Electronic unit
Option: Air conditioning – Refrigeration
126 Refrigeration relay
127 Relay for electric cooling fans (low speed: refrigeration)
128 Electrovalve for fast idle
129 Pressure switch
130 Compressor
131 Control thermostat

Key to Fig. 13.90 (CX 25 GTi Turbo models)

No	Item	Current track
1	Cigar lighter (front)	189 to 203
3	Cigar lighter (LH rear)	124
4	Cigar lighter (RH rear)	132
10	Alternator	86 to 89
44	Digital display unit	67 to 74
45	Battery	2
46	Instrument panel	63 to 108, 211 to 214
51	Ignition coil (cyls 1 and 4)	57, 58
52	Ignition coil (cyls 2 and 3)	61, 62
57	Fuel calculator	47, 48
60	Air conditioning control unit	12 to 15
76	Front window winder unit (LH)	113 to 115
81	Heating control unit	27 to 30
84	Coolant level sensor control unit	76 to 78
89	Central locking indicator lamp	183, 184
90	Central locking control unit	176 to 186
91	Remote locking control unit	172 to 174
92	Interior lighting timer (delay)	169 to 173
93	Bulb failure monitoring unit	33, 81, 83 109, 110, 147 208, 217
127	Warning buzzer	174, 175
131	TDC sensor	60, 61
132	Flywheel sensor	58, 59
136	Vacuum sensor	59 to 61
137	Anti-knock sensor	57, 58
140	Distance sensor	50
141	Ignition ECU	54 to 65
142	Fuel injection ECU	36 to 48
170	Boot light switch	198
174	Boot lock switch	179
180	Reversing lamp switch	33
185	Stop-lamp switch	147
190	Handbrake switch	90
192	Throttle switch	45 to 47
229	Ignition/starter switch	5, 27, 38, 138
230	Door switch (LH front)	171
231	Door switch (RH front)	172
232	Door switch (LH rear)	174
233	Door switch (RH rear)	175
234	Glovebox switch	187
235	Hydraulic fluid pressure switch	81
236	Hydraulic fluid level switch	80

No	Item	Current track
237	Coolant level sensor	76, 77
238	Door ajar switch (RH front)	99
239	Door ajar switch (LH front)	98
241	Door ajar switch (RH rear)	101
242	Door ajar switch (LH rear)	100
243	Boot ajar switch	102
244	Bonnet ajar switch	97
251	Height control switch	139 to 143
254	Lighting/direction indicator switch	107 to 110, 209 to 215
255	Windscreen wiper/washer and horn switch	133 to 138, 159
268	Air recycling switch	16 to 18
269	Air conditioning switch	20 to 23
270	Maximum air conditioning switch	17 to 19
271	Air distribution switch	19 to 21
276	Mirror switch	152 to 157
278	Heater blower speed control	23 to 25, 29 to 31
279	Heater control lighting	103, 104
280	Supplementary air control	44
285	HT suppressors	59, 60
295	Horn compressor	160
300	Starter motor	3 to 5
302	Airflow meter	40 to 44
345	Fast idle valve	14
365	Ashtray lighting	204
370	Boot lighting	188
375	Glovebox lighting	187
380	Under-bonnet lighting	202
385	Number plate light (LH)	218
386	Number plate light (RH)	219
390	Ignition switch lighting	208
410	Air conditioning compressor clutch	13
430	Brake caliper (LH front)	83, 84
431	Brake caliper (RH front)	85, 86
440	Sidelamp (LH front)	201
441	Sidelamp (RH front)	203
442	Tail lamp (LH)	217
443	Tail lamp (RH)	218
447	Front foglamp (LH)	206
448	Front foglamp (RH)	207
457	Stop-lamp (LH)	147
458	Stop-lamp (RH)	148

Key to Fig. 13.90 (CX 25 GTi Turbo models) (continued)

No	Item	Current track	No	Item	Current track
460	Rear foglamp (LH)	208	630	Fuel flap lock motor	179
461	Rear foglamp (RH)	209	634	Engine cooling fan (RH)	9
462	Reversing lamp (LH)	33	635	Engine cooling fan (LH)	9
463	Reversing lamp (RH)	34	650	Low oil pressure switch	79
480	Direction indicator (LH front)	108	658	Heater blower speed control unit	25, 26
481	Direction indicator (RH front)	111	660	Computer	50 to 53
482	Direction indicator (LH rear)	109	680	Windscreen washer pump	138
483	Direction indicator (RH rear)	110	683	Fuel pump	45
486	Auxiliary headlamp (LH)	211	690	Interior light (central)	165 to 167
487	Auxiliary headlamp (RH)	216	695	Interior light (front spot)	165
488	Headlamp (LH)	212, 213	698	Headphone socket	195 to 198
489	Headlamp (RH)	214, 215	700	Air conditioning pressure switch	13
500	Loudspeaker (LH front)	191	710	Accessory supply socket	123
501	Loudspeaker (RH front)	193	721	Radio connections	191 to 199
502	Loudspeaker (LH rear)	194	731	Fuel injection relay	38 to 46
503	Loudspeaker (RH rear)	199	733	Cooling fan relay (air conditioning)	12, 13
506	Tweeter (LH)	192	734	Injector relay	35, 36
507	Tweeter (RH)	192	735	Main beam relay	215, 216
510	Front foglamp switch	204 to 206	739	Weight control relay	142 to 145
511	Rear foglamp switch	208 to 210	743	Horn relay	159, 160
519	Driver's door LH window switch	120 to 122	745	Heater blower relay (high speed)	24 to 26
520	Driver's door RH window switch	115 to 118	750	Foglamp relay	206 to 208
521	Front passenger door window switch	120 to 122	772	Cooling fan high speed relay	10 to 11
522	Rear LH window switch	125 to 127	773	Cooling fan series/parallel relay	7 to 9
523	Rear RH window switch	129 to 131	795	Panel lighting rheostat	97
532	Heated rear window switch	162 to 164	810	Direction indicator repeater (LH)	107
545	Interior lighting switch	166 to 168	811	Direction indicator repeater (RH)	112
570	Hazard warning switch	109 to 113	814	Door mirror (LH)	151 to 154
575	Cold start injector	38	815	Door mirror (RH)	155 to 157
576	Fuel injectors	40 to 43	831	Heater flap motor	29 to 31
580	Fuel gauge	94 to 96	835	Engine oil level sensor	92, 93
600	Windscreen wiper motor	133 to 137	837	Evaporator temperature sensor (air conditioning)	12, 13
608	Height control motor	140 to 146	838	Ambient air temperature sensor	71, 72
615	Window motor (RH front)	116	839	Cabin air temperature sensor	30
616	Window motor (LH front)	121	840	Coolant temperature sensor (for display)	73, 74
617	Window motor (RH rear)	126	841	Coolant temperature sensor (for EFi)	39
618	Window motor (LH rear)	130	842	Engine oil pressure sender	91
621	Air intake flap motor	17	843	Engine oil temperature sender	70, 71
622	Air distribution flap motor	20	850	Engine cooling fan thermoswitch	9, 10
625	Door lock motor (LH front)	177 to 179	870	Thermotime switch	37, 38
626	Door lock motor (RH front)	181 to 183	935	Heater blower motor	25
627	Door lock motor (LH rear)	177 to 179	945	Heated rear window	163
628	Door lock motor (RH rear)	181 to 183	980	Door locking warning lamp	184
629	Boot lock motor	183			

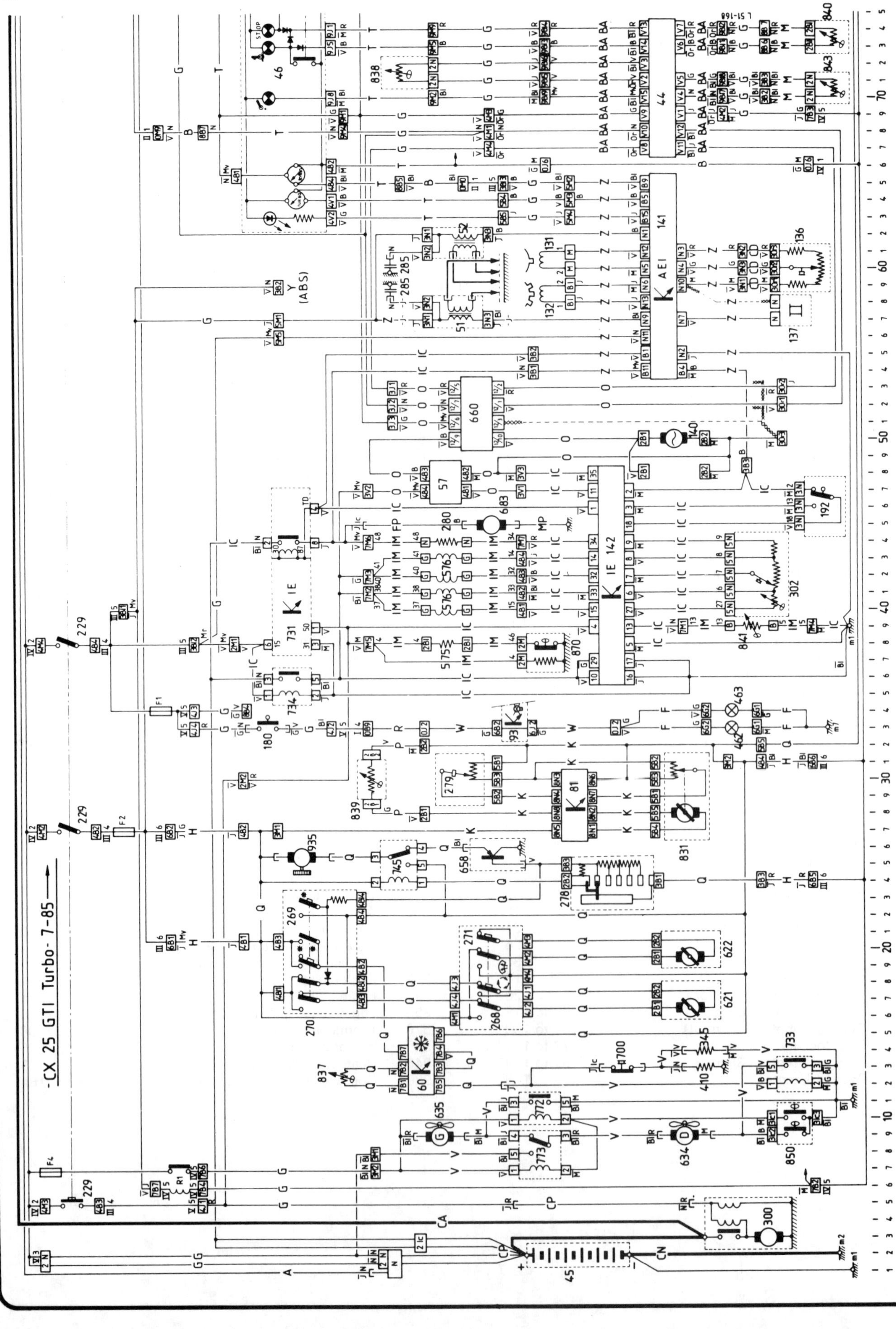

CX 25 GTI Turbo - 7-85 →

Fig. 13.90 Wiring diagram for CX 25 GTi Turbo models

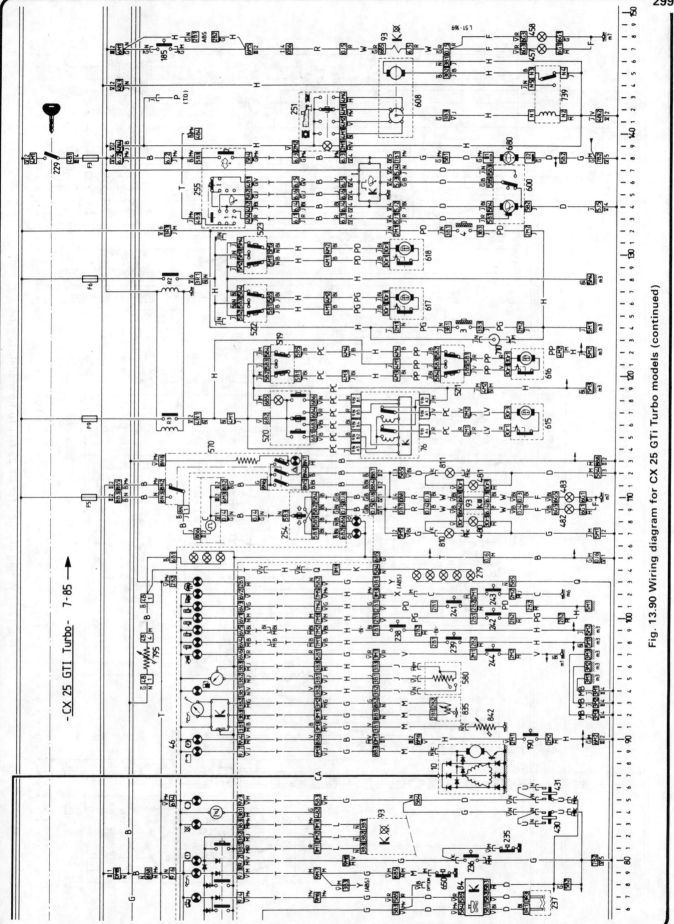

Fig. 13.90 Wiring diagram for CX 25 GTi Turbo models (continued)

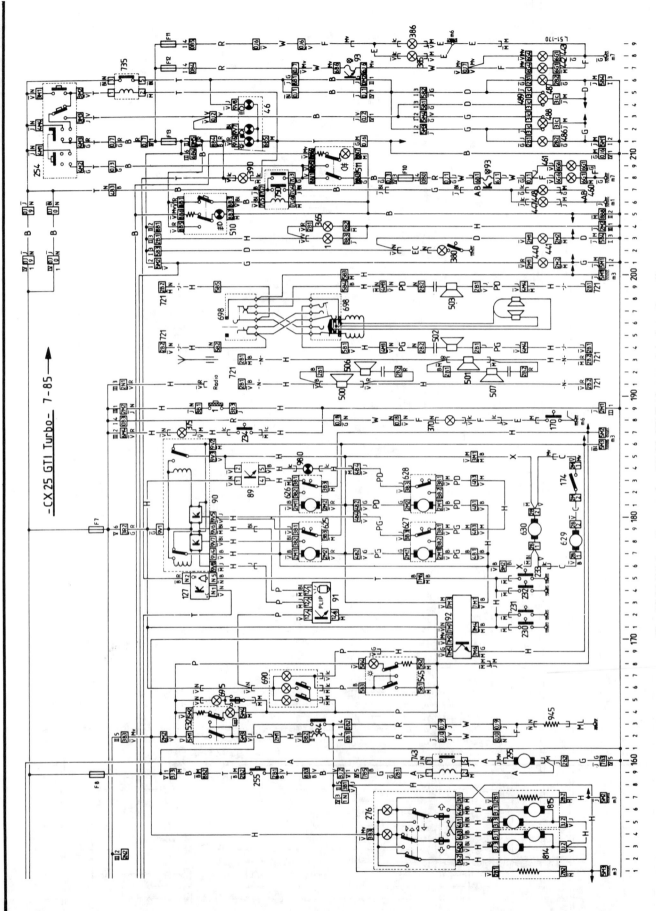

Fig. 13.90 Wiring diagram for CX 25 GTi Turbo models (continued)

-CX 25 GTI Turbo- 7-85 →

General repair procedures

Whenever servicing, repair or overhaul work is carried out on the car or its components, it is necessary to observe the following procedures and instructions. This will assist in carrying out the operation efficiently and to a professional standard of workmanship.

Joint mating faces and gaskets

Where a gasket is used between the mating faces of two components, ensure that it is renewed on reassembly, and fit it dry unless otherwise stated in the repair procedure. Make sure that the mating faces are clean and dry with all traces of old gasket removed. When cleaning a joint face, use a tool which is not likely to score or damage the face, and remove any burrs or nicks with an oilstone or fine file.

Make sure that tapped holes are cleaned with a pipe cleaner, and keep them free of jointing compound if this is being used unless specifically instructed otherwise.

Ensure that all orifices, channels or pipes are clear and blow through them, preferably using compressed air.

Oil seals

Whenever an oil seal is removed from its working location, either individually or as part of an assembly, it should be renewed.

The very fine sealing lip of the seal is easily damaged and will not seal if the surface it contacts is not completely clean and free from scratches, nicks or grooves. If the original sealing surface of the component cannot be restored, the component should be renewed.

Protect the lips of the seal from any surface which may damage them in the course of fitting. Use tape or a conical sleeve where possible. Lubricate the seal lips with oil before fitting and, on dual lipped seals, fill the space between the lips with grease.

Unless otherwise stated, oil seals must be fitted with their sealing lips toward the lubricant to be sealed.

Use a tubular drift or block of wood of the appropriate size to install the seal and, if the seal housing is shouldered, drive the seal down to the shoulder. If the seal housing is unshouldered, the seal should be fitted with its face flush with the housing top face.

Screw threads and fastenings

Always ensure that a blind tapped hole is completely free from oil, grease, water or other fluid before installing the bolt or stud. Failure to do this could cause the housing to crack due to the hydraulic action of the bolt or stud as it is screwed in.

When tightening a castellated nut to accept a split pin, tighten the nut to the specified torque, where applicable, and then tighten further to the next split pin hole. Never slacken the nut to align a split pin hole unless stated in the repair procedure.

When checking or retightening a nut or bolt to a specified torque setting, slacken the nut or bolt by a quarter of a turn, and then retighten to the specified setting.

Locknuts, locktabs and washers

Any fastening which will rotate against a component or housing in the course of tightening should always have a washer between it and the relevant component or housing.

Spring or split washers should always be renewed when they are used to lock a critical component such as a big-end bearing retaining nut or bolt.

Locktabs which are folded over to retain a nut or bolt should always be renewed.

Self-locking nuts can be reused in non-critical areas, providing resistance can be felt when the locking portion passes over the bolt or stud thread.

Split pins must always be replaced with new ones of the correct size for the hole.

Special tools

Some repair procedures in this manual entail the use of special tools such as a press, two or three-legged pullers, spring compressors etc. Wherever possible, suitable readily available alternatives to the manufacturer's special tools are described, and are shown in use. In some instances, where no alternative is possible, it has been necessary to resort to the use of a manufacturer's tool and this has been done for reasons of safety as well as the efficient completion of the repair operation. Unless you are highly skilled and have a thorough understanding of the procedure described, never attempt to bypass the use of any special tool when the procedure described specifies its use. Not only is there a very great risk of personal injury, but expensive damage could be caused to the components involved.

Fault diagnosis

Introduction

The vehicle owner who does his or her own maintenance according to the recommended schedules should not have to use this section of the manual very often. Modern component reliability is such that, provided those items subject to wear or deterioration are inspected or renewed at the specified intervals, sudden failure is comparatively rare. Faults do not usually just happen as a result of sudden failure, but develop over a period of time. Major mechanical failures in particular are usually preceded by characteristic symptoms over hundreds or even thousands of miles. Those components which do occasionally fail without warning are often small and easily carried in the vehicle.

With any fault finding, the first step is to decide where to begin investigations. Sometimes this is obvious, but on other occasions a little detective work will be necessary. The owner who makes half a dozen haphazard adjustments or replacements may be successful in curing a fault (or its symptoms), but he will be none the wiser if the fault recurs and he may well have spent more time and money than was necessary. A calm and logical approach will be found to be more satisfactory in the long run. Always take into account any warning signs or abnormalities that may have been noticed in the period preceding the fault – power loss, high or low gauge readings, unusual noises or smells, etc – and remember that failure of components such as fuses or spark plugs may only be pointers to some underlying fault.

The pages which follow here are intended to help in cases of failure to start or breakdown on the road. There is also a Fault Diagnosis Section at the end of each Chapter which should be consulted if the preliminary checks prove unfruitful. Whatever the fault, certain basic principles apply. These are as follows:

Verify the fault. This is simply a matter of being sure that you know what the symptoms are before starting work. This is particularly important if you are investigating a fault for someone else who may not have described it very accurately.

Don't overlook the obvious. For example, if the vehicle won't start, is there petrol in the tank? (Don't take anyone else's word on this particular point, and don't trust the fuel gauge either!) If an electrical fault is indicated, look for loose or broken wires before digging out the test gear.

Cure the disease, not the symptom. Substituting a flat battery with a fully charged one will get you off the hard shoulder, but if the underlying cause is not attended to, the new battery will go the same way. Similarly, changing oil-fouled spark plugs for a new set will get you moving again, but remember that the reason for the fouling (if it wasn't simply an incorrect grade of plug) will have to be established and corrected.

Don't take anything for granted. Particularly, don't forget that a 'new' component may itself be defective (especially if it's been rattling round in the boot for months), and don't leave components out of a fault diagnosis sequence just because they are new or recently fitted. When you do finally diagnose a difficult fault, you'll probably realise that all the evidence was there from the start.

Electrical faults

Electrical faults can be more puzzling than straightforward mechanical failures, but they are no less susceptible to logical analysis if the basic principles of operation are understood. Vehicle electrical wiring exists in extremely unfavourable conditions – heat, vibration and chemical attack – and the first things to look for are loose or corroded connections and broken or chafed wires, especially where the wires pass through holes in the bodywork or are subject to vibration.

All metal-bodied vehicles in current production have one pole of the battery 'earthed', ie connected to the vehicle bodywork, and in nearly all modern vehicles it is the negative (–) terminal. The various electrical components – motors, bulb holders etc – are also connected to earth, either by means of a lead or directly by their mountings. Electric current flows through the component and then back to the battery via the bodywork. If the component mounting is loose or corroded, or if a good path back to the battery is not available, the circuit will be incomplete and malfunction will result. The engine and/or gearbox are also earthed by means of flexible metal straps to the body or subframe; if these straps are loose or missing, starter motor, generator and ignition trouble may result.

Assuming the earth return to be satisfactory, electrical faults will be due either to component malfunction or to defects in the current supply. Individual components are dealt with in Chapter 10. If supply wires are broken or cracked internally this results in an open-circuit, and the easiest way to check for this is to bypass the suspect wire temporarily with a length of wire having a crocodile clip or suitable connector at each end. Alternatively, a 12V test lamp can be used to verify the presence of supply voltage at various points along the wire and the break can be thus isolated.

If a bare portion of a live wire touches the bodywork or other earthed metal part, the electricity will take the low-resistance path thus formed back to the battery: this is known as a short-circuit. Hopefully a short-circuit will blow a fuse, but otherwise it may cause burning of the insulation (and possibly further short-circuits) or even a

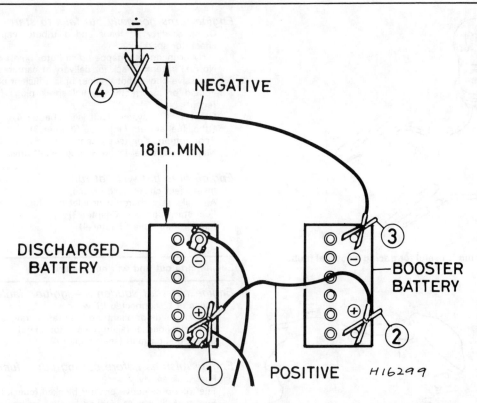

Jump start lead connections for negative earth vehicles – connect leads in order shown

fire. This is why it is inadvisable to bypass persistently blowing fuses with silver foil or wire.

Spares and tool kit

Most vehicles are supplied only with sufficient tools for wheel changing; the *Maintenance and minor repair* tool kit detailed in *Tools and working facilities,* with the addition of a hammer, is probably sufficient for those repairs that most motorists would consider attempting at the roadside. In addition a few items which can be fitted without too much trouble in the event of a breakdown should be carried. Experience and available space will modify the list below, but the following may save having to call on professional assistance:

Spark plugs, clean and correctly gapped
HT lead and plug cap – long enough to reach the plug furthest from the distributor
Distributor rotor, condenser and contact breaker points
Drivebelt(s) – emergency type may suffice
Spare fuses
Set of principal light bulbs
Tin of radiator sealer and hose bandage
Exhaust bandage
Roll of insulating tape
Length of soft iron wire
Length of electrical flex
Torch or inspection lamp (can double as test lamp)
Battery jump leads
Tow-rope
Ignition waterproofing aerosol
Litre of engine oil
Sealed can of hydraulic fluid
Emergency windscreen
Worm-drive clips
Tube of filler paste

If spare fuel is carried, a can designed for the purpose should be used to minimise risks of leakage and collision damage. A first aid kit and a warning triangle, whilst not at present compulsory in the UK, are obviously sensible items to carry in addition to the above.

When touring abroad it may be advisable to carry additional

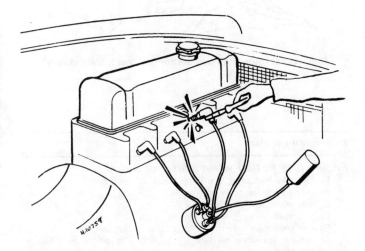

Crank engine and check for spark. Note use of insulated tool!

spares which, even if you cannot fit them yourself, could save having to wait while parts are obtained. The items below may be worth considering:

Clutch and throttle cables
Cylinder head gasket
Alternator brushes
Fuel pump repair kit
Tyre valve core

One of the motoring organisations will be able to advise on availability of fuel etc in foreign countries.

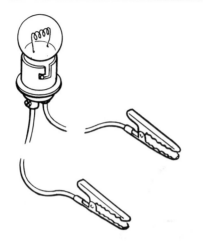

A simple test lamp is useful for tracing electrical faults

Remove fuel pipe from carburettor and check fuel delivery

Engine will not start

Engine fails to turn when starter operated
Flat battery (recharge, use jump leads, or push start)
Battery terminals loose or corroded
Battery earth to body defective
Engine earth strap loose or broken
Starter motor (or solenoid) wiring loose or broken
Automatic transmission selector in wrong position, or inhibitor switch faulty
Ignition/starter switch faulty
Major mechanical failure (seizure)
Starter or solenoid internal fault (see Chapter 10)

Starter motor turns engine slowly
Partially discharged battery (recharge, use jump leads, or push start)
Battery terminals loose or corroded
Battery earth to body defective
Engine earth strap loose
Starter motor (or solenoid) wiring loose
Starter motor internal fault (see Chapter 10)

Starter motor spins without turning engine
Flat battery
Starter motor pinion sticking on sleeve
Flywheel gear teeth damaged or worn
Starter motor mounting bolts loose

Engine turns normally but fails to start
Damp or dirty HT leads and distributor cap (crank engine and check for spark)
Dirty or incorrectly gapped distributor points (if applicable)
No fuel in tank (check for delivery at carburettor)
Excessive choke (hot engine) or insufficient choke (cold engine)
Fouled or incorrectly gapped spark plugs (remove, clean and regap)
Other ignition system fault (see Chapter 4)
Other fuel system fault (see Chapter 3)
Poor compression (see Chapter 1)
Major mechanical failure (eg camshaft drive)

Engine fires but will not run
Insufficient choke (cold engine)
Air leaks at carburettor or inlet manifold
Fuel starvation (see Chapter 3)
Ignition fault (see Chapter 4)

Engine cuts out and will not restart

Engine cuts out suddenly – ignition fault
Loose or disconnected LT wires
Wet HT leads or distributor cap (after traversing water splash)
Coil or condenser failure (check for spark)
Other ignition fault (see Chapter 4)

Engine misfires before cutting out – fuel fault
Fuel tank empty
Fuel pump defective or filter blocked (check for delivery)
Fuel tank filler vent blocked (suction will be evident on releasing cap)
Carburettor needle valve sticking
Carburettor jets blocked (fuel contaminated)
Other fuel system fault (see Chapter 3)

Engine cuts out – other causes
Serious overheating
Major mechanical failure (eg camshaft drive)

Engine overheats

Ignition (no-charge) warning light illuminated
Slack or broken drivebelt – retension or renew (Chapter 2)

Ignition warning light not illuminated
Coolant loss due to internal or external leakage (see Chapter 2)
Thermostat defective
Low oil level
Brakes binding
Radiator clogged externally or internally
Electric cooling fan not operating correctly
Engine waterways clogged
Ignition timing incorrect or automatic advance malfunctioning
Mixture too weak

Note: *Do not add cold water to an overheated engine or damage may result*

Low engine oil pressure

Gauge reads low or warning light illuminated with engine running
Oil level low or incorrect grade
Defective gauge or sender unit
Wire to sender unit earthed
Engine overheating
Oil filter clogged or bypass valve defective
Oil pressure relief valve defective
Oil pick-up strainer clogged

Oil pump worn or mountings loose
Worn main or big-end bearings
Note: *Low oil pressure in a high-mileage engine at tickover is not necessarily a cause for concern. Sudden pressure loss at speed is far more significant. In any event, check the gauge or warning light sender before condemning the engine.*

Engine noises

Pre-ignition (pinking) on acceleration
Incorrect grade of fuel
Ignition timing incorrect
Distributor faulty or worn
Worn or maladjusted carburettor
Excessive carbon build-up in engine

Whistling or wheezing noises
Leaking vacuum hose

Leaking carburettor or manifold gasket
Blowing head gasket

Tapping or rattling
Incorrect valve clearances
Worn valve gear
Worn timing chain or belt
Broken piston ring (ticking noise)

Knocking or thumping
Unintentional mechanical contact (eg fan blades)
Worn fanbelt
Peripheral component fault (generator, water pump etc)
Worn big-end bearings (regular heavy knocking, perhaps less under load)
Worn main bearings (rumbling and knocking, perhaps worsening under load)
Piston slap (most noticeable when cold)

Conversion factors

Length (distance)
Inches (in)	X	25.4	= Millimetres (mm)		X	0.0394	= Inches (in)
Feet (ft)	X	0.305	= Metres (m)		X	3.281	= Feet (ft)
Miles	X	1.609	= Kilometres (km)		X	0.621	= Miles

Volume (capacity)
Cubic inches (cu in; in^3)	X	16.387	= Cubic centimetres (cc; cm^3)	X	0.061	= Cubic inches (cu in; in^3)
Imperial pints (Imp pt)	X	0.568	= Litres (l)	X	1.76	= Imperial pints (Imp pt)
Imperial quarts (Imp qt)	X	1.137	= Litres (l)	X	0.88	= Imperial quarts (Imp qt)
Imperial quarts (Imp qt)	X	1.201	= US quarts (US qt)	X	0.833	= Imperial quarts (Imp qt)
US quarts (US qt)	X	0.946	= Litres (l)	X	1.057	= US quarts (US qt)
Imperial gallons (Imp gal)	X	4.546	= Litres (l)	X	0.22	= Imperial gallons (Imp gal)
Imperial gallons (Imp gal)	X	1.201	= US gallons (US gal)	X	0.833	= Imperial gallons (Imp gal)
US gallons (US gal)	X	3.785	= Litres (l)	X	0.264	= US gallons (US gal)

Mass (weight)
Ounces (oz)	X	28.35	= Grams (g)	X	0.035	= Ounces (oz)
Pounds (lb)	X	0.454	= Kilograms (kg)	X	2.205	= Pounds (lb)

Force
Ounces-force (ozf; oz)	X	0.278	= Newtons (N)	X	3.6	= Ounces-force (ozf; oz)
Pounds-force (lbf; lb)	X	4.448	= Newtons (N)	X	0.225	= Pounds-force (lbf; lb)
Newtons (N)	X	0.1	= Kilograms-force (kgf; kg)	X	9.81	= Newtons (N)

Pressure
Pounds-force per square inch (psi; lbf/in^2; lb/in^2)	X	0.070	= Kilograms-force per square centimetre (kgf/cm^2; kg/cm^2)	X	14.223	= Pounds-force per square inch (psi; lbf/in^2; lb/in^2)
Pounds-force per square inch (psi; lbf/in^2; lb/in^2)	X	0.068	= Atmospheres (atm)	X	14.696	= Pounds-force per square inch (psi; lbf/in^2; lb/in^2)
Pounds-force per square inch (psi; lbf/in^2; lb/in^2)	X	0.069	= Bars	X	14.5	= Pounds-force per square inch (psi; lbf/in^2; lb/in^2)
Pounds-force per square inch (psi; lbf/in^2; lb/in^2)	X	6.895	= Kilopascals (kPa)	X	0.145	= Pounds-force per square inch (psi; lbf/in^2; lb/in^2)
Kilopascals (kPa)	X	0.01	= Kilograms-force per square centimetre (kgf/cm^2; kg/cm^2)	X	98.1	= Kilopascals (kPa)
Millibar (mbar)	X	100	= Pascals (Pa)	X	0.01	= Millibar (mbar)
Millibar (mbar)	X	0.0145	= Pounds-force per square inch (psi; lbf/in^2; lb/in^2)	X	68.947	= Millibar (mbar)
Millibar (mbar)	X	0.75	= Millimetres of mercury (mmHg)	X	1.333	= Millibar (mbar)
Millibar (mbar)	X	0.401	= Inches of water (inH$_2$O)	X	2.491	= Millibar (mbar)
Millimetres of mercury (mmHg)	X	0.535	= Inches of water (inH$_2$O)	X	1.868	= Millimetres of mercury (mmHg)
Inches of water (inH$_2$O)	X	0.036	= Pounds-force per square inch (psi; lbf/in^2; lb/in^2)	X	27.68	= Inches of water (inH$_2$O)

Torque (moment of force)
Pounds-force inches (lbf in; lb in)	X	1.152	= Kilograms-force centimetre (kgf cm; kg cm)	X	0.868	= Pounds-force inches (lbf in; lb in)
Pounds-force inches (lbf in; lb in)	X	0.113	= Newton metres (Nm)	X	8.85	= Pounds-force inches (lbf in; lb in)
Pounds-force inches (lbf in; lb in)	X	0.083	= Pounds-force feet (lbf ft; lb ft)	X	12	= Pounds-force inches (lbf in; lb in)
Pounds-force feet (lbf ft; lb ft)	X	0.138	= Kilograms-force metres (kgf m; kg m)	X	7.233	= Pounds-force feet (lbf ft; lb ft)
Pounds-force feet (lbf ft; lb ft)	X	1.356	= Newton metres (Nm)	X	0.738	= Pounds-force feet (lbf ft; lb ft)
Newton metres (Nm)	X	0.102	= Kilograms-force metres (kgf m; kg m)	X	9.804	= Newton metres (Nm)

Power
Horsepower (hp)	X	745.7	= Watts (W)	X	0.0013	= Horsepower (hp)

Velocity (speed)
Miles per hour (miles/hr; mph)	X	1.609	= Kilometres per hour (km/hr; kph)	X	0.621	= Miles per hour (miles/hr; mph)

Fuel consumption
Miles per gallon, Imperial (mpg)	X	0.354	= Kilometres per litre (km/l)	X	2.825	= Miles per gallon, Imperial (mpg)
Miles per gallon, US (mpg)	X	0.425	= Kilometres per litre (km/l)	X	2.352	= Miles per gallon, US (mpg)

Temperature

Degrees Fahrenheit = (°C x 1.8) + 32

Degrees Celsius (Degrees Centigrade; °C) = (°F − 32) x 0.56

It is common practice to convert from miles per gallon (mpg) to litres/100 kilometres (l/100km), where mpg (Imperial) x l/100 km = 282 and mpg (US) x l/100 km = 235

Index

Printed by
J H Haynes & Co Ltd
Sparkford Nr Yeovil
Somerset BA22 7JJ England